WILD WORLD

Dedicated to, and in memory of Emily Owen
A fierce supporter of my work, and the most special friend.

It pains me that you aren't here to see the fruits
of your encouragement and friendship,
but wherever you are, this is for you.

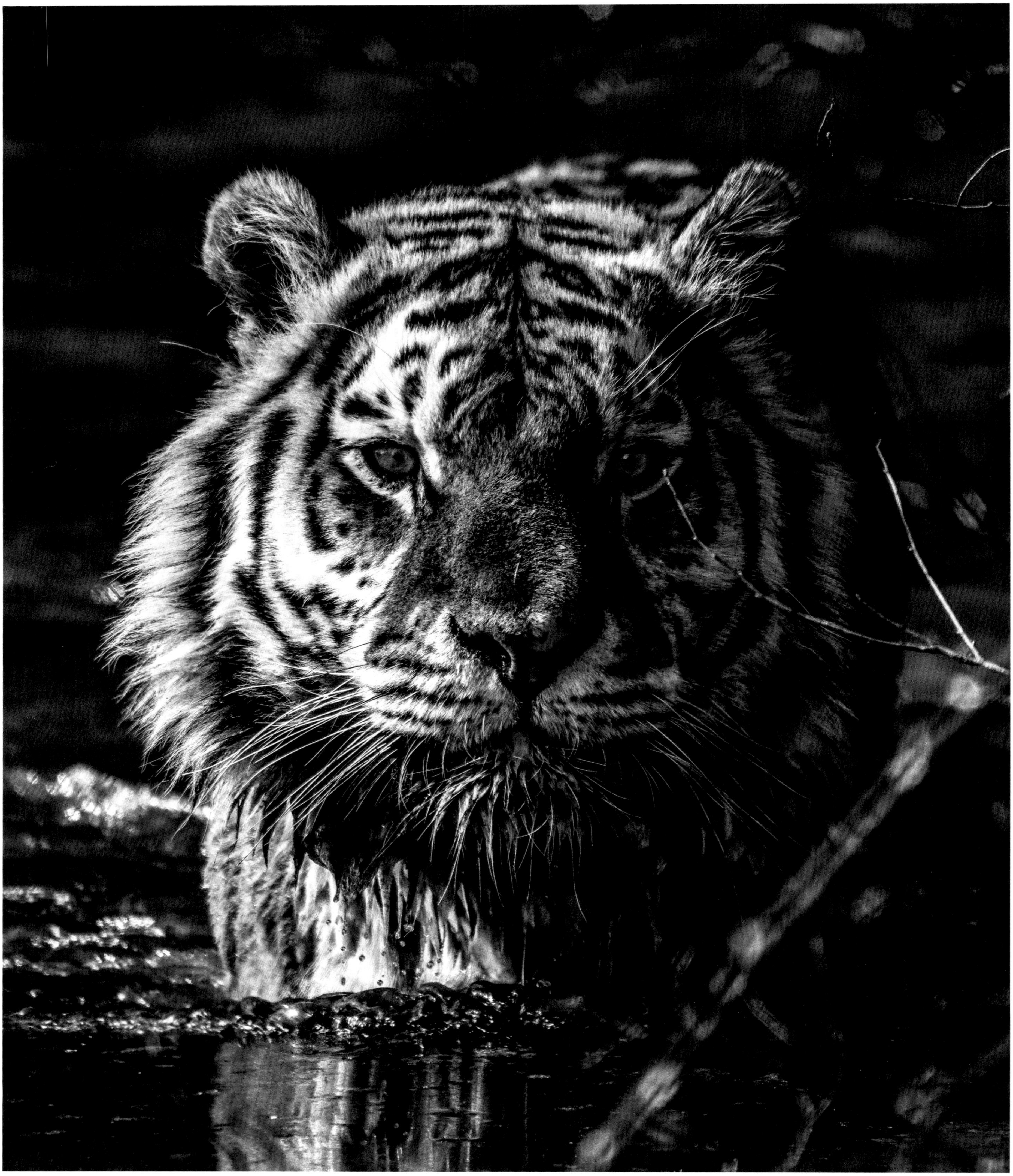

WILD WORLD

Alfie Bowen
Foreword by Chris Packham

Alfie Bowen has given us a feast for the eye – his stunning images capture the beauty and majesty of the natural world and its wildlife; you will want to revisit them over and over again. But this is also a moving book – in which Alfie talks openly about the challenges he has faced, and the inspiration he has drawn from nature. WWF is delighted to be able to work with Alfie, and hugely grateful that part of the proceeds from his book will go towards our vital work, including protecting some of the amazing wildlife that are the stars of his photos.

Tanya Steele
Chief Executive, WWF

ACC ART BOOKS

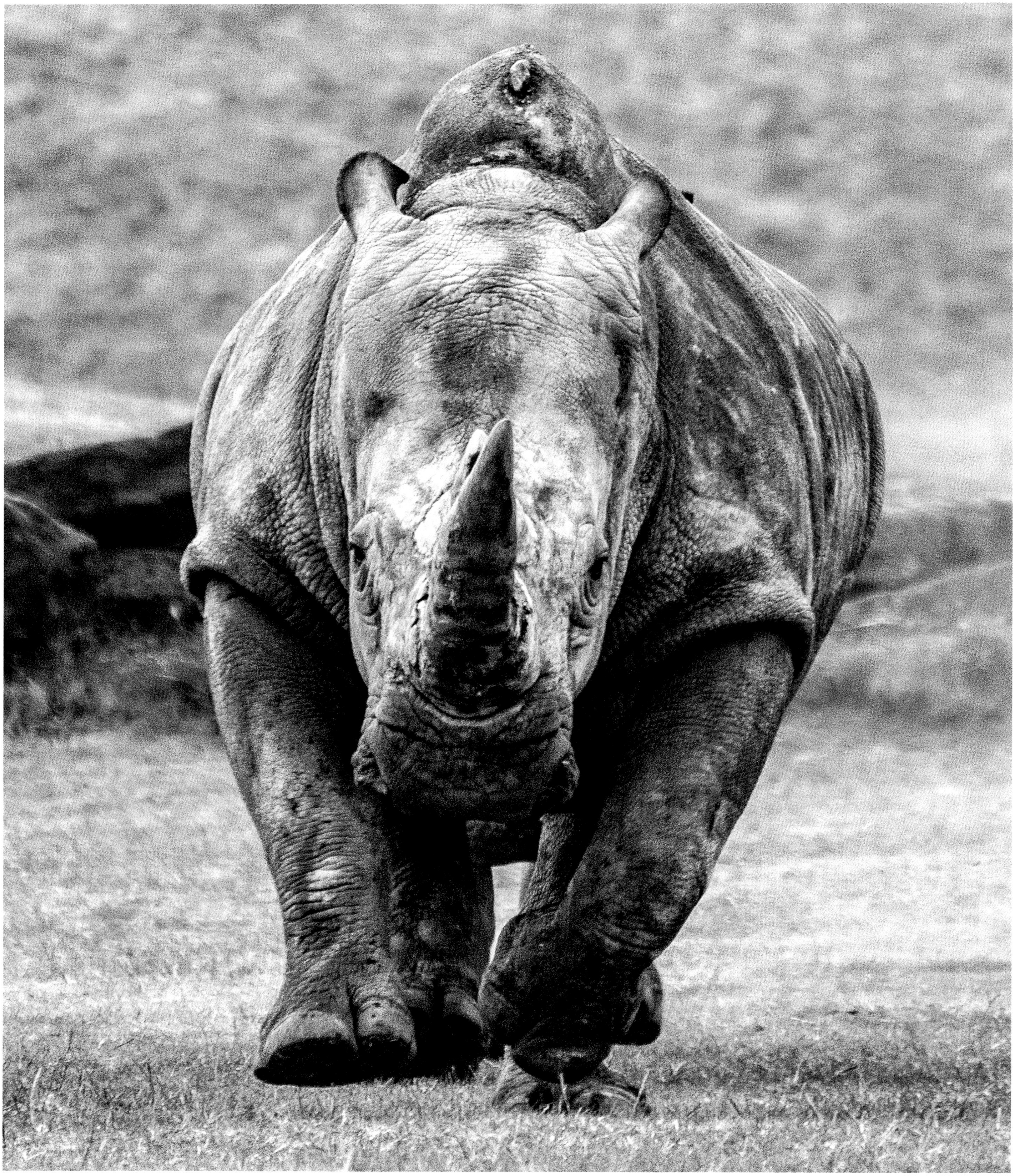

Contents

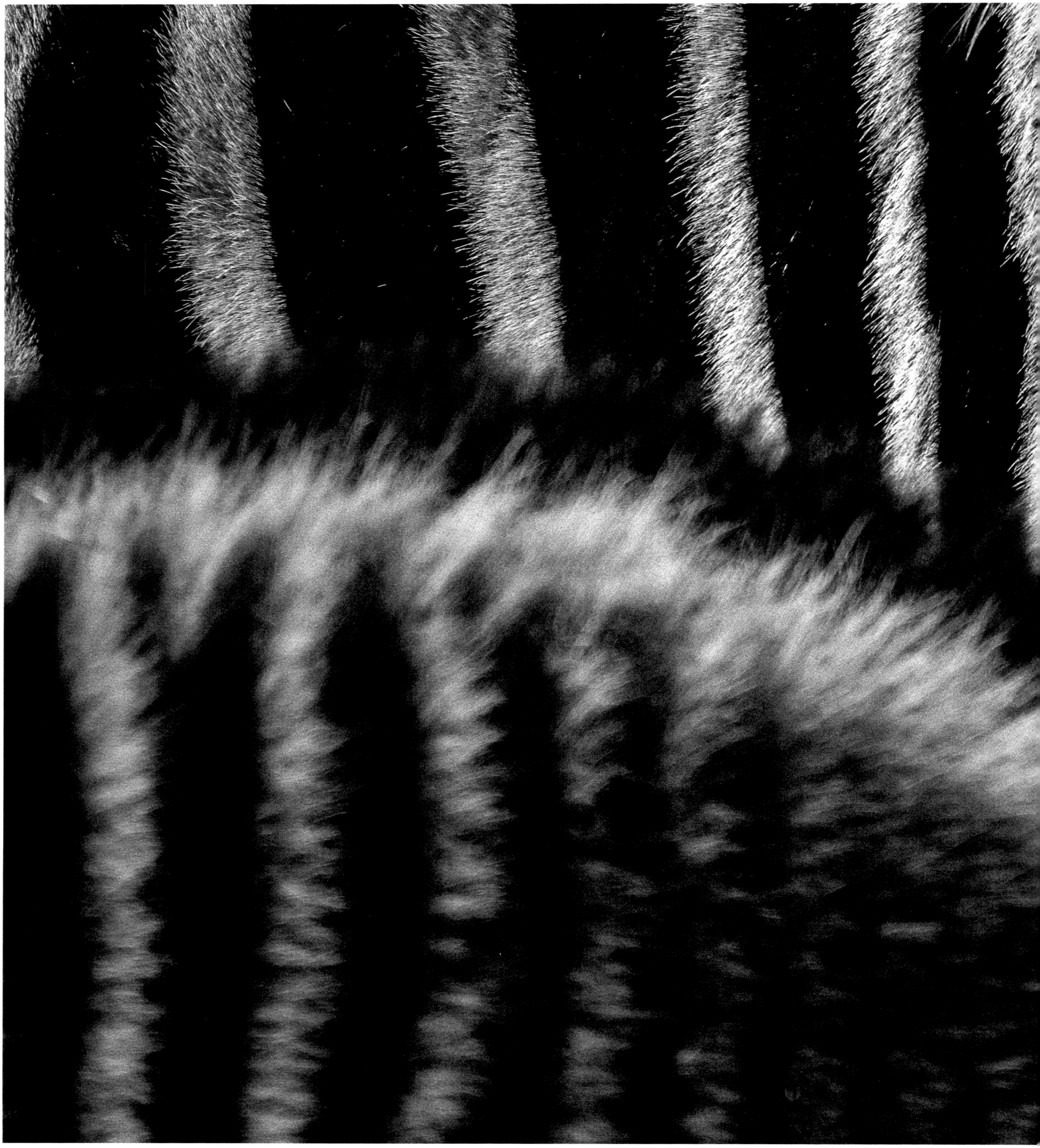

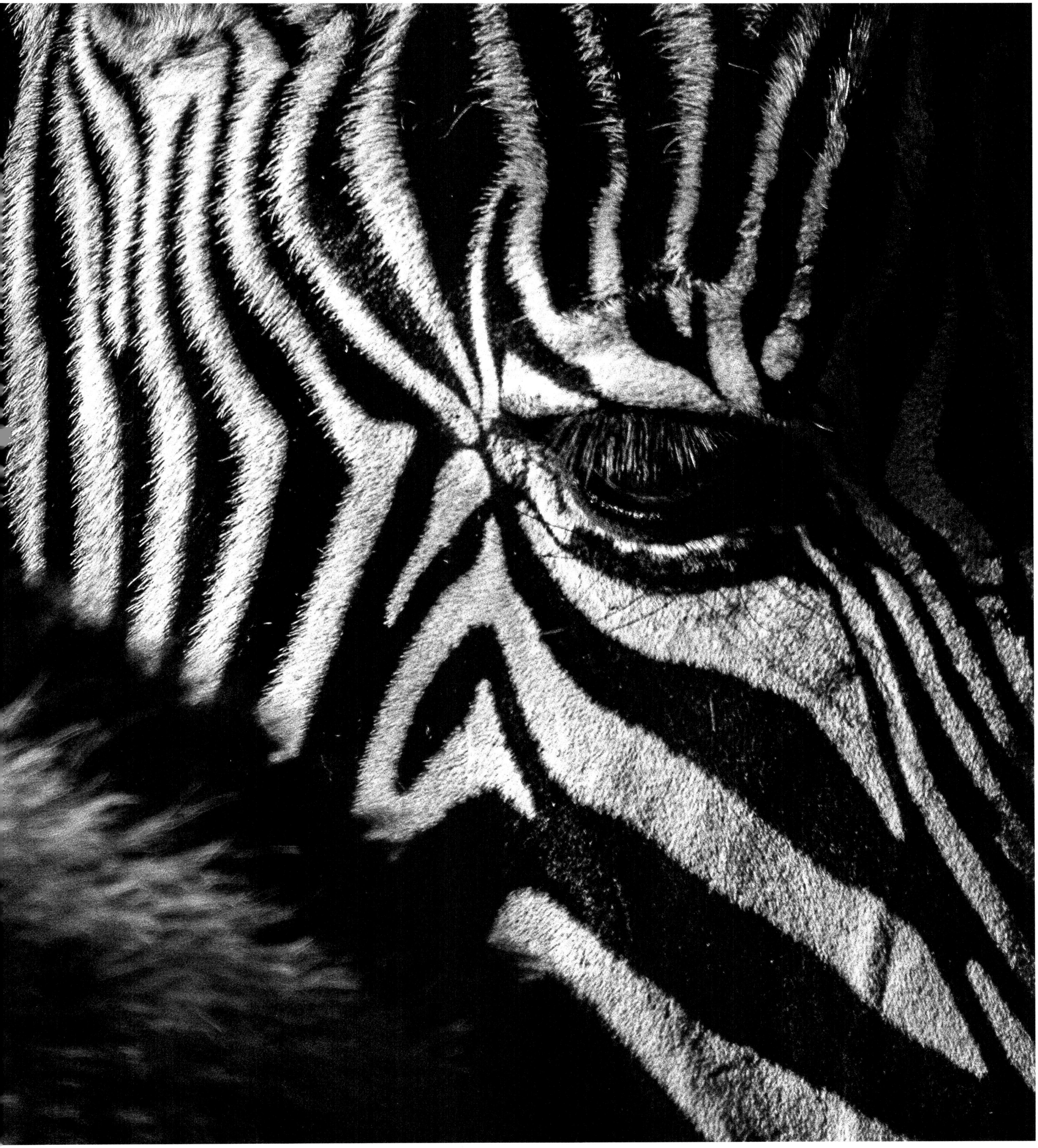

Foreword
by Chris Packham

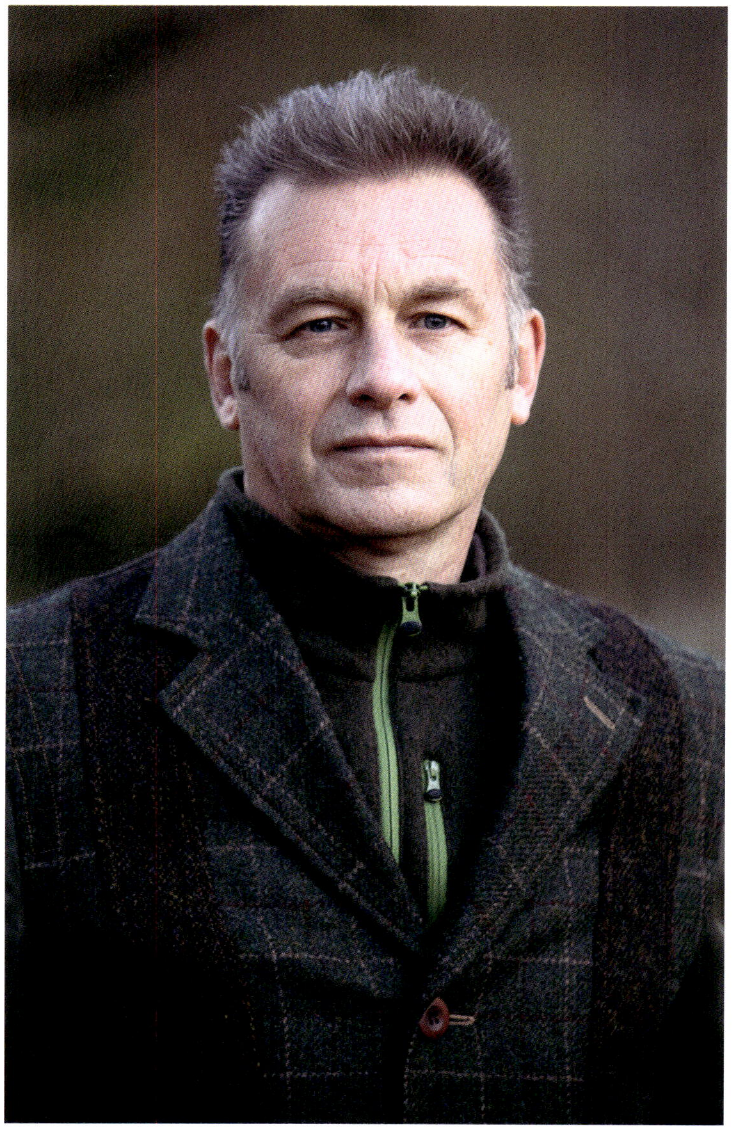

Billions of photographs are made each day. Perhaps a few, probably only one will be really good – good enough to endure beyond the moment that the photographer makes all the decisions and presses the shutter. On some days I think that despite the statistical odds none will make that grade. Not a single image will be captured which will endure beyond a frivolous instant, a lazy click, a laugh, a tear, not one will capture that single opportunity in the entire history of our universe to completely align to something so momentous, so special, so nearly perfect that it will be cherished forever as part of our species unique vision and creativity. And given this is what any serious photographer aspires too, with those sorts of odds stacked against you, who would actually pick up a camera?

Well, maybe someone with an obsessional desire to create something perfect. Something new, something entirely unique, some deeply personal response to a situation which is transcribed by a camera into a form that can instantaneously be read and understood and loved, or loathed, by whoever looks at that image. Whoooaaaah! That ambition takes around fifty words to describe . . . but what does it take to achieve? Don't ask me, ask Alfie. By my reckoning I've never achieved it, and I am still trying. That's the obsessional bit, the need to aspire to perfection, even though it's patently unobtainable.

I like Alfie's photos. He's looking at the light a lot, he is mastering it, playing with it. He likes pattern and simplicity, he likes colour but equally loves monochrome. His photographs are bold, sometimes graphic, and always eye-catching. But more importantly he sees his subjects rather than just looking at them. He is not only responding to their form, but their feeling and emotional energy. He has a keen eye for detail, ultra-detail, not in terms of resolution, but in terms of connection. I think he sees more than what is psychically presented to him, each photograph offers a little glimpse of his soul. And, hats off, he is producing this outstanding work whilst focusing on captive animals in the UK. He is not merely a photographer, but also a highly skilled artist.

In some ways captive animals are easier, accessibility, familiarity. . . but in other ways they are very, very hard subjects. Over exposed, often compromised by their enclosures and the restrictions that they generate, they offer quite a limited scope for proper photography. And yet, despite these many challenges, Alfie has found something special in each study which lifts his photographs far beyond their predicted scope. And that is a rare and magnificent success.

The photographs are outstanding, and the story behind them inspirational. Given the odds stacked against Alfie throughout his life, this book is a significant success and bodes very well for a continued and very inspiring career as a world-class photographer.

Chris Packham
New Forest

Introduction

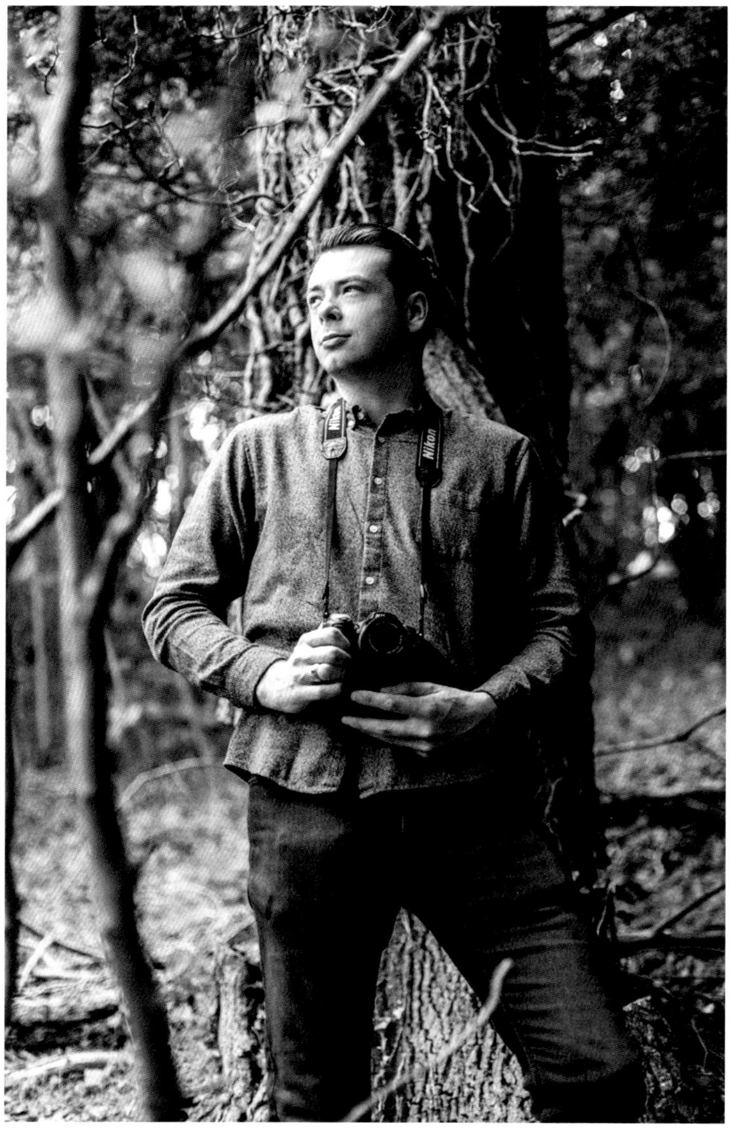

‘After many years of social exclusion, I have finally found my calling and the obsessive and non-stop nature of my mind is being put to good use in the creation of these vignettes. I am a dreamer, and I am living my dream.’

It was back in 2013 that this incredible journey began . . . well, the photography part anyway, because the obsession with wildlife began the day I was born.

Wildlife has always been a passion of mine, and almost all of my childhood was spent either playing with pretend animals or feeding the nearby ducks. I always remember being told that I was a difficult child to entertain, because if it wasn’t animal-related then, quite simply, I couldn’t care less! Many tantrums were thrown about going on shopping trips because, at the time, these seemed pointless to me; I’d have much rather stayed at home with a good animal book.

Many happy hours were spent outside in all weathers exploring the garden, playing in the mud and watching the many creatures that called it home. These experiences fuelled a great respect for the natural world, something so many children are deprived of thanks to the modern, technologically driven society we now live in. I’ll always remember the holidays of my childhood in Weybourne Forest, Norfolk. These were family affairs, with my grandparents, aunty and uncle joining me, Mum and my sister Amie. I spent much of my time in this magical woodland observing the numerous pigs, ducks, chickens and rabbits that were the owners’ much-loved pets. I used to sit on the veranda of our lodge for hours, peering into the abundance of swaying pine trees and glistening, needle-laden branches for a glimpse of the elusive red squirrel. This often led to disappointment, but it never deterred me from doing the same the following morning. The buzz from the occasional sighting set my soul on fire.

Perhaps my favourite childhood pastime was visiting my local wildlife park, where I could experience the sights and smells of wildlife from around the world. I spent hours reading about these species but seeing them in person was invigorating. I hold many memories from these

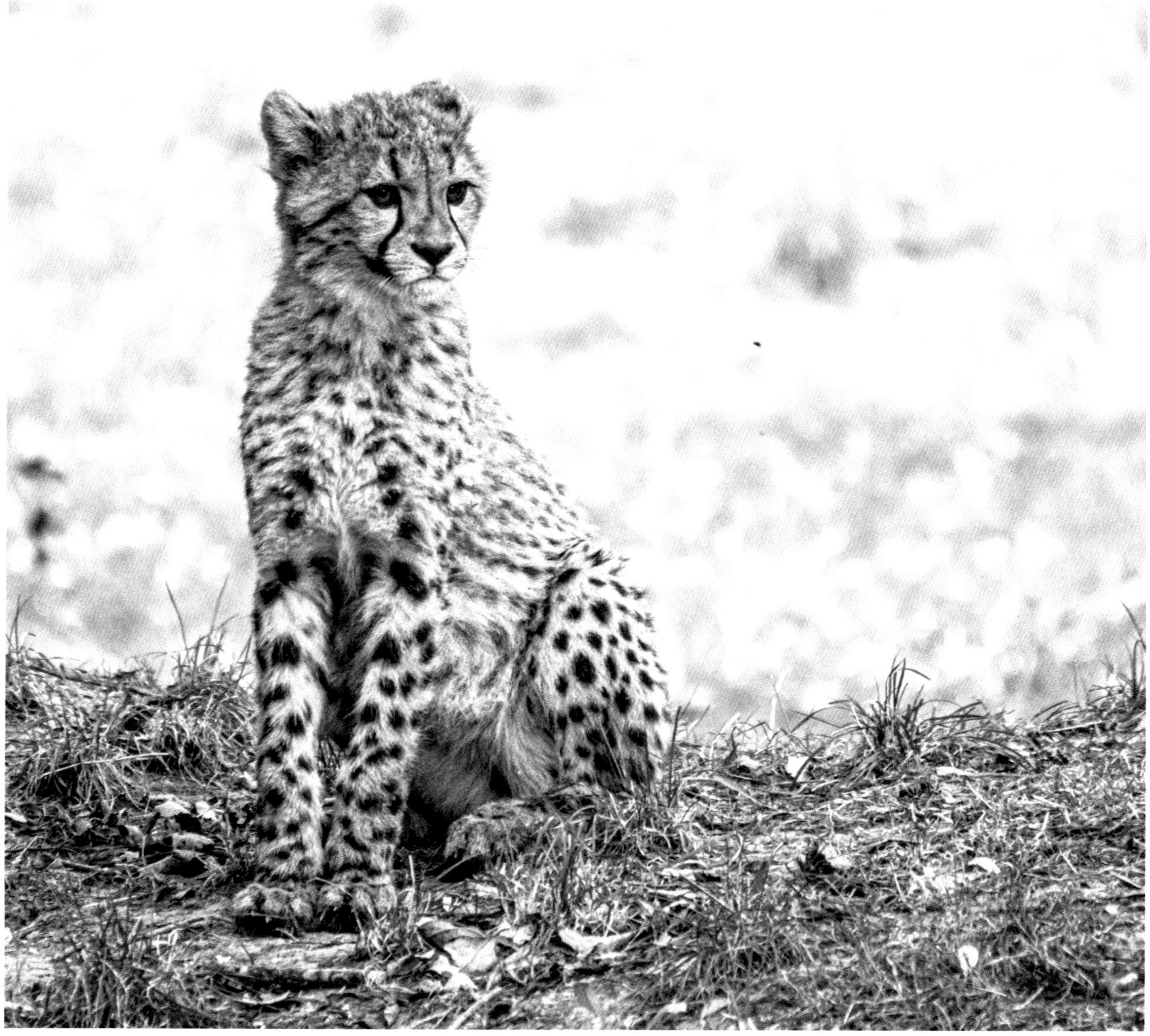

childhood explorations but, perhaps, the one that remains most fresh in my mind is witnessing my first giraffe birth. I watched this calf enter the world, watched her grow from a six-foot calf to a sixteen-foot adult; it broke my heart when she passed away in 2016. The experience taught me so much, and I will hold its teachings dear for the rest of my life. We must protect these most beautiful creatures.

Now, having turned 23, I am still as obsessed with the natural world and wildlife as I was at four years old, and I now know that I have autism to thank for that because autism brings with it obsessions.

It was only shortly before changing schools to Centre Academy East Anglia in 2014 that I reinvigorated my passion for wildlife, and during a period out of school, I began regular visits to my local wildlife park and spent many happy hours losing myself amongst the many fascinating articles that I found whilst trawling the internet. Having exhausted all the ways of satisfying my obsession with wildlife, I then stumbled across my mum's little Lumix compact camera – and set about attempting to photograph wildlife.

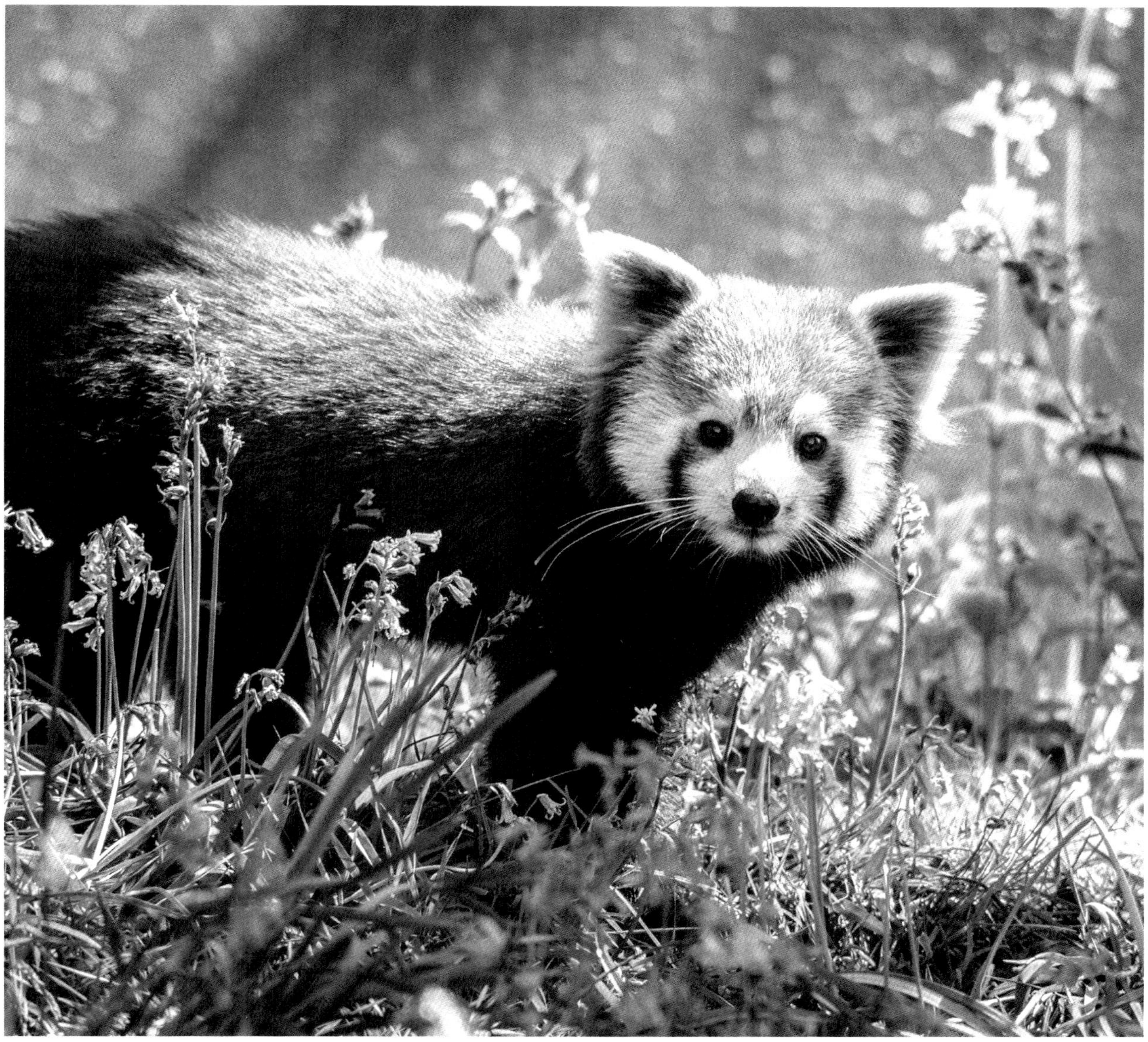

Much to my delight, she invested in a newer compact camera in the spring of 2015, meaning I became the proud new owner of her old Lumix. I took the camera everywhere with me, but quickly became frustrated by its limited functions. Autism allowed me to mentally envisage many different images, but my camera would not allow me to turn those mental sketches into reality. I began my Christmas list in October hoping for a DSLR camera. I wasn't disappointed: Christmas Day 2015 will always remain in my heart and my mind as the day that changed everything.

Ansel Adams, the American landscape photographer and environmentalist, said, 'You don't make a photograph just with a camera. You bring to the act of photography all the pictures you have seen, the books you have read, the music you have heard, the people you have loved.' This couldn't be more accurate. Photography provides me with an output for my emotional energy, and I often travel back to the tougher times in my life to provide the emotional energy for my imagery.

There are many highs as a photographer and few lows, but the consistent failure to successfully photograph the cheetah has proven to be one of those lows. I have learnt how to cope with lows over the years and, as the great Henry Ford said, "Failure is simply the opportunity to begin again, this time more intelligently". With this quote firmly in my mind, I began again and set out to photograph the cheetah for the fourth year in a row. My first three attempts – in 2016, 2017 and 2018 – had proven unsuccessful. 2019 was finally the year in which I broke through that dismal barrier.

The challenges associated with capturing each image are considerable, but I would be concerned if the job was easy. The world has seen many images of animals; the challenge is to garner unique imagery, and that is never going to be easy. It can be lonely, cold and frustrating, and I often fail; but that's all part of the game and, as I've learnt throughout life, nothing worth having comes easy.

I work largely in wildlife conservancies, investing many hours into every image. I think those who are very vocal about whether an animal is 'wild or not' are missing the point – we should be thankful to have these most gracious of animals living alongside us, and very thankful to those conservancies that champion these species and do their all to maintain the genetic pool.

Conservancies around the world also provide an effective method for countries to raise the funds required to finance extensive protection, rehabilitation and breeding programmes. As the global human population continues to grow, we must find new and effective methods in order to live in harmony with the world's wildlife, otherwise we face the stark reality of losing them forever.

The natural world always did, and still does, offer me a source of solace and that begins with the landscapes that surround me. A walk in the woods, or a stroll along East Anglia's coastline has always proved a very effective method of easing my anxiety or lifting my mood on a down day. Of course, a walk in the East Anglian countryside is a feast for my increased senses, and this proved challenging during my younger years. A beach is not just a beach for someone with autism – it is an ocean that is an ever-changing shade of blue, a thousand pebbles in a myriad of colours, billions of grains of sand, and a range of bird species squawking in a range of frequencies. It is emotionally exhausting and overwhelming for the senses. Learning how to process these elements has taken time but it is, of course, this level of attention to detail that allows me to do what I do.

With each day spent outdoors I am reminded of what a beautiful world we all call home, and the challenges that face ecosystems across the world.

Shortly before going to press, I was sent the WWF's groundbreaking *Below The Canopy* report, an investigation into the decline of the world's forests and of the species that live within them. The report suggests that forest vertebrate populations have declined by a staggering 53% since

1970, a decline that has serious consequences for the integrity of the forested environments around the world.

It is important to note that forests are home to over half of the world's land-dwelling species, and act as the world's largest carbon sinks. Essentially, if we are to reverse the effects of climate change before they become irreversible, we must stop deforestation and begin restoring the world's forested ecosystems. They are essential to our survival and I do hope that the photographs that follow these words inspire you to care a little more about the world in which you live.

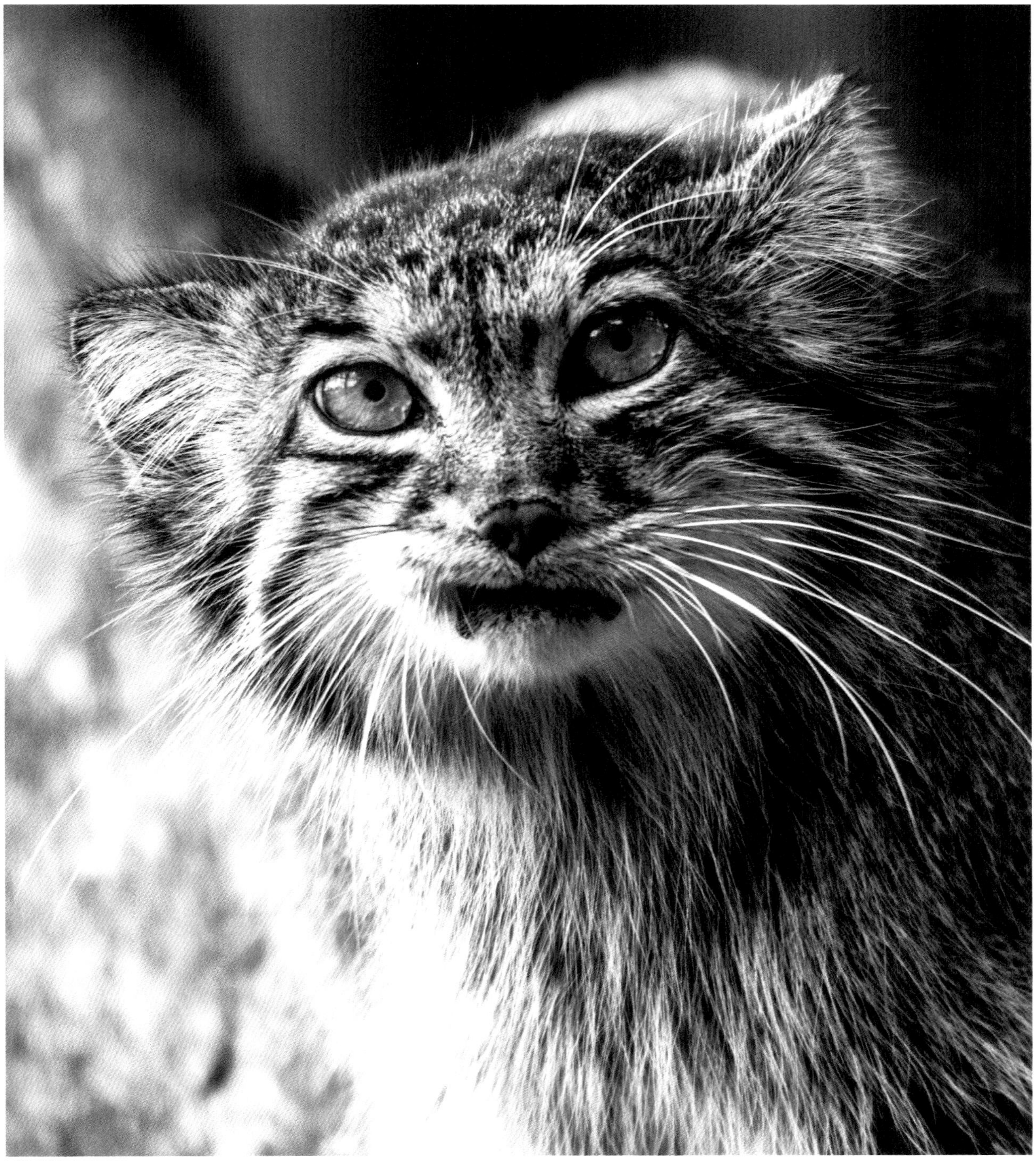

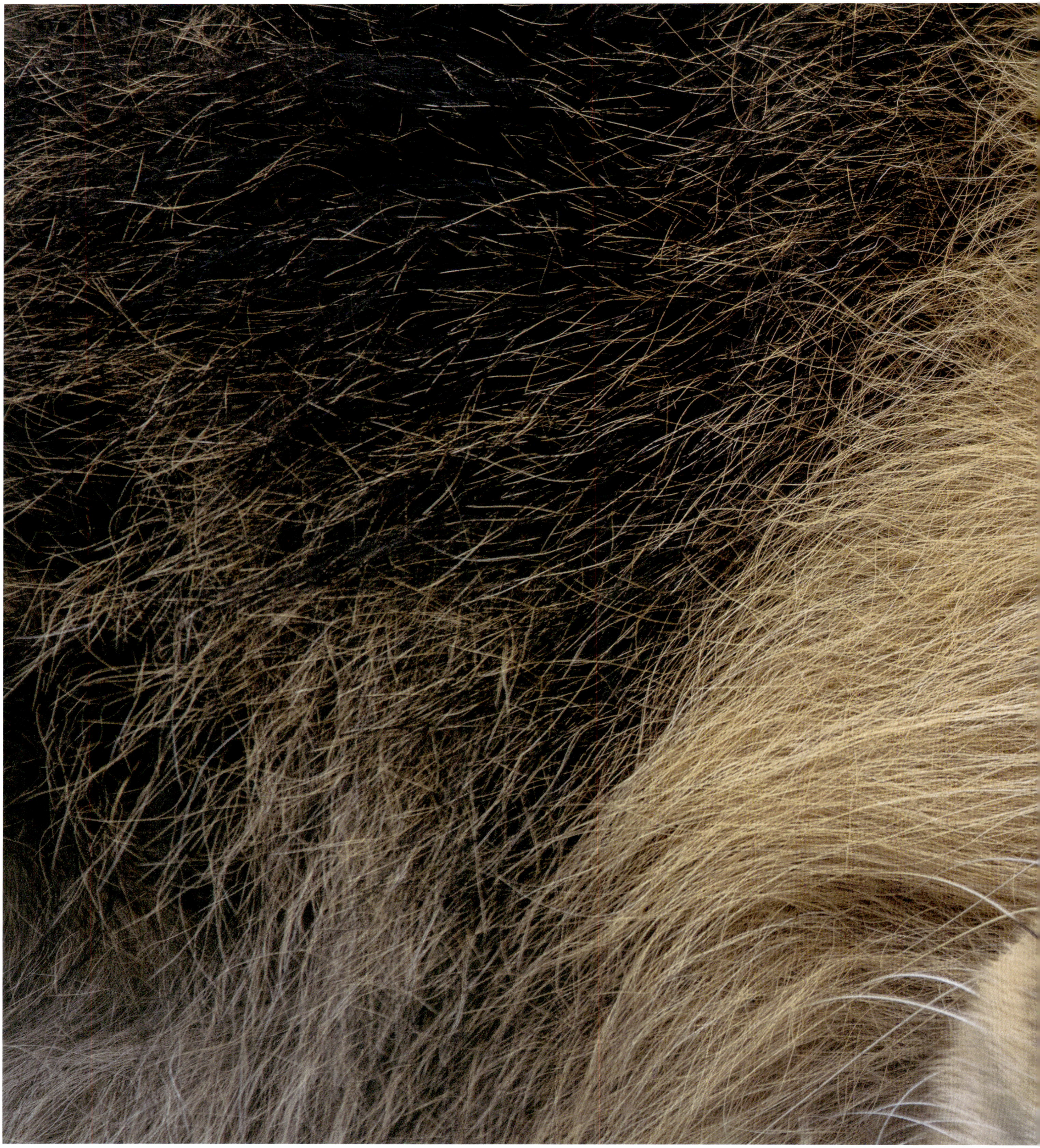

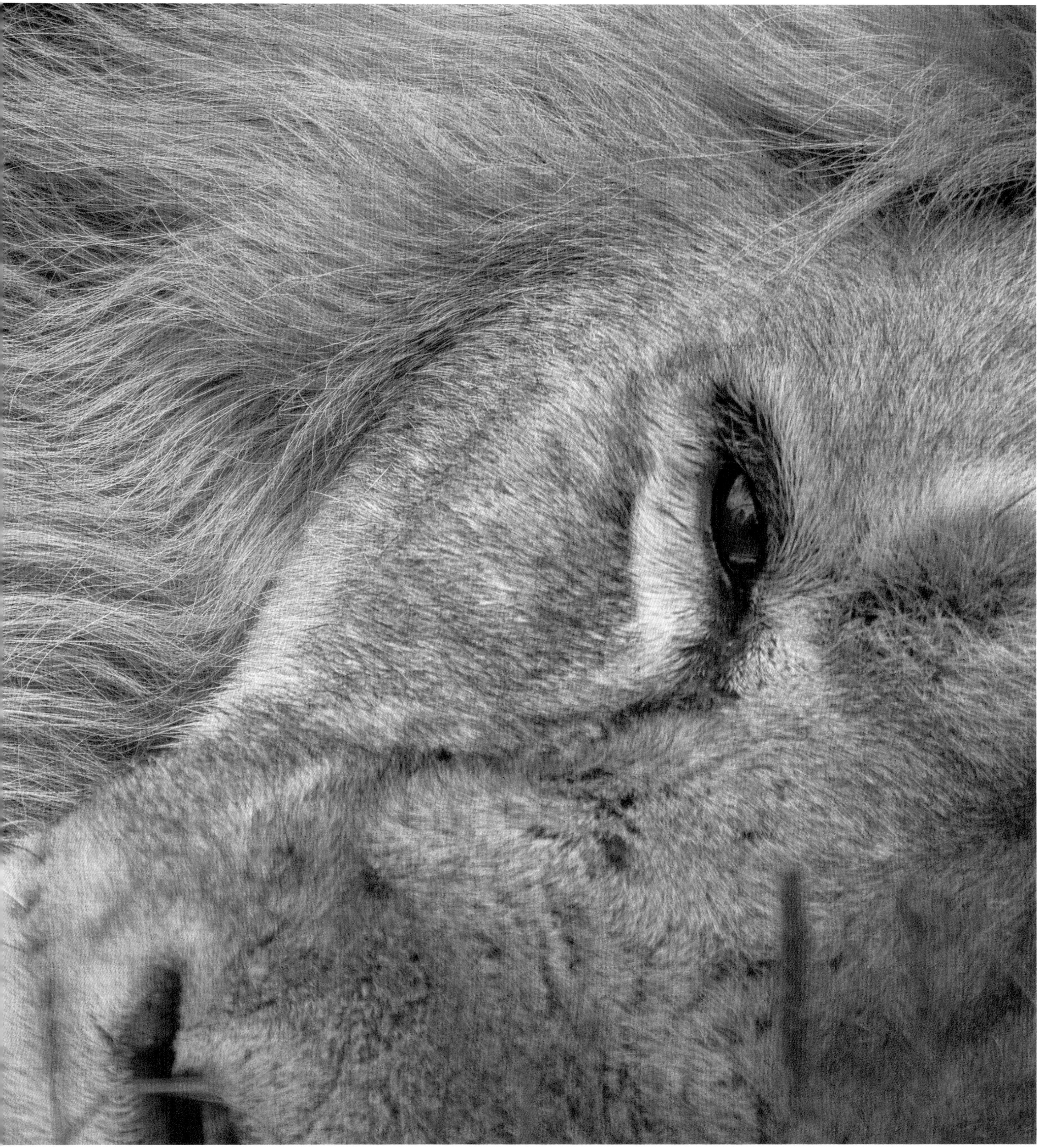

The lion is at grave risk of extinction and I hope that this book will serve as a catalyst for changes not just with regard to autism but also conservation. We must not allow these beautiful animals to disappear on our watch. We are extremely lucky to share our planet with this beautiful species, and we should do all we can to preserve them for future generations.

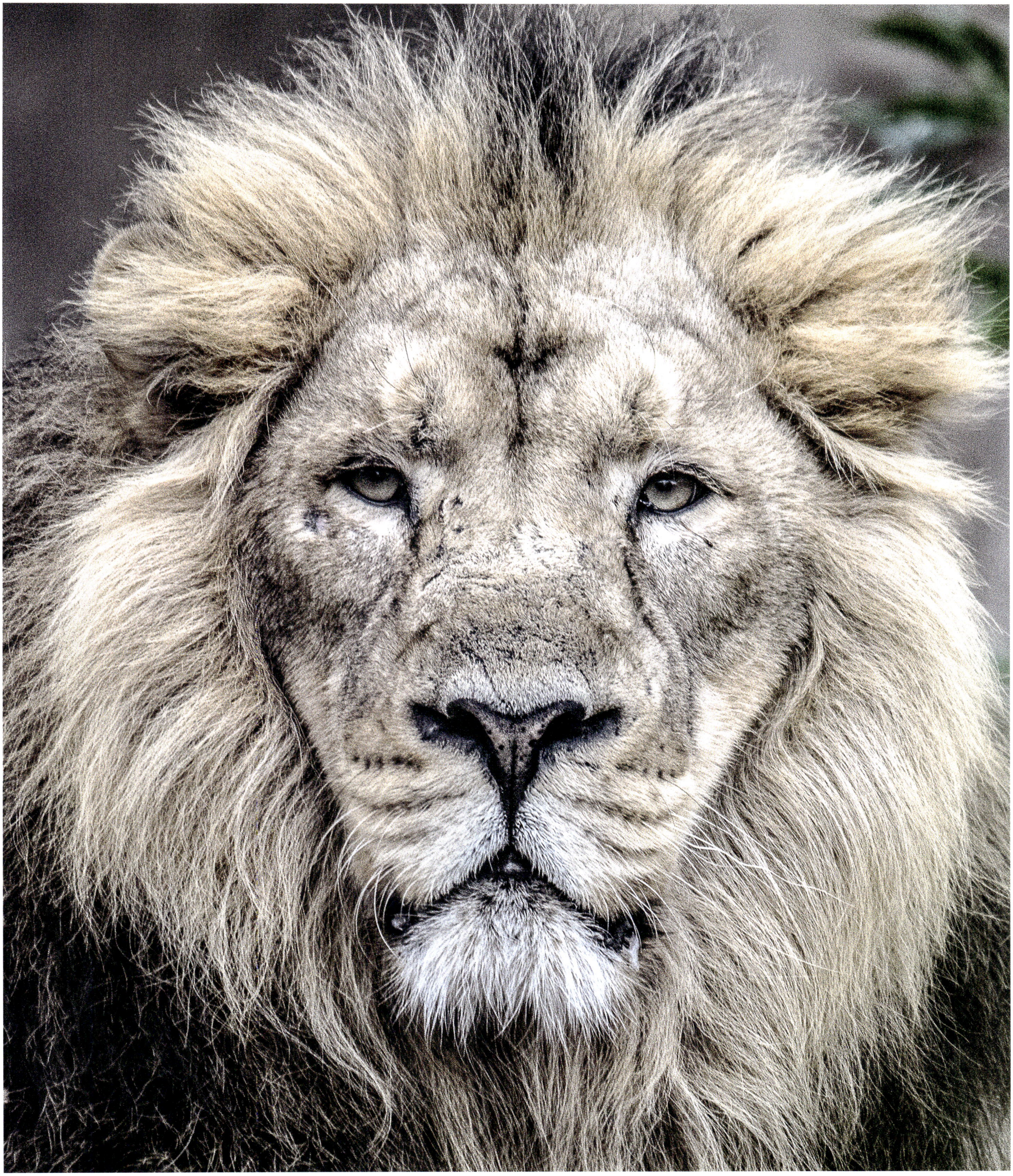

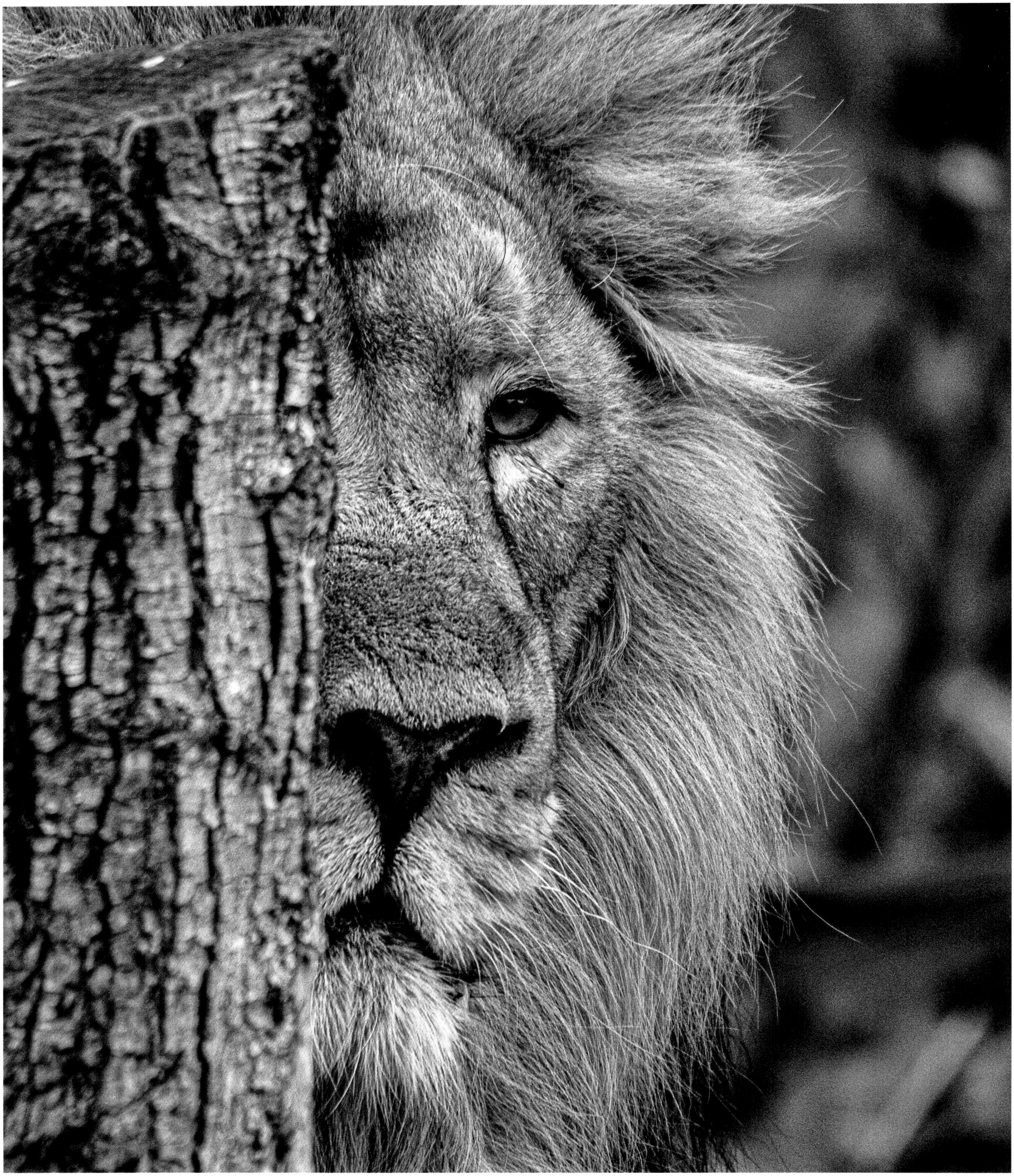

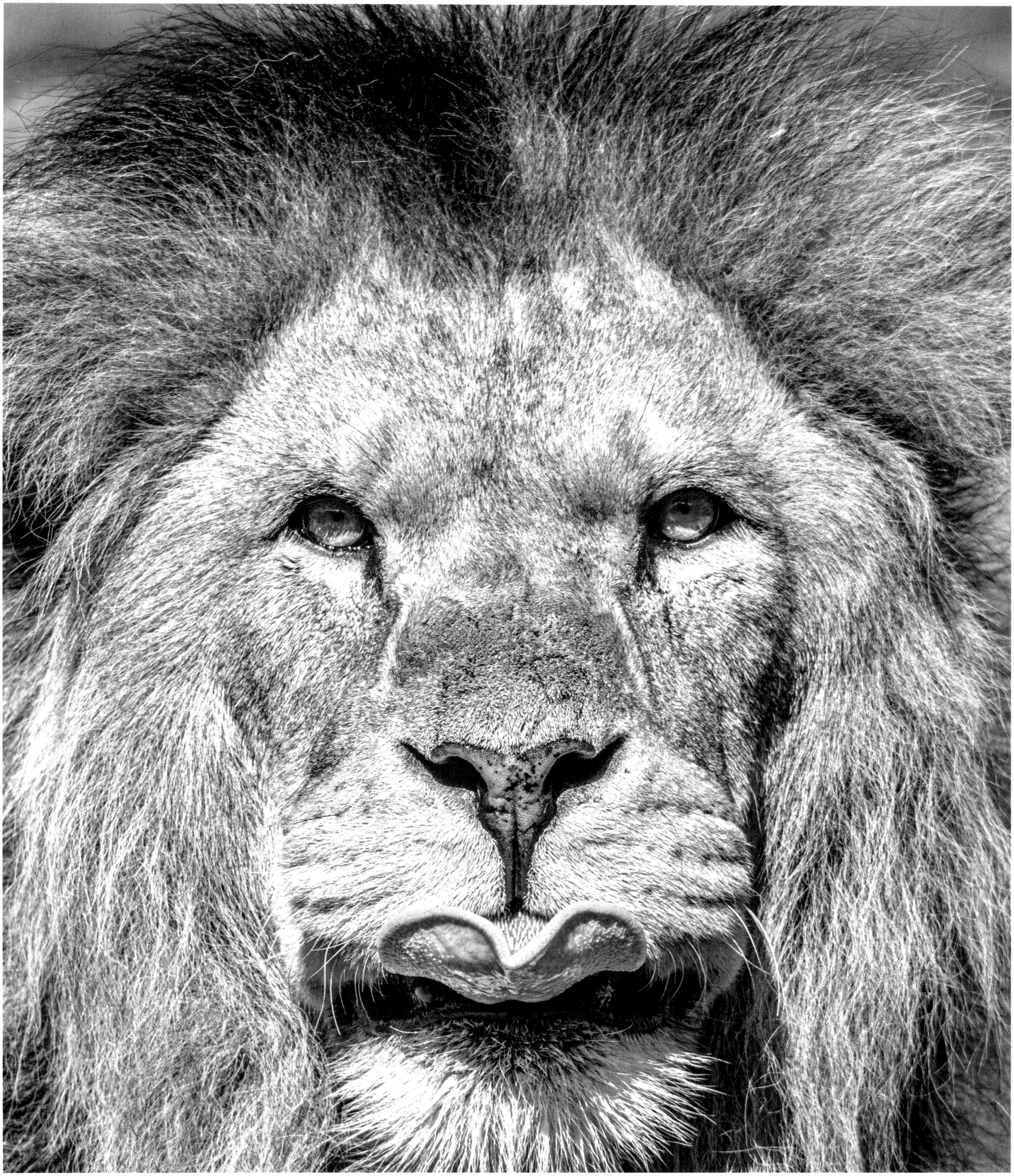

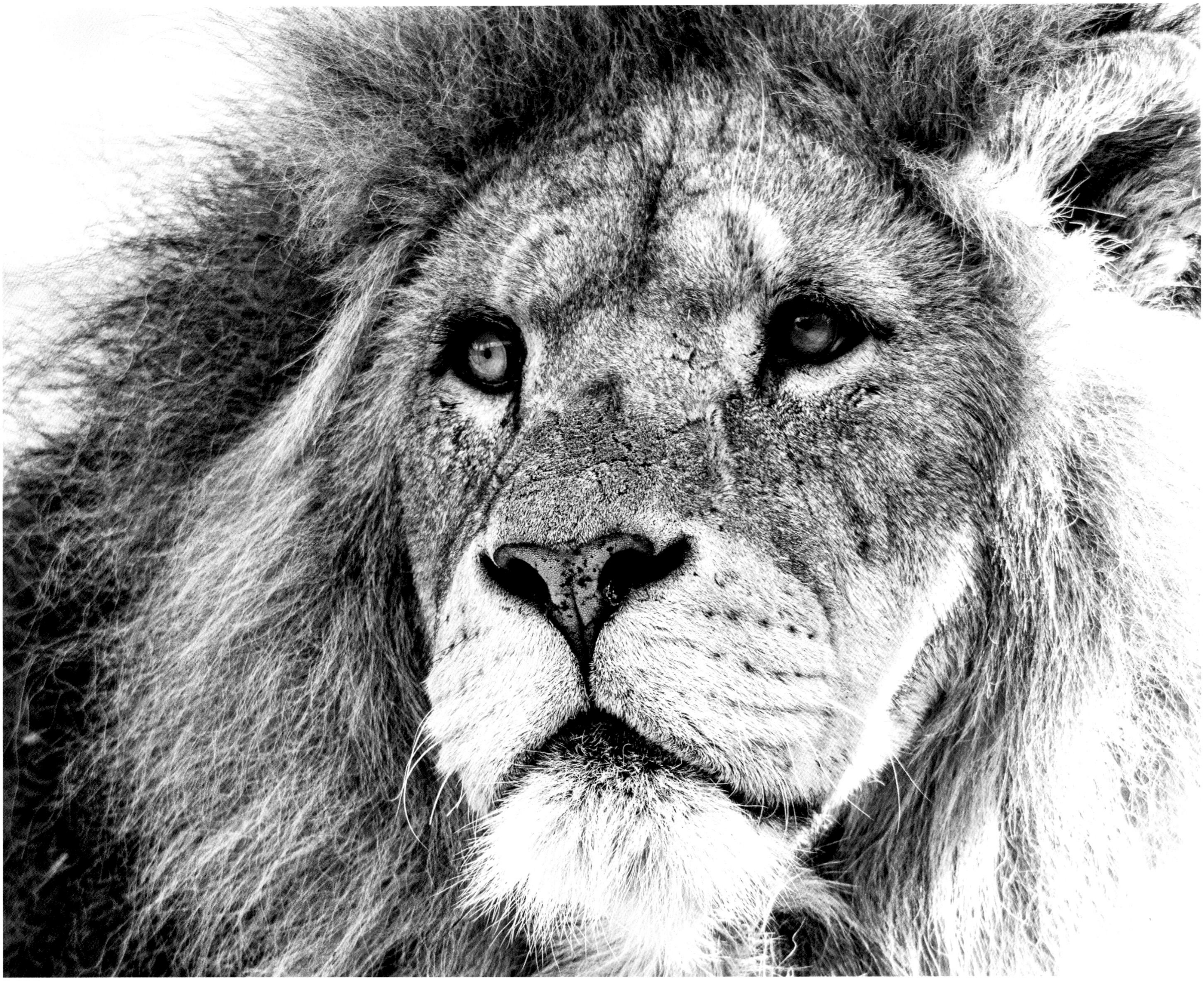

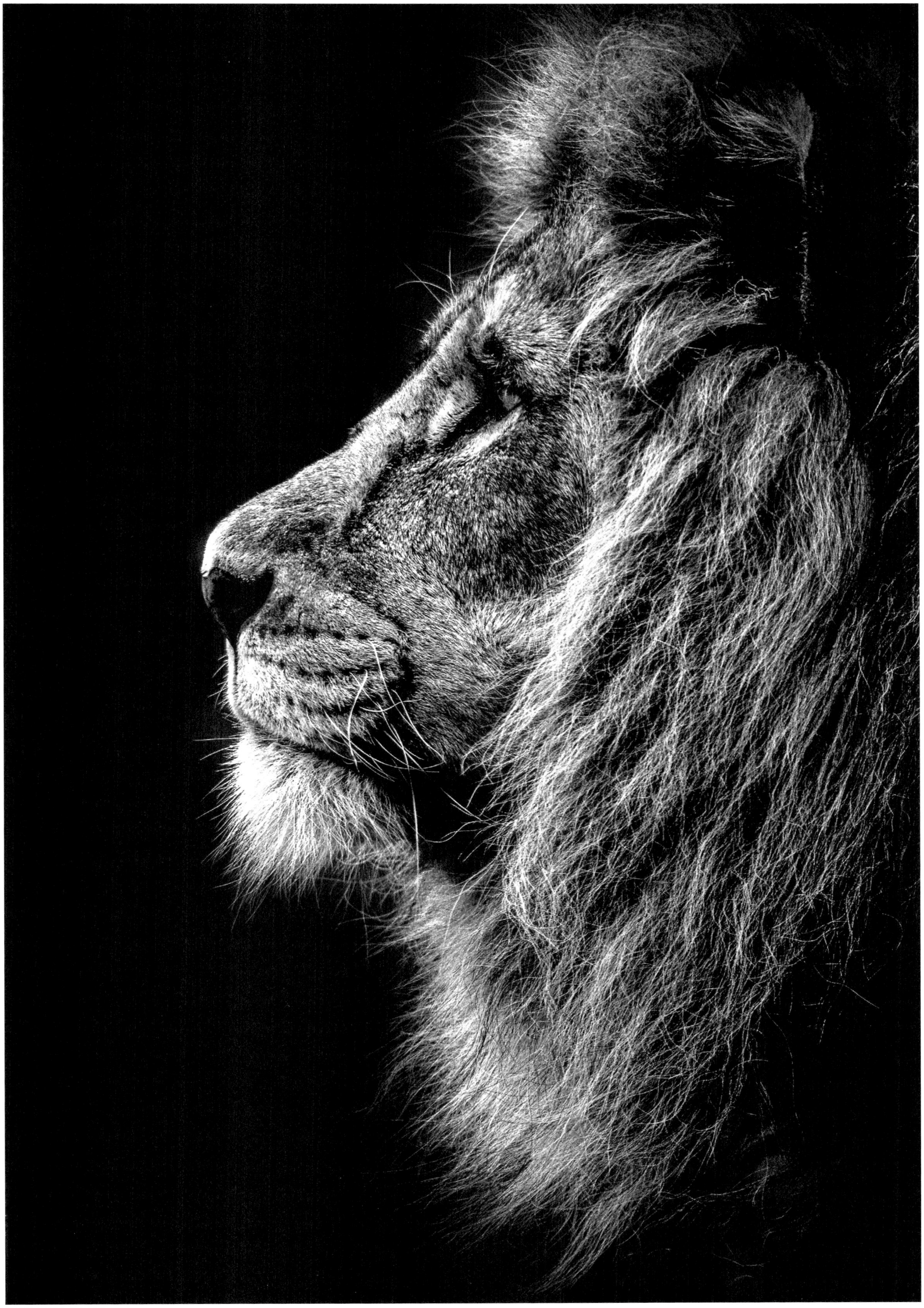

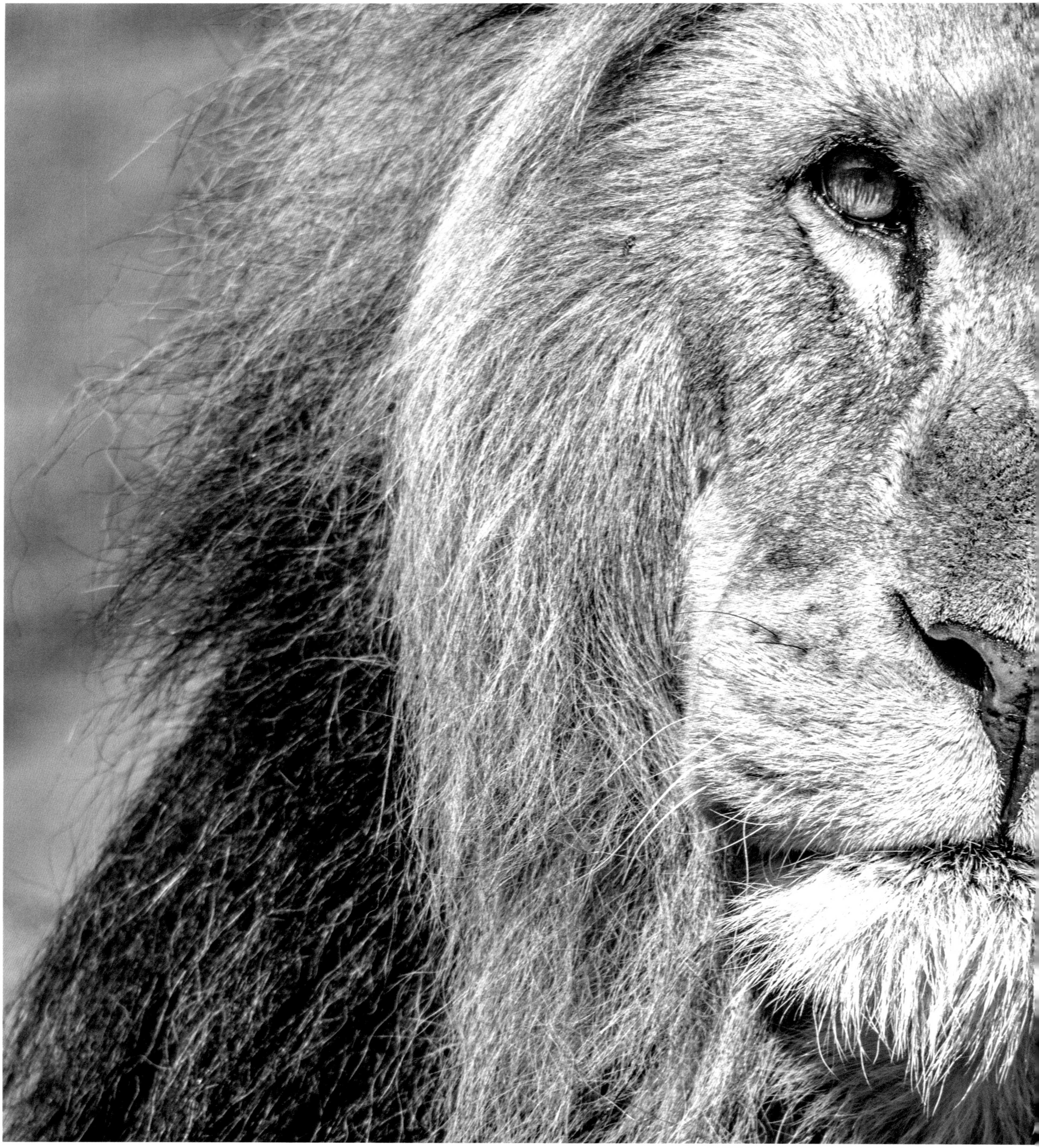

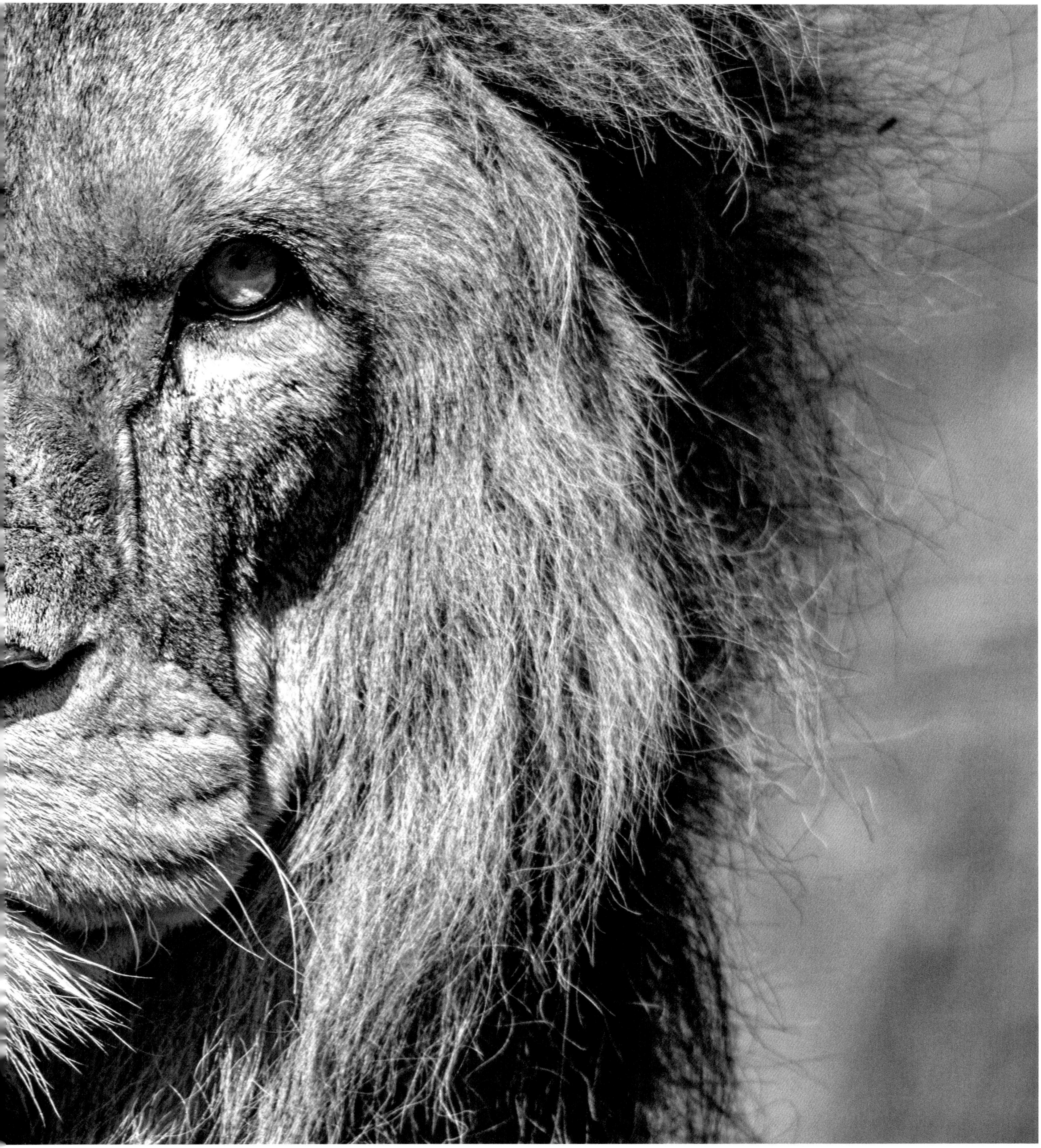

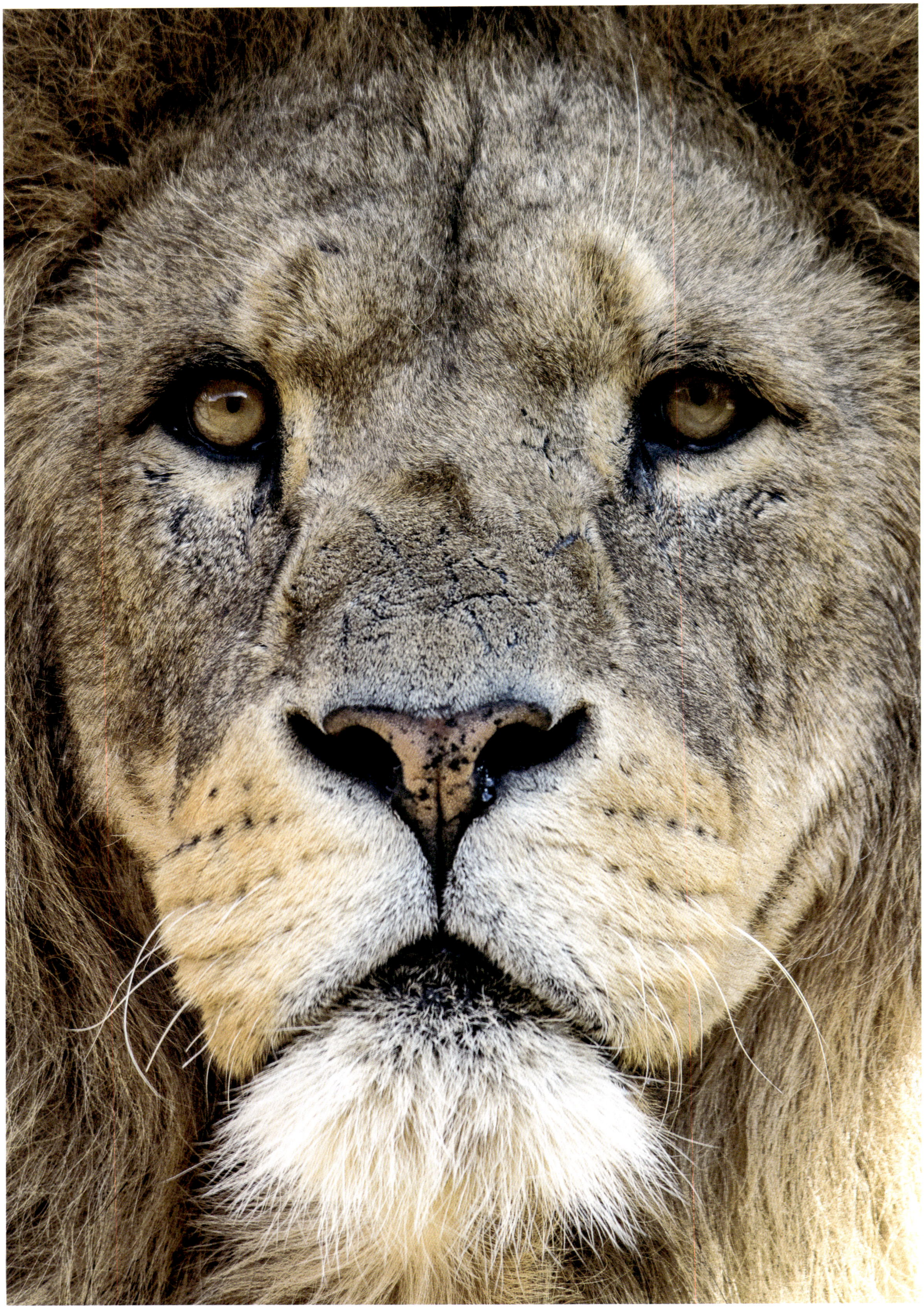

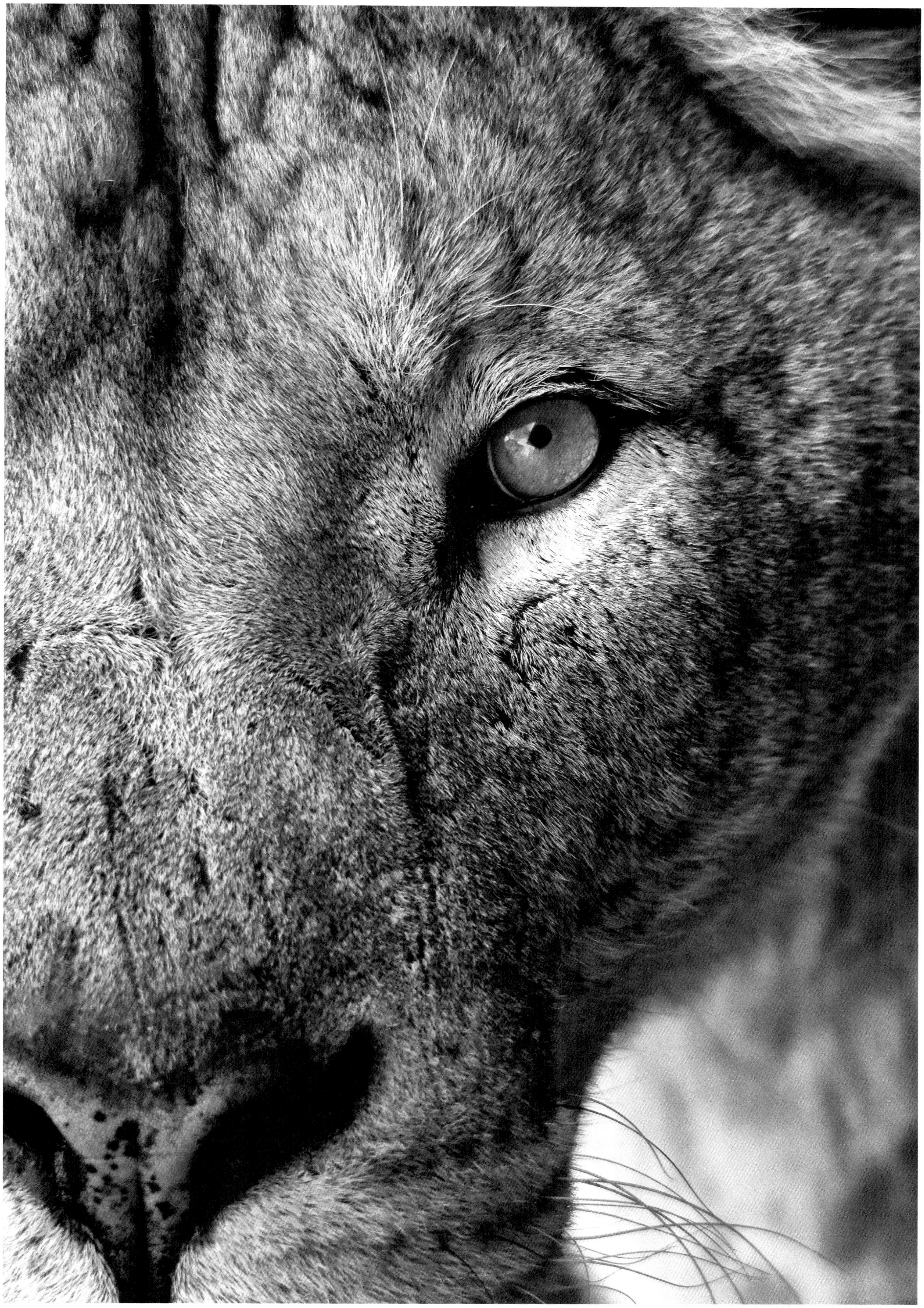

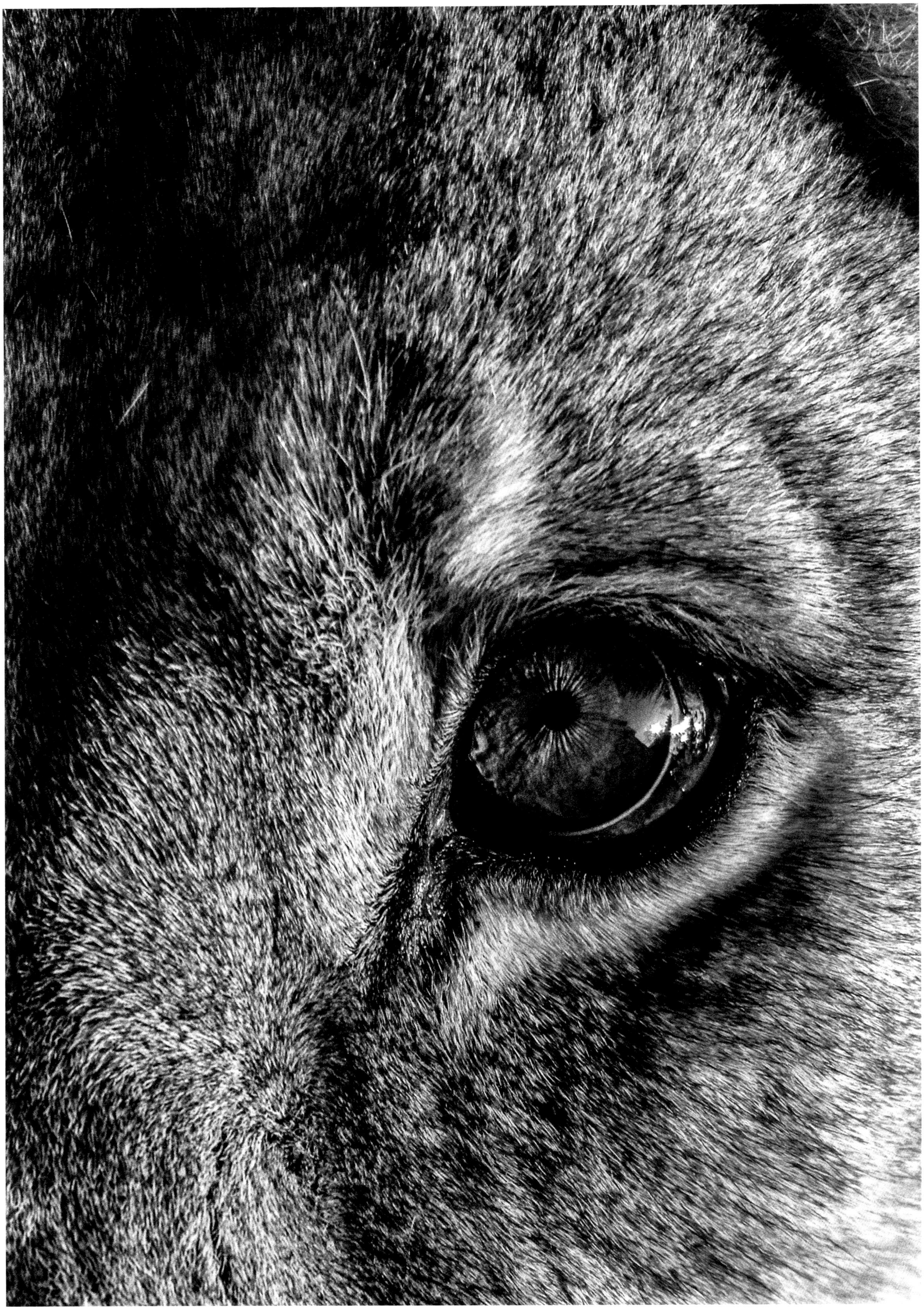

‘Her Eye’ is the favourite of those I have taken of this iconic species. I took it back in 2016 but I still get emotional when I look at it. It says so much: love, pride, determination and loyalty. I hope that the image strikes an emotional chord with you.

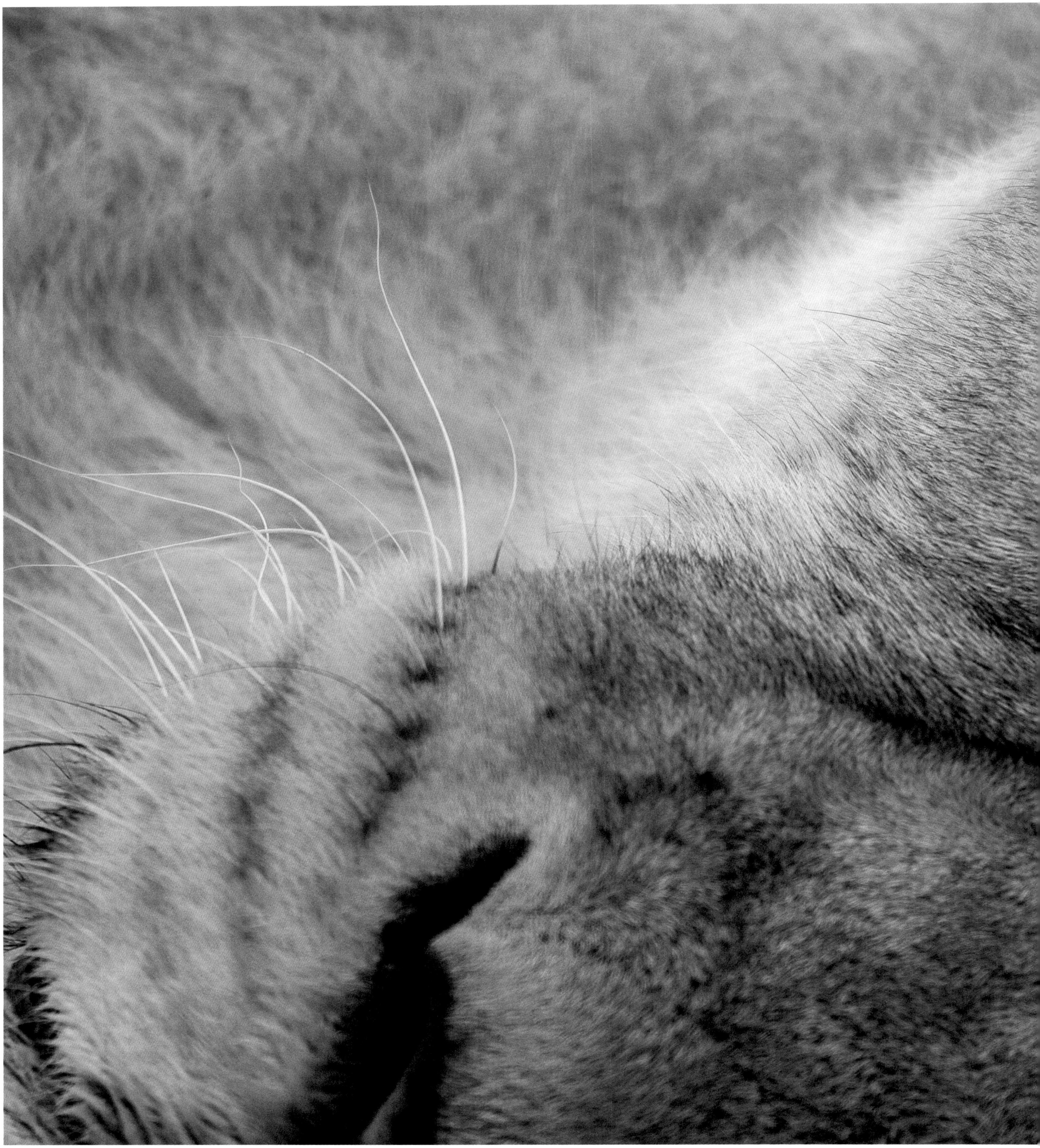

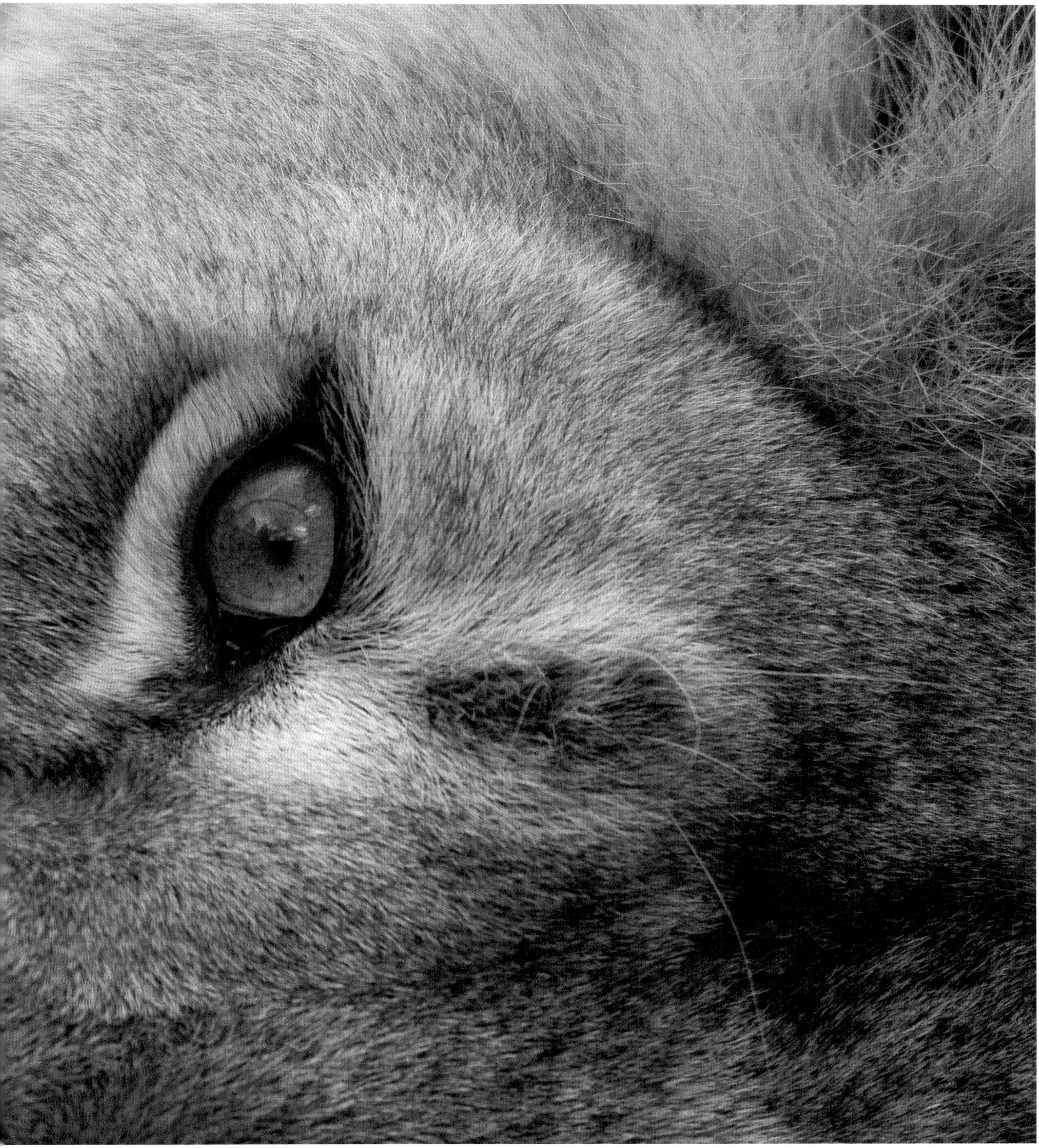

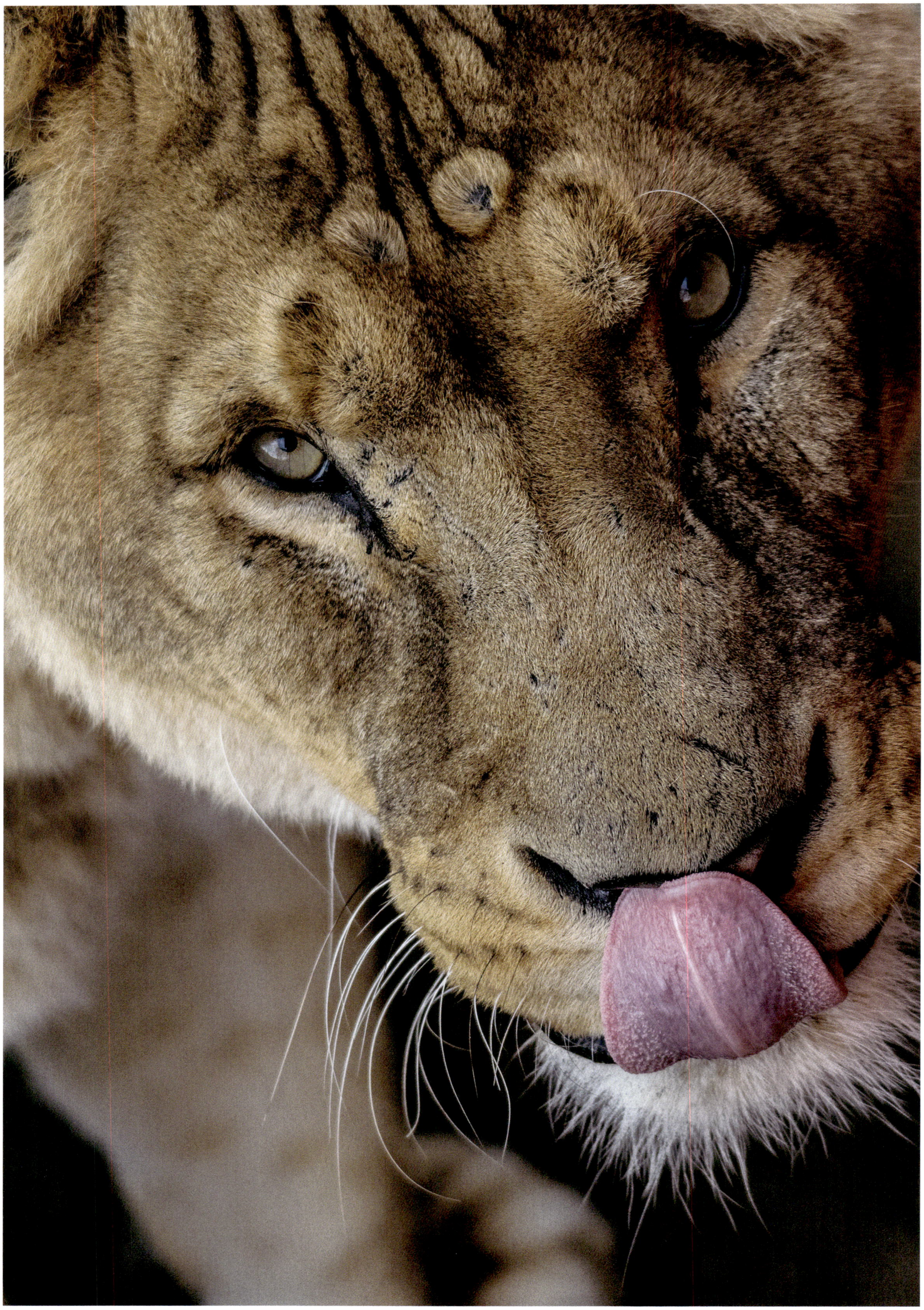

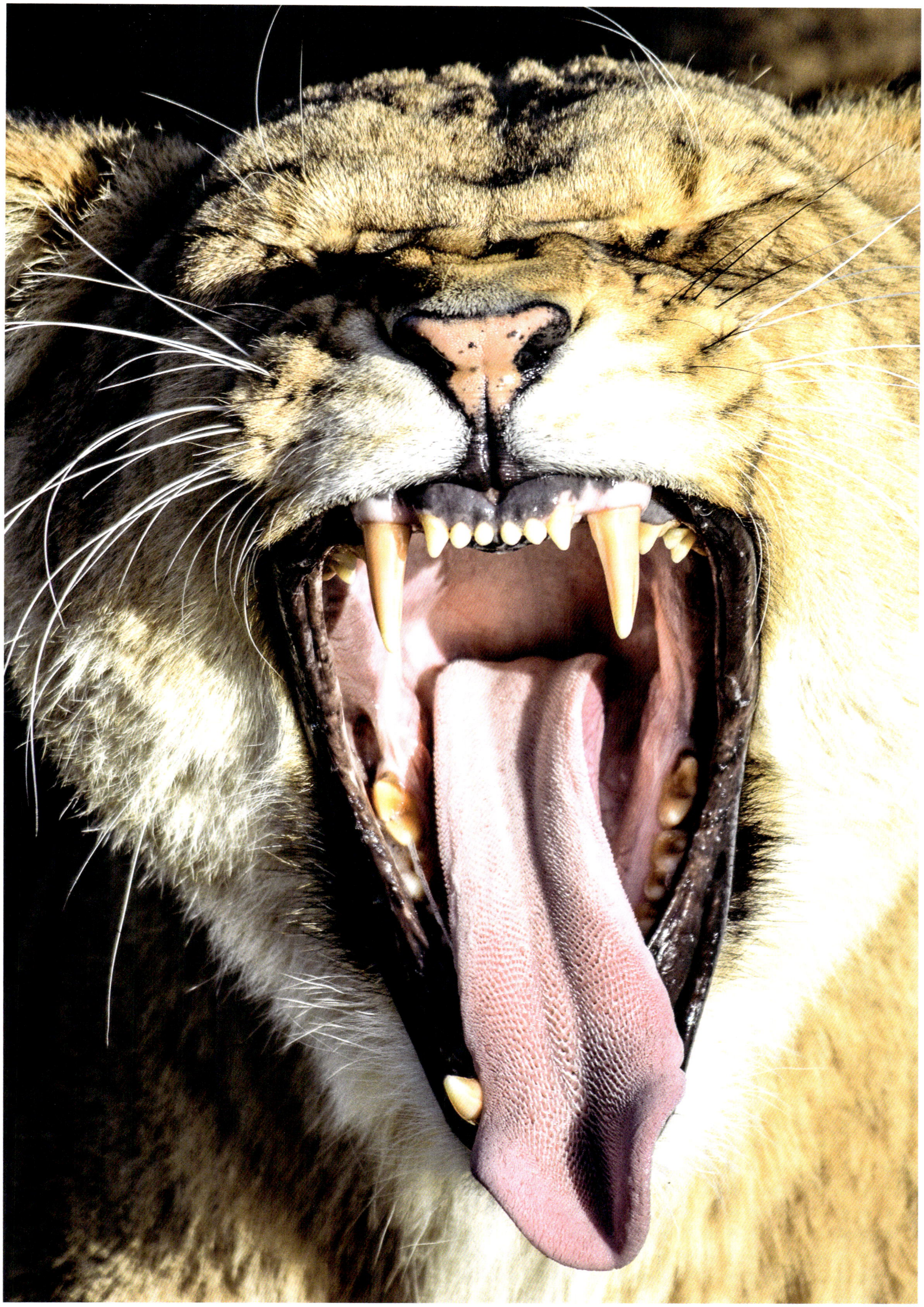

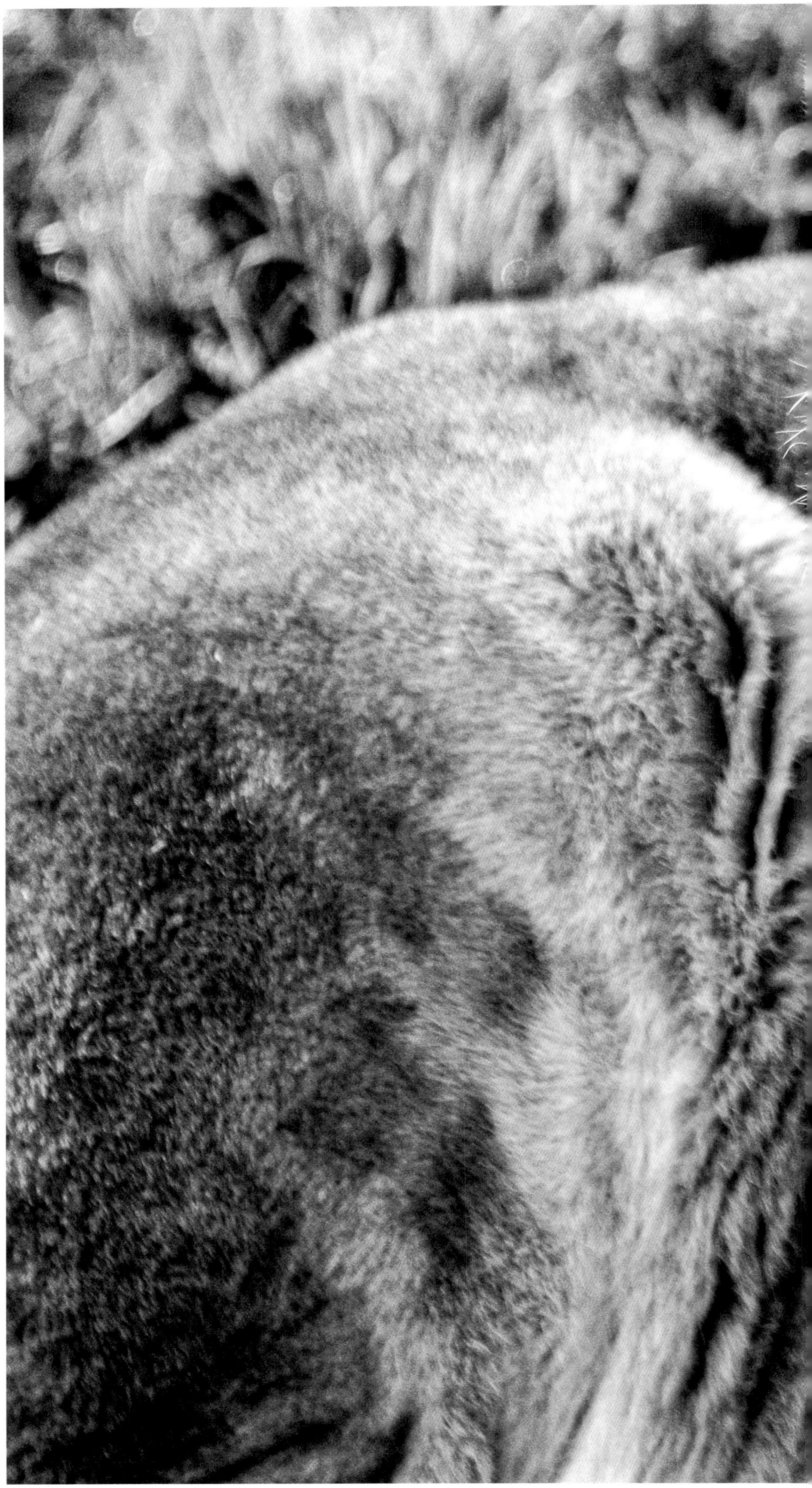

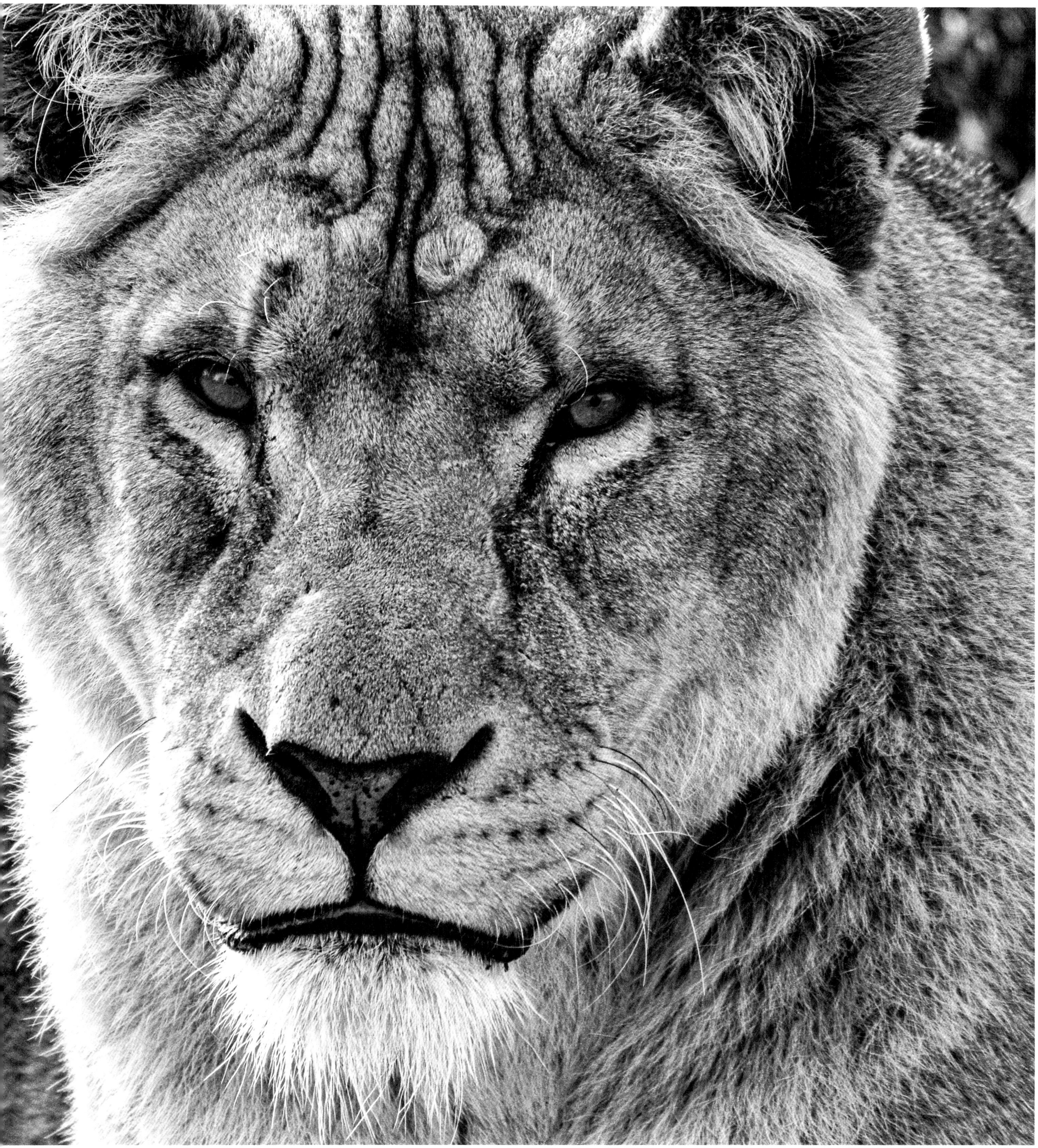

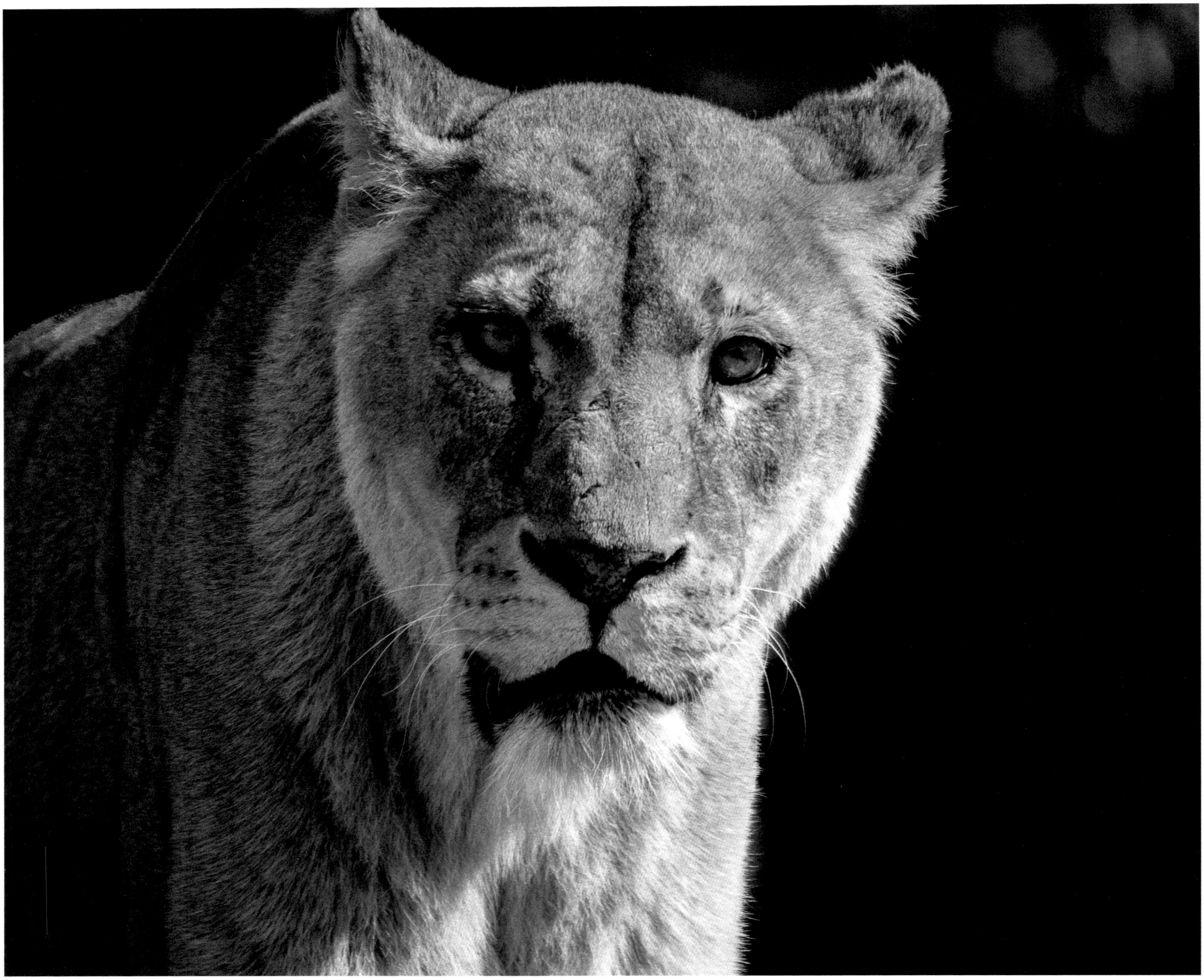

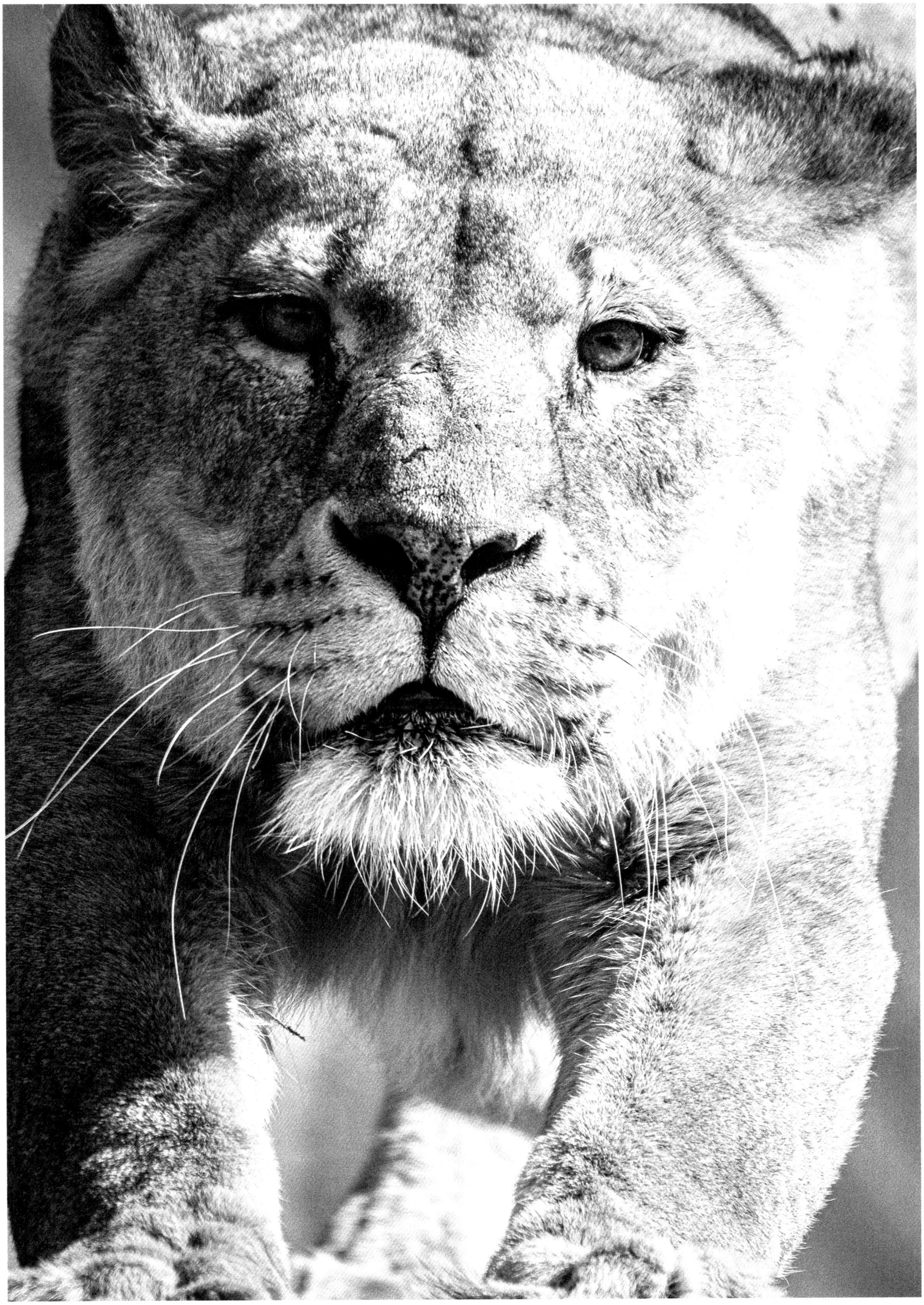

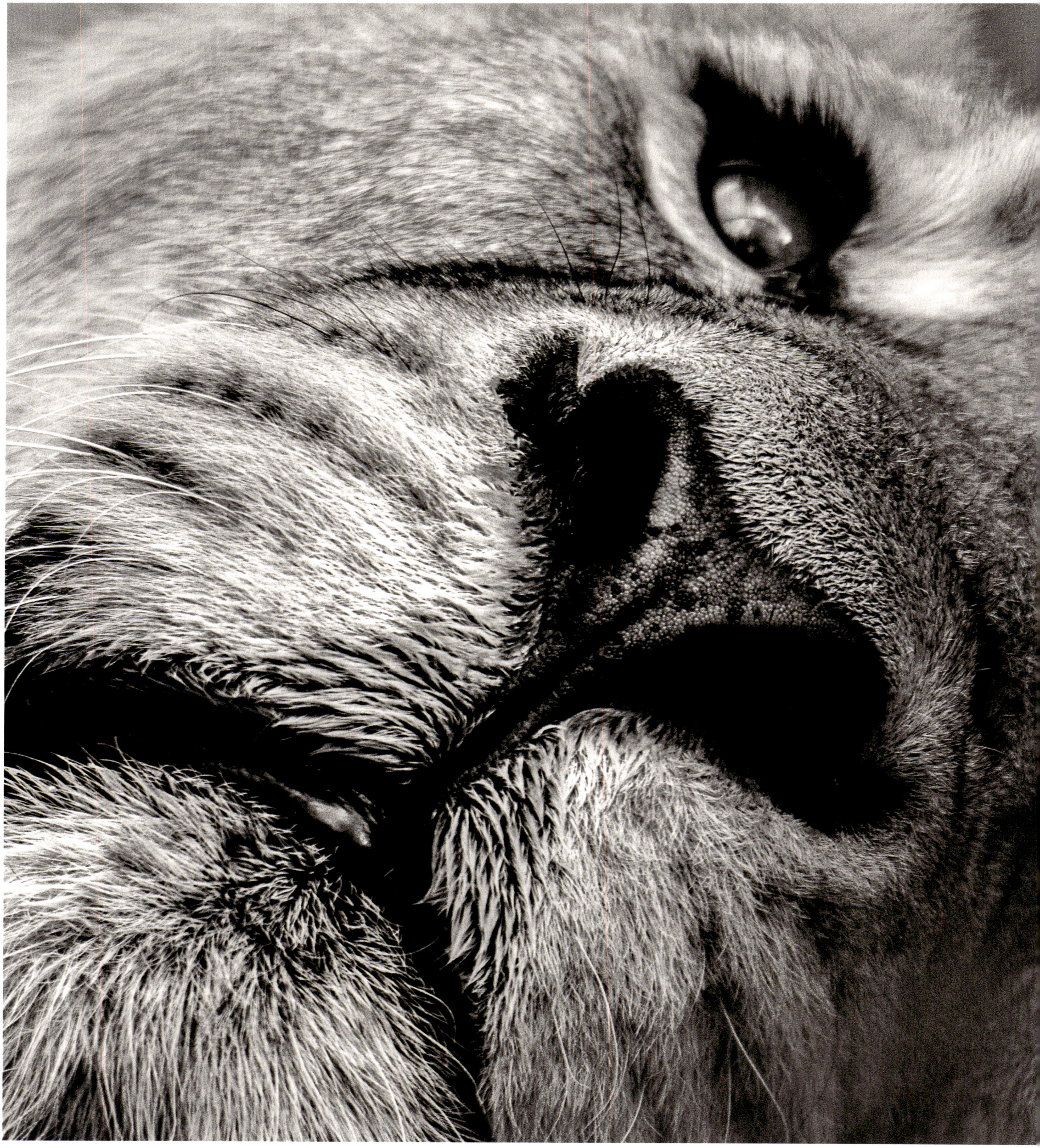

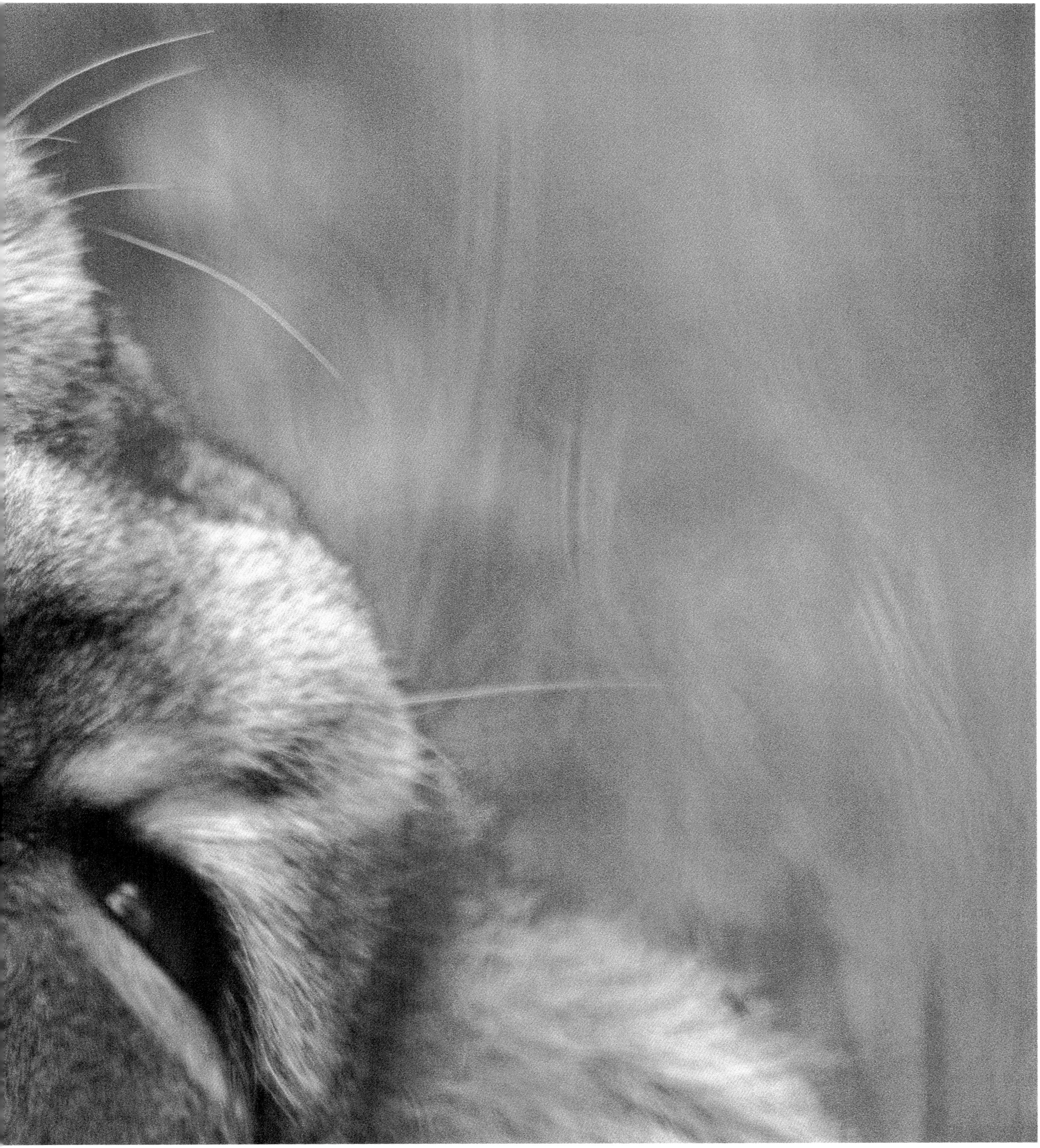

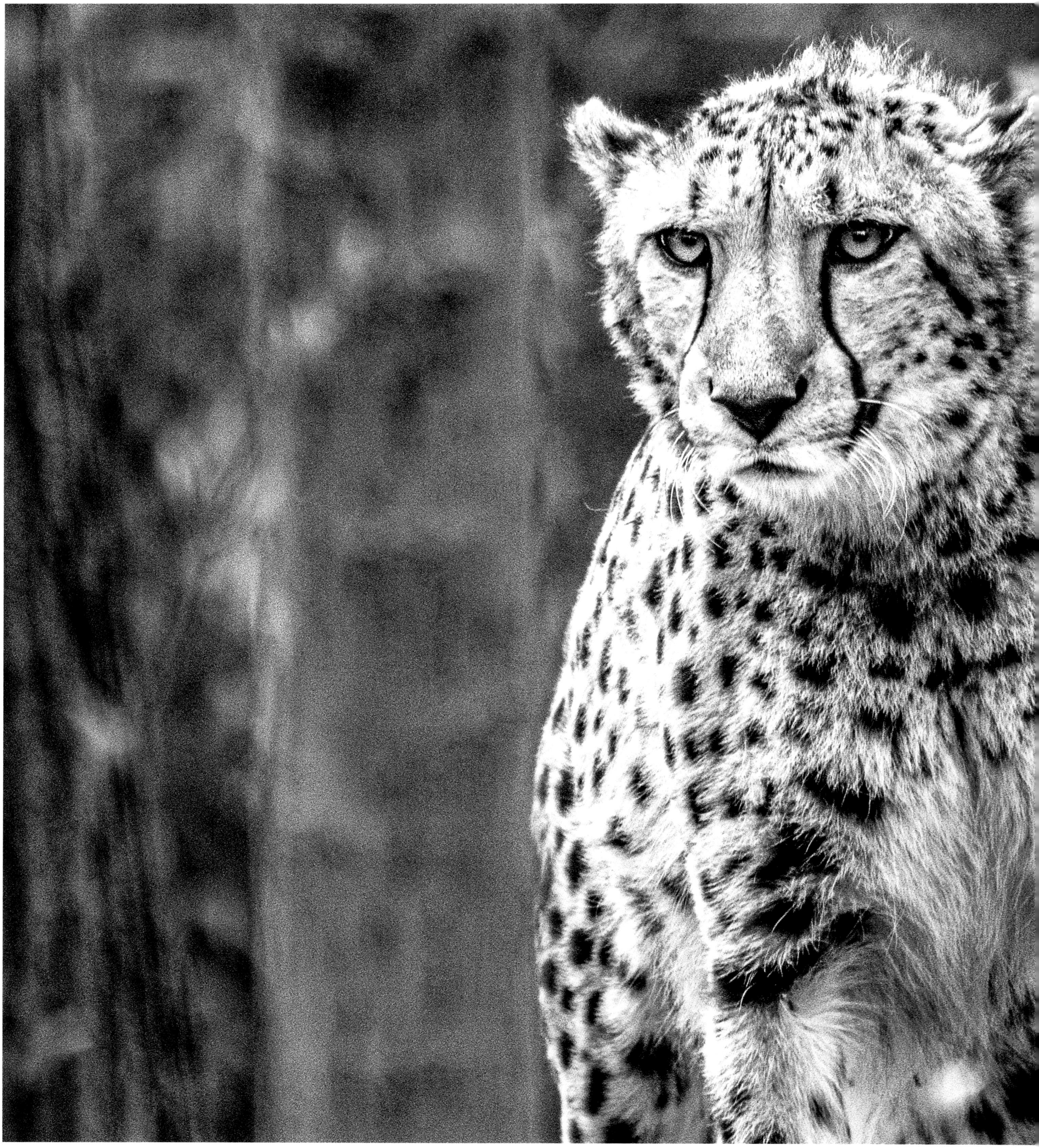

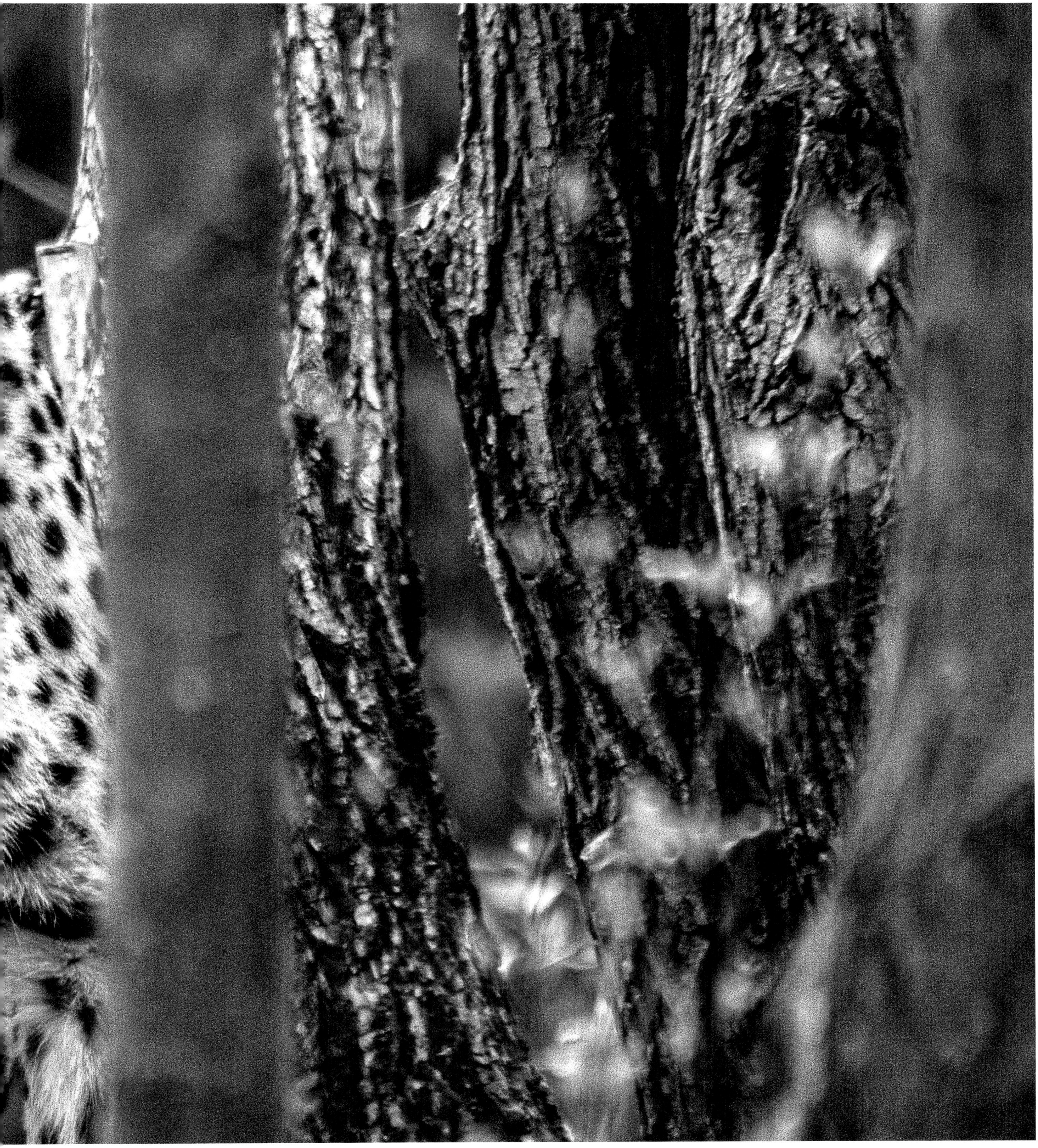

After years of failing to get a good enough shot of a cheetah, this April afternoon in 2019 I managed to capture 'Stealth'. That day will live long in my memory, it is yet another reminder to never give up when things aren't going your way.

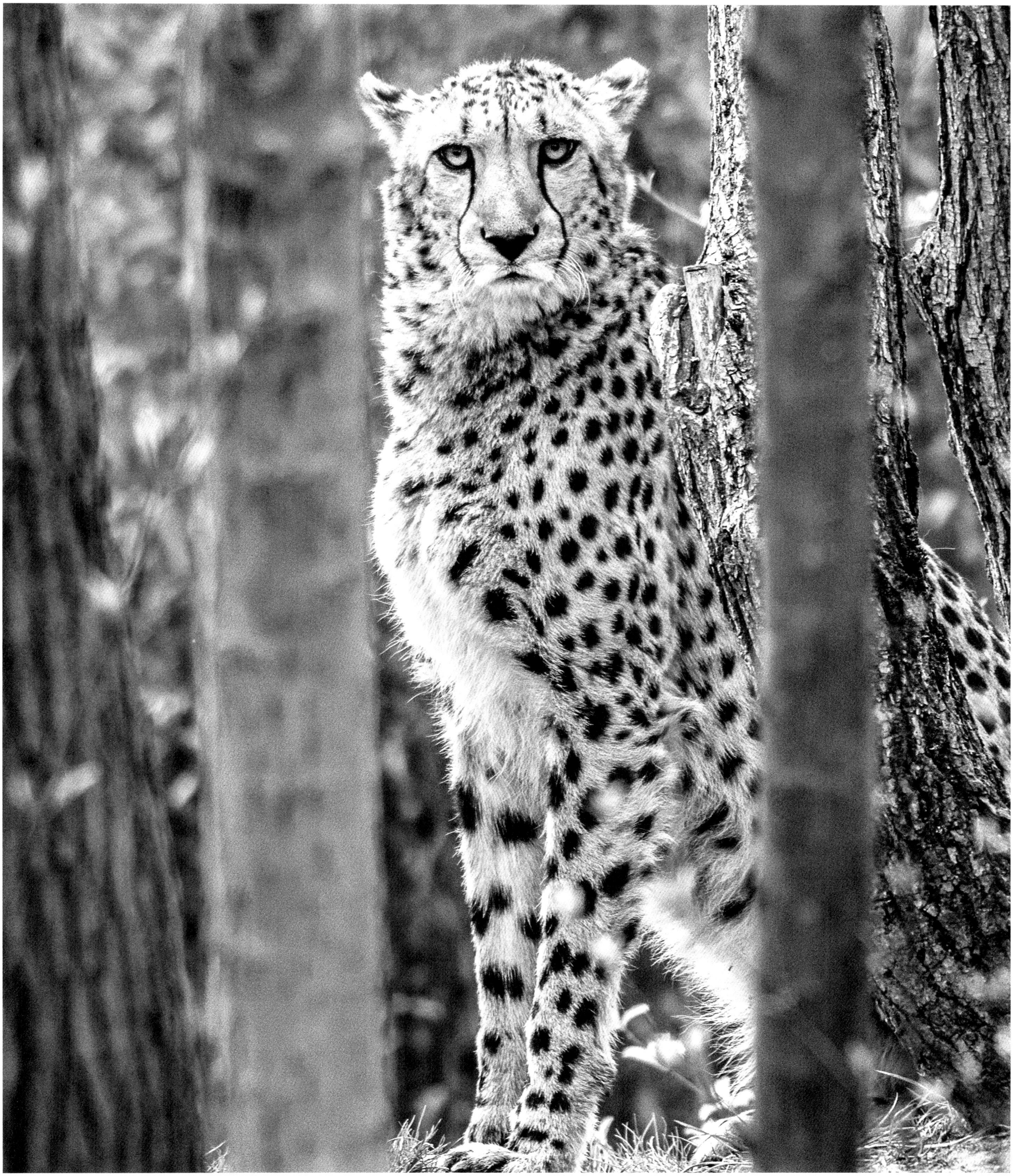

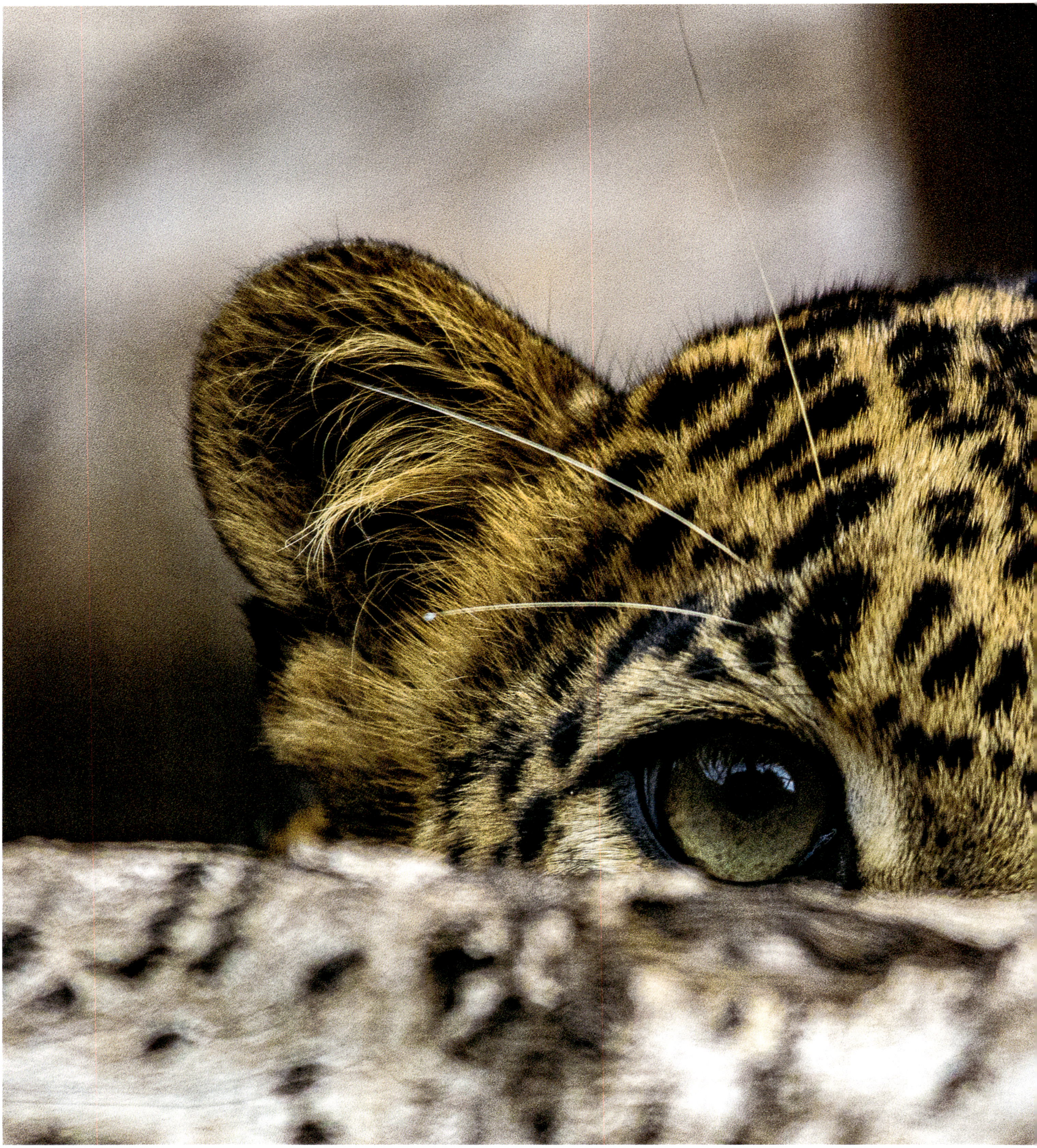

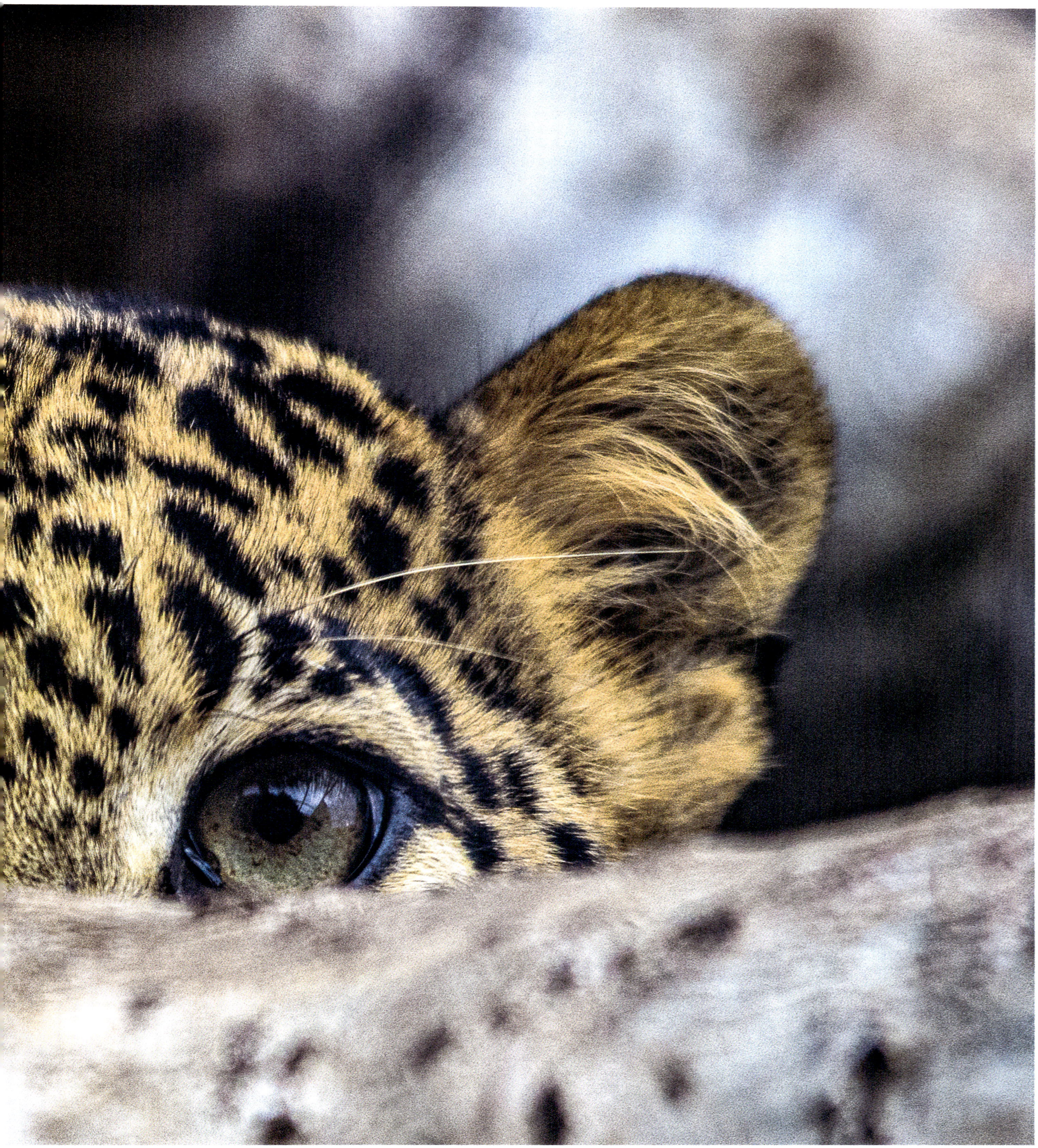

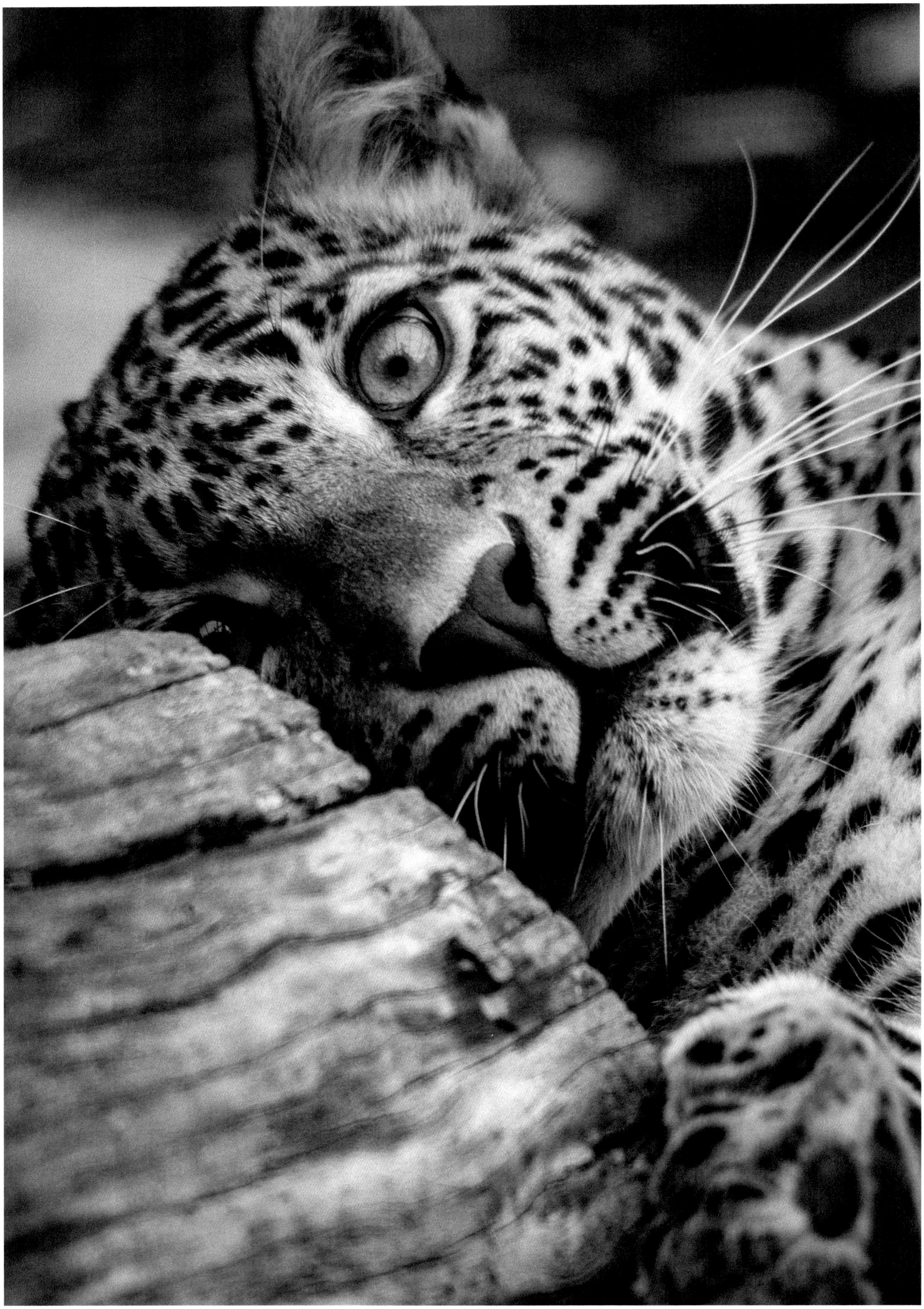

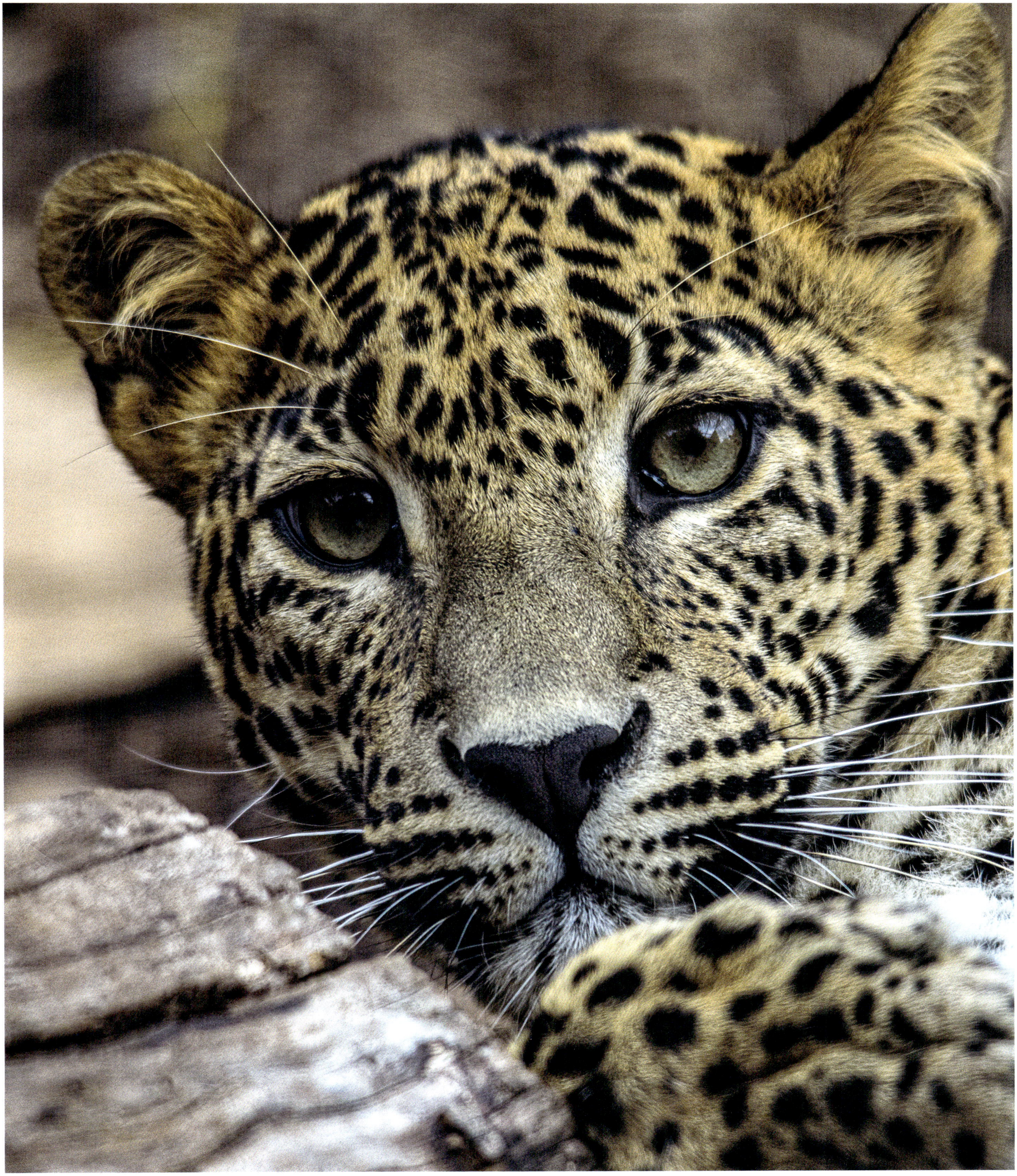

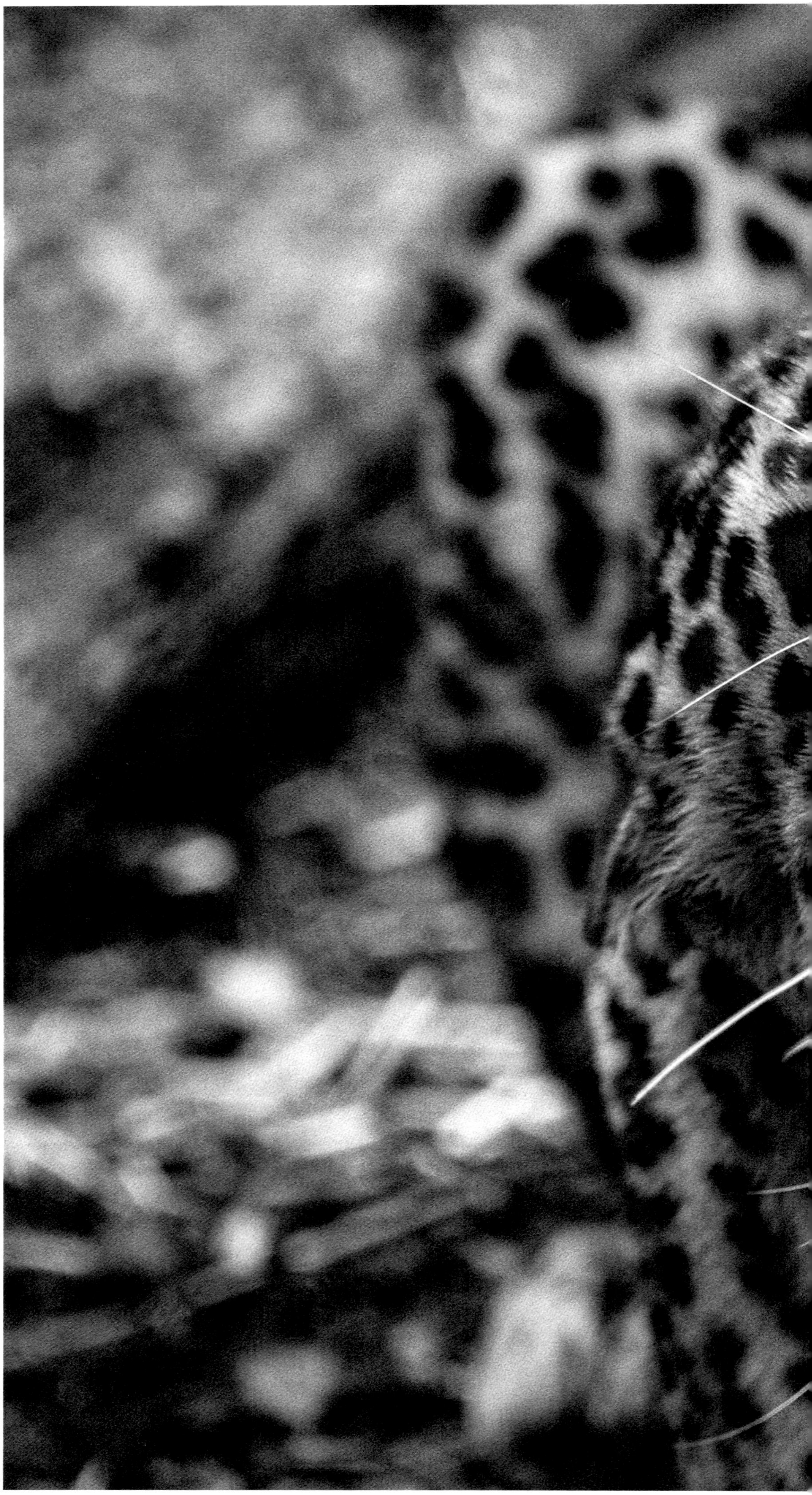

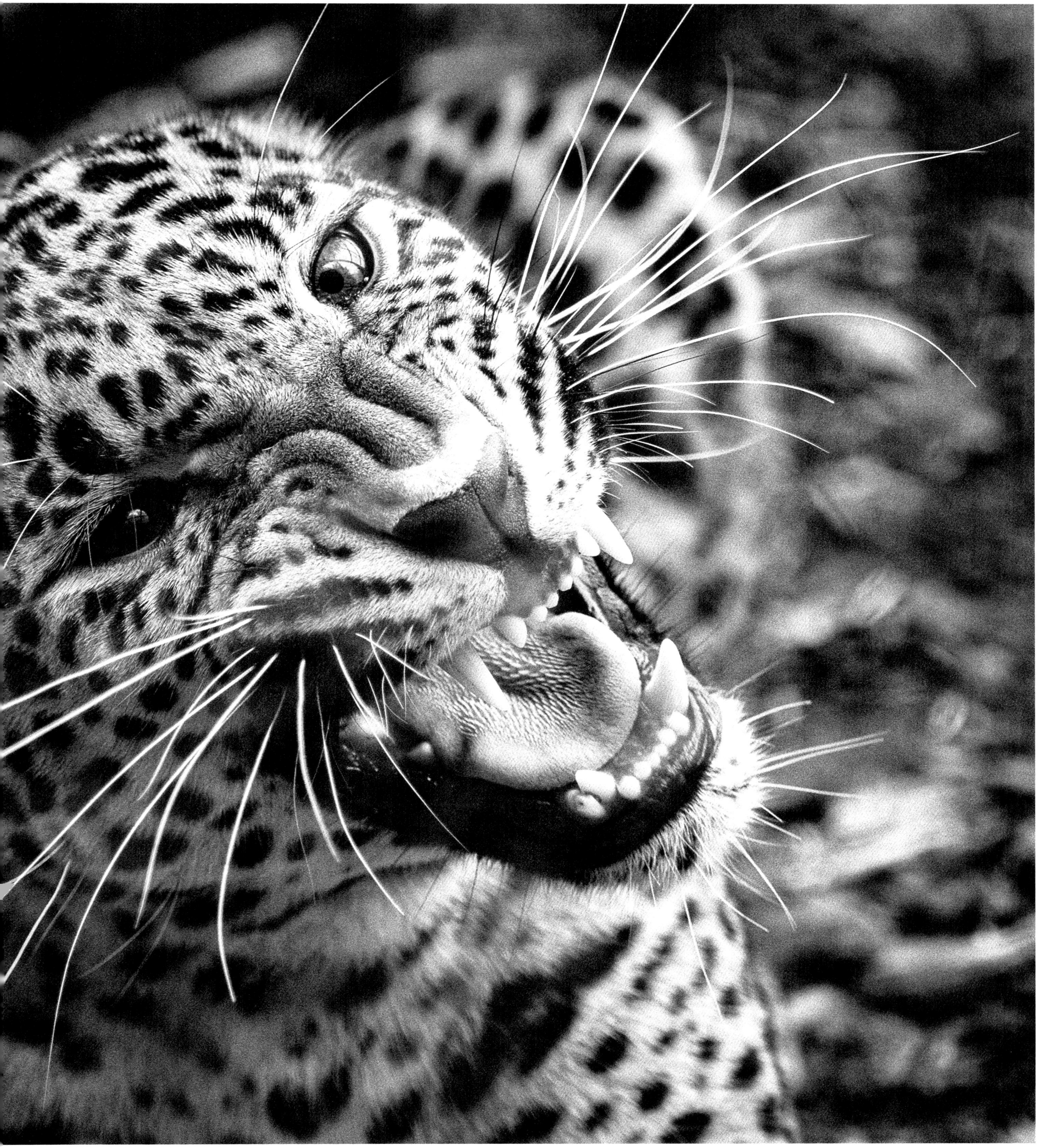

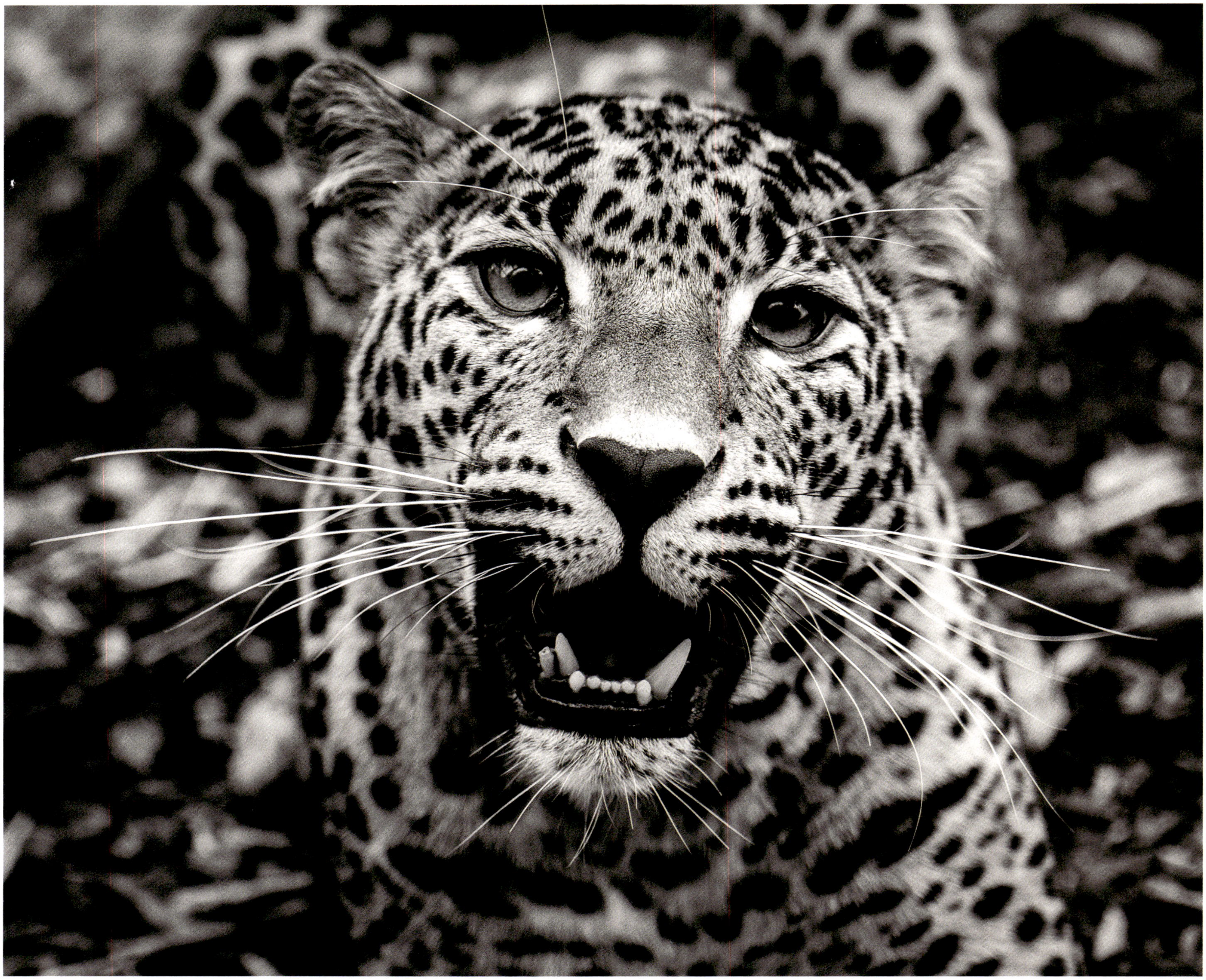

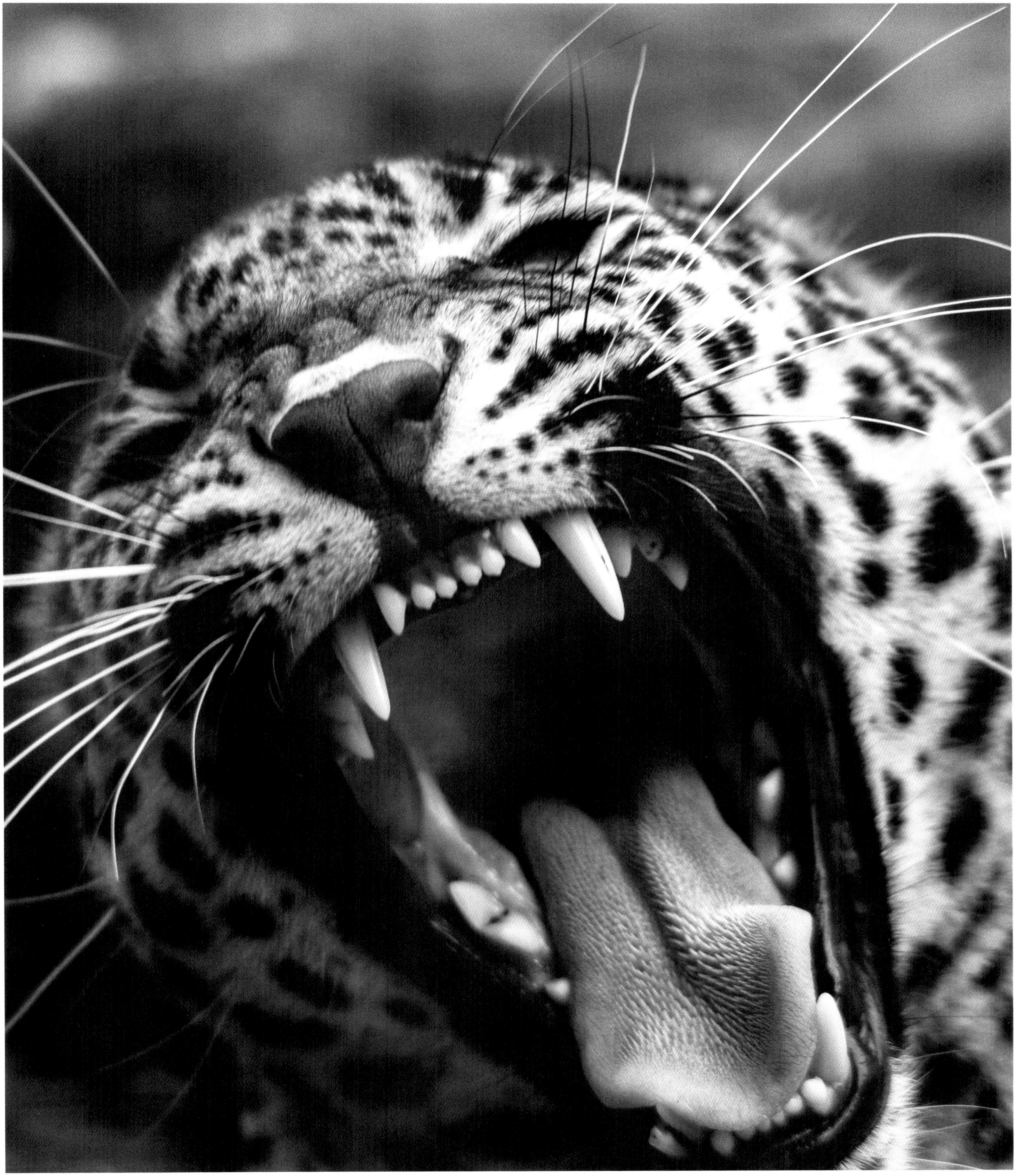

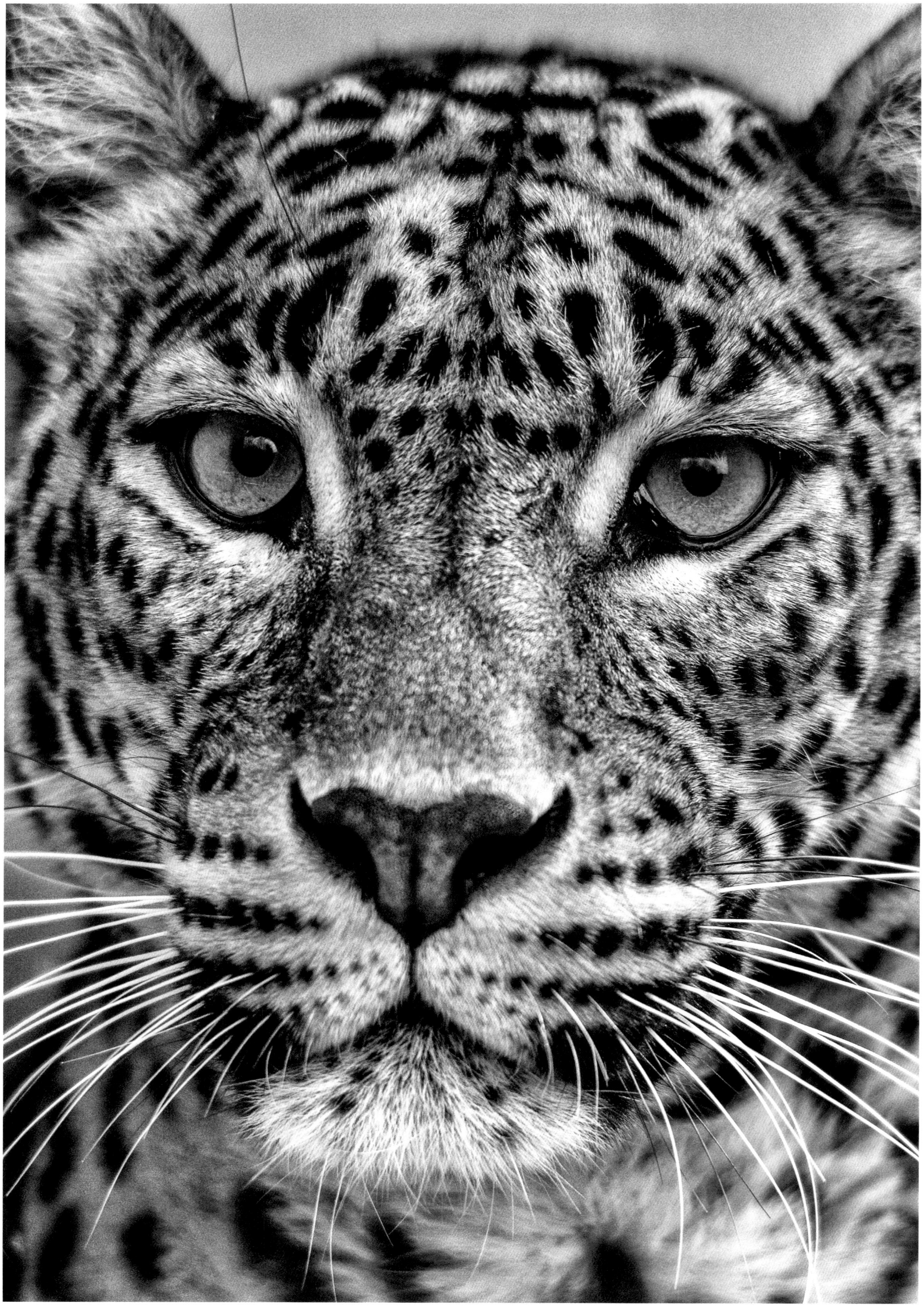

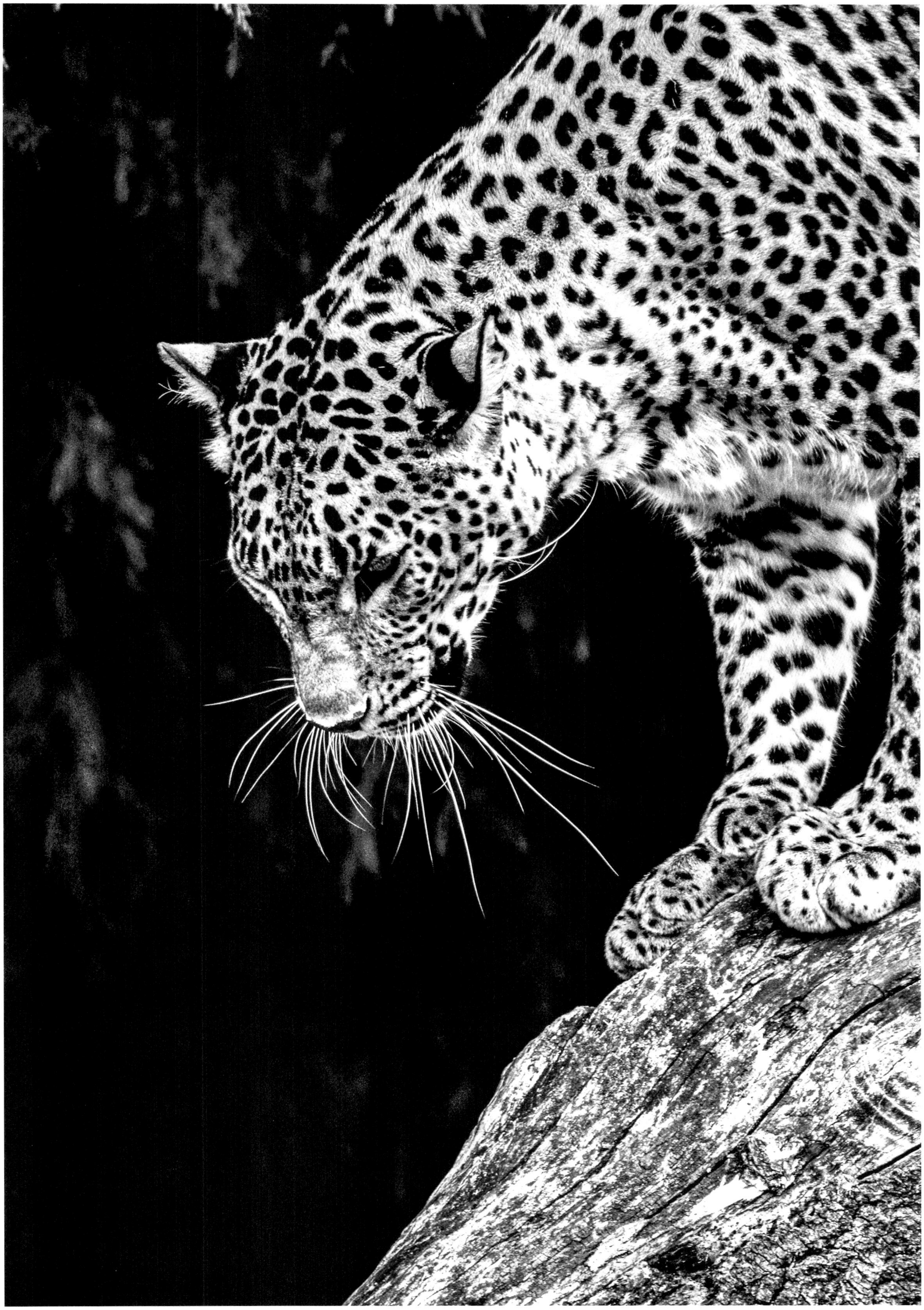

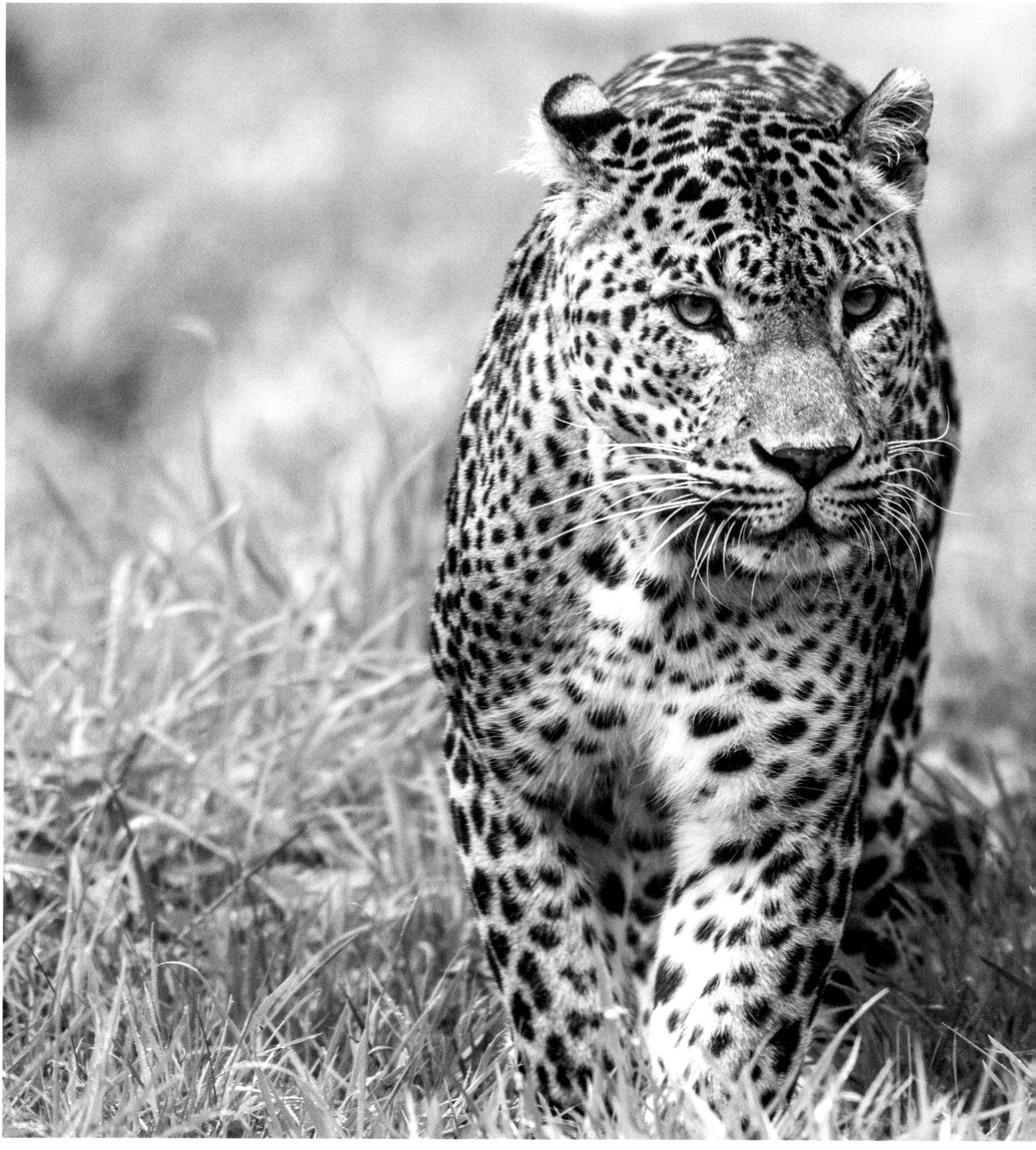

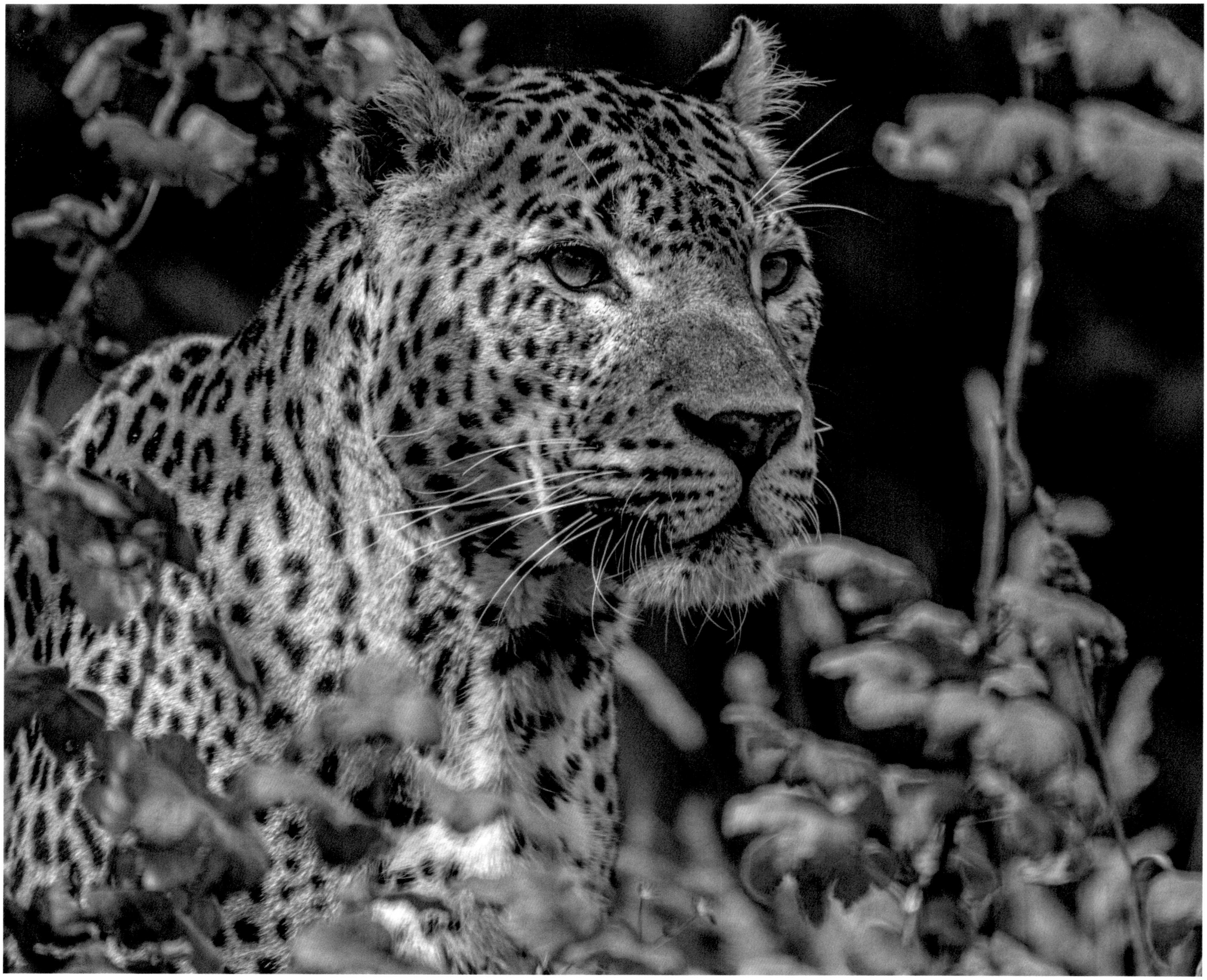

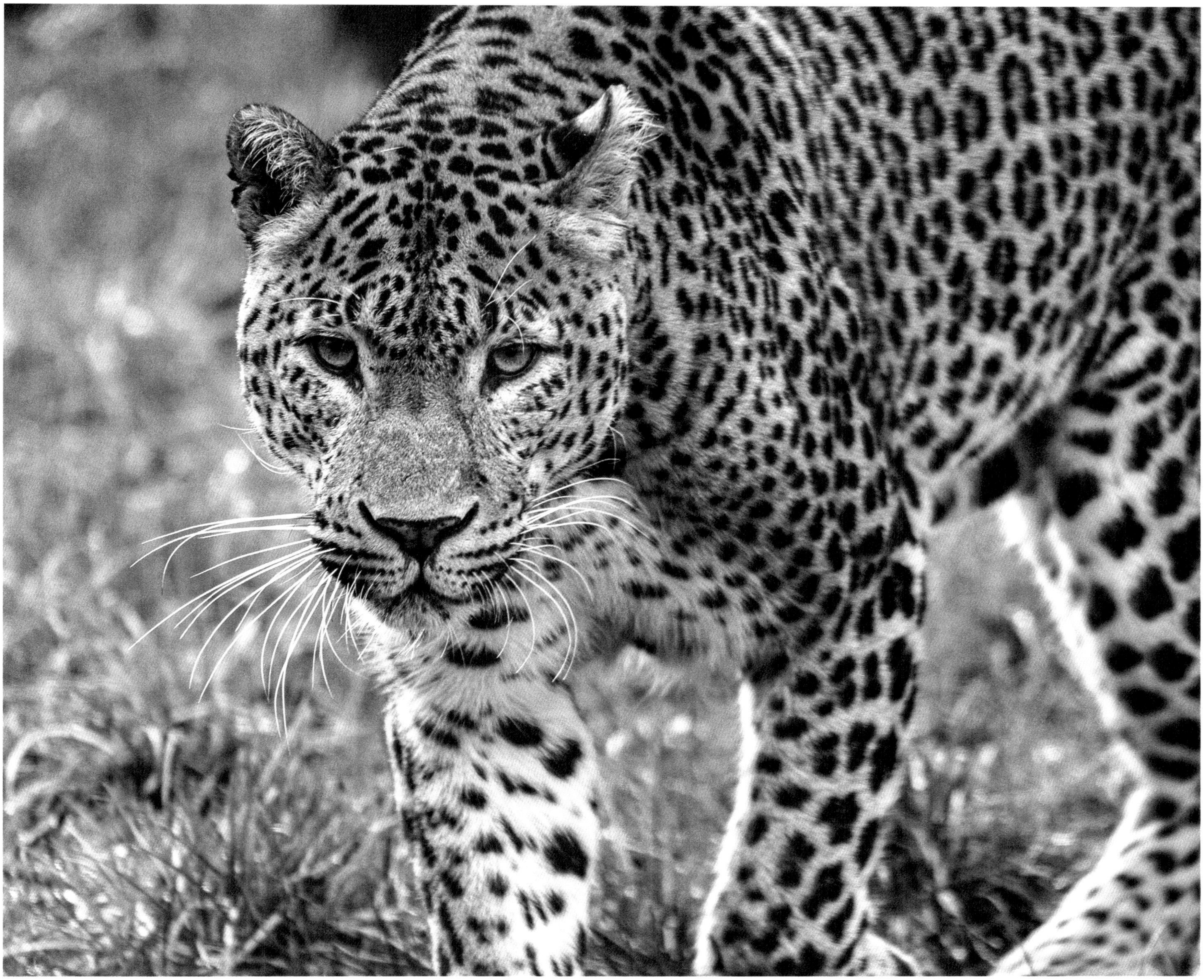

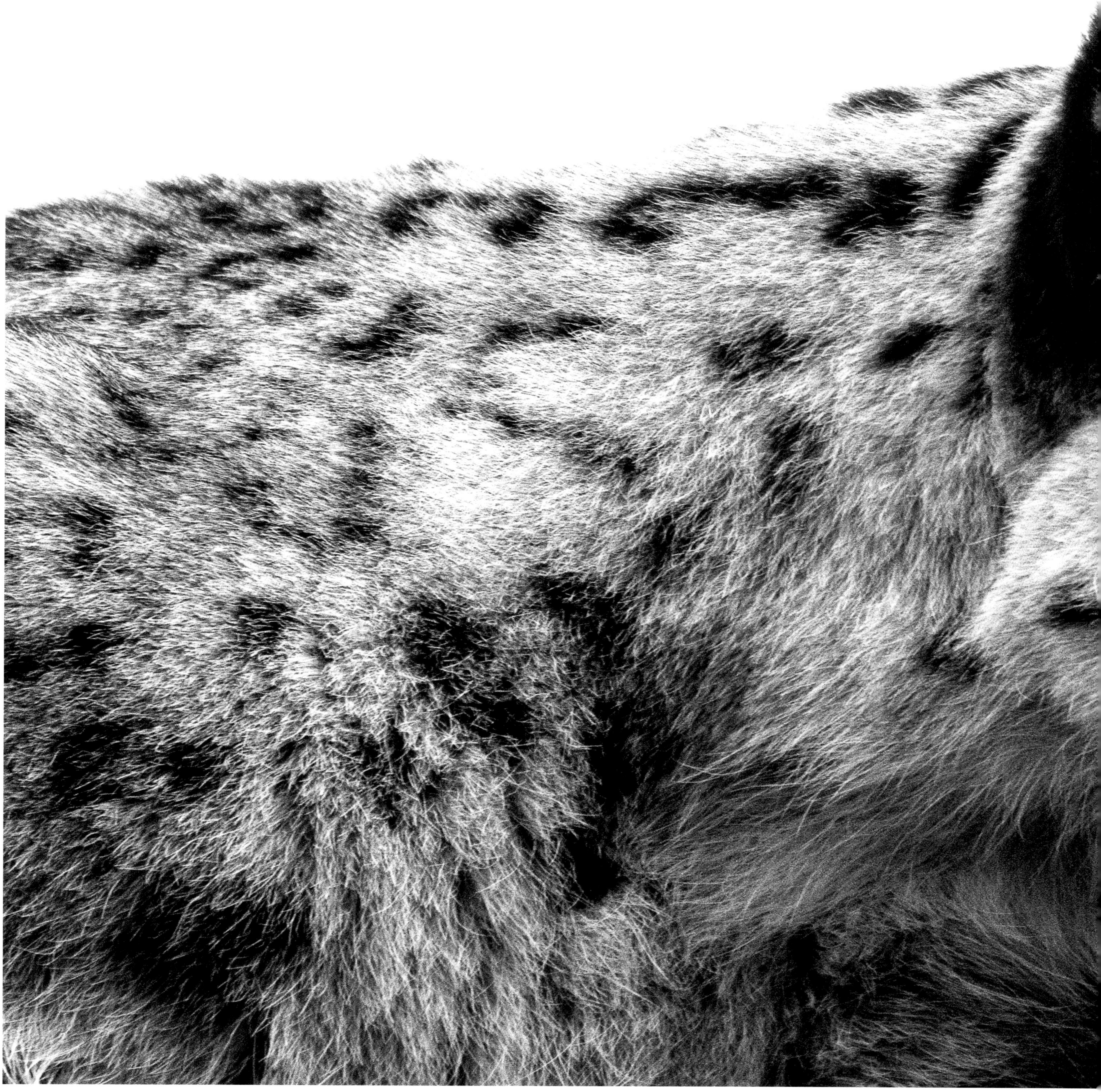

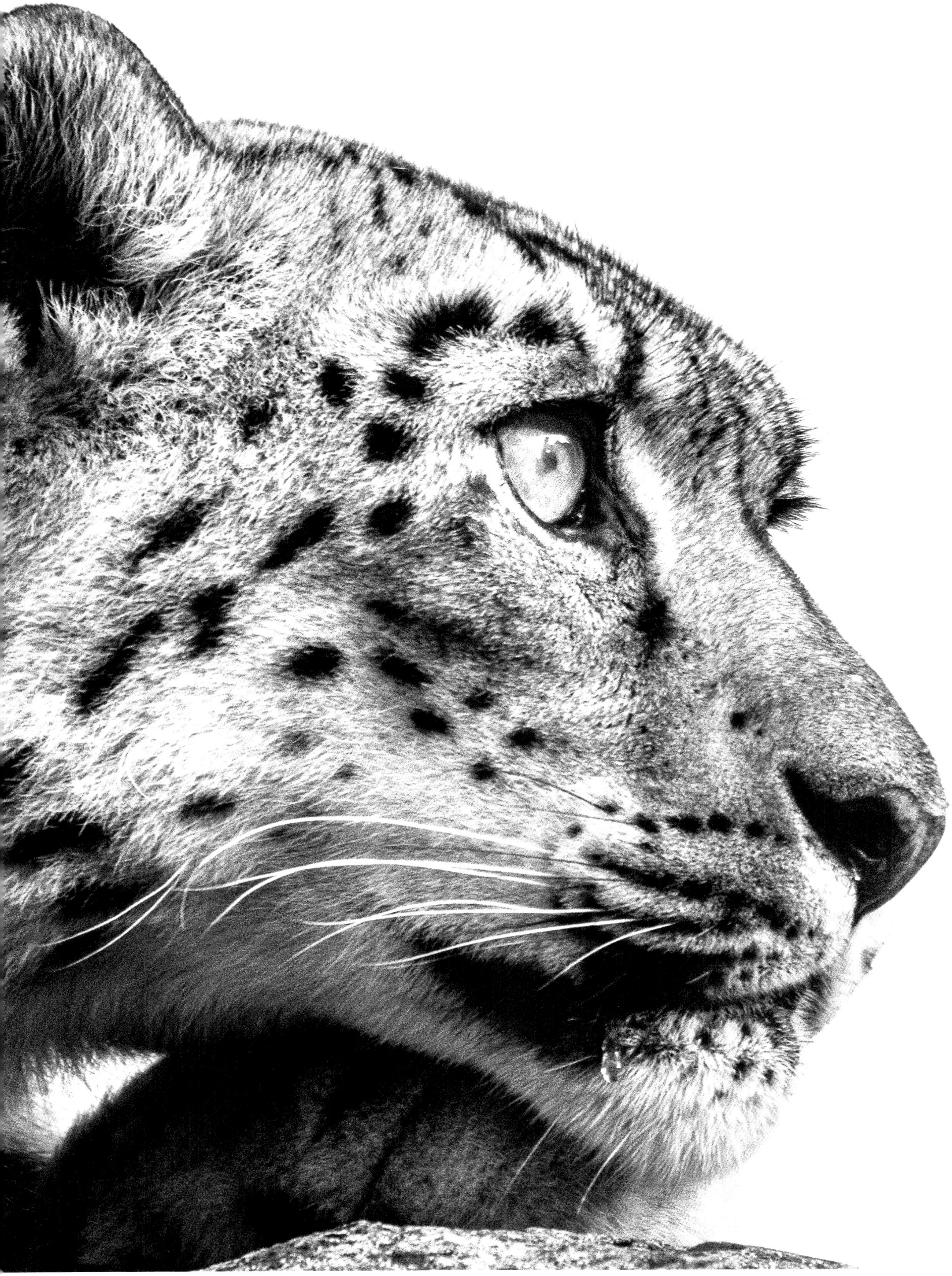

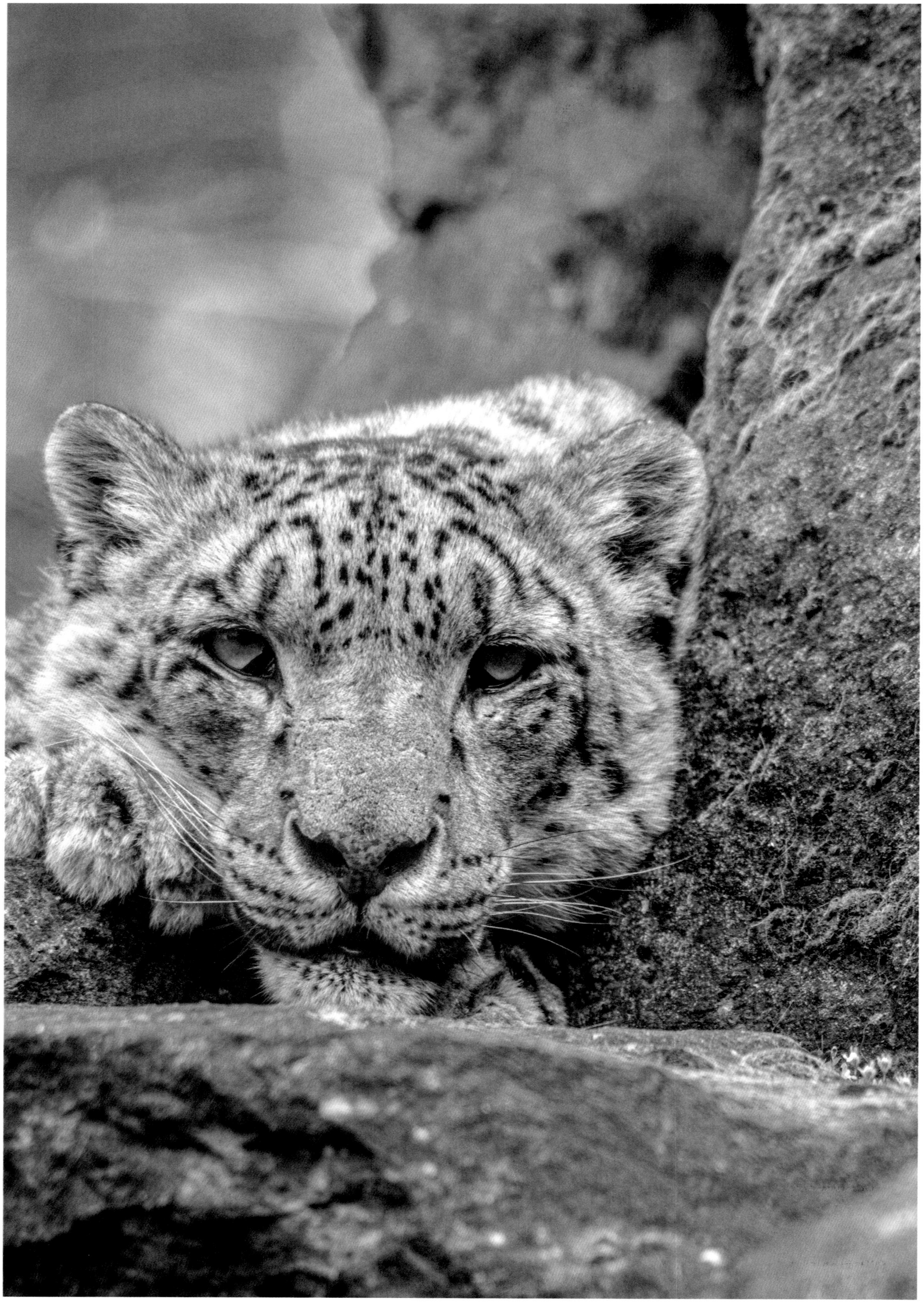

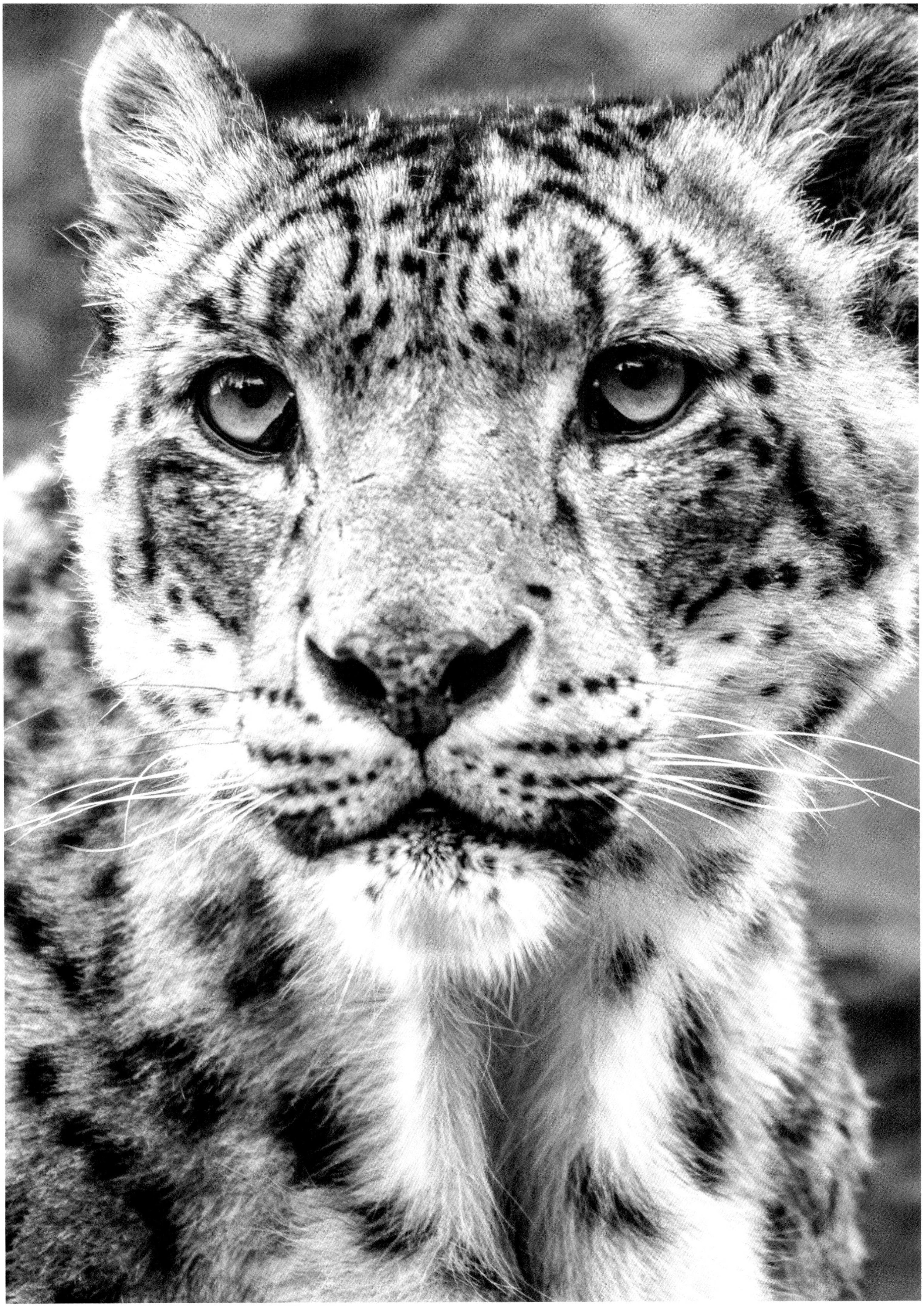

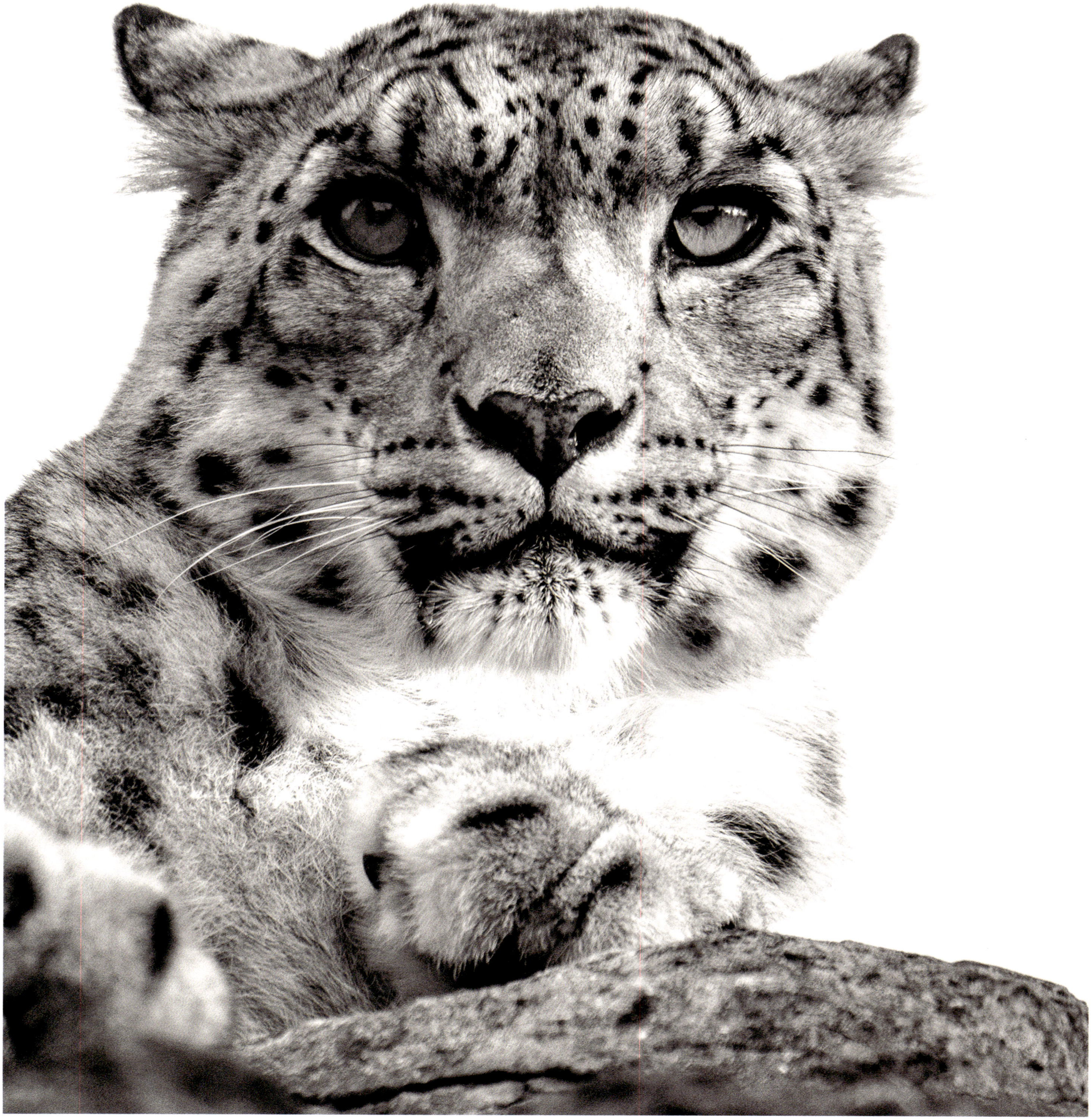

The snow leopard is rare, shy and aggressive – getting close takes a large amount of research and emotional investment. I wanted to capture an intimate portrait of this extremely elusive cat, which I knew was going to be a massive challenge and it was likely that I would leave the assignment empty-handed. That is part of the gamble we take as photographers, but the occasional successful assignment makes up for the failures.

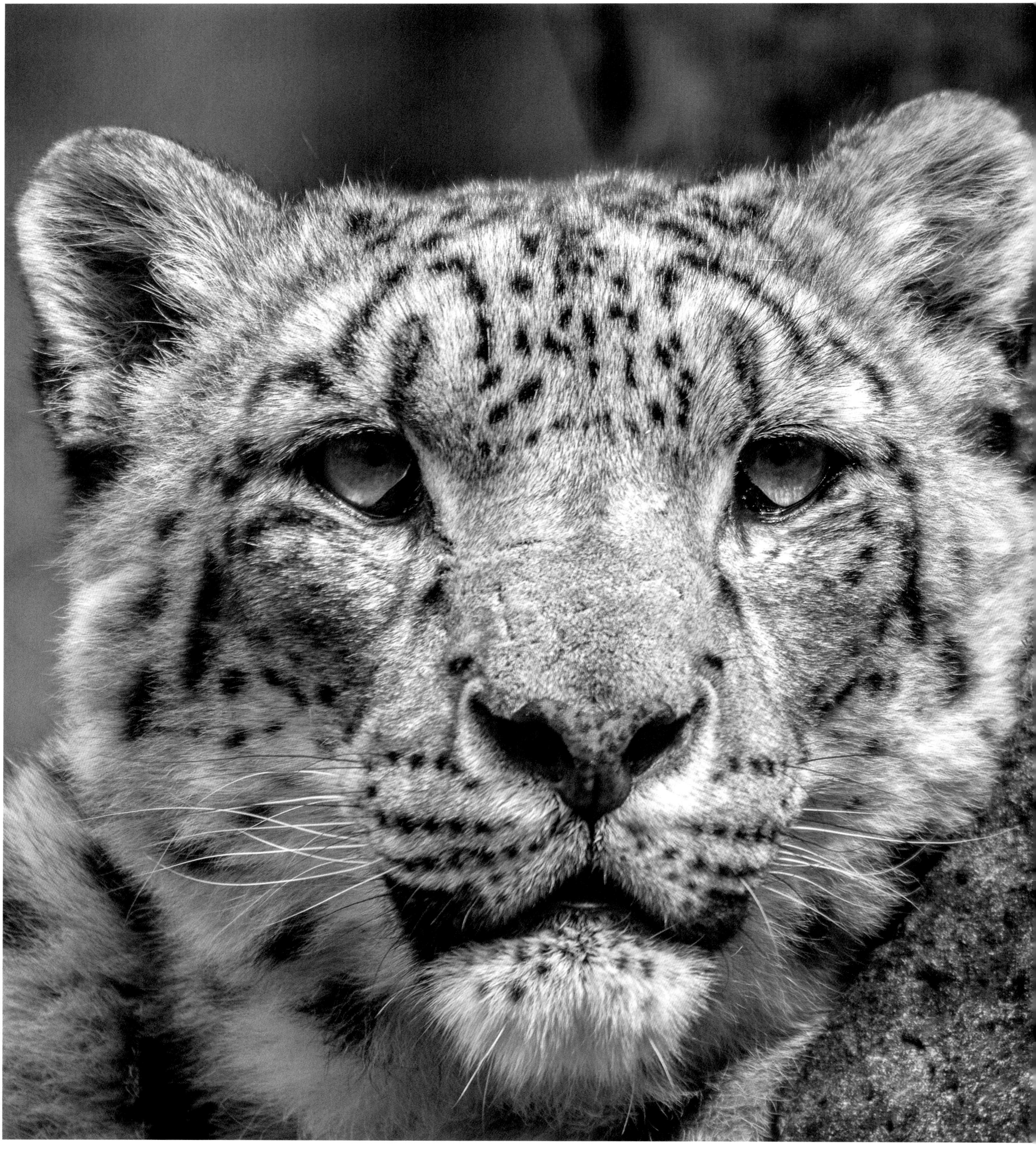

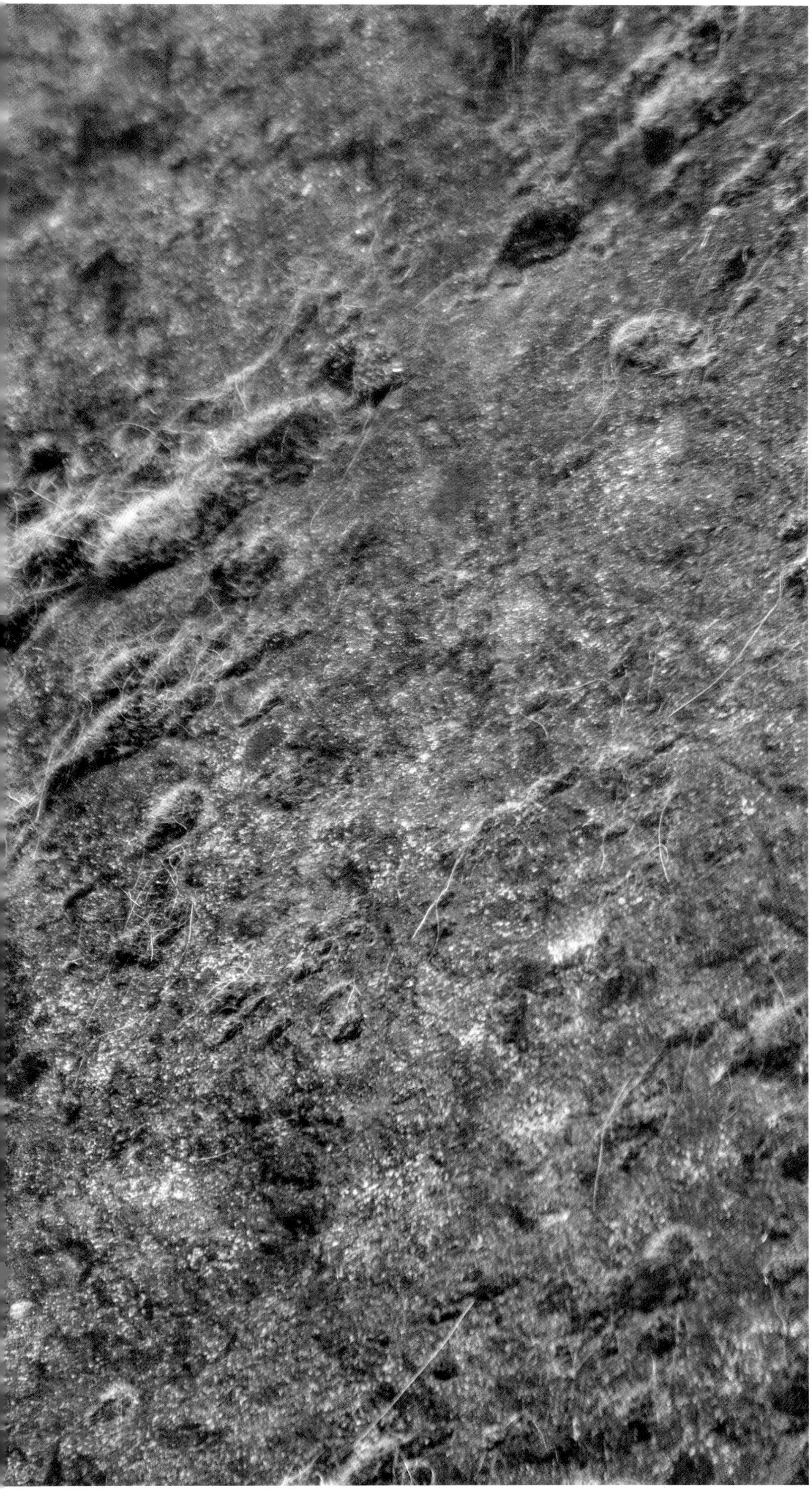

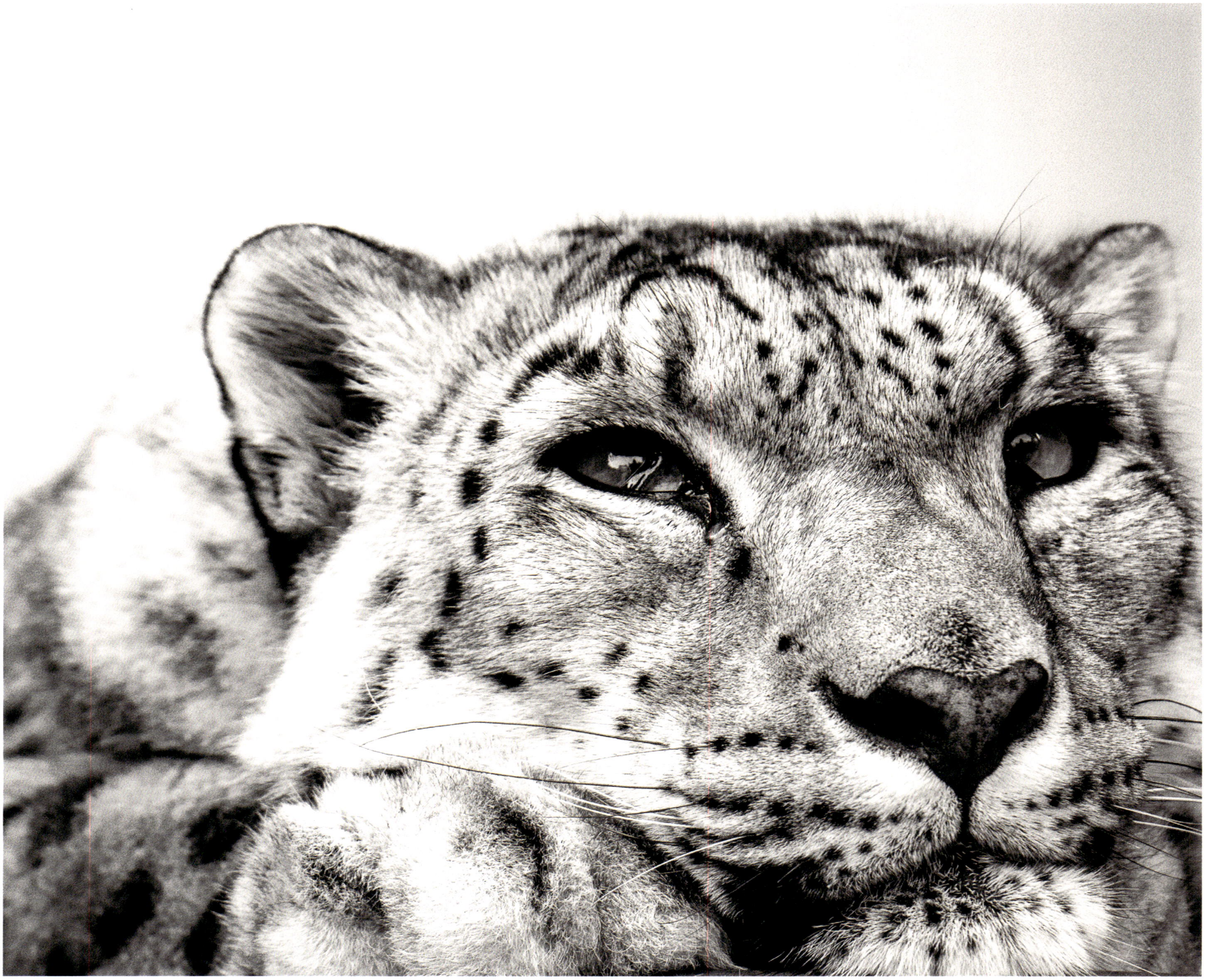

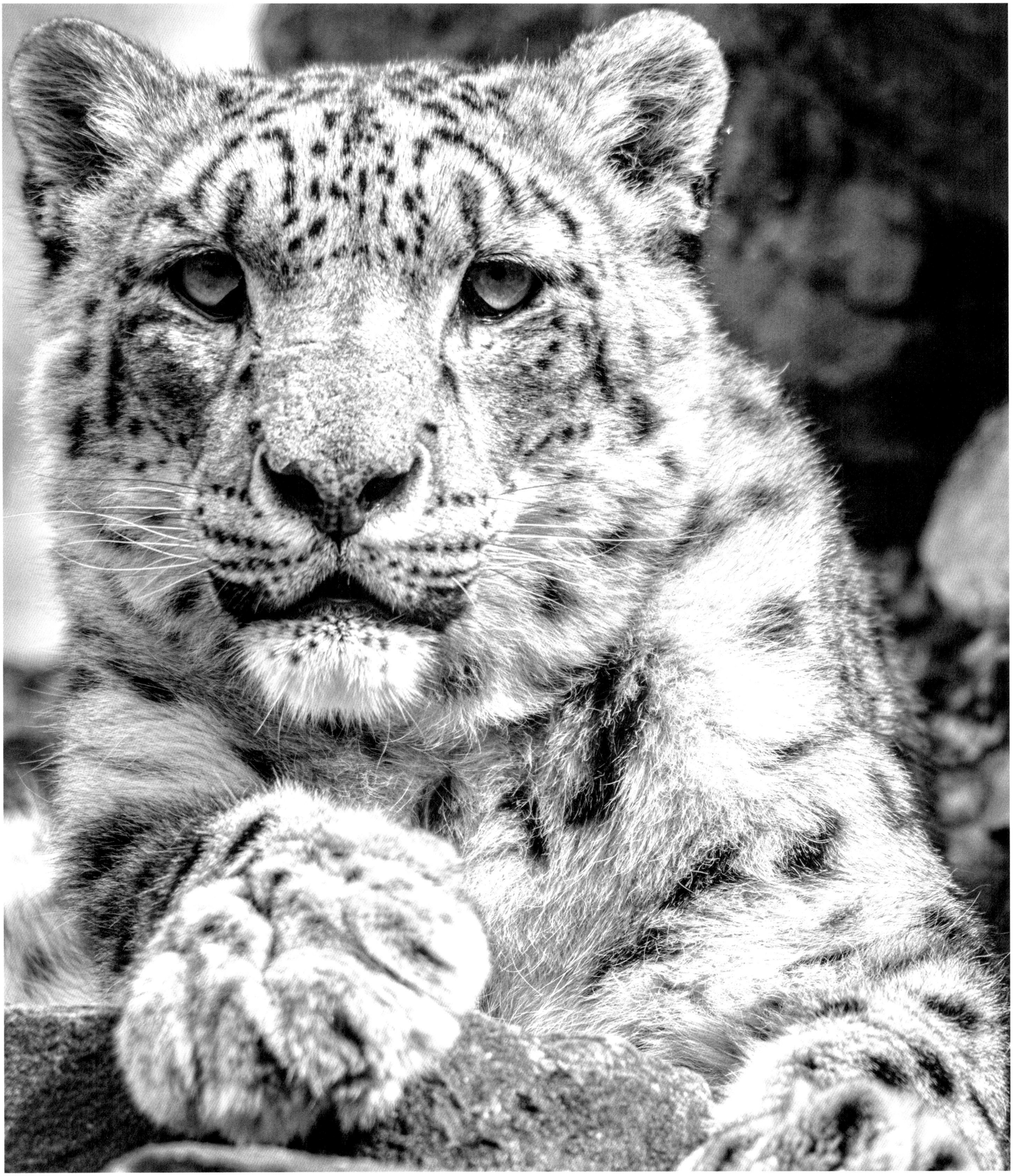

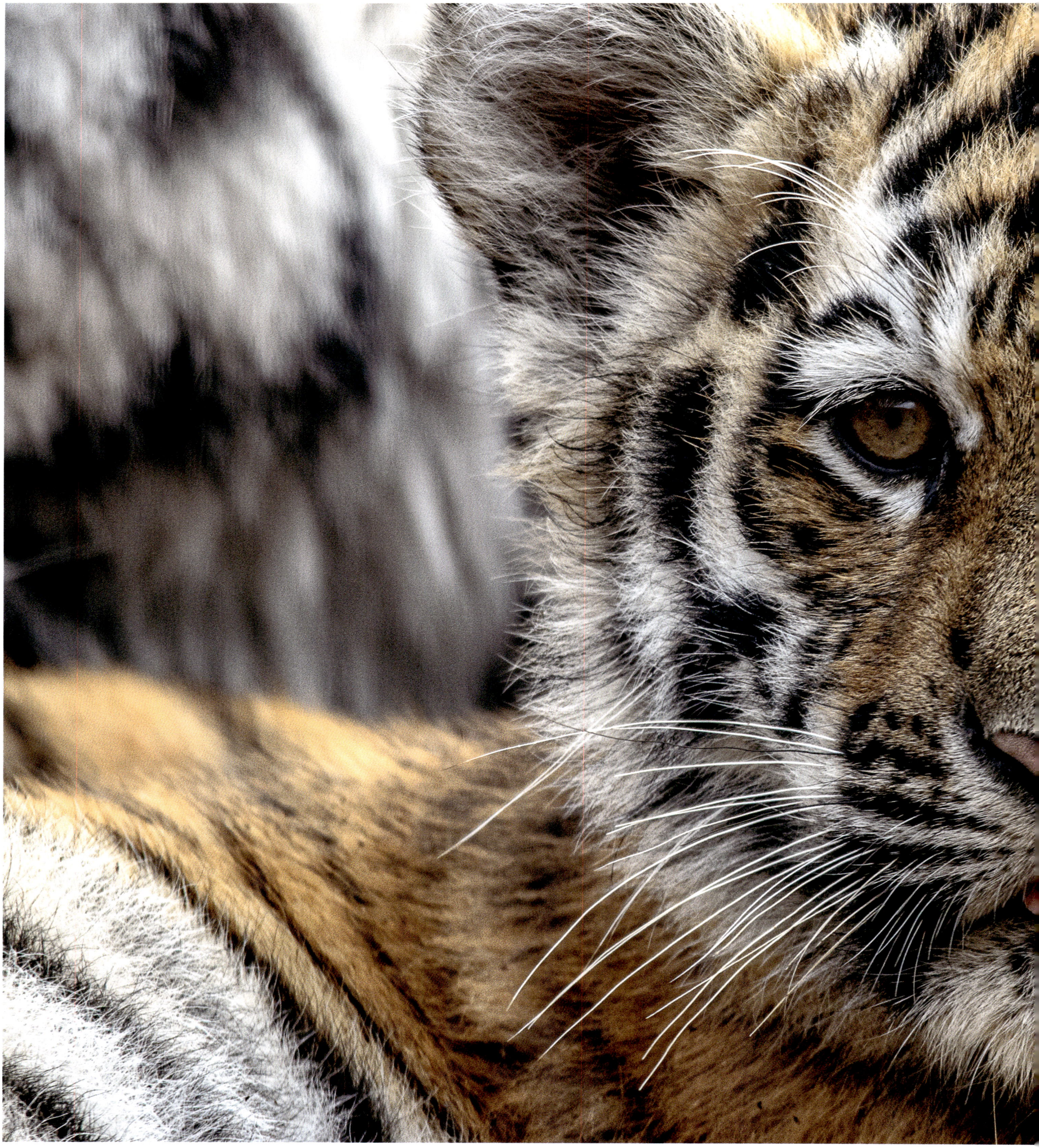

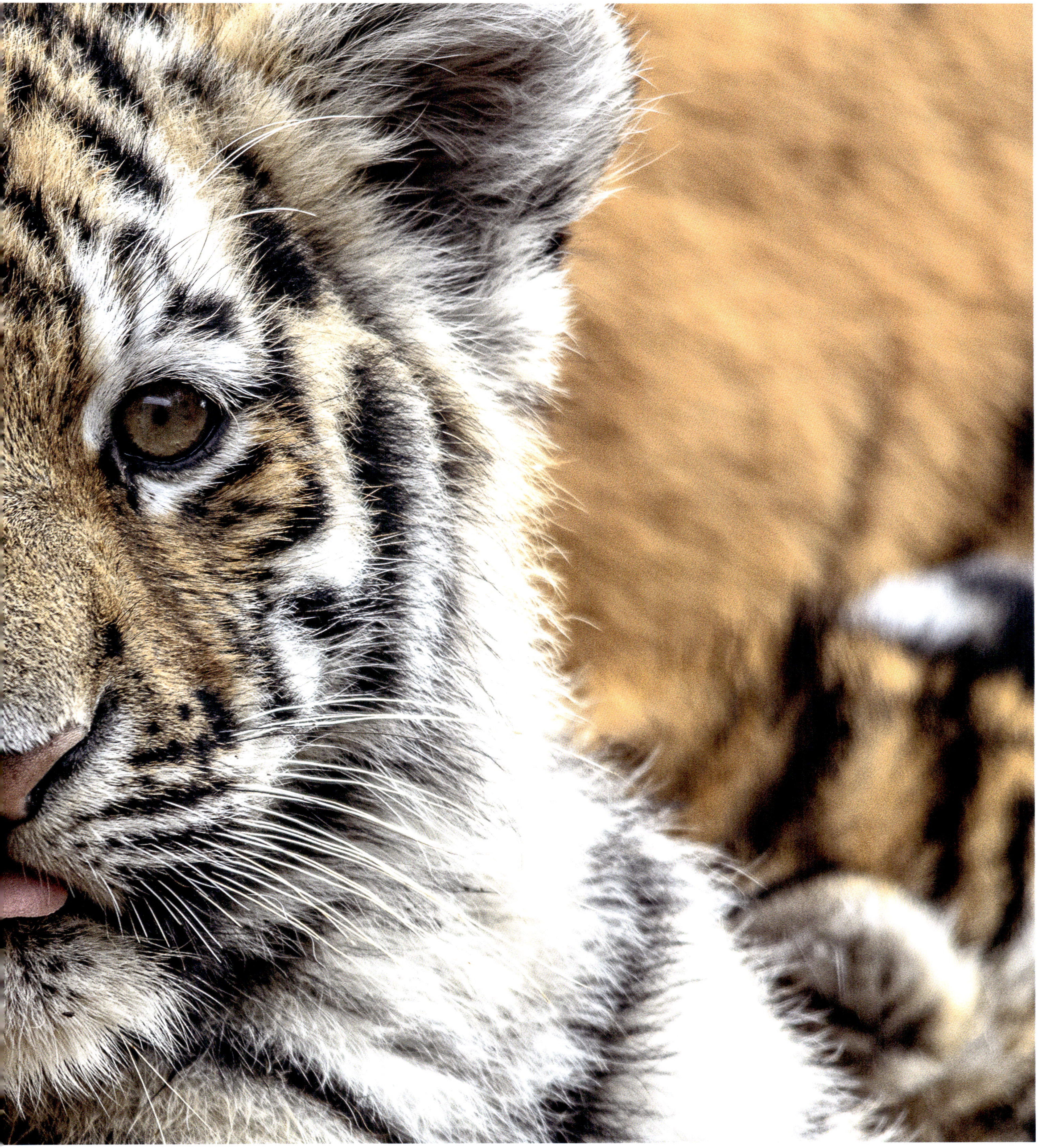

The tiger is a symbol of the important role that wildlife conservancies play in conservation efforts. There are now thought to be around 400 Amur tigers left in the wilds of Russia and China and were it not for captive breeding efforts, this tiger sub-species would now be extinct.

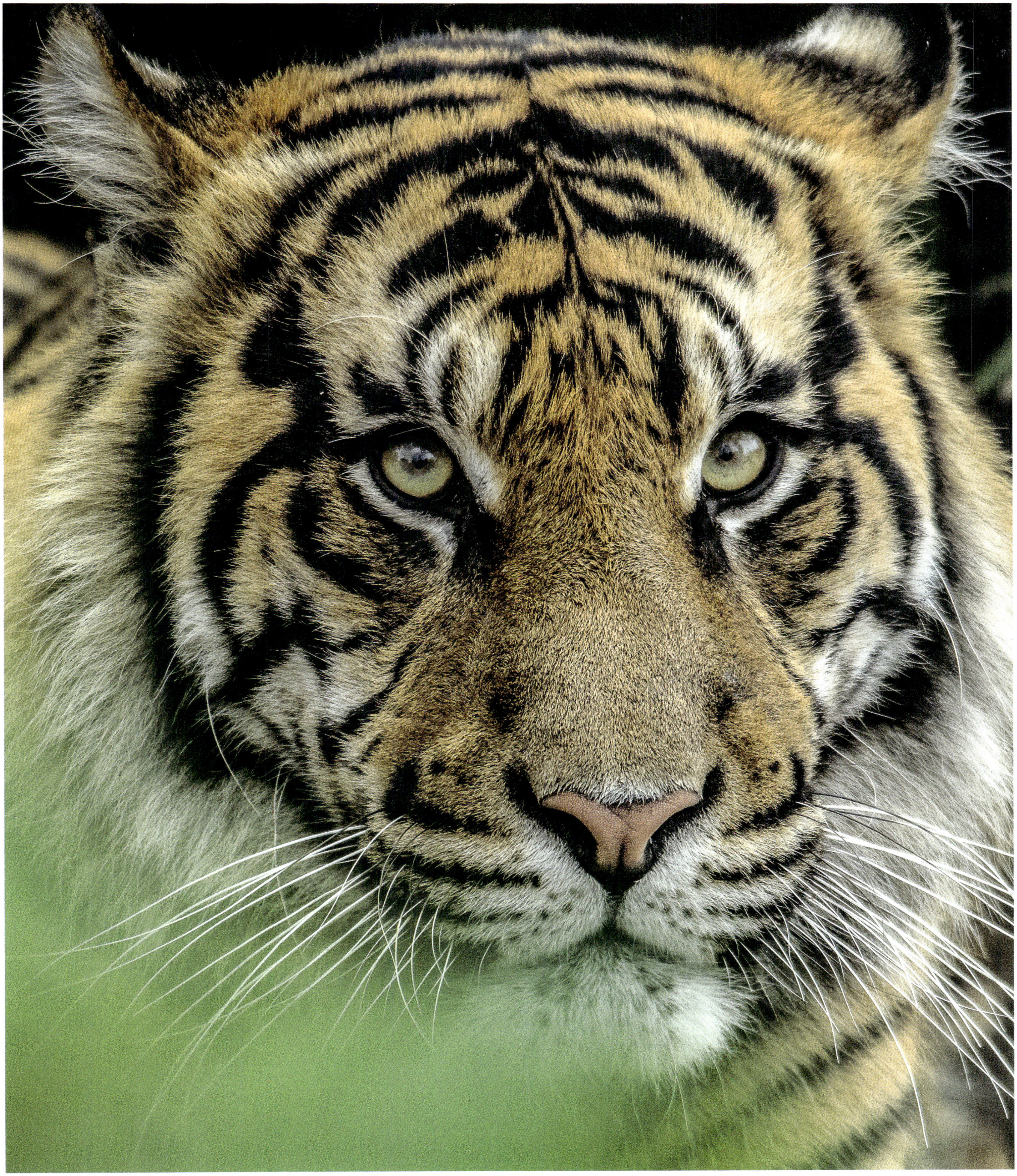

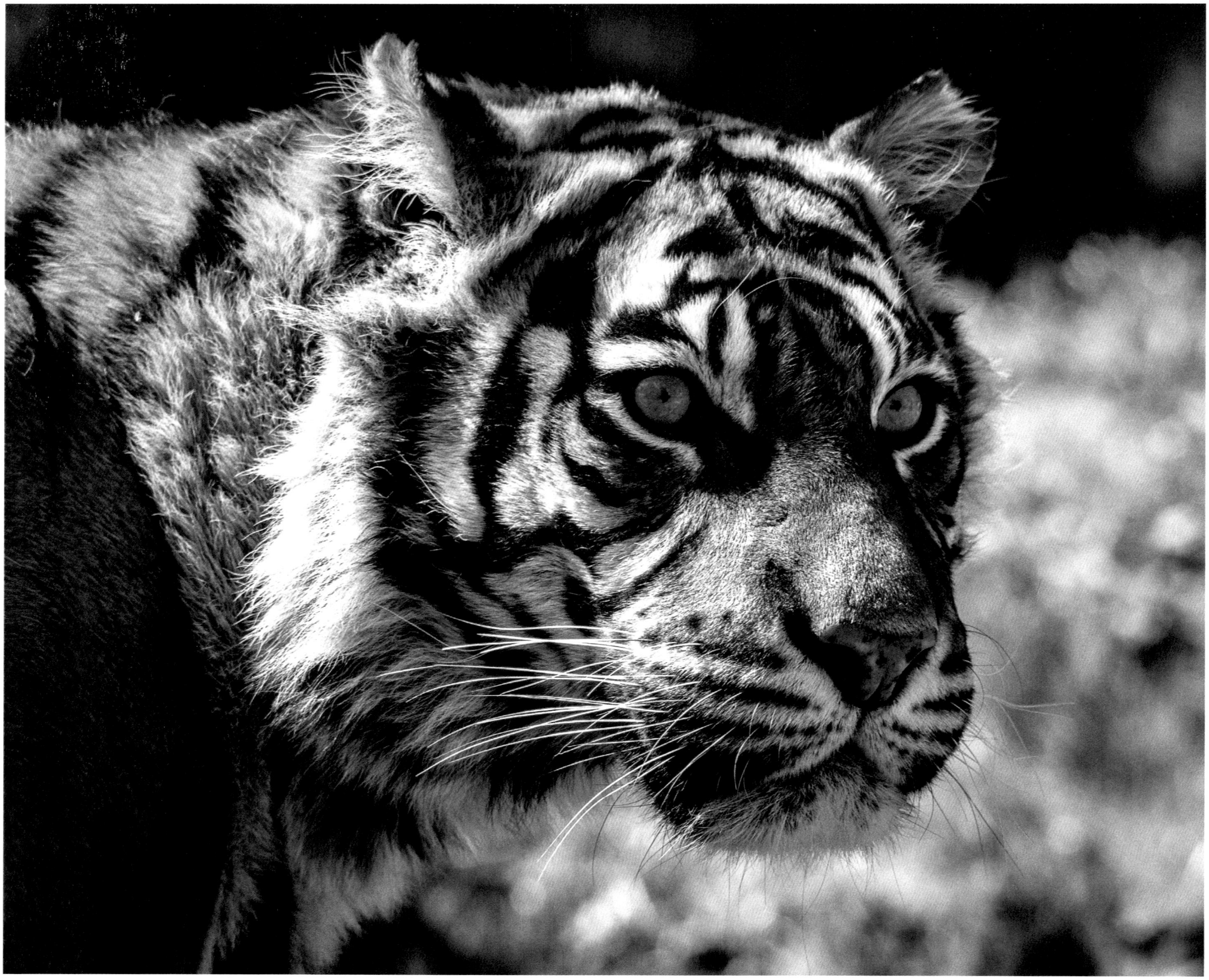

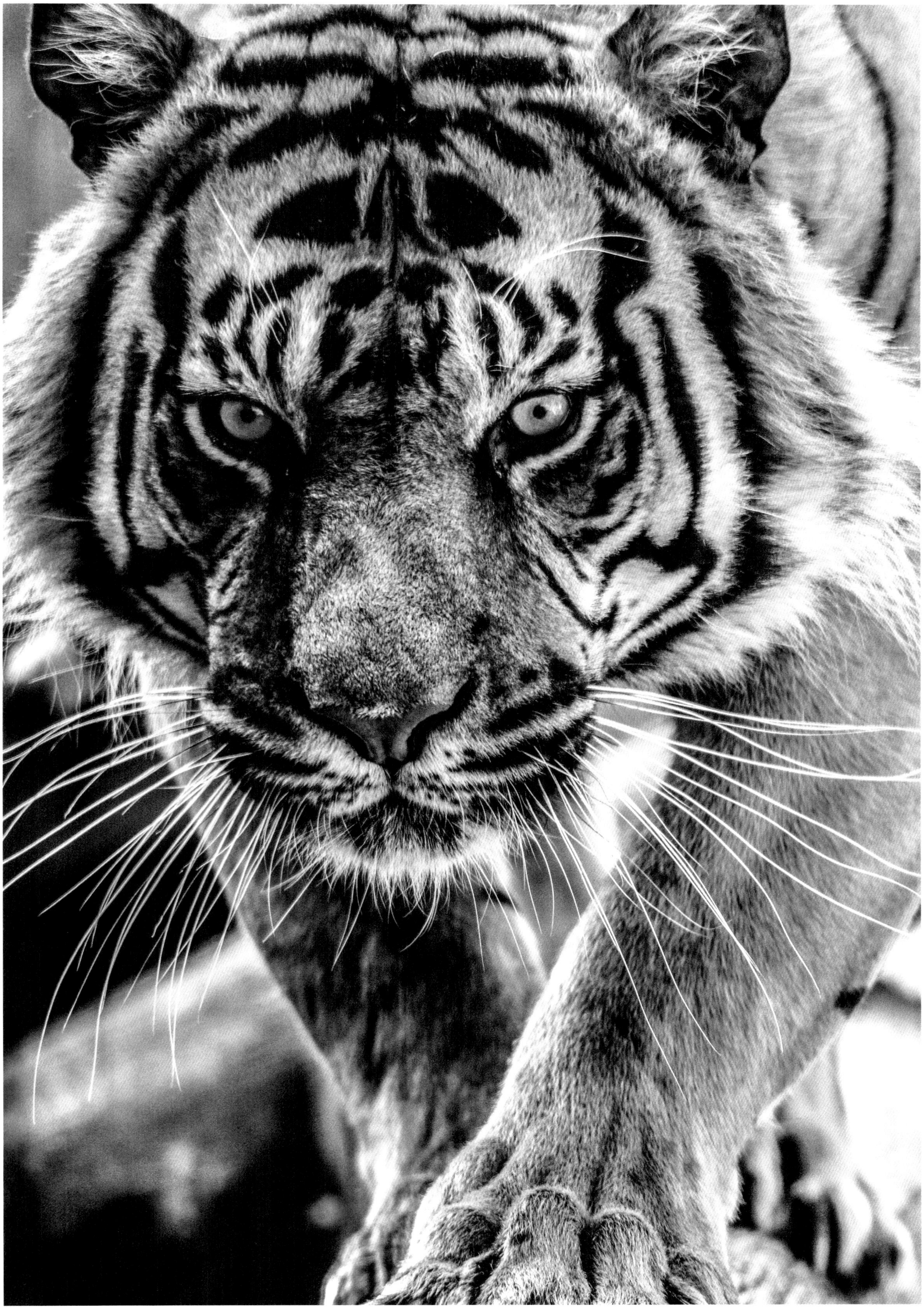

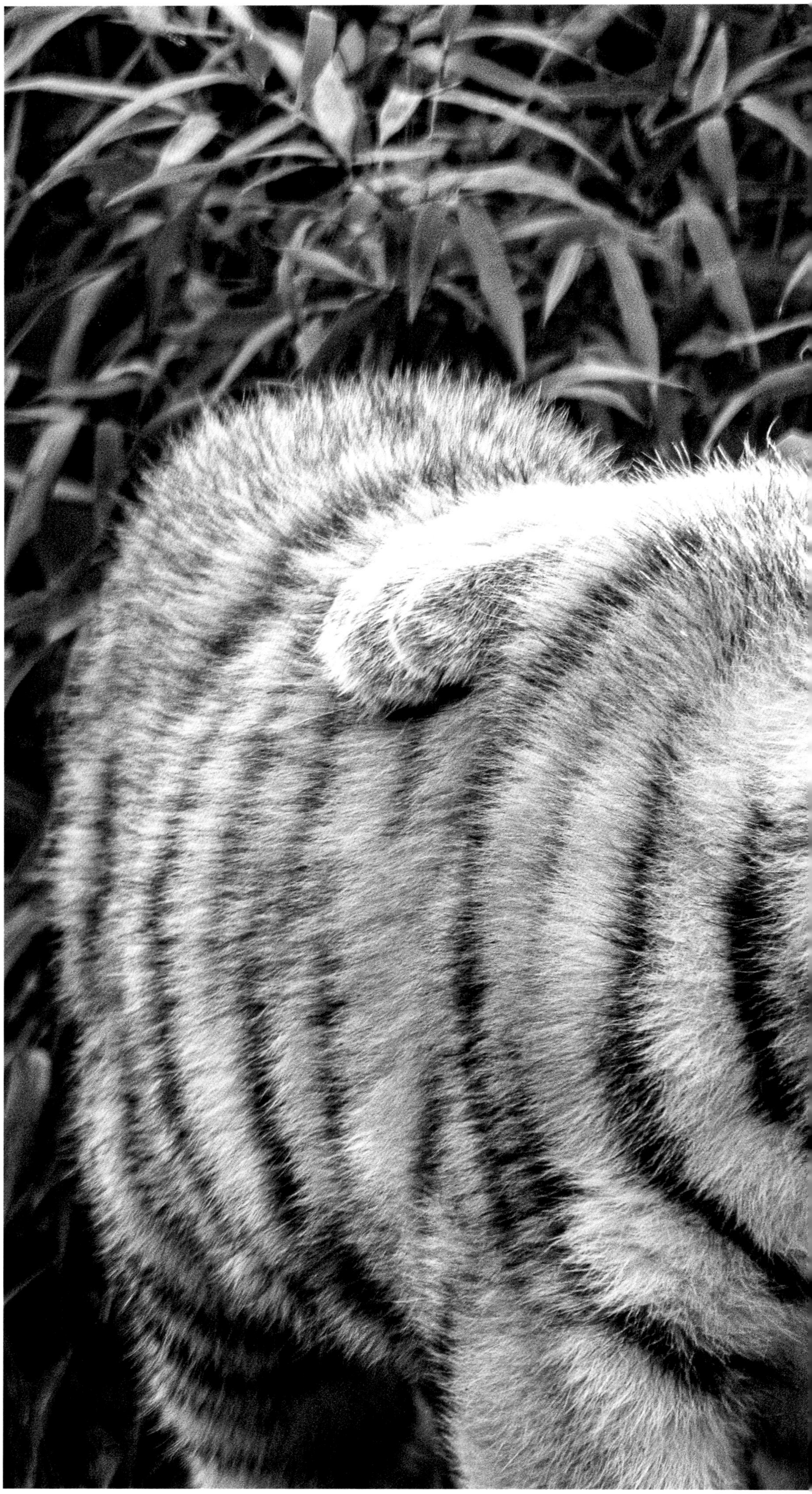

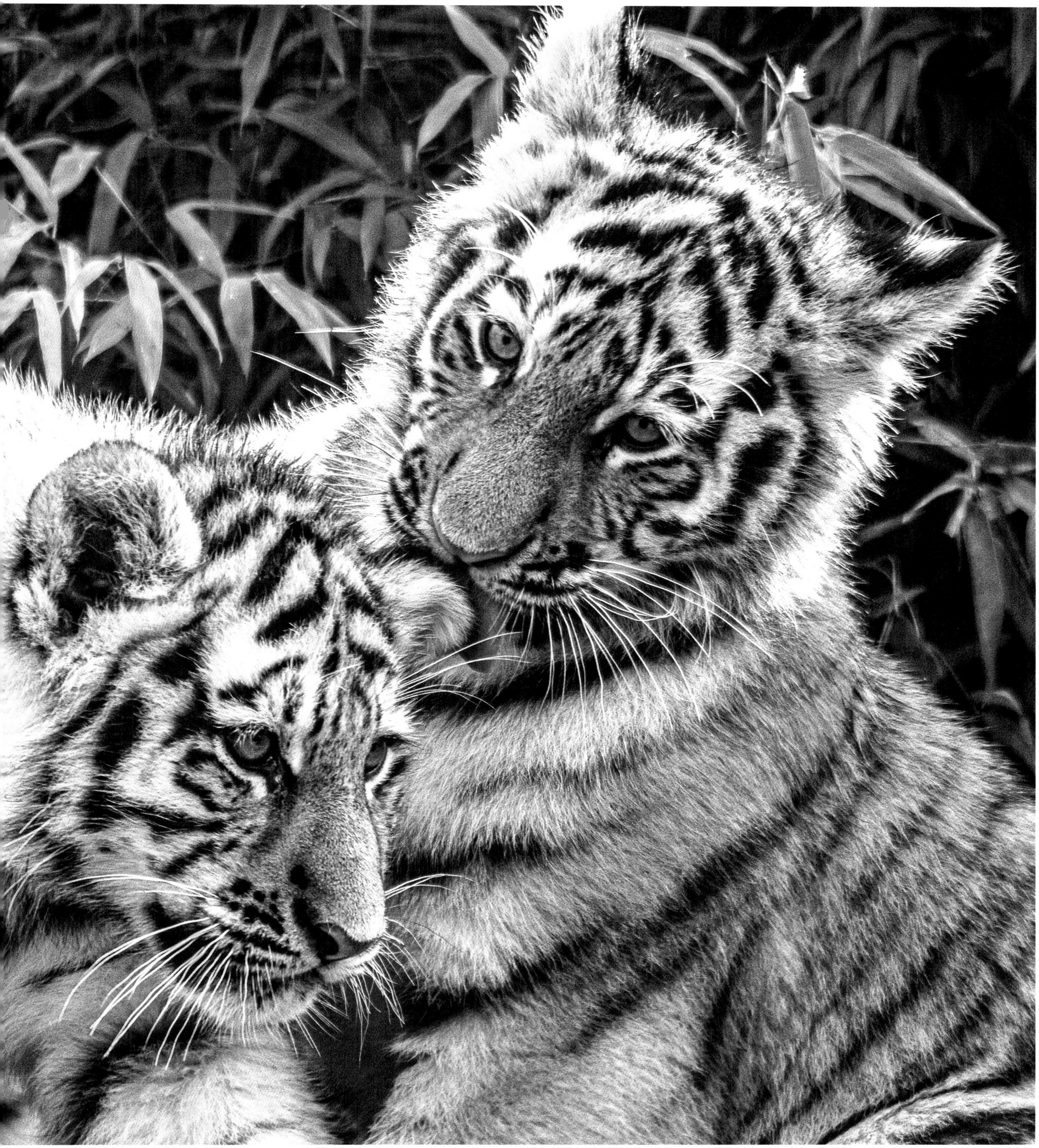

I think this image, ‘Savage Beauty’, plays with people’s romantic visions of the tiger, the image certainly reminds me of Kipling’s Shere Khan, but it also touches the viewer in a very direct way, which, I hope, encourages them to do their bit to save the tiger.

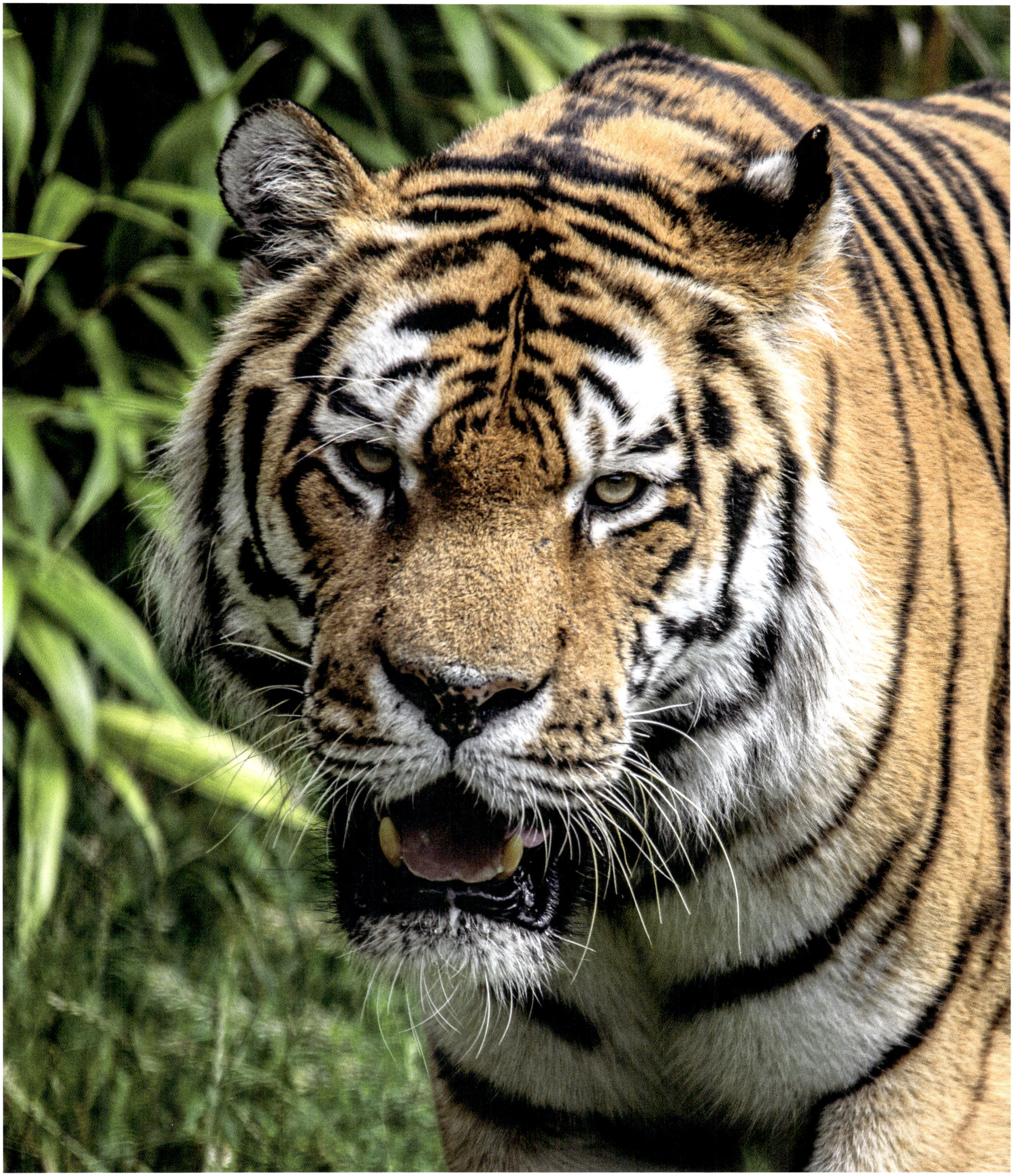

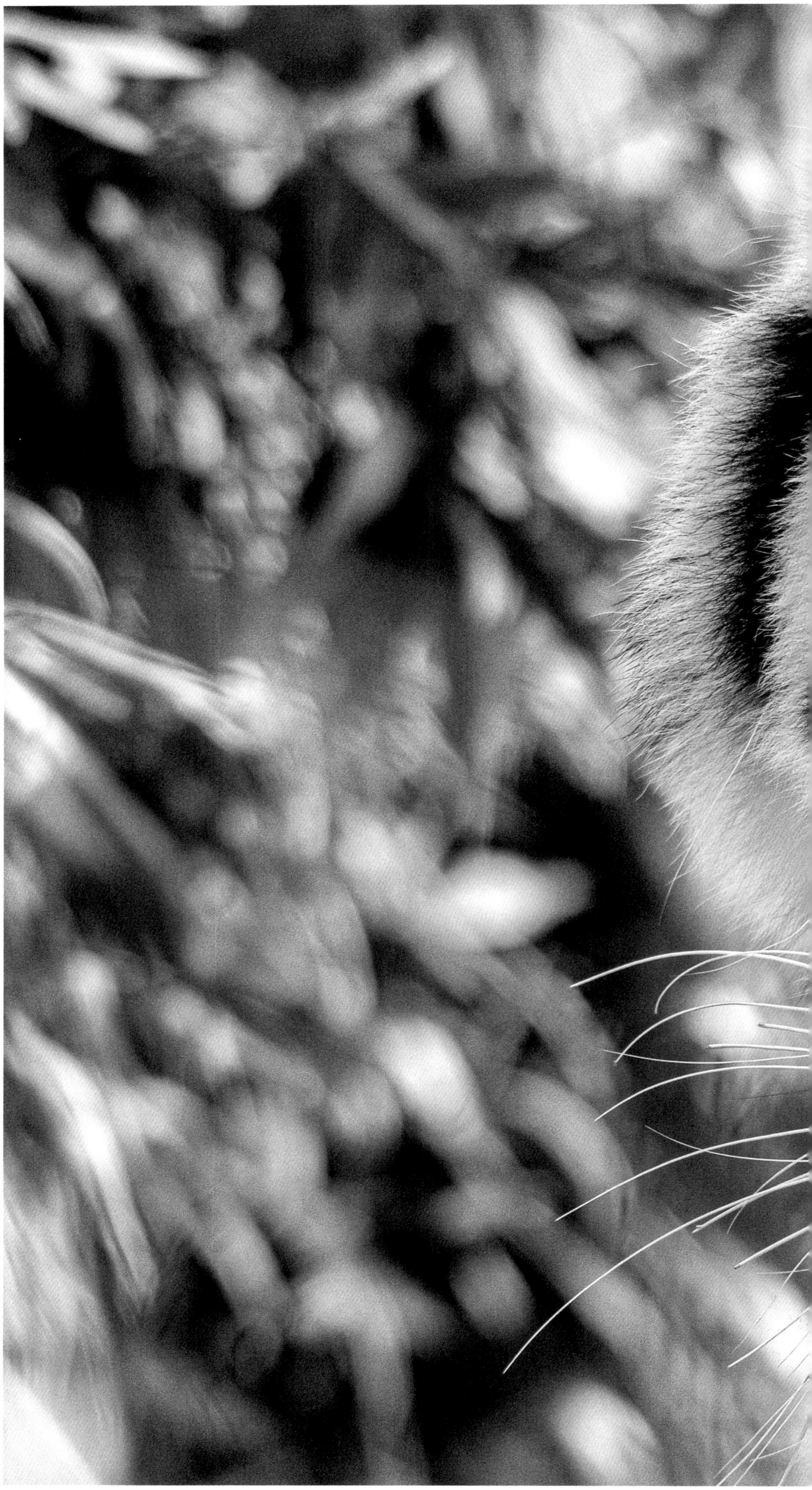

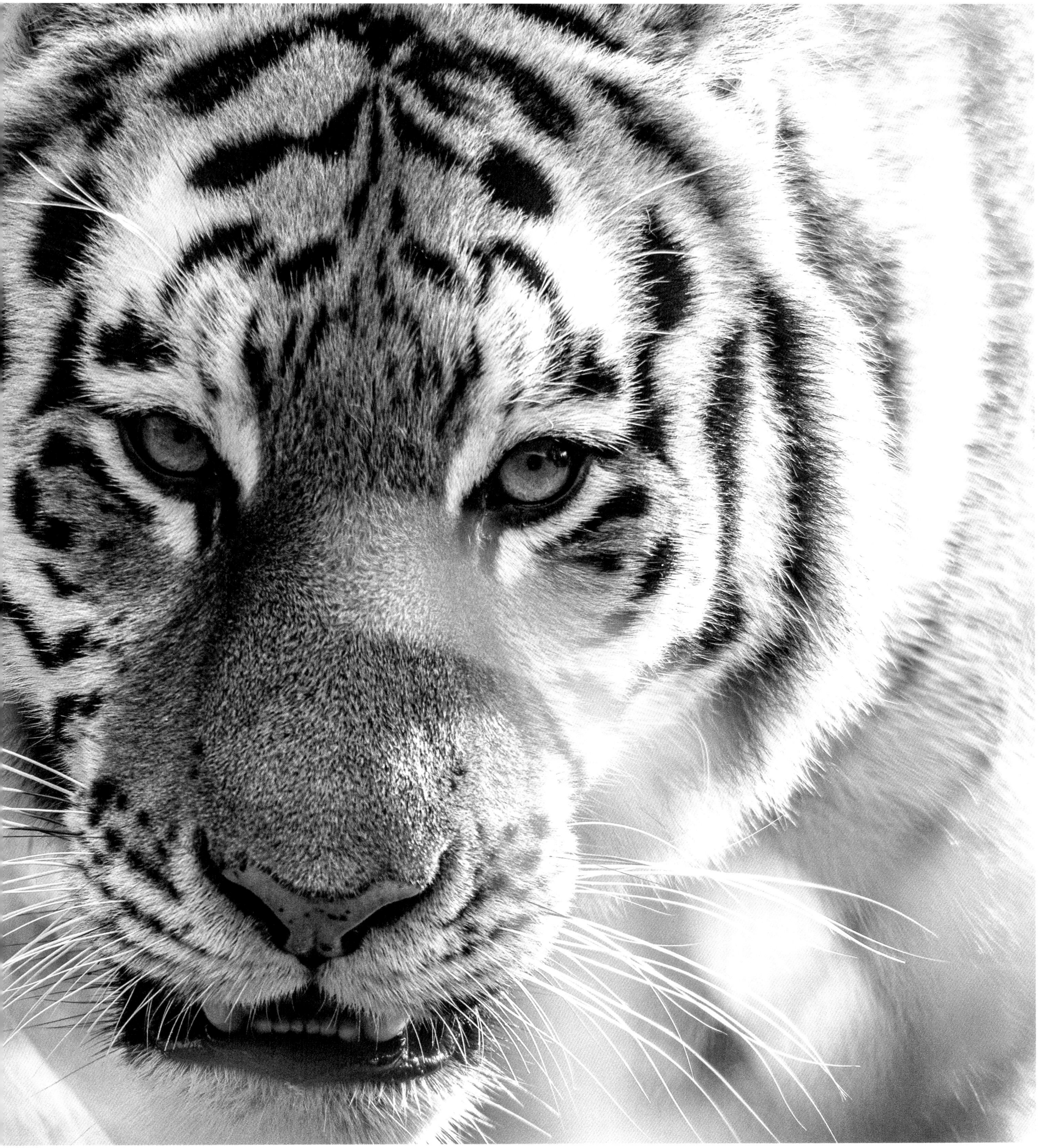

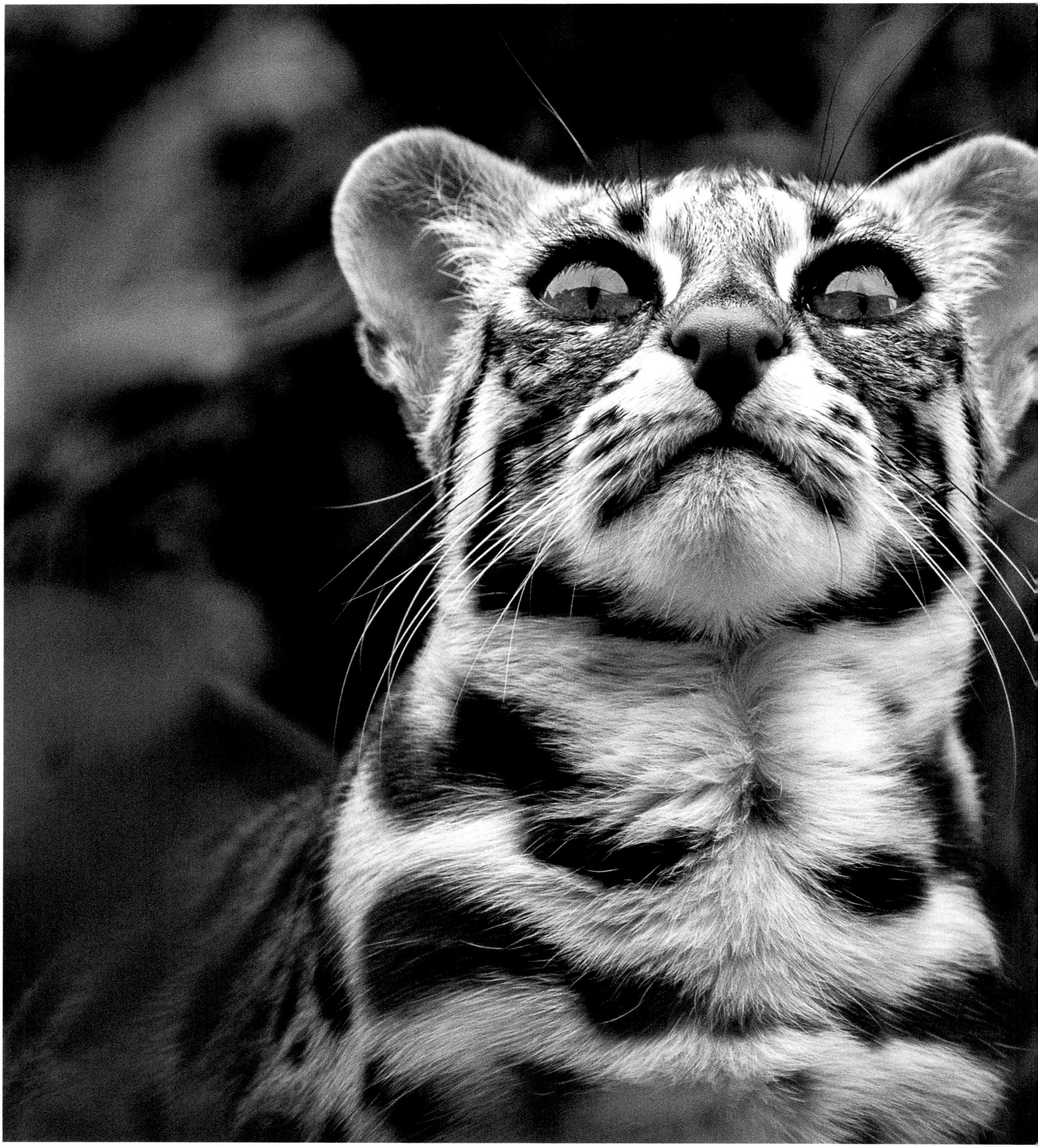

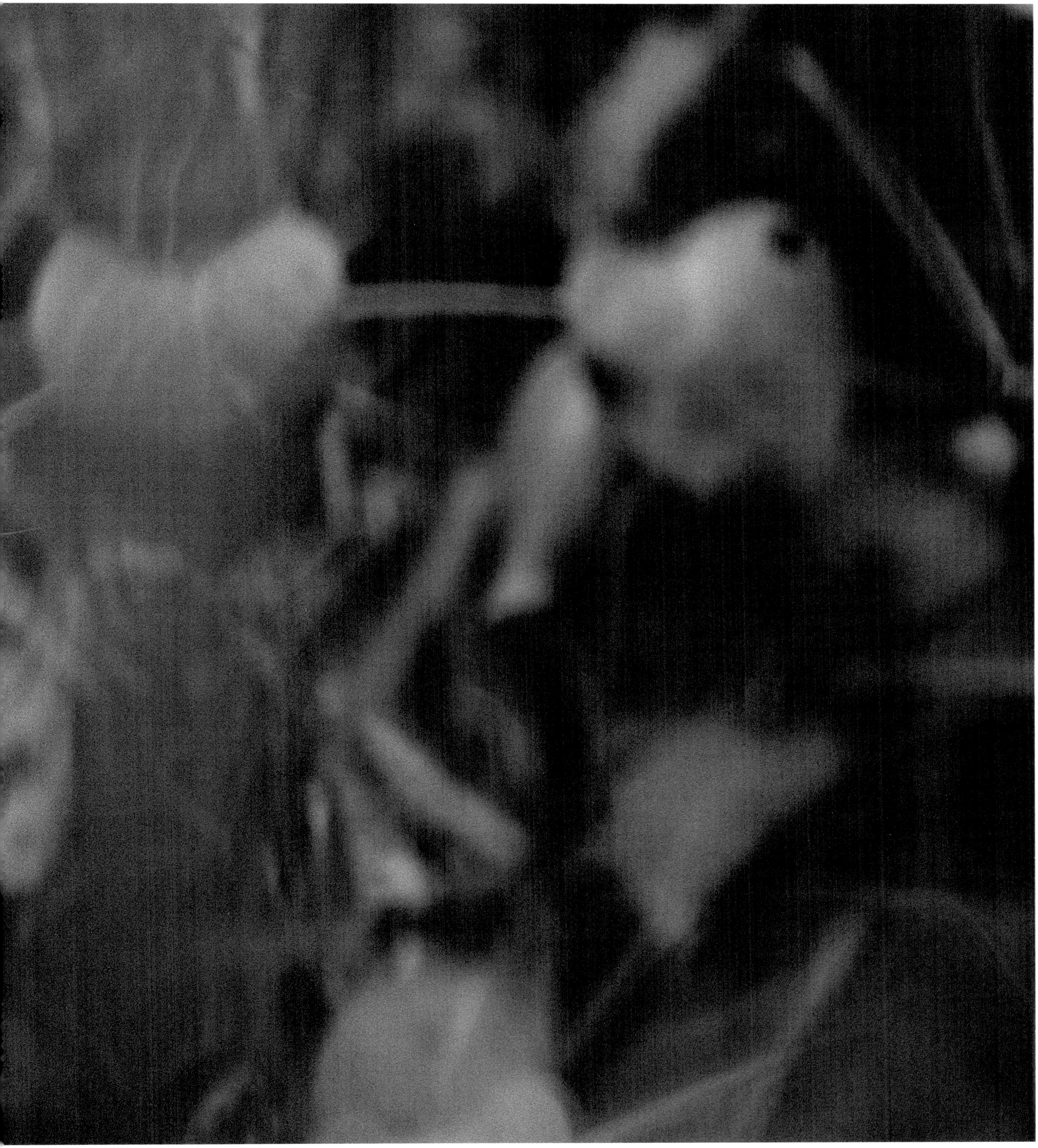

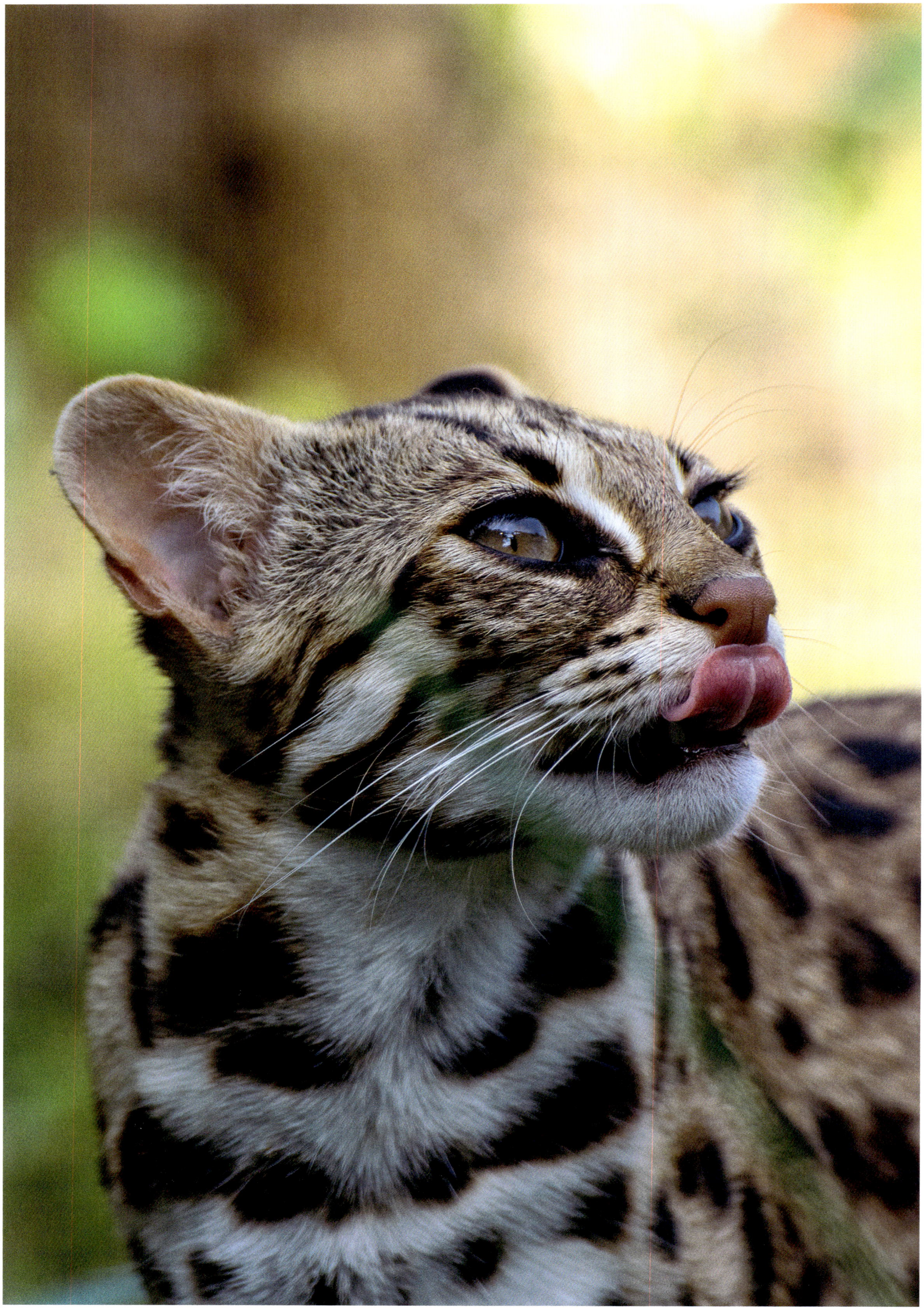

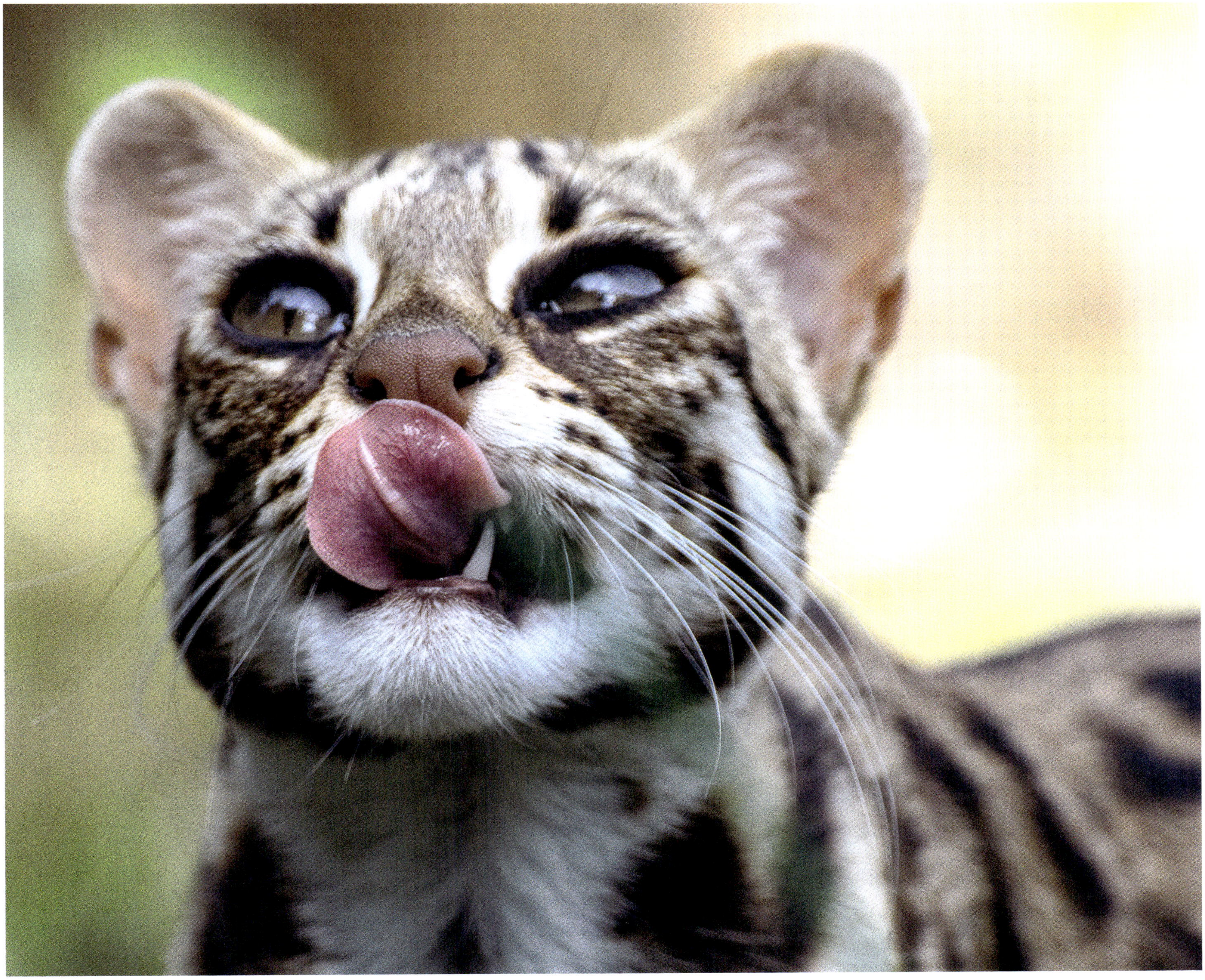

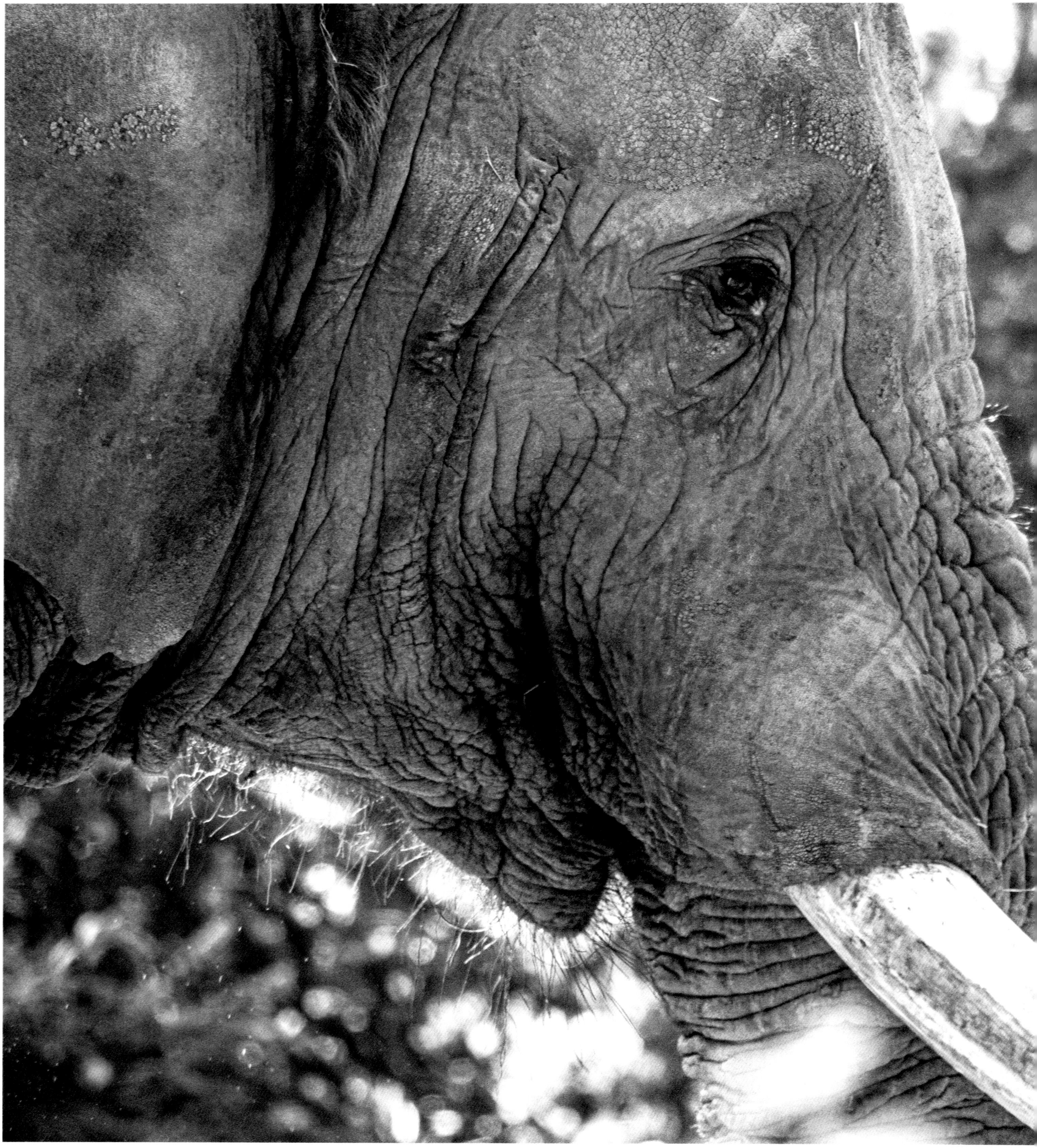

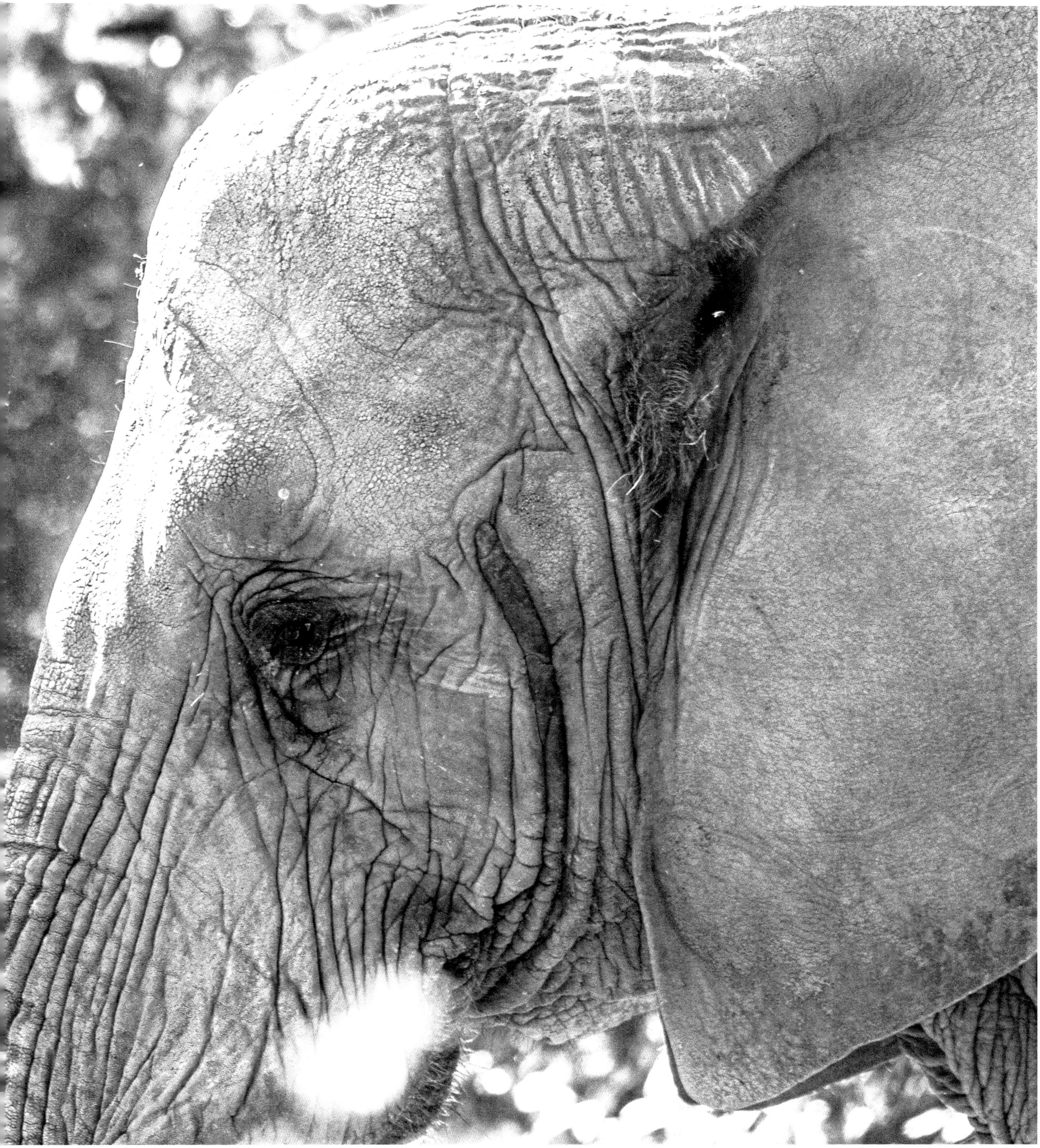

I've spent many hours staring into the eyes of the world's third biggest animal, the elephant. It is a very humbling experience and one that I will always cherish. Bullying left me with a major distrust in humans, many of whom had caused me nothing but pain and that only increased my love for animals. The very species that bullied me is now wiping out this beautiful creature, I think that says something profoundly negative about the human race.

We should all spend some time looking into the eyes of an elephant – we could learn a thing or two.

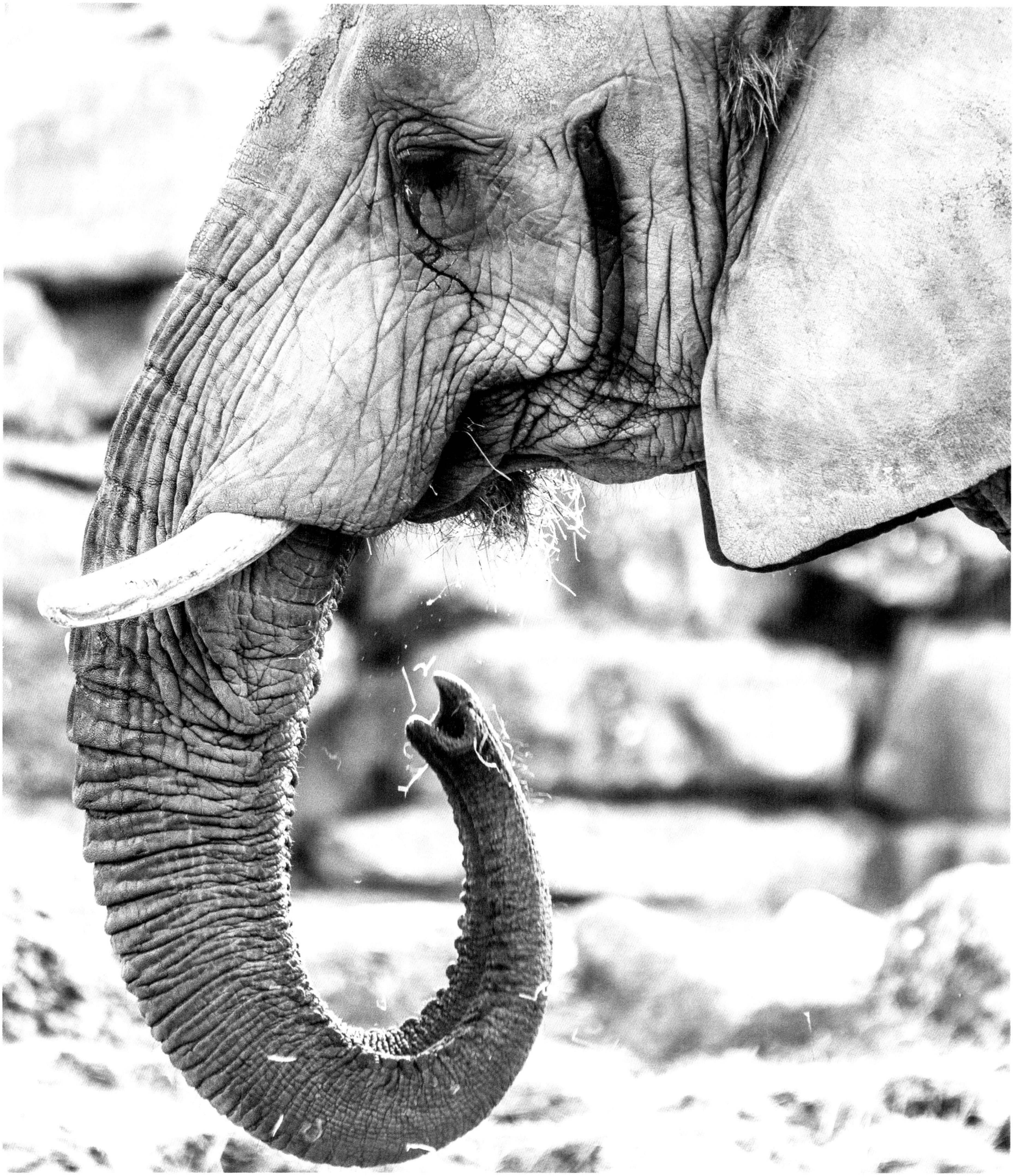

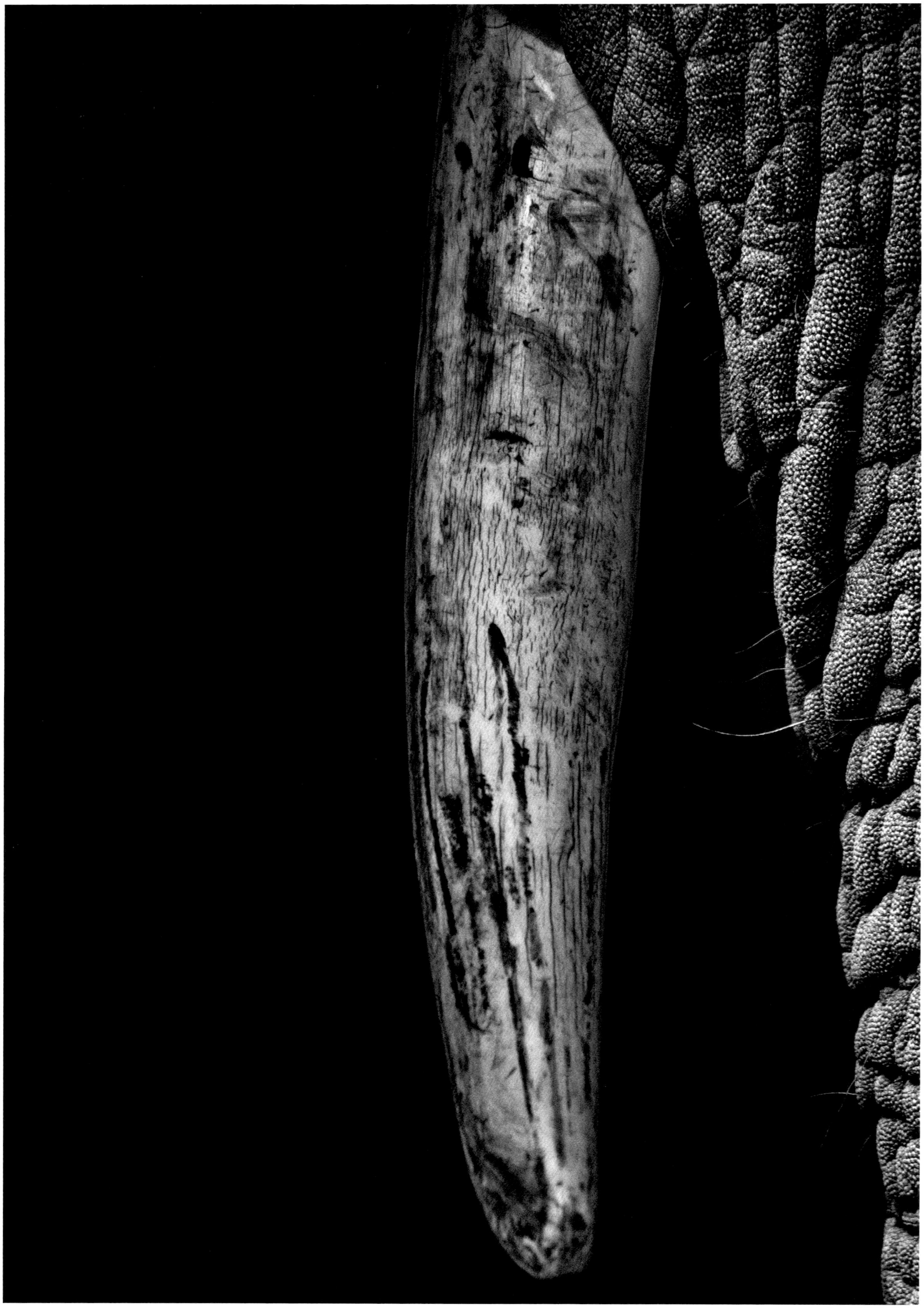

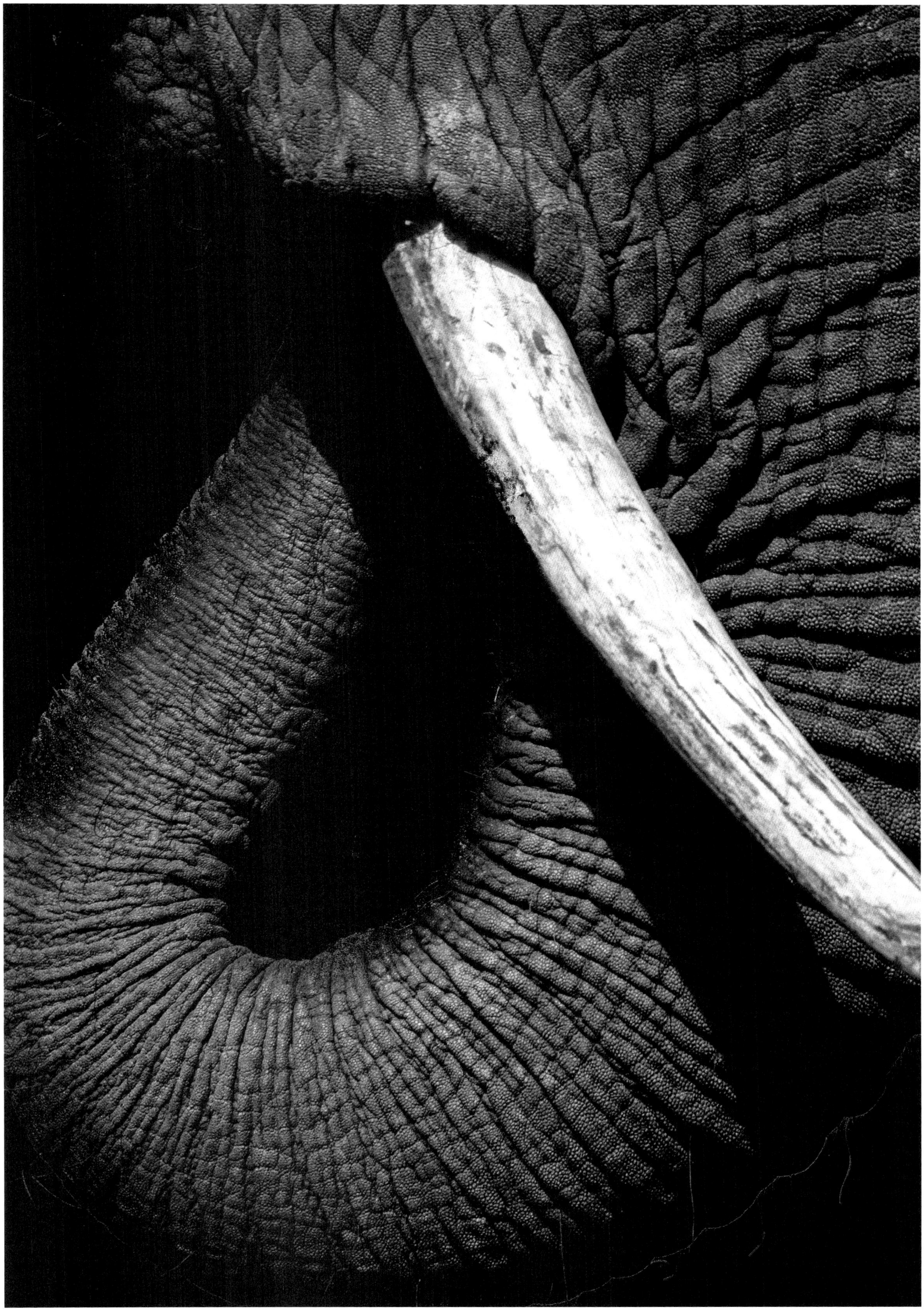

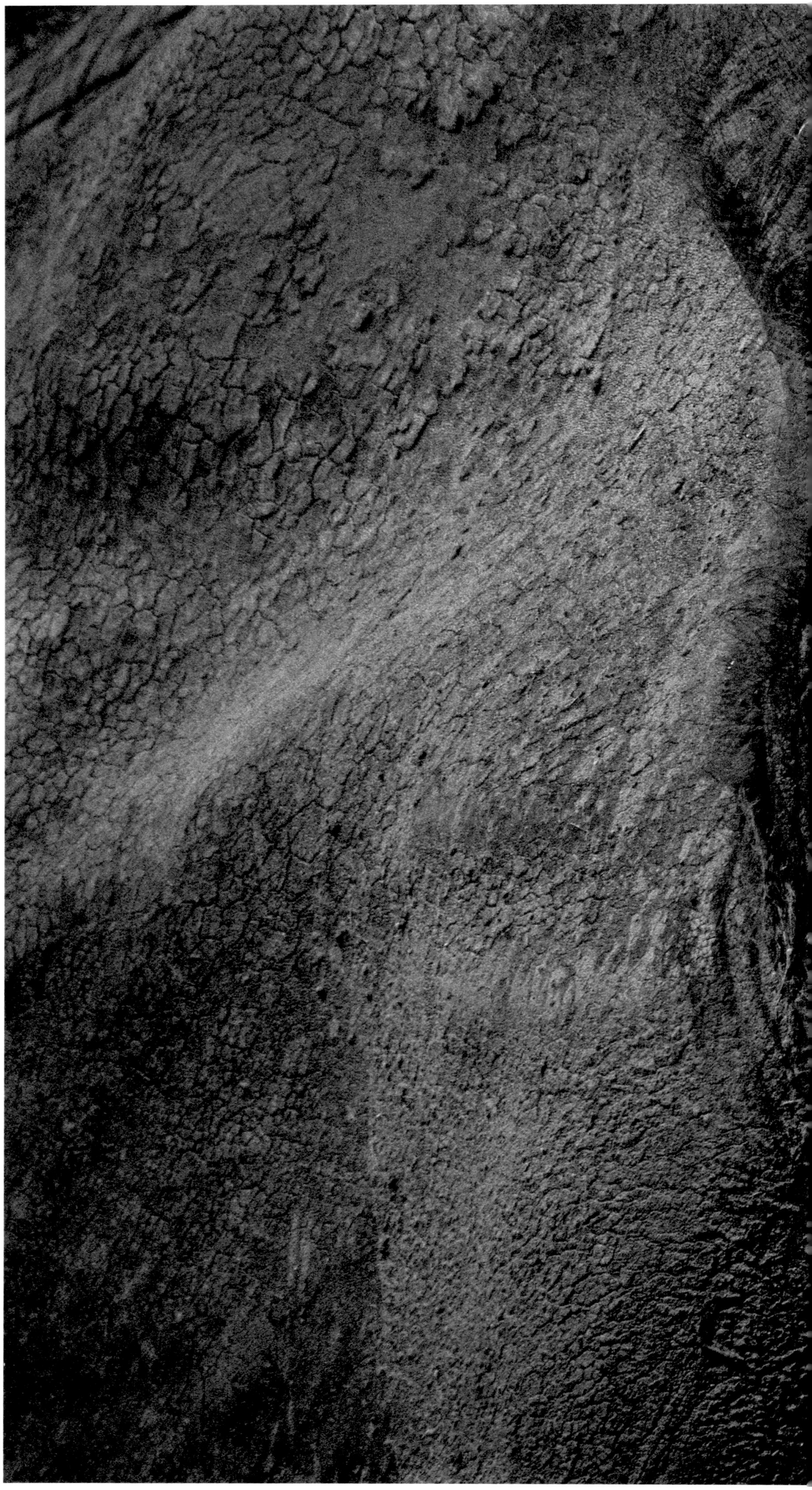

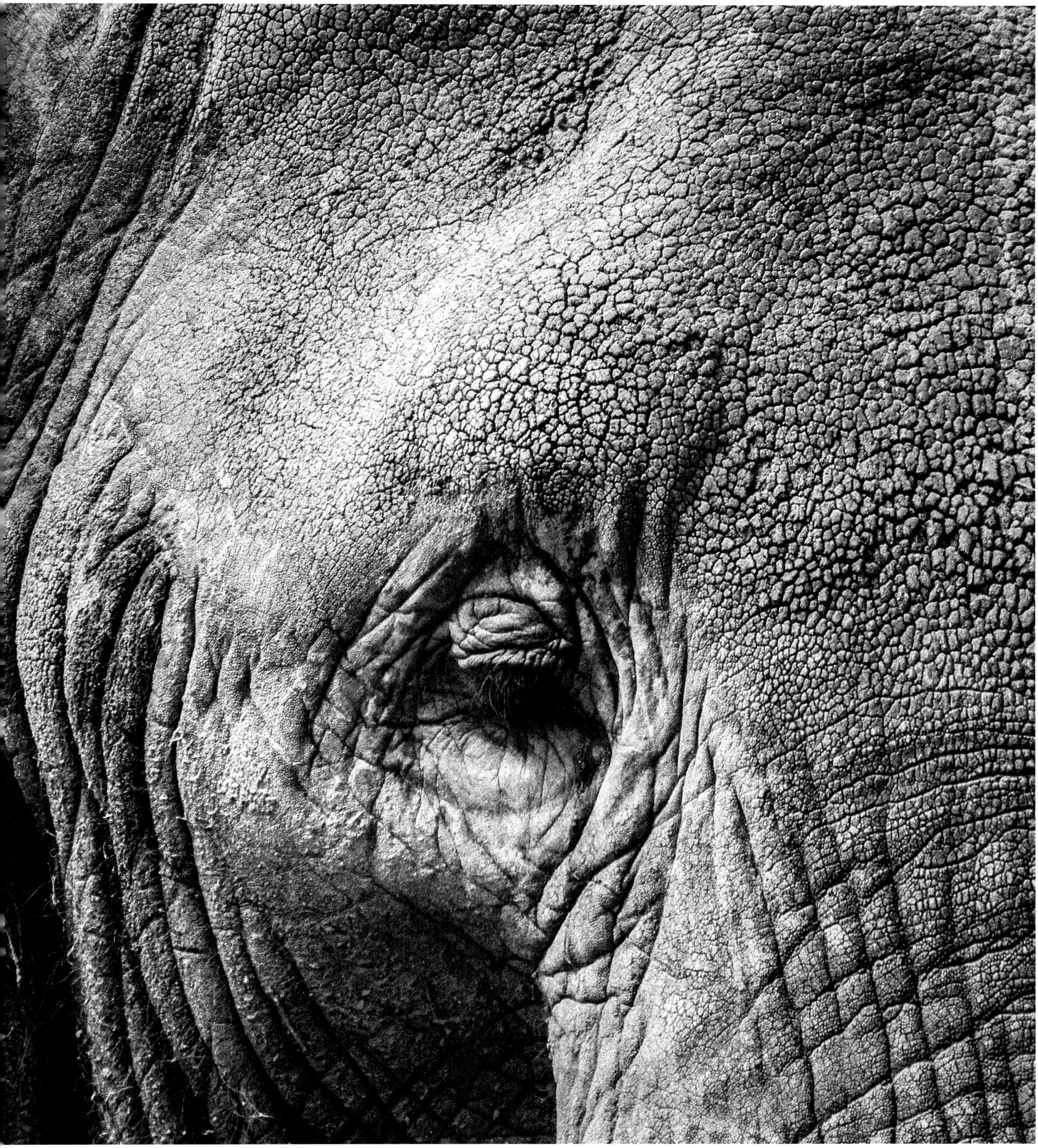

“People are so difficult. Give me an elephant any day.” These words from conservationist and author, Mark Shand, resonate with me on several levels. Autism brings with it an inherent and very genuine fear of social situations and I spent much of my childhood avoiding any situation in which I would be forced to communicate with another person.

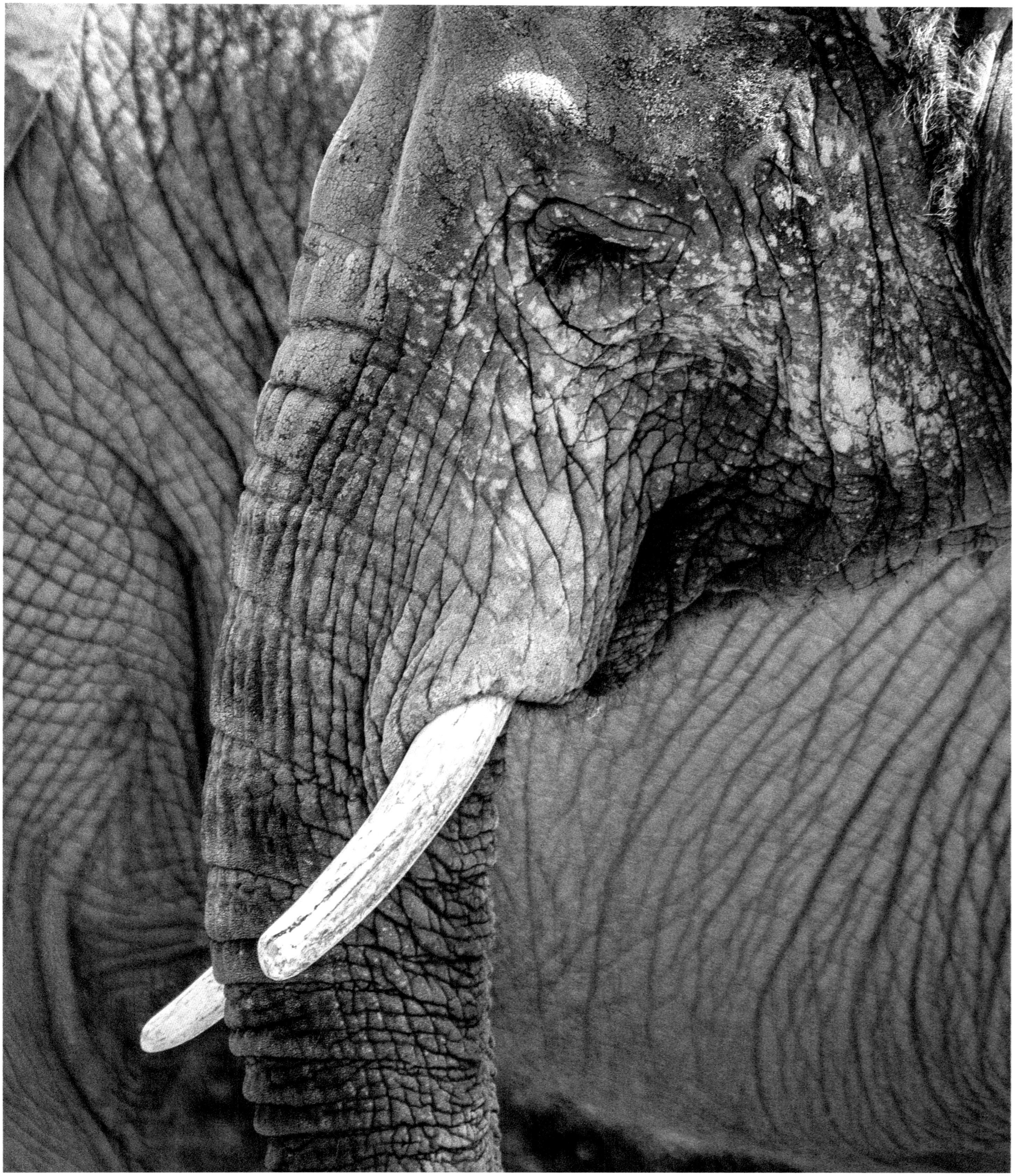

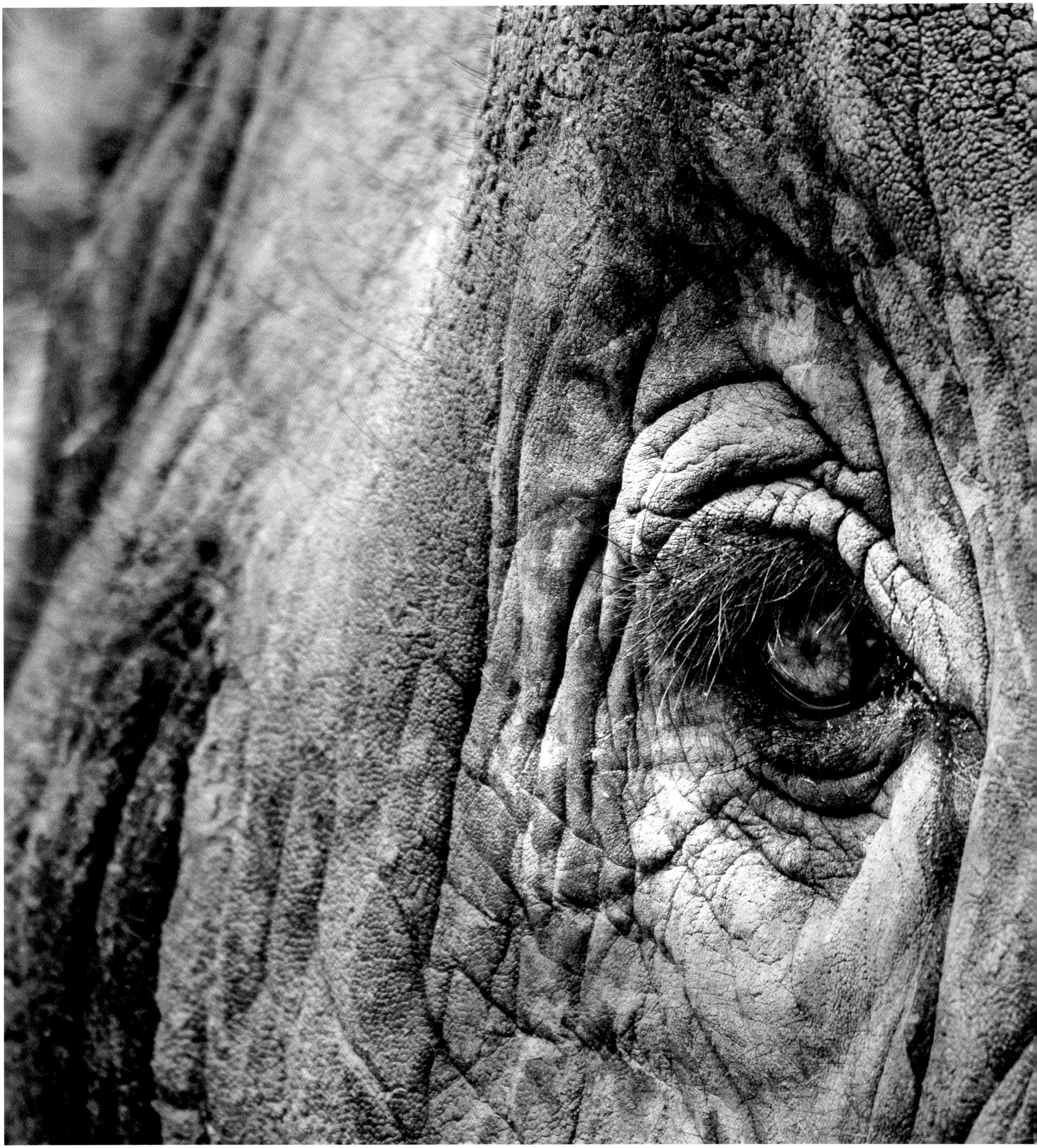

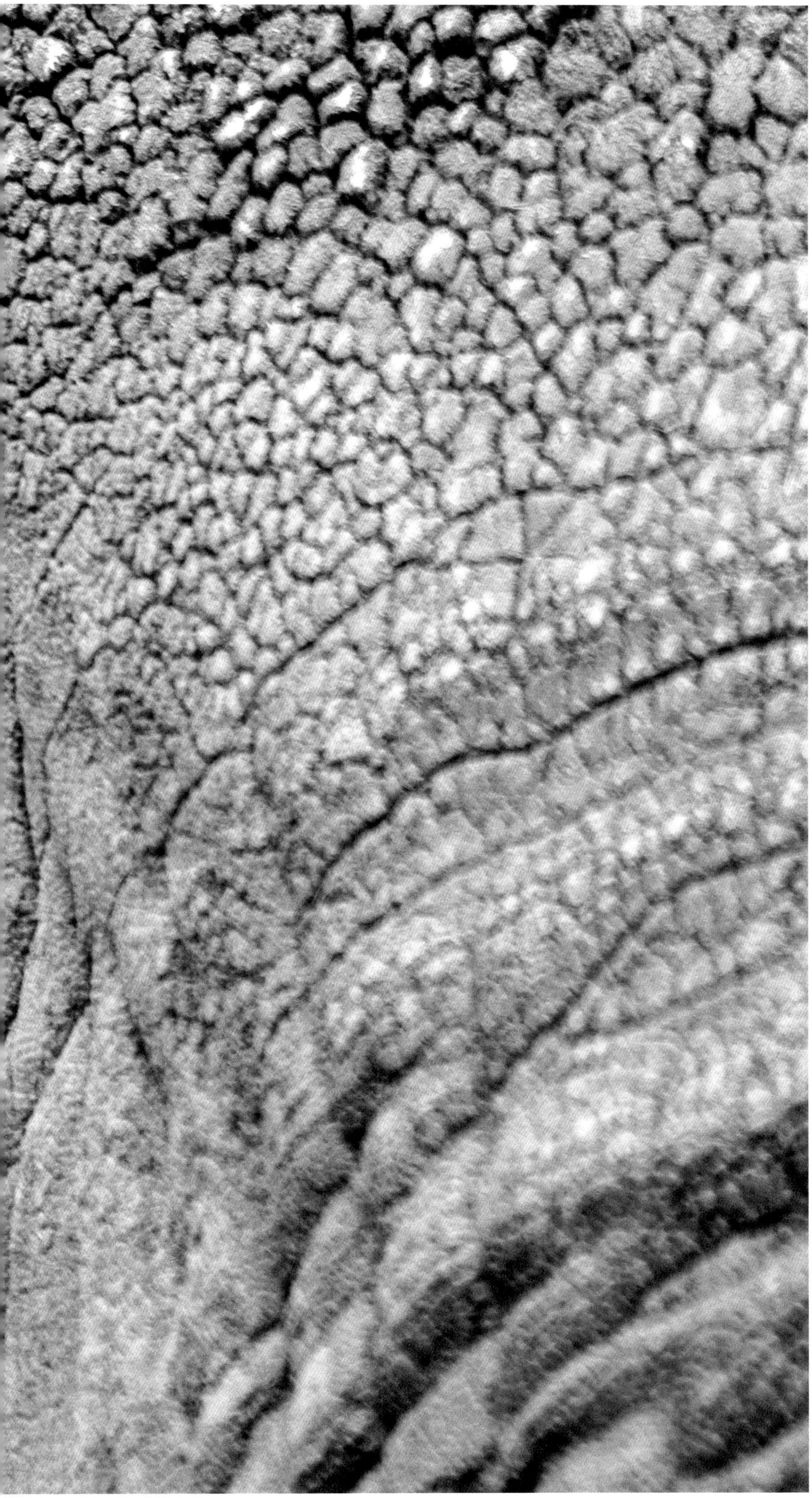

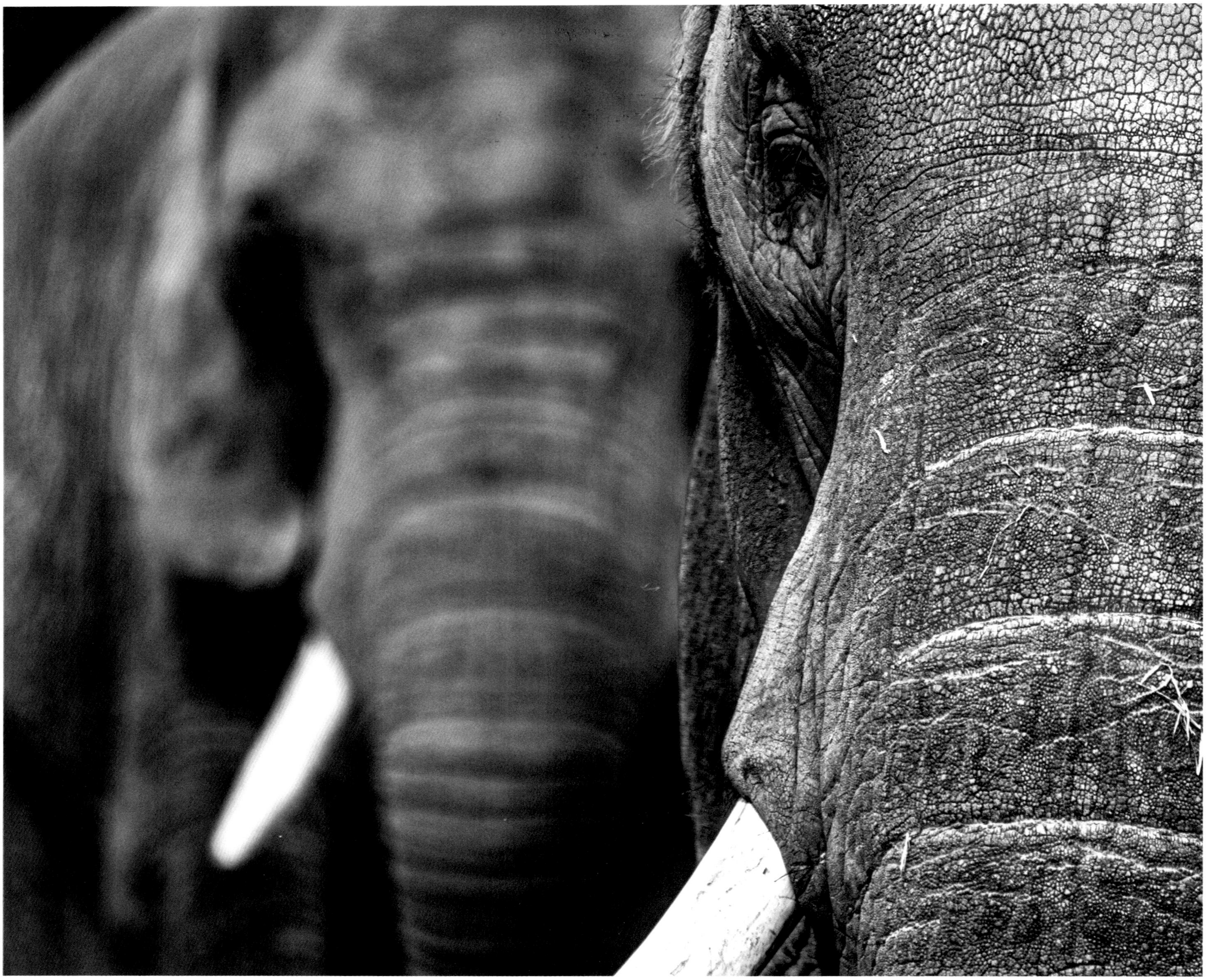

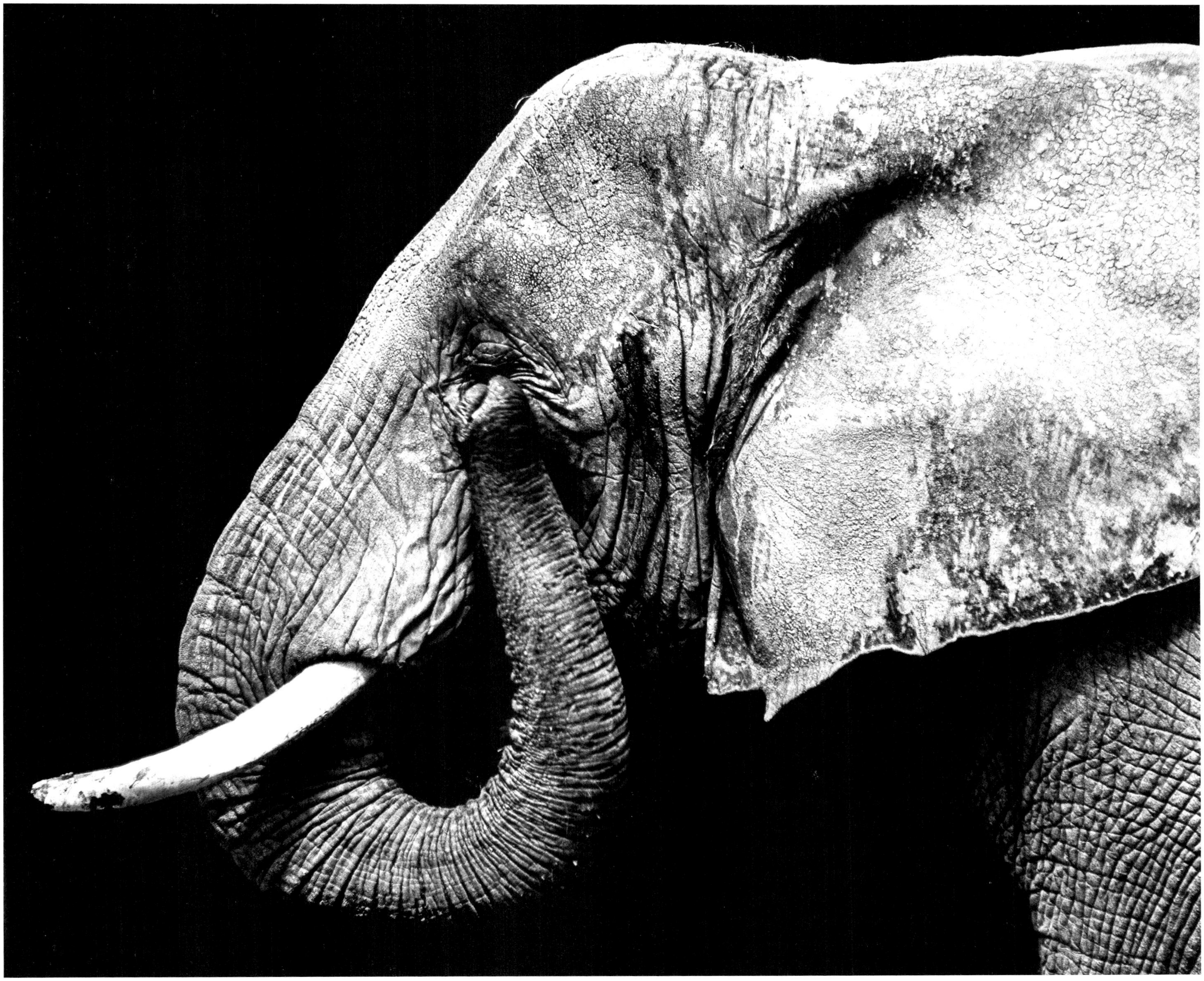

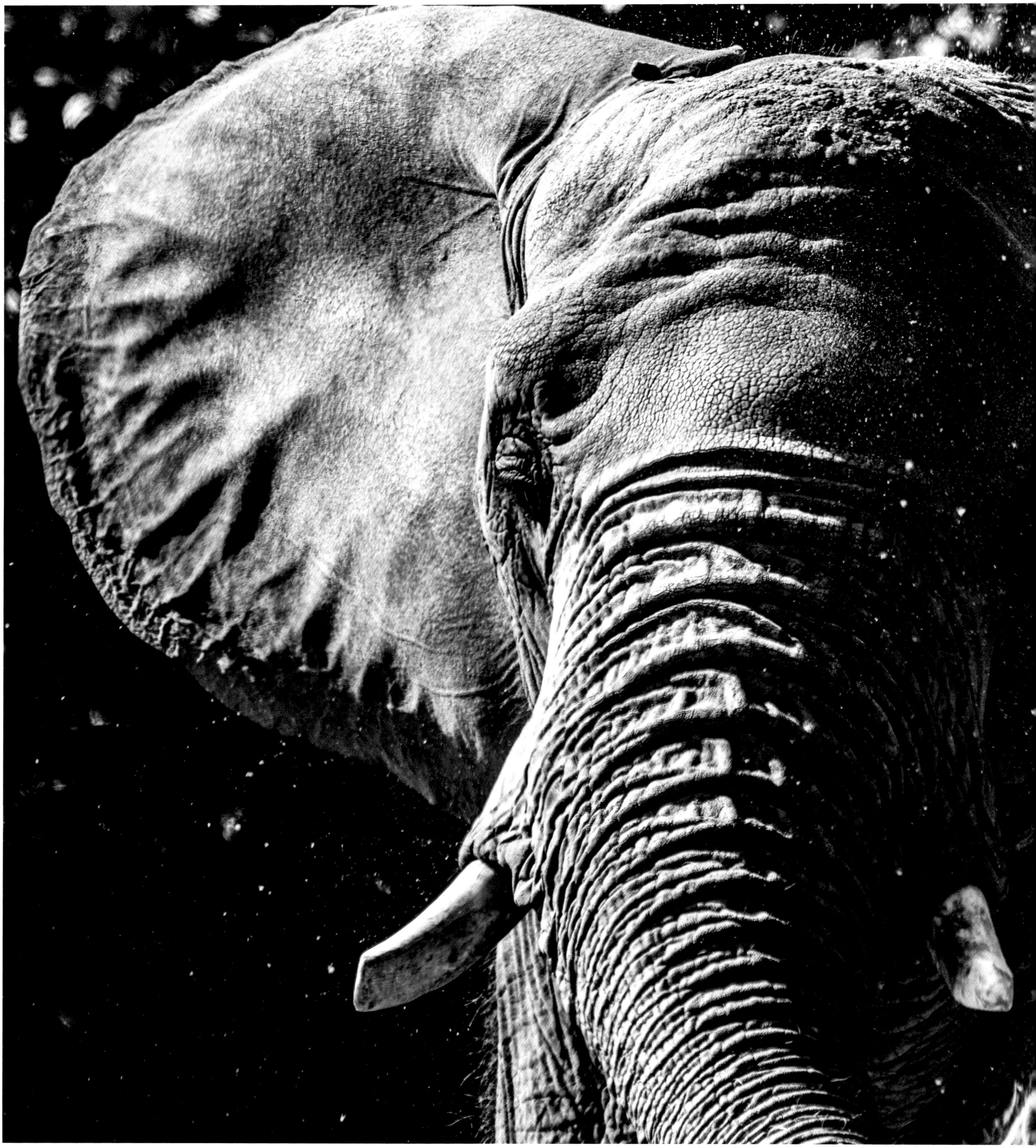

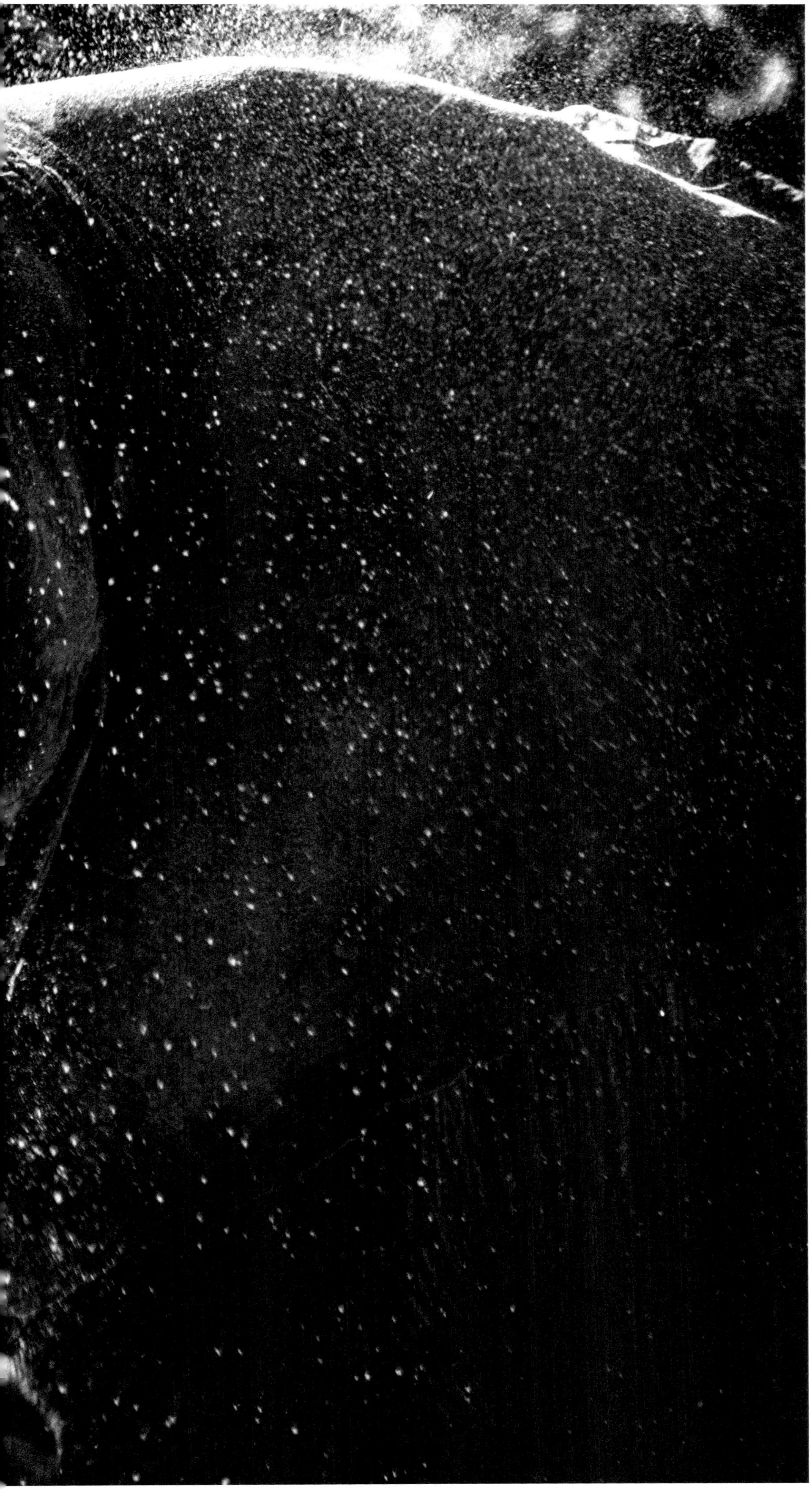

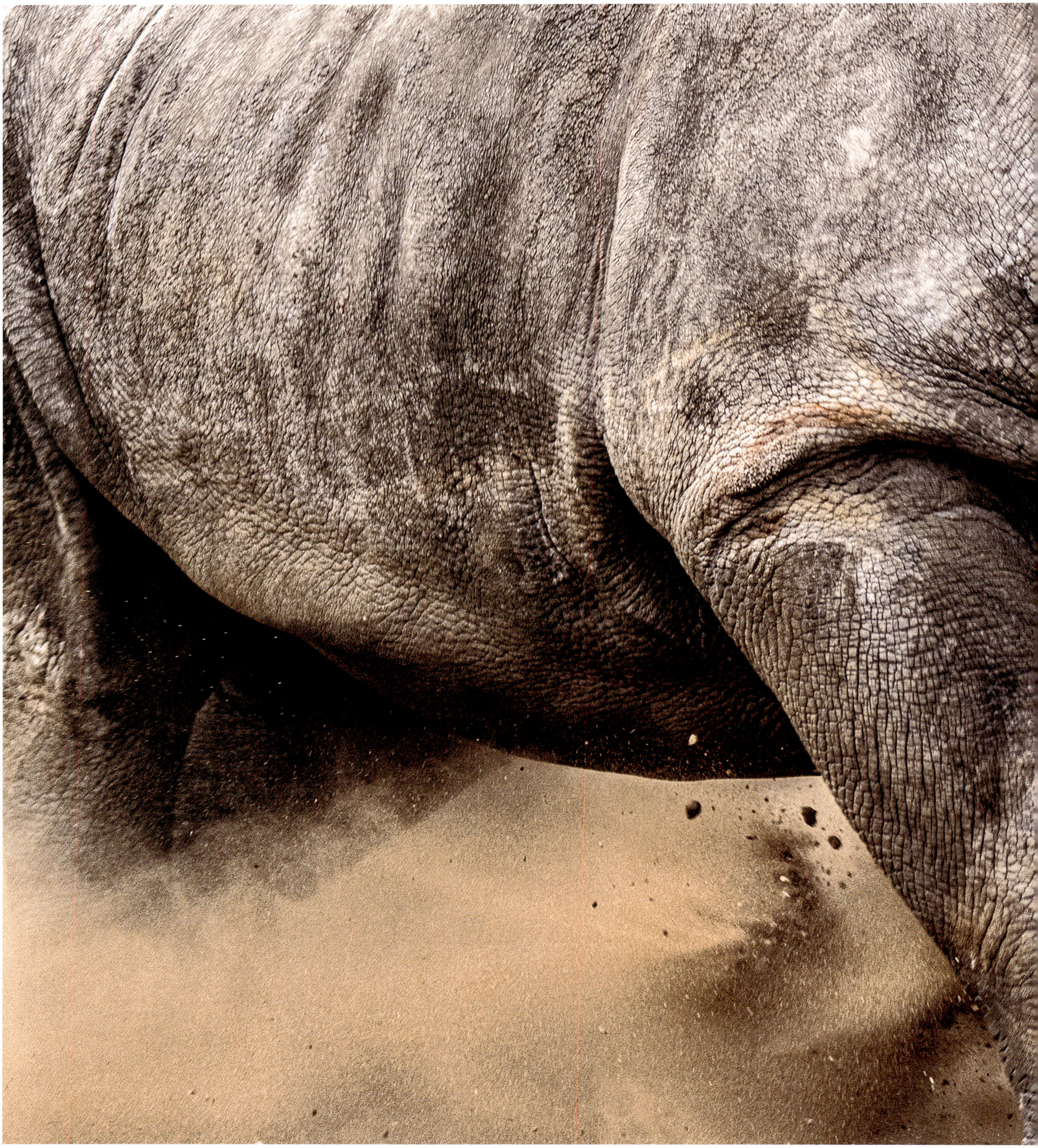

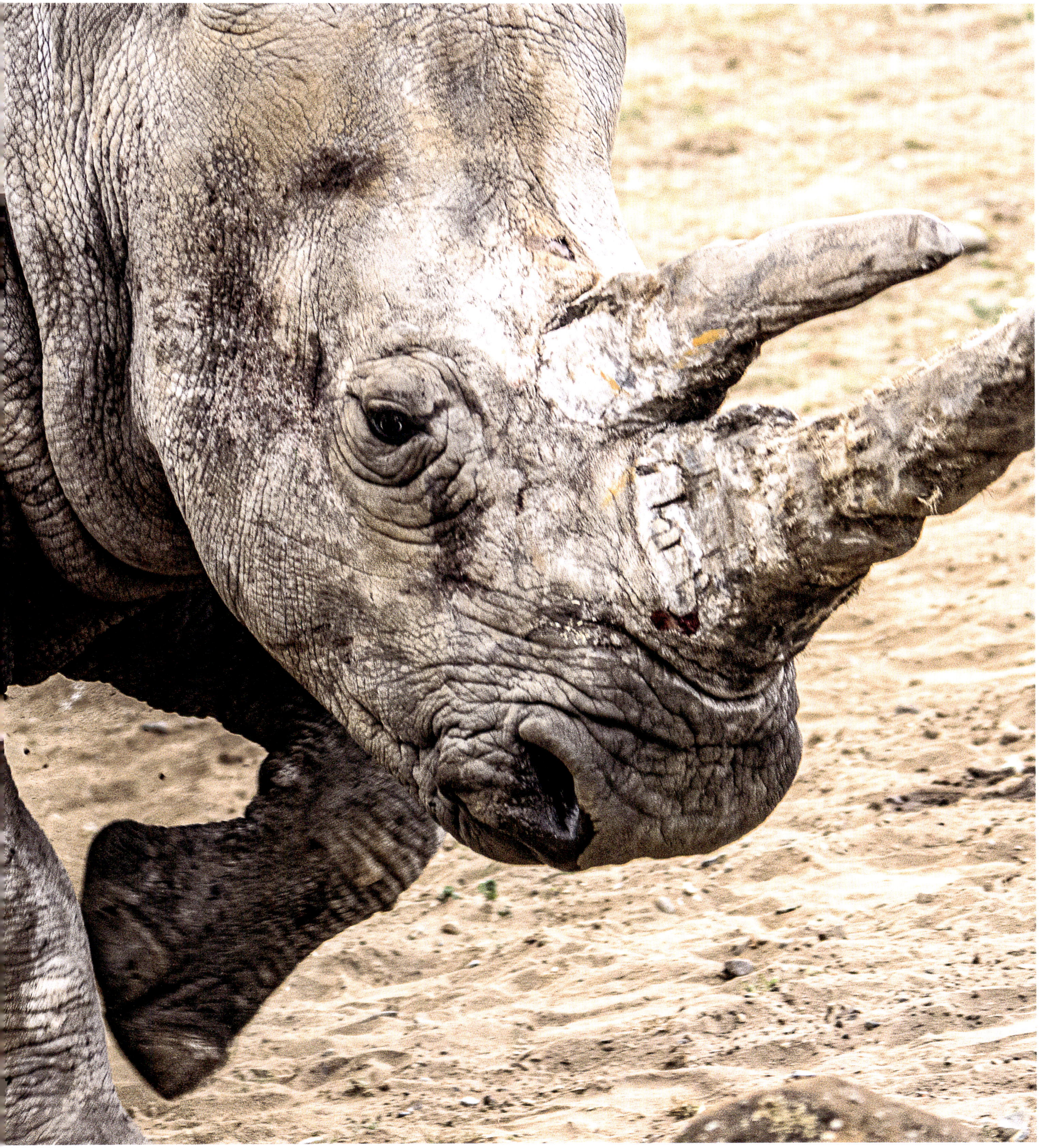

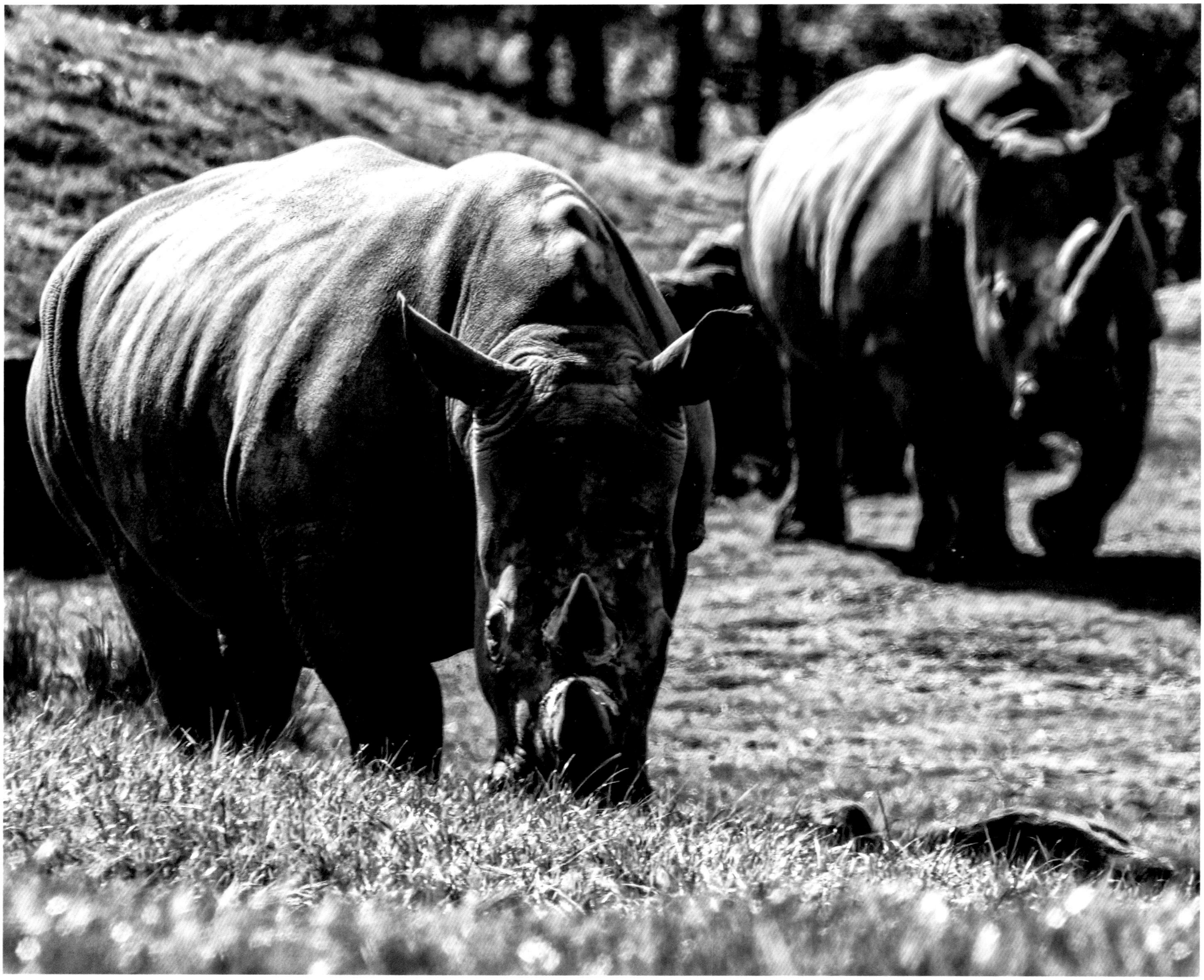

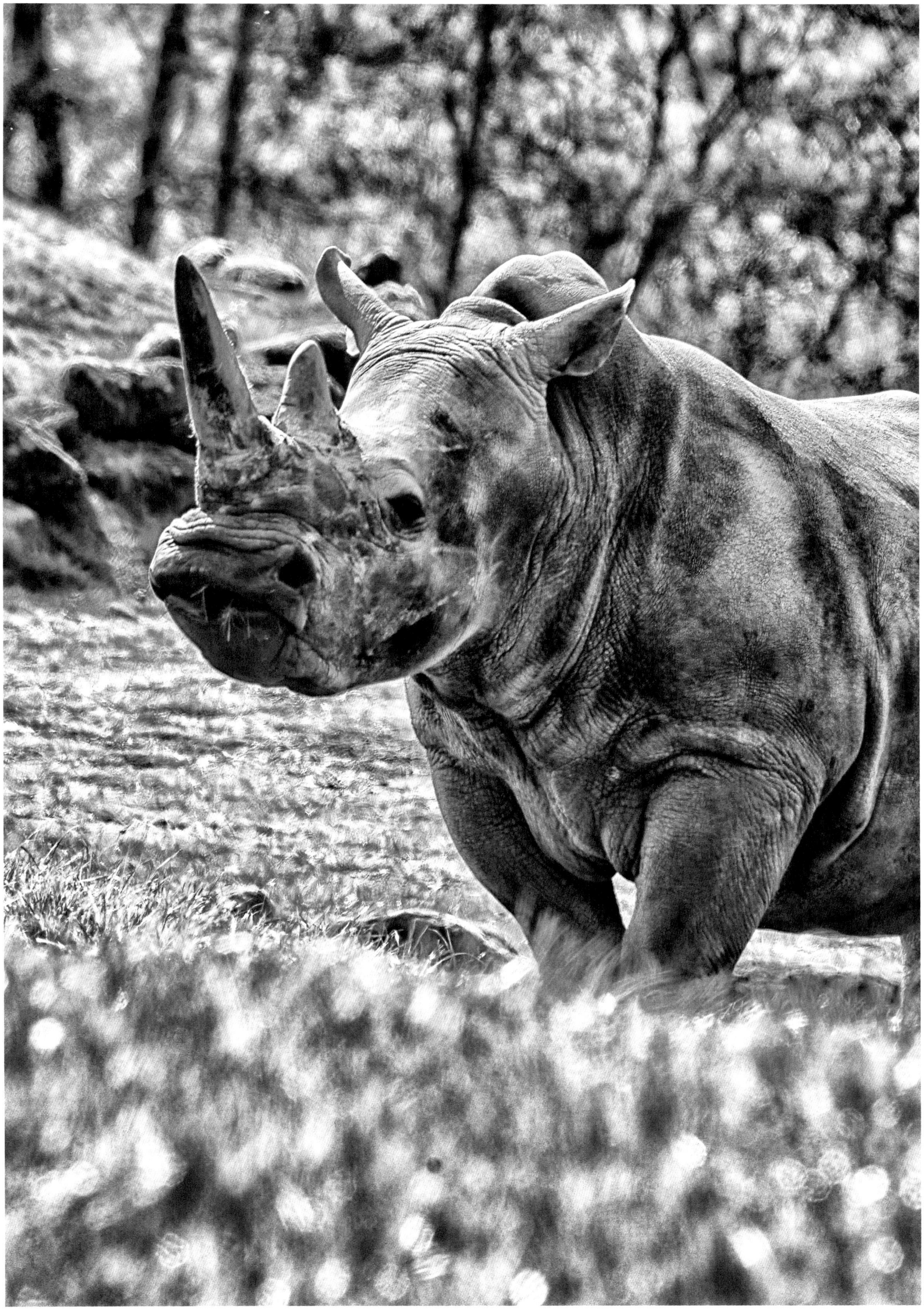

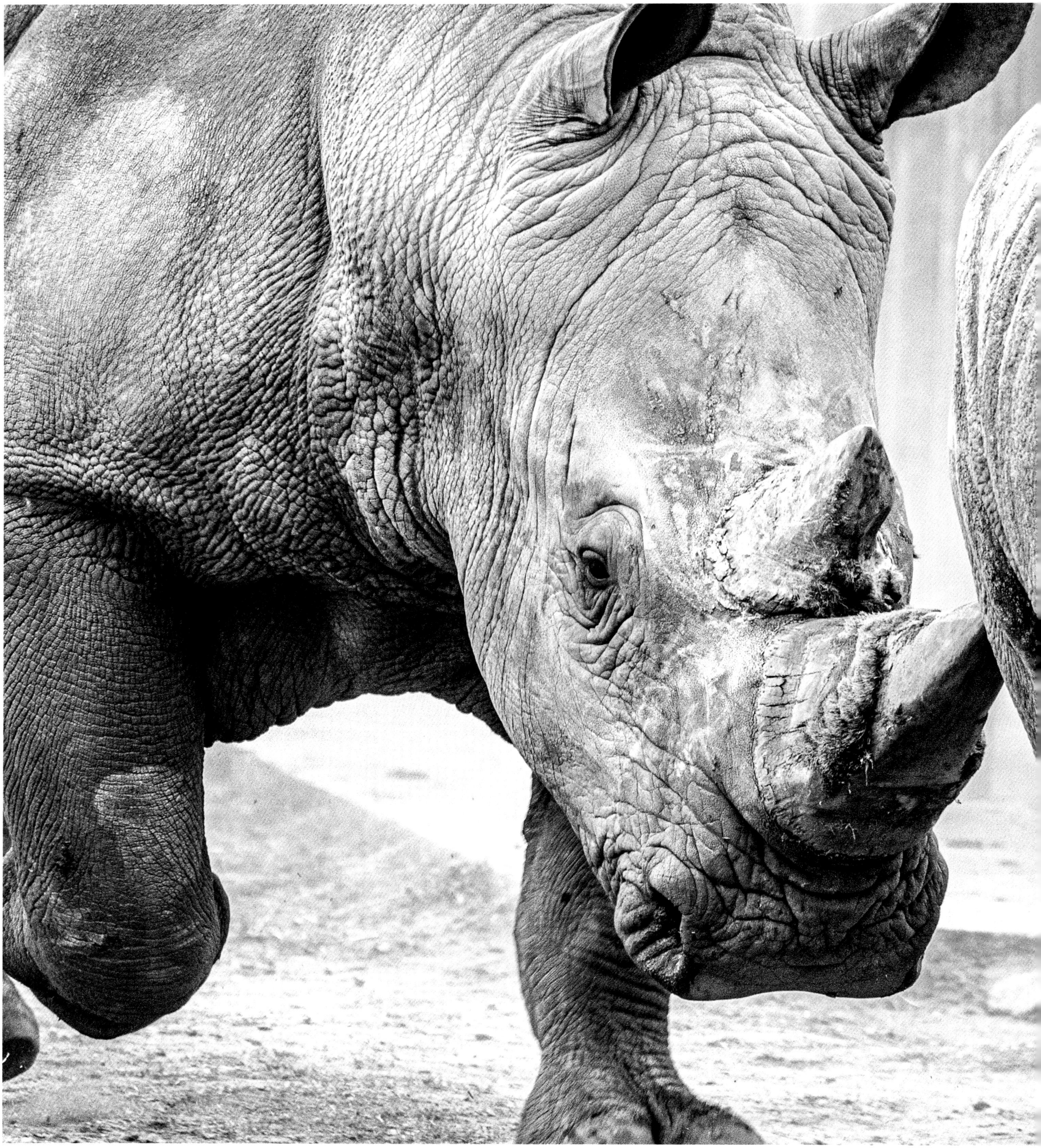

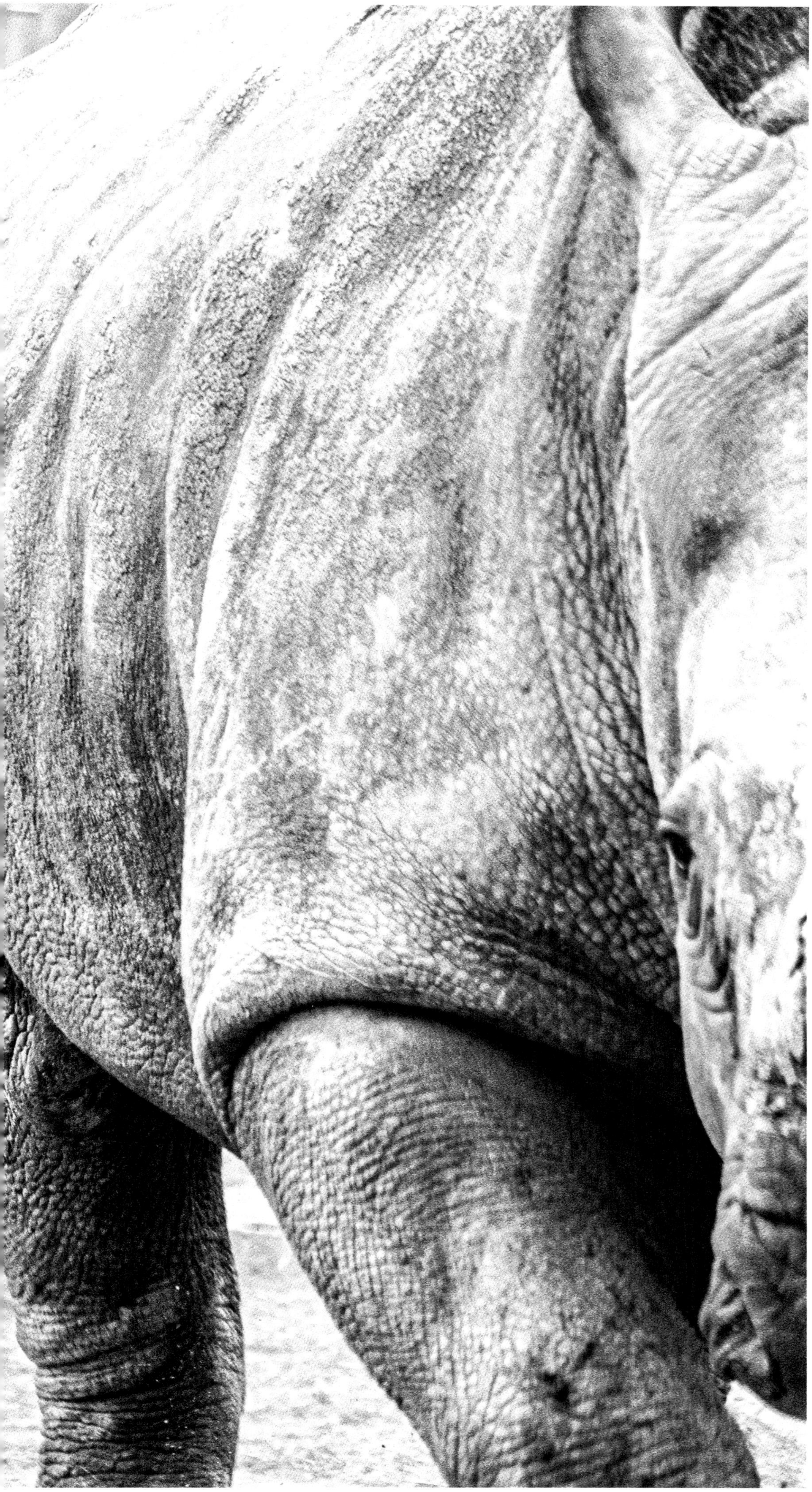

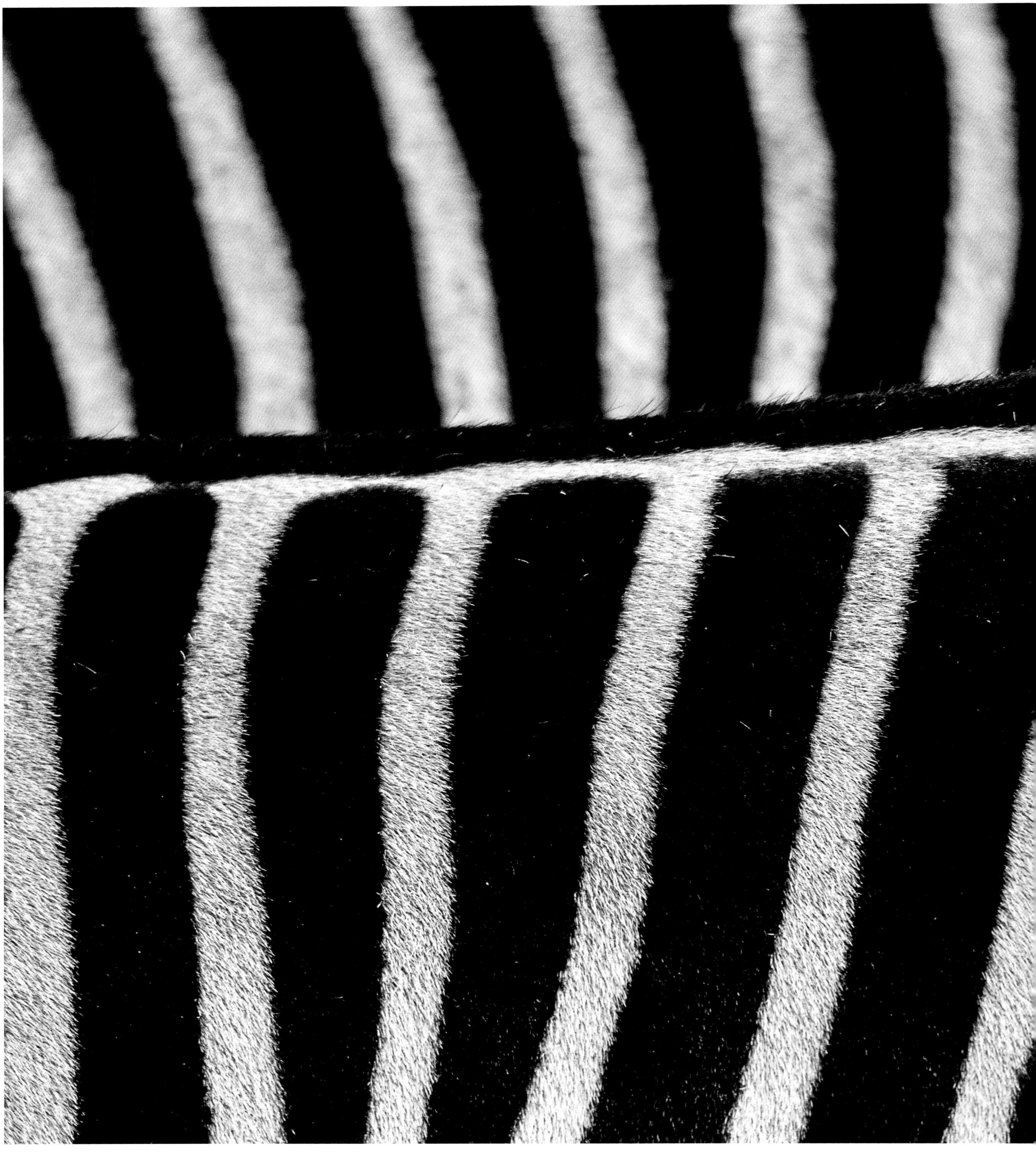

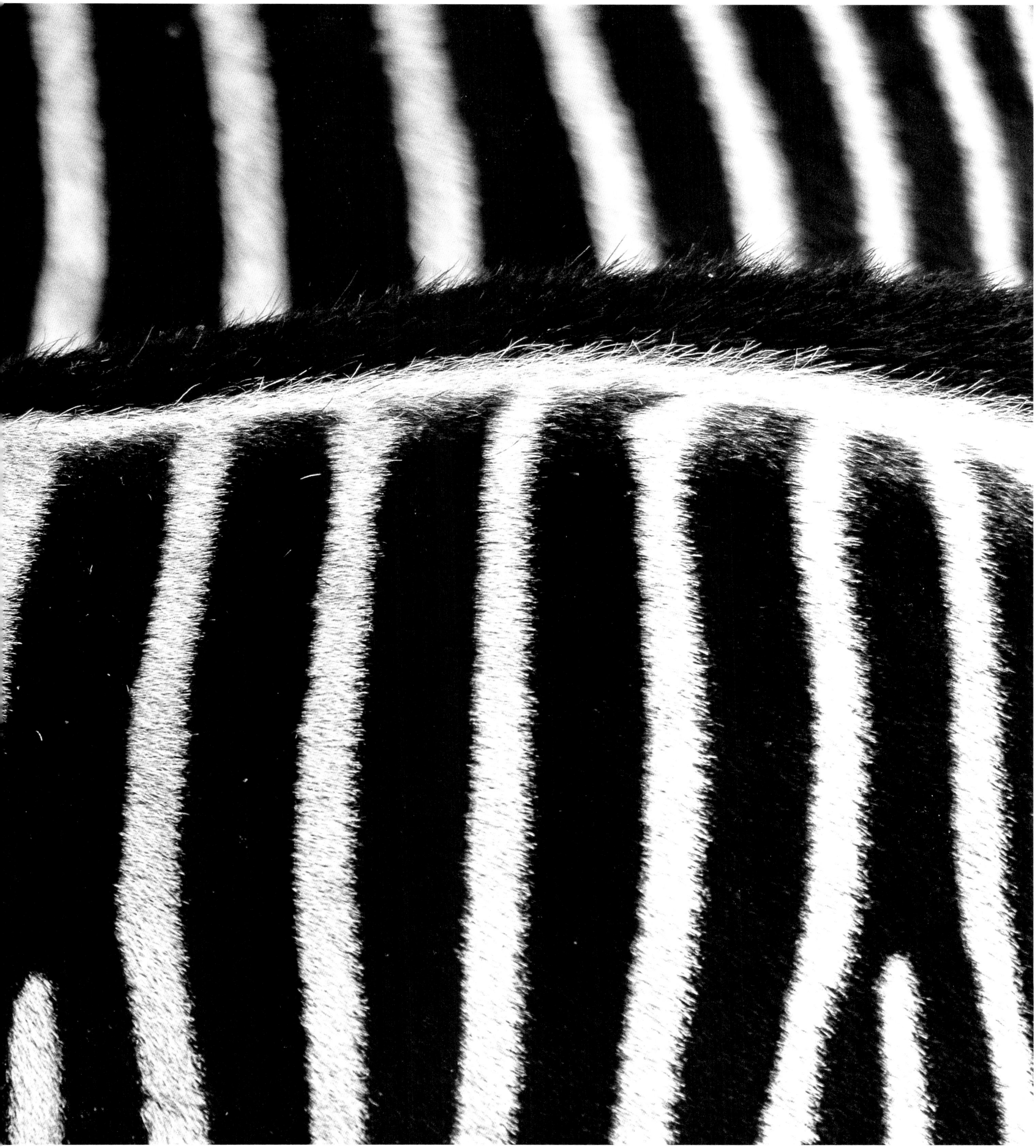

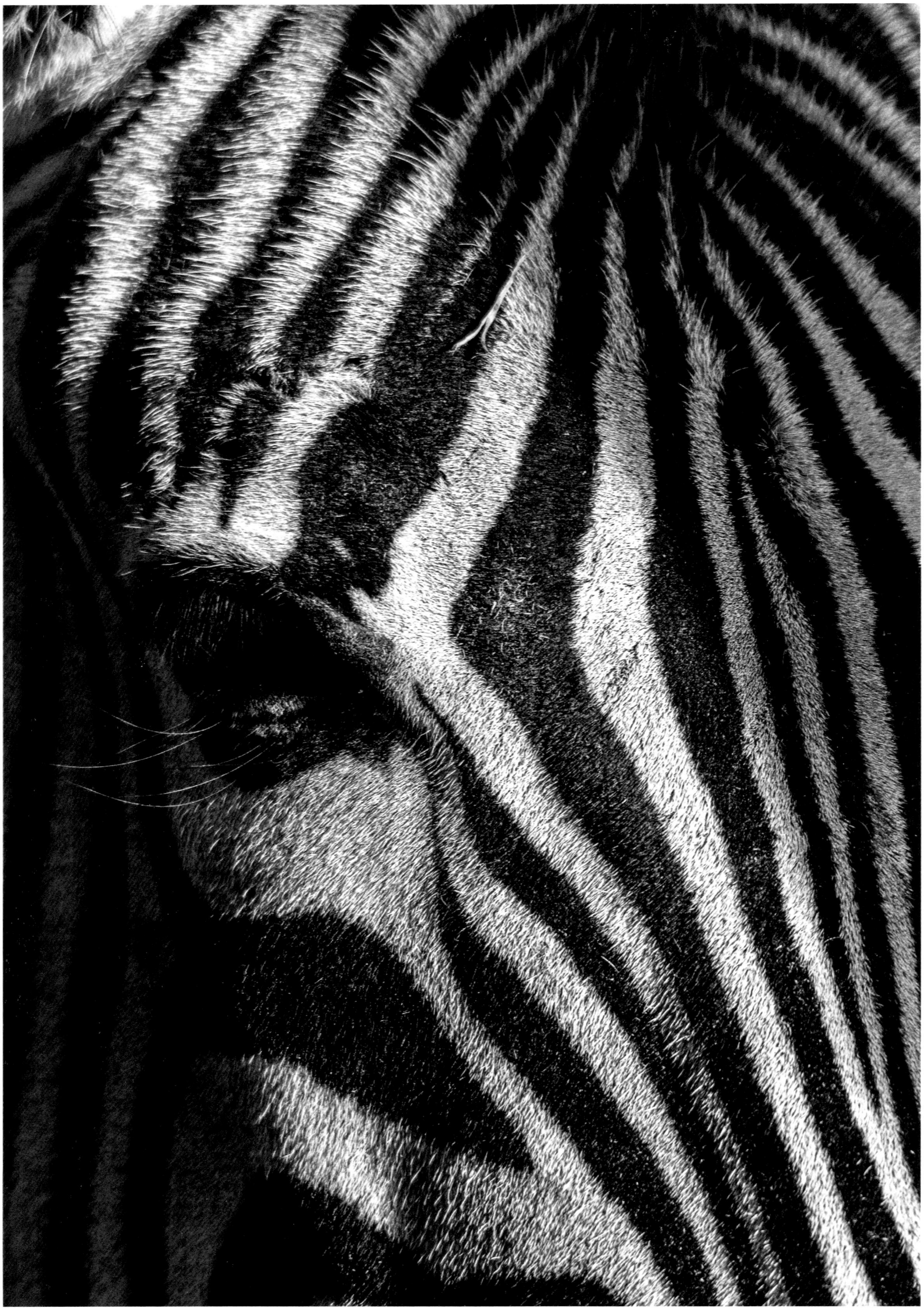

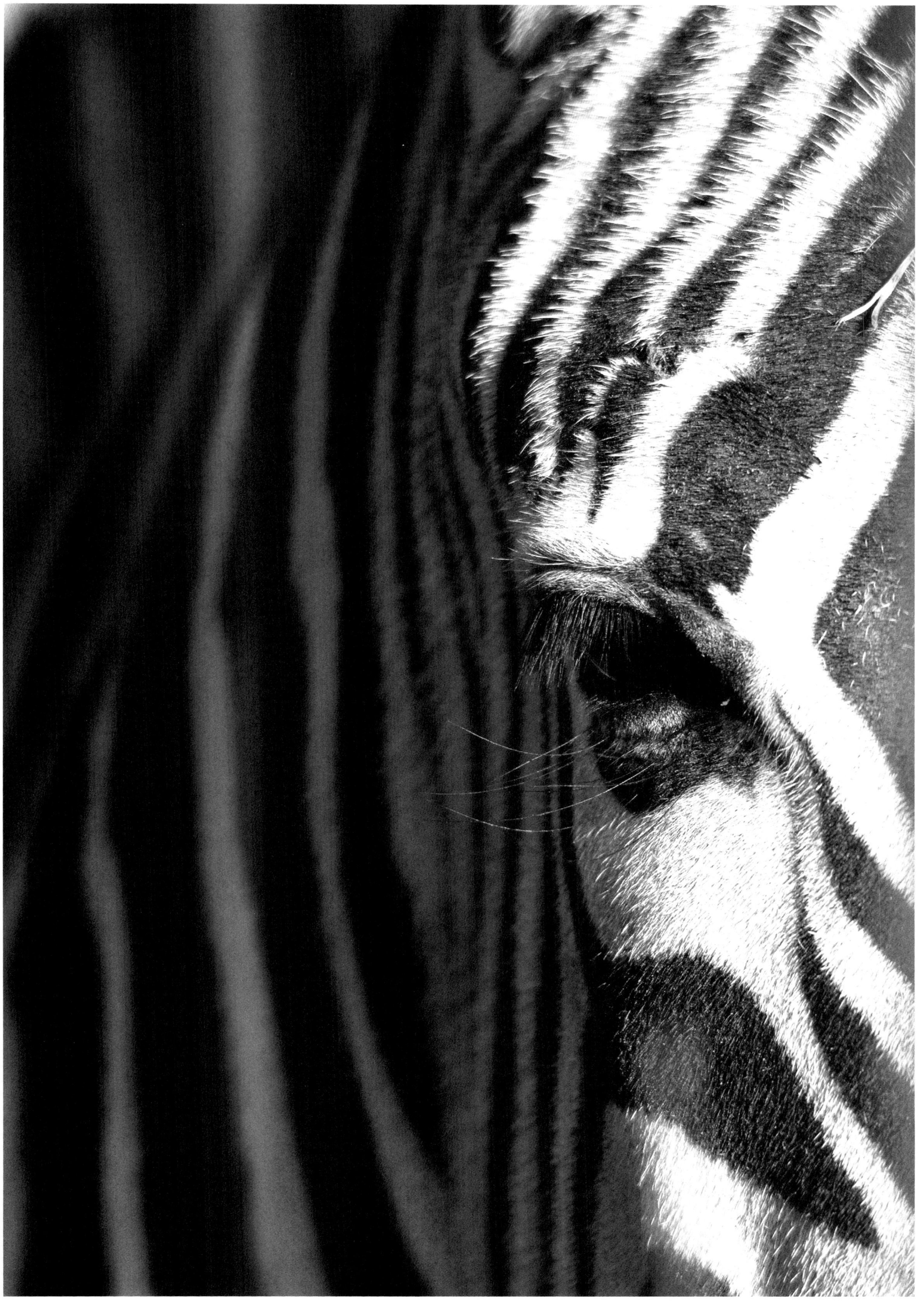

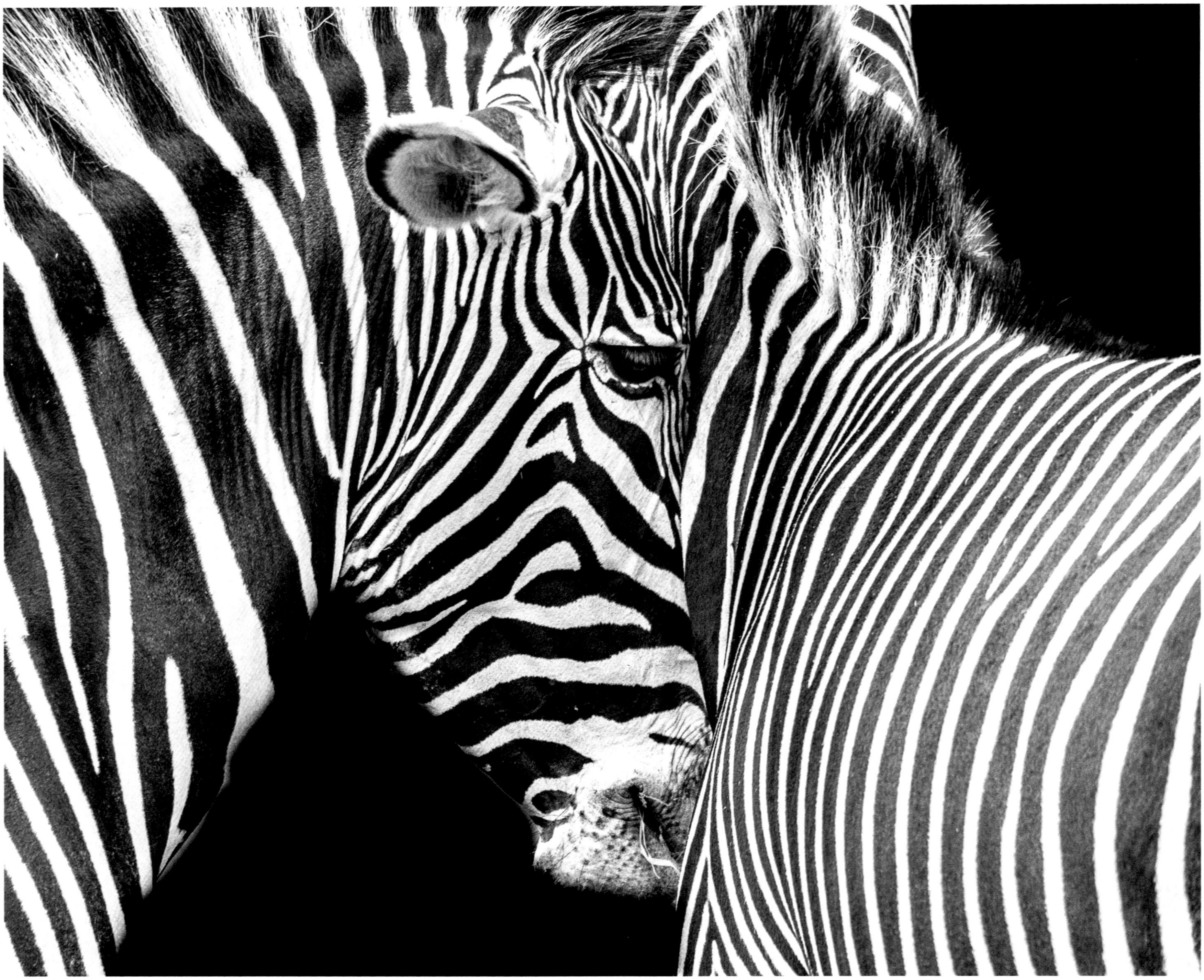

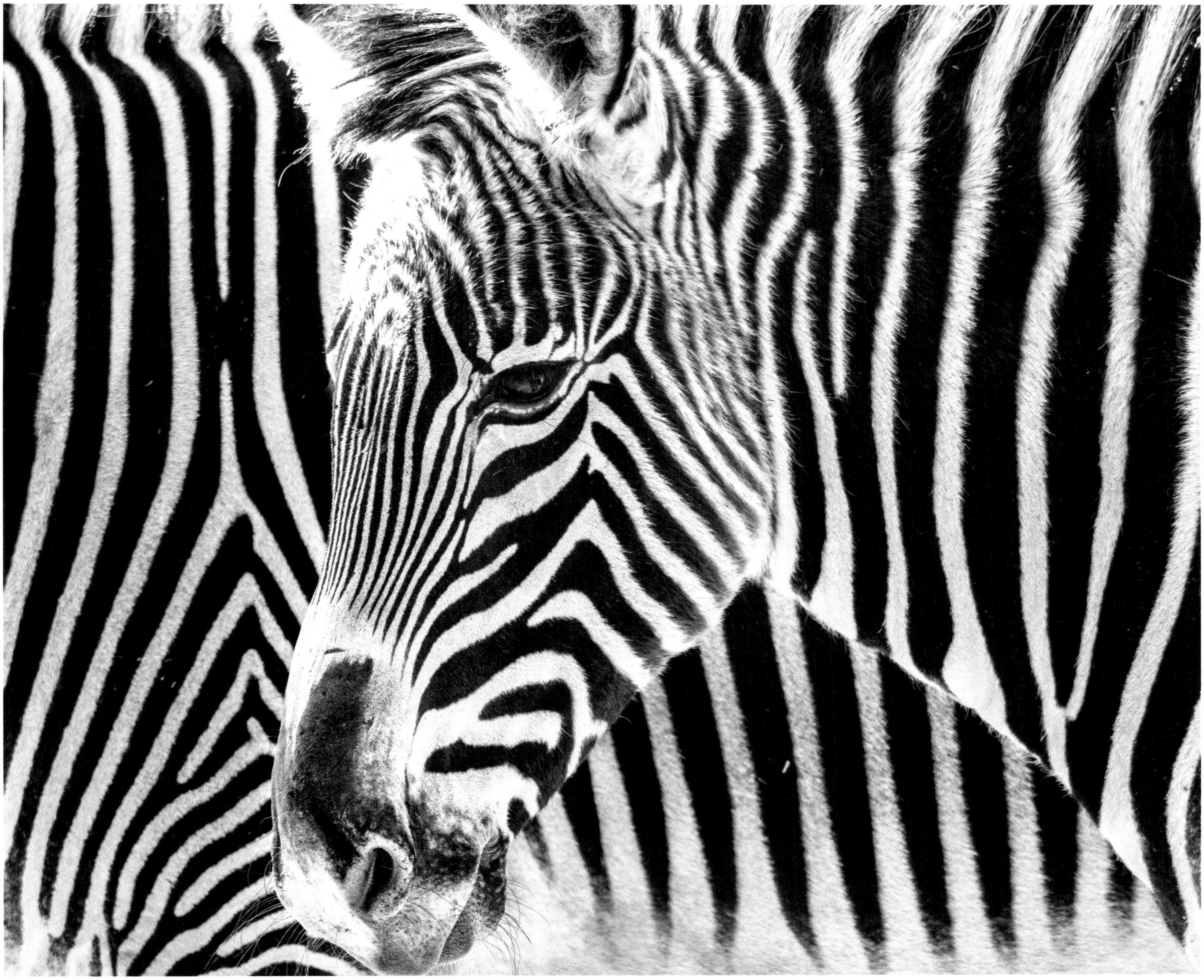

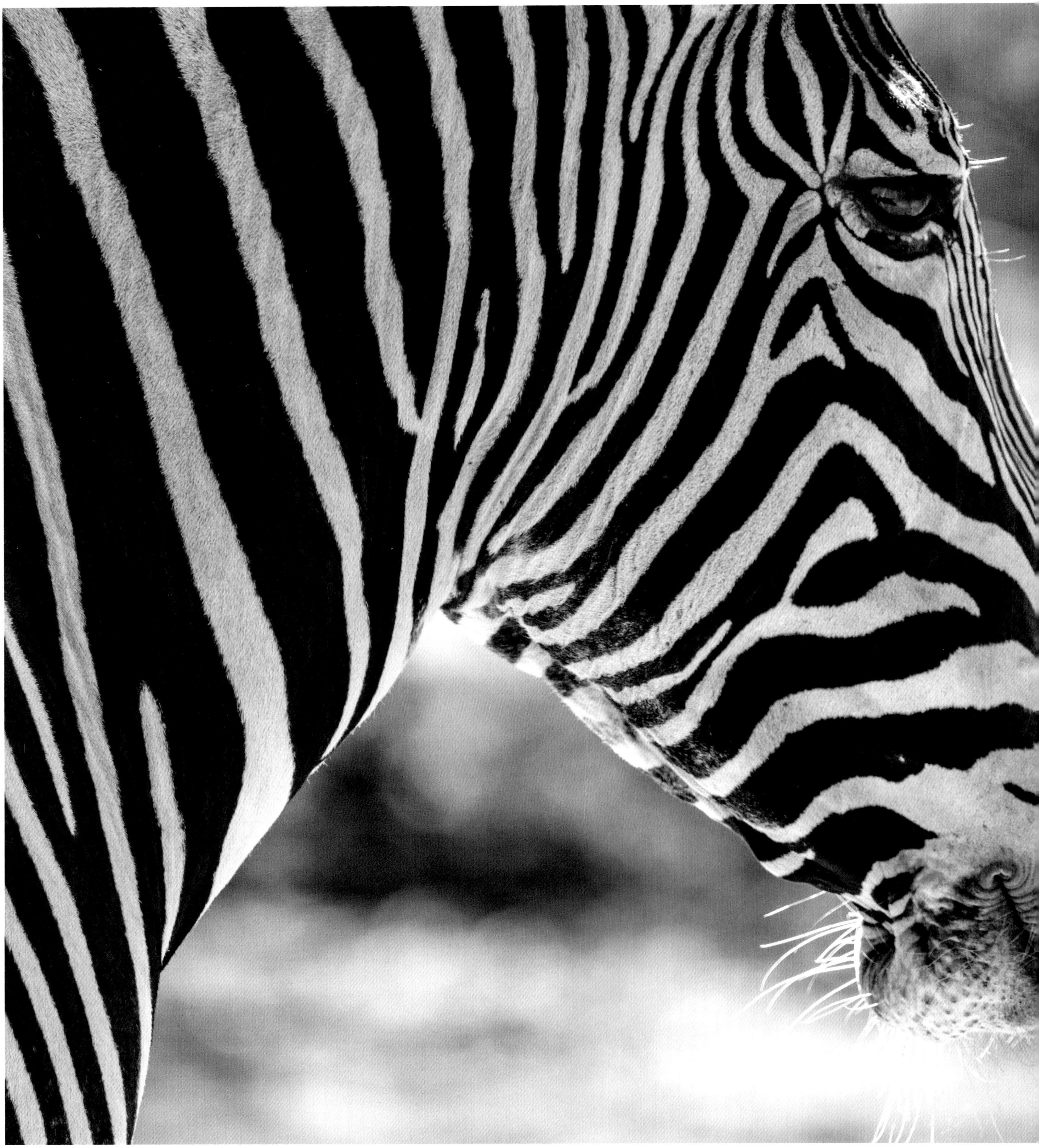

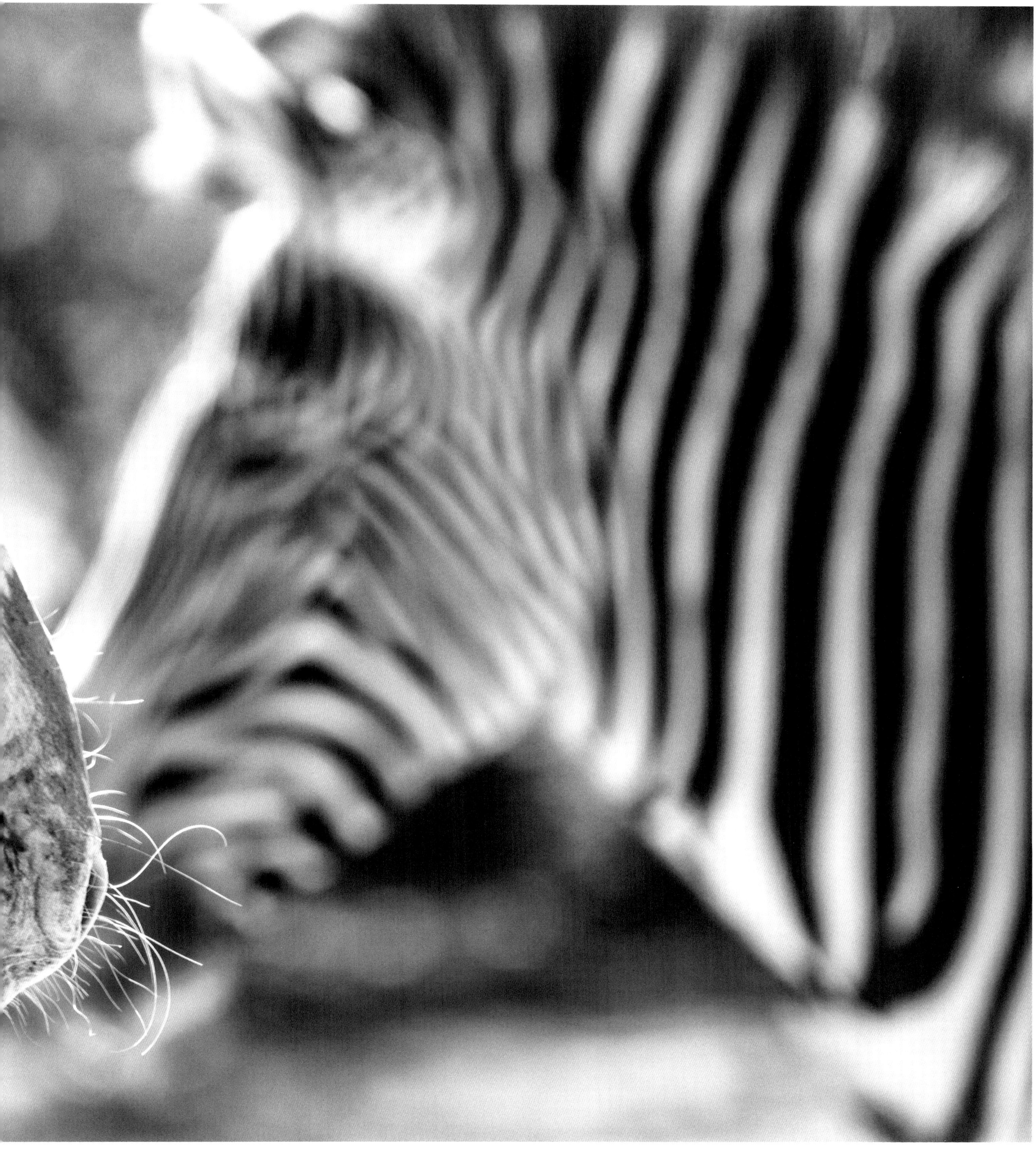

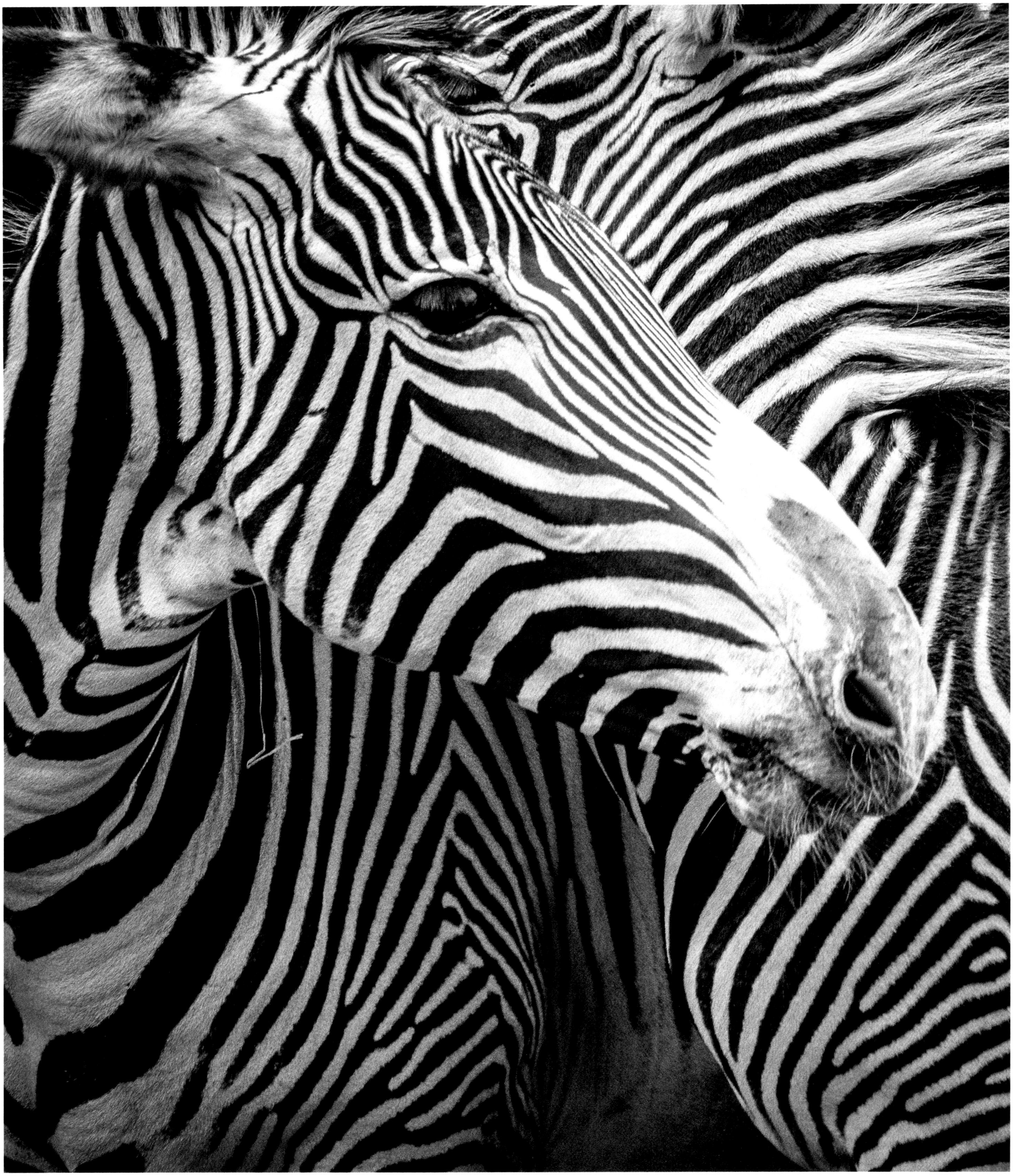

I am often asked which my favourite animal is to photograph and, thus, I have spent many hours wrangling with myself as to the answer. I arrived, finally, at a conclusion: the zebra, there are few animals as visually pleasing.

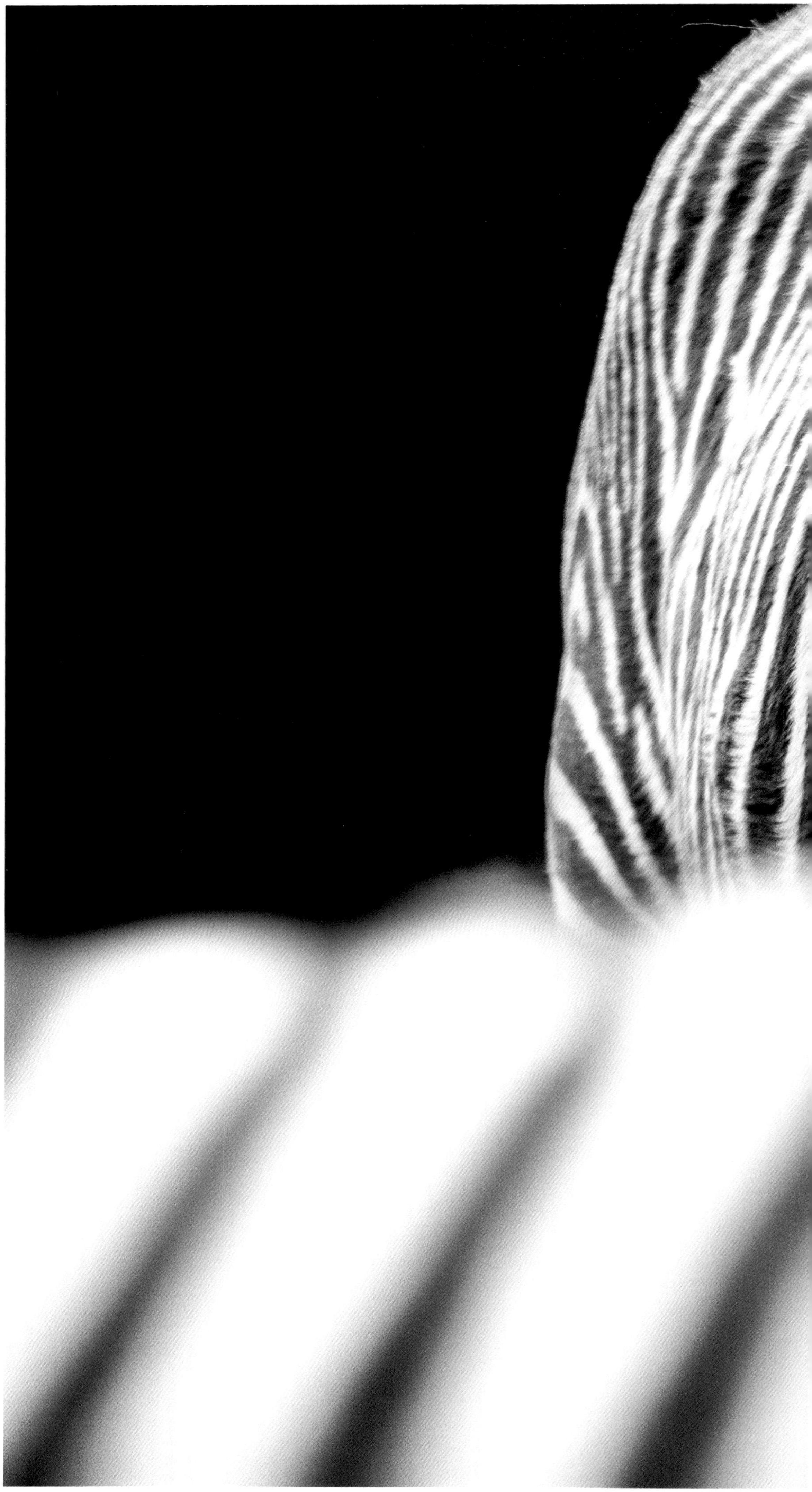

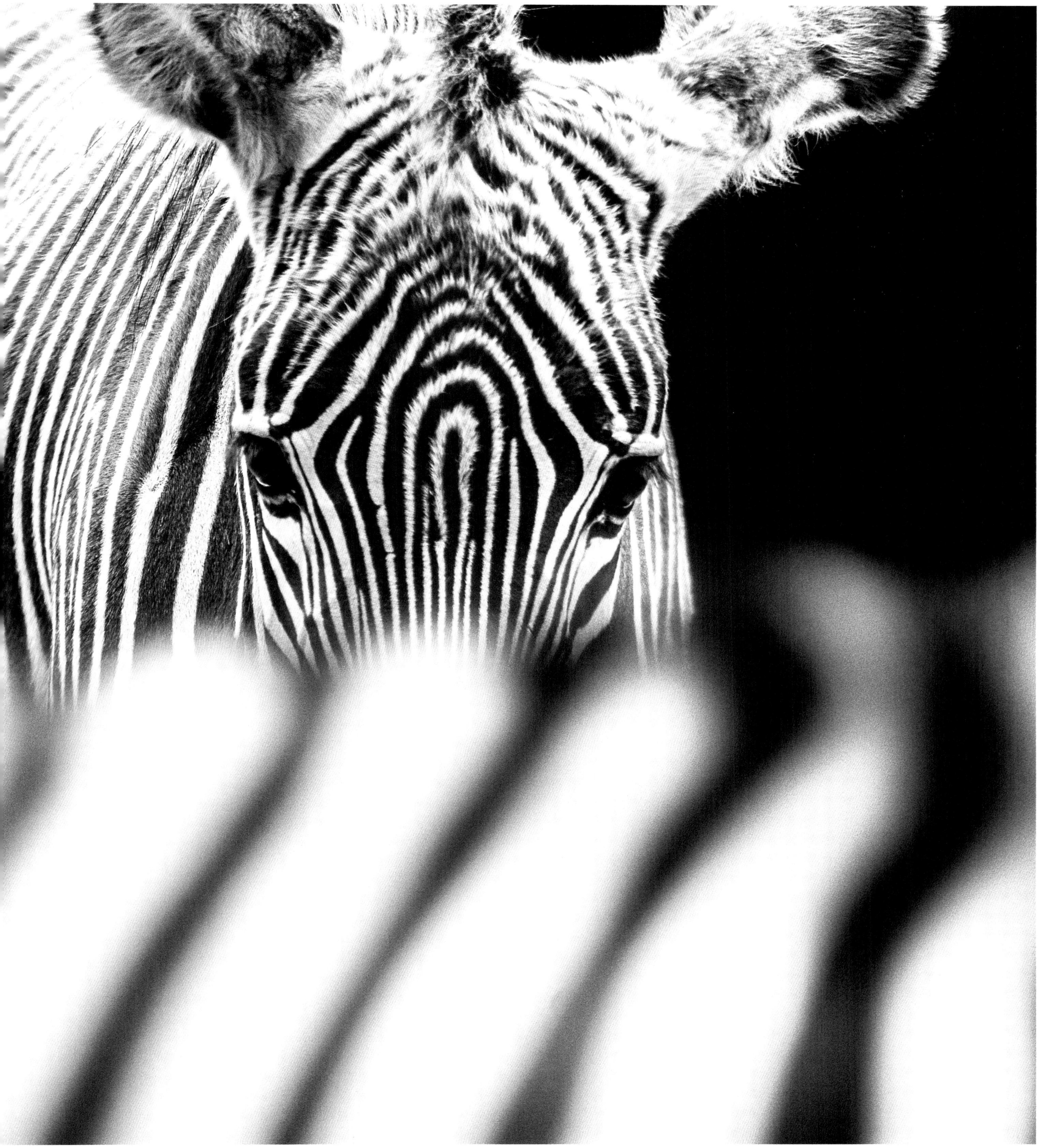

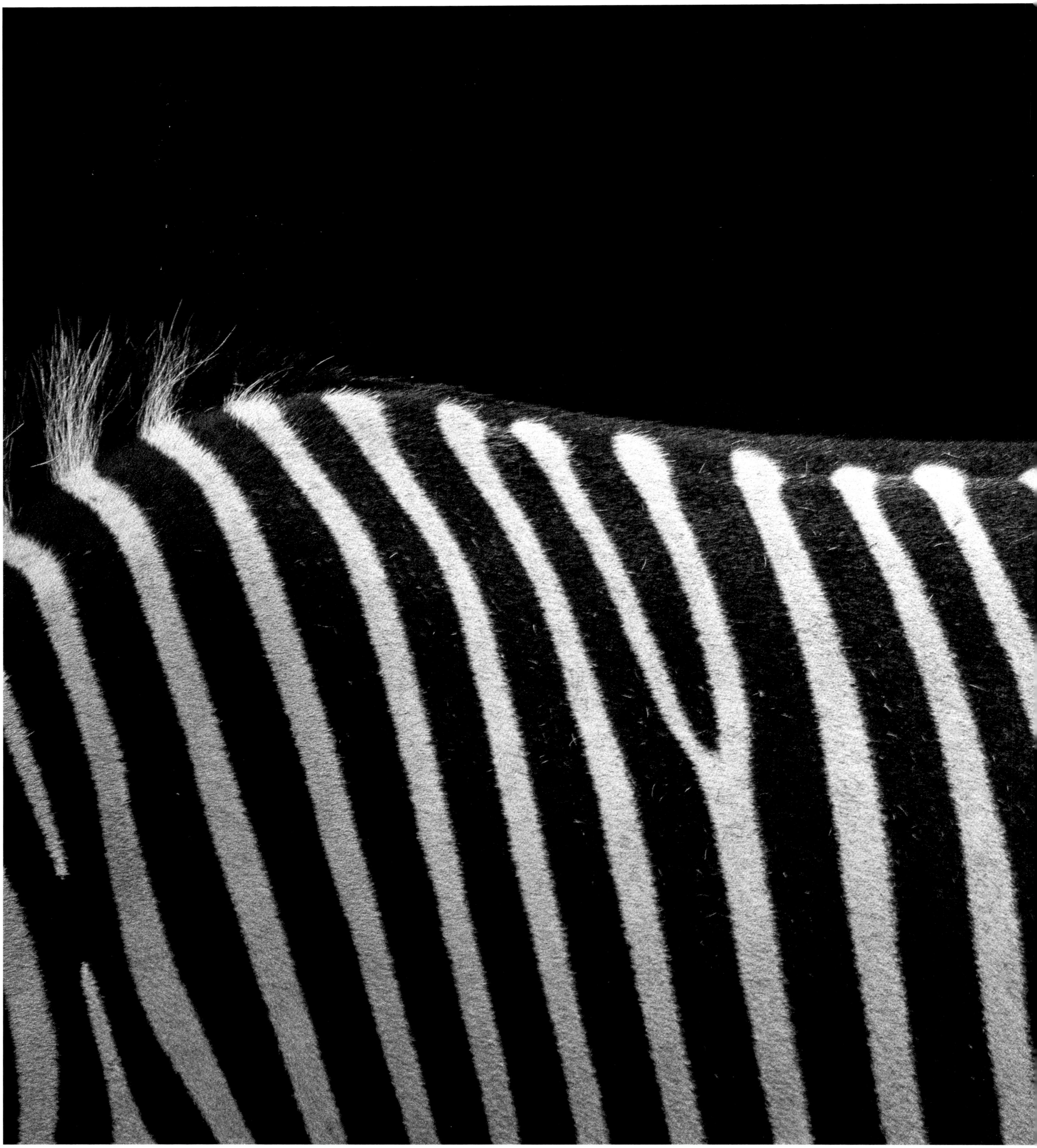

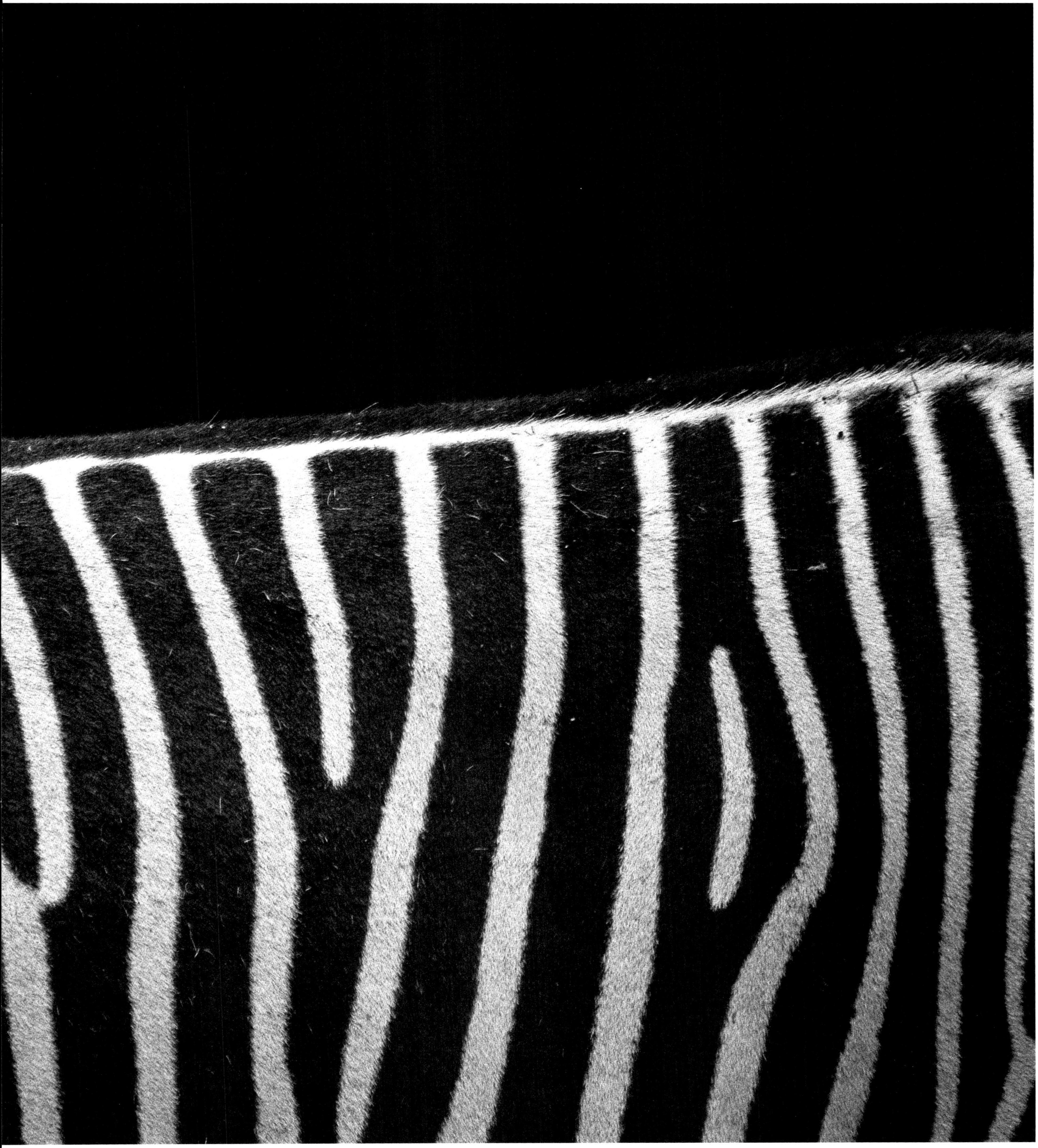

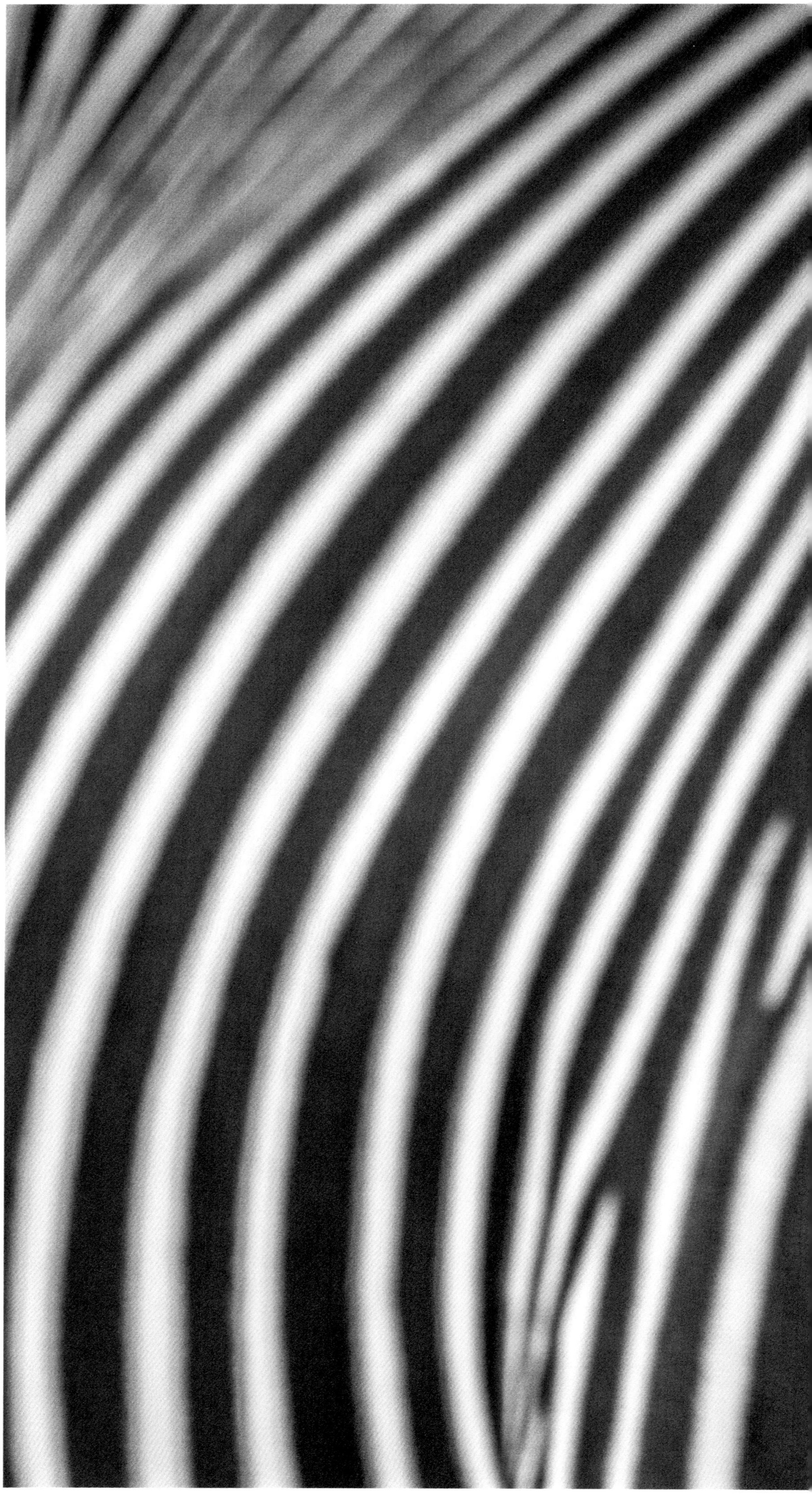

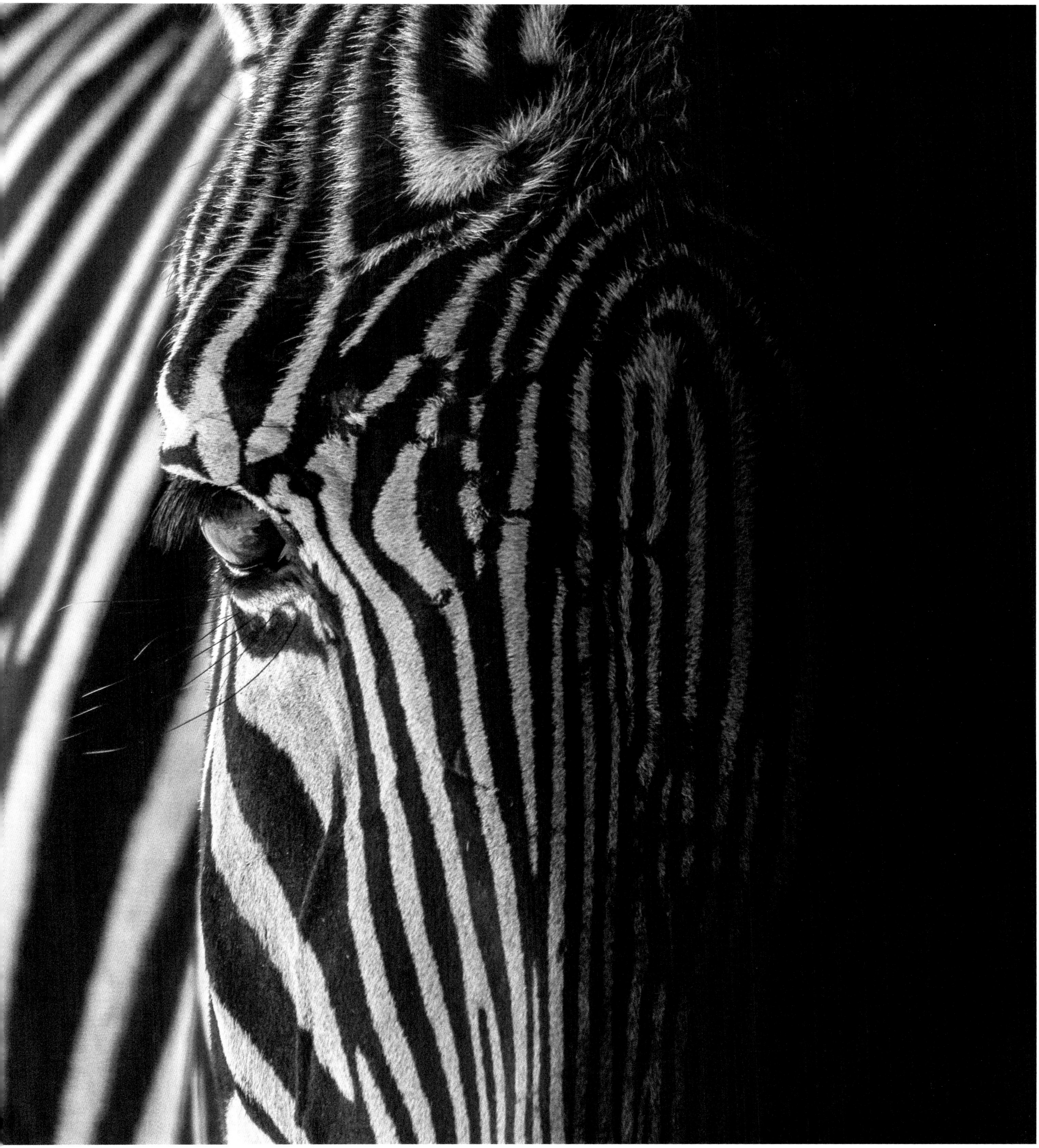

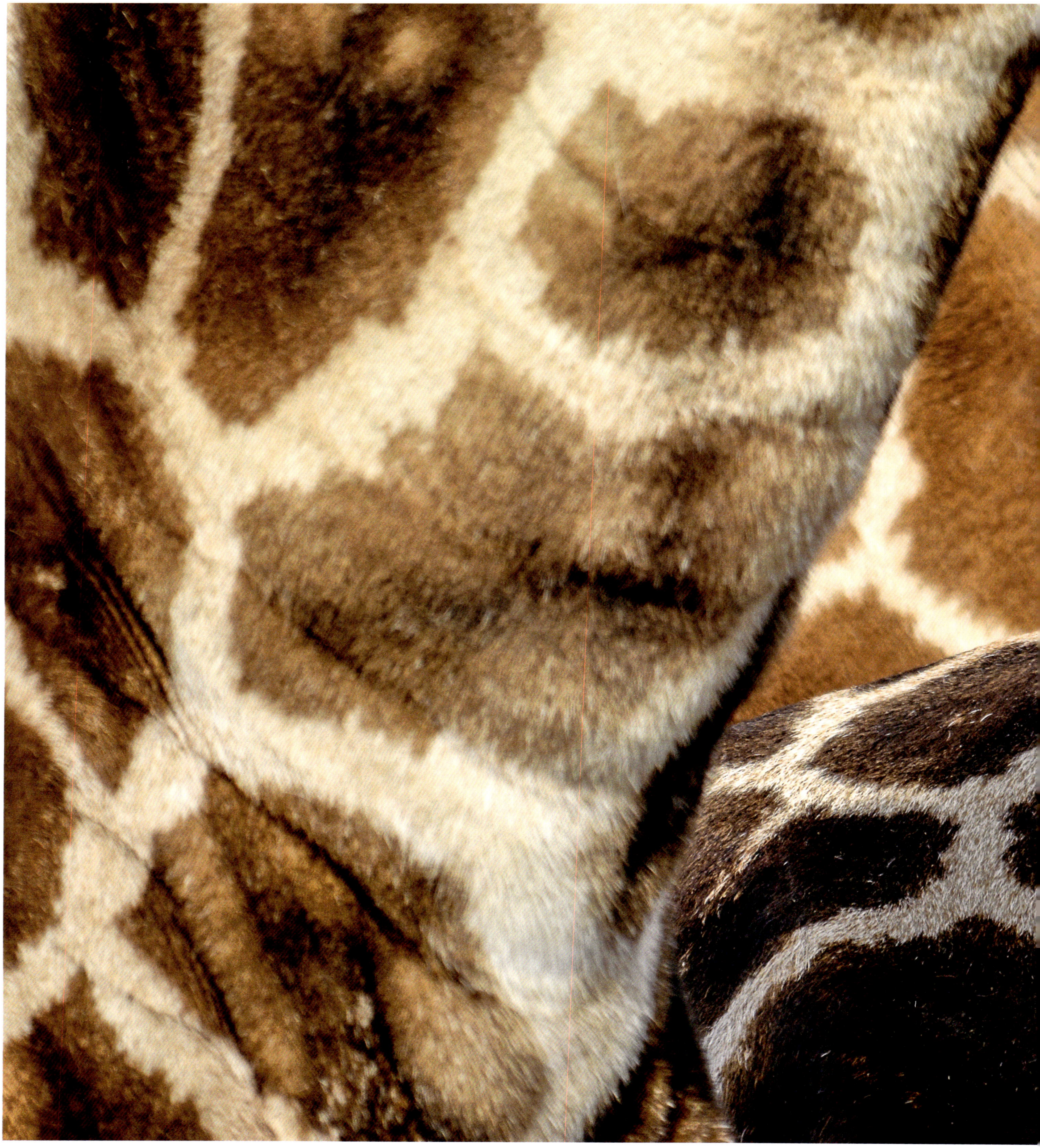

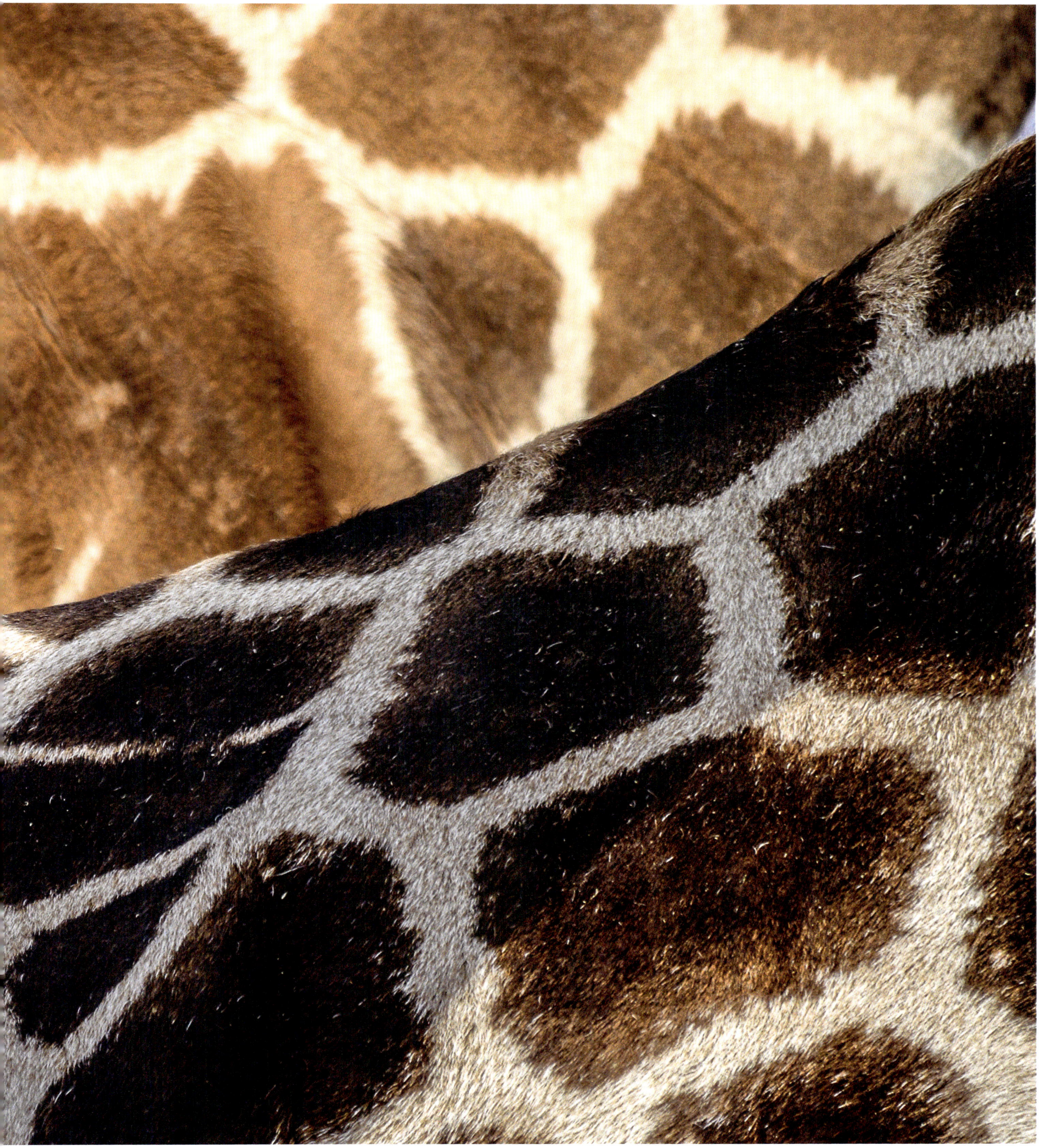

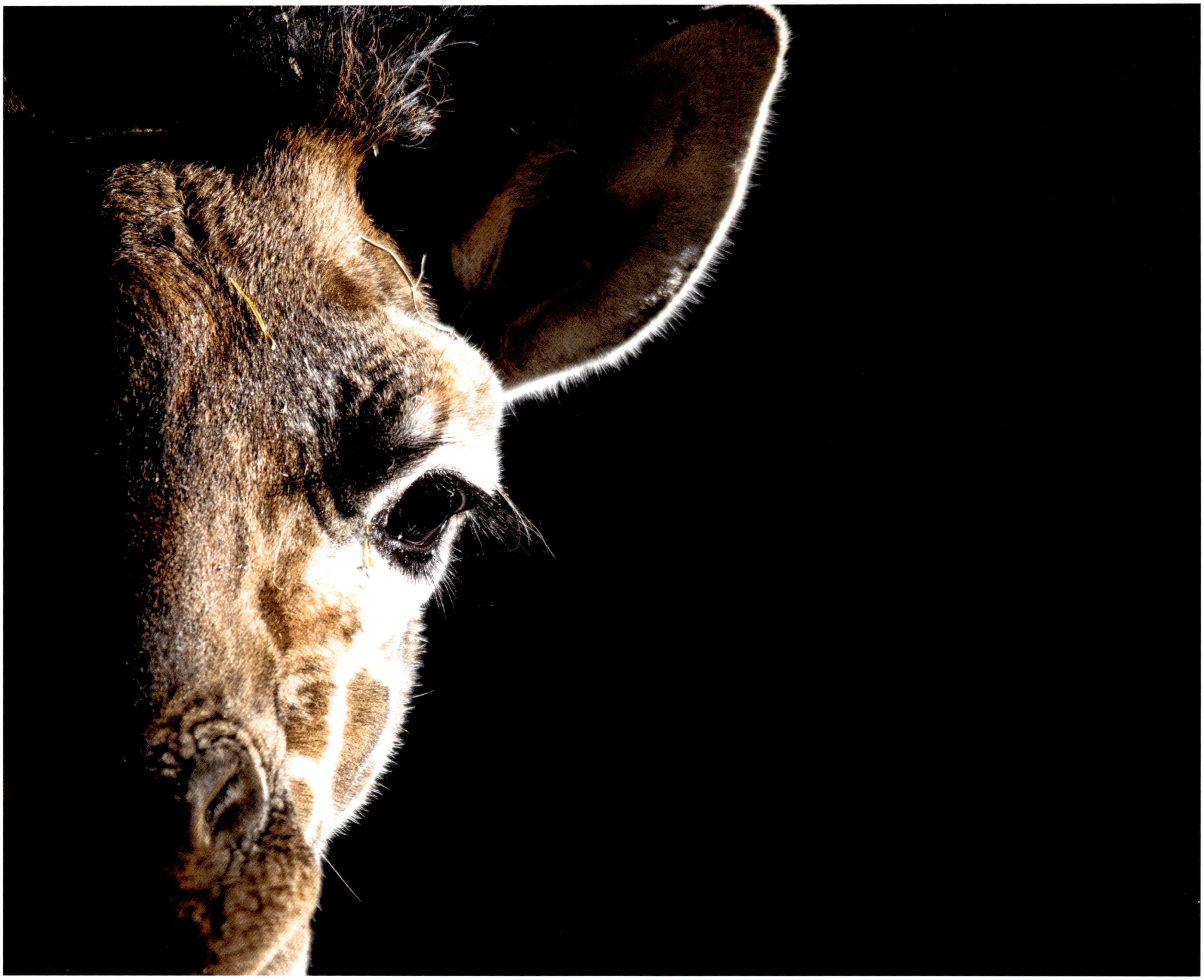

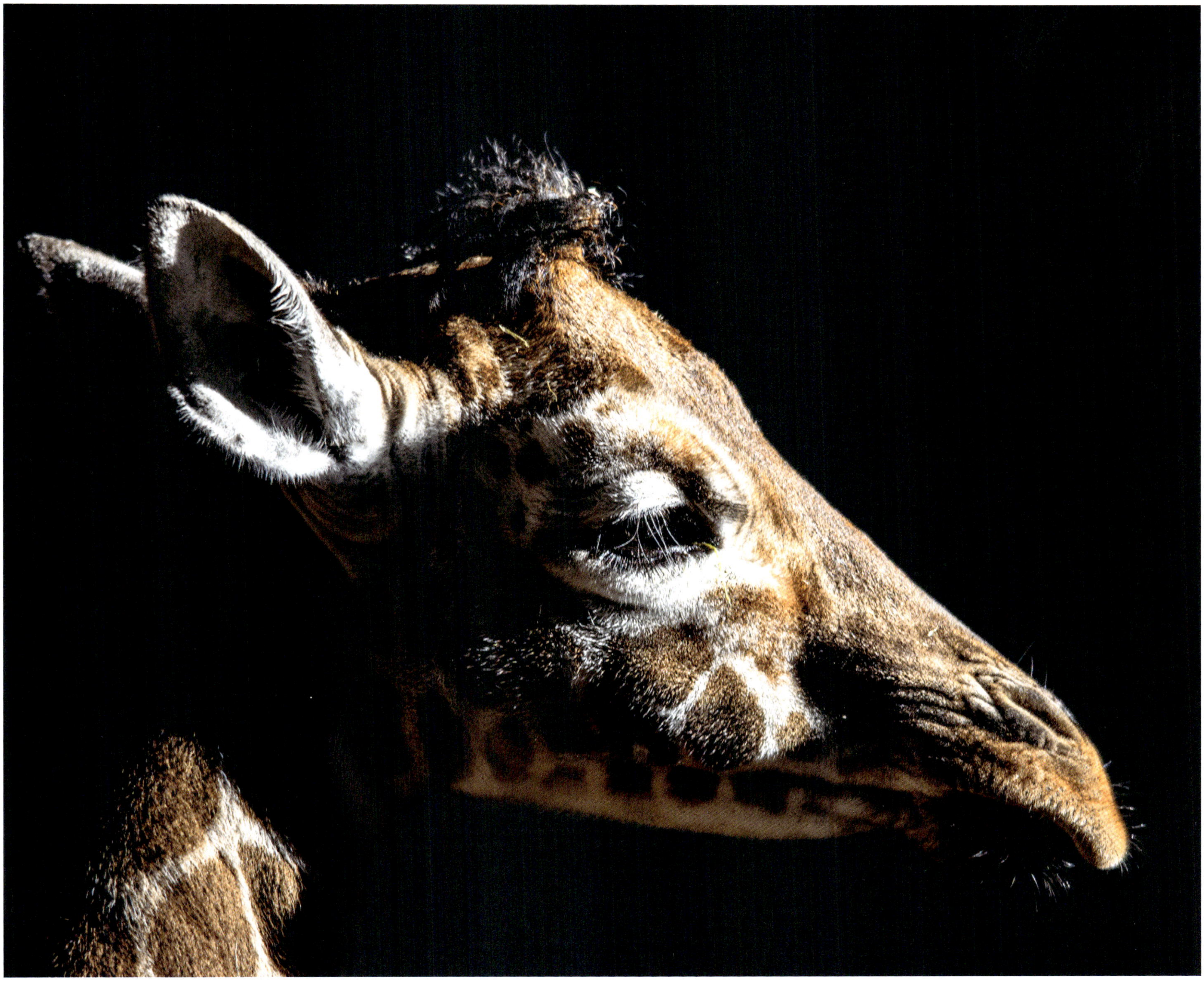

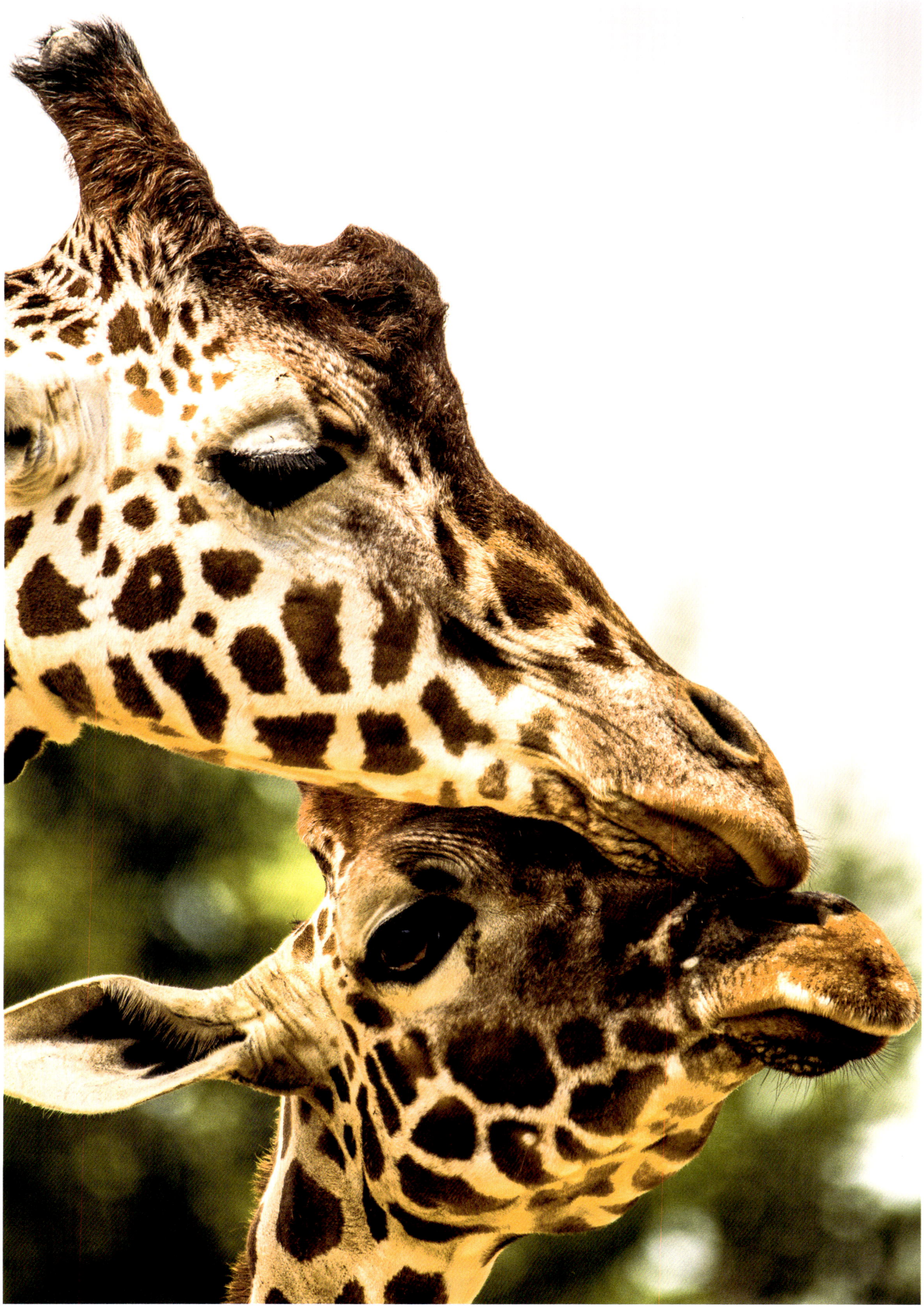

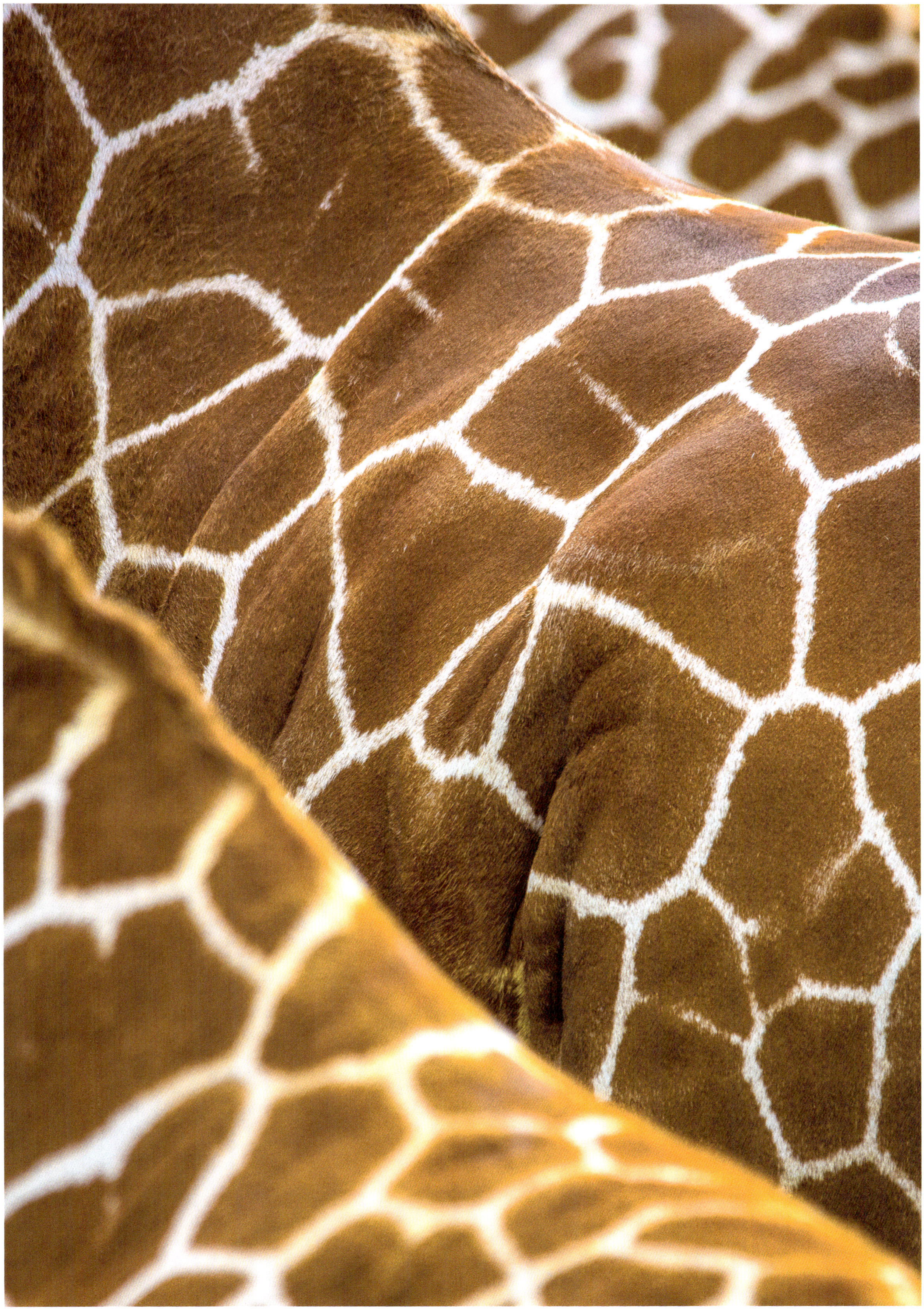

Giraffes are shy animals and getting close enough to capture the desired face-on portrait took time, energy and a lot of patience. It is a tough and often frustrating method but I think I finally have a strong image of these most beautiful creatures in ‘Big Friendly Giant’ and I am very proud.

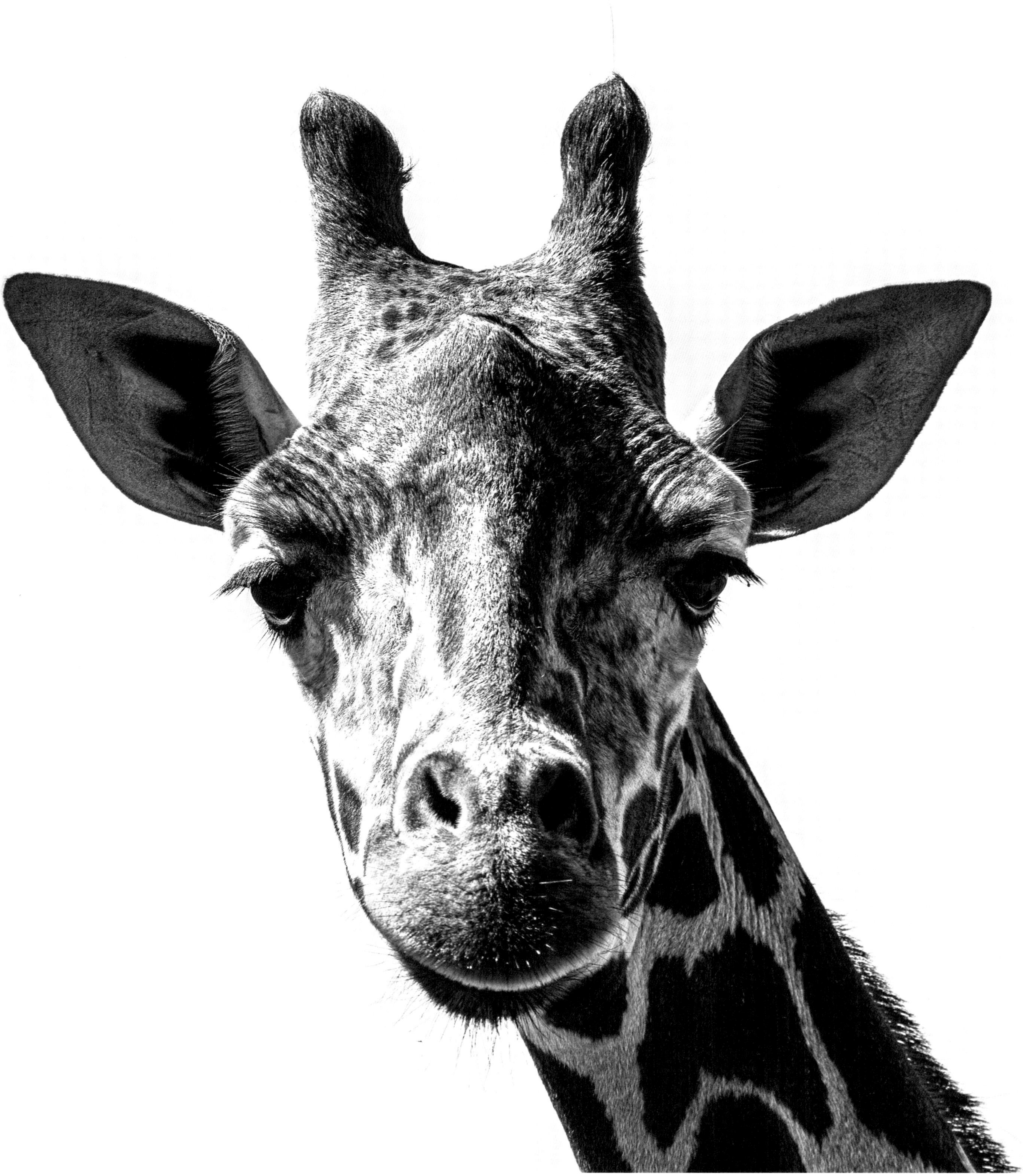

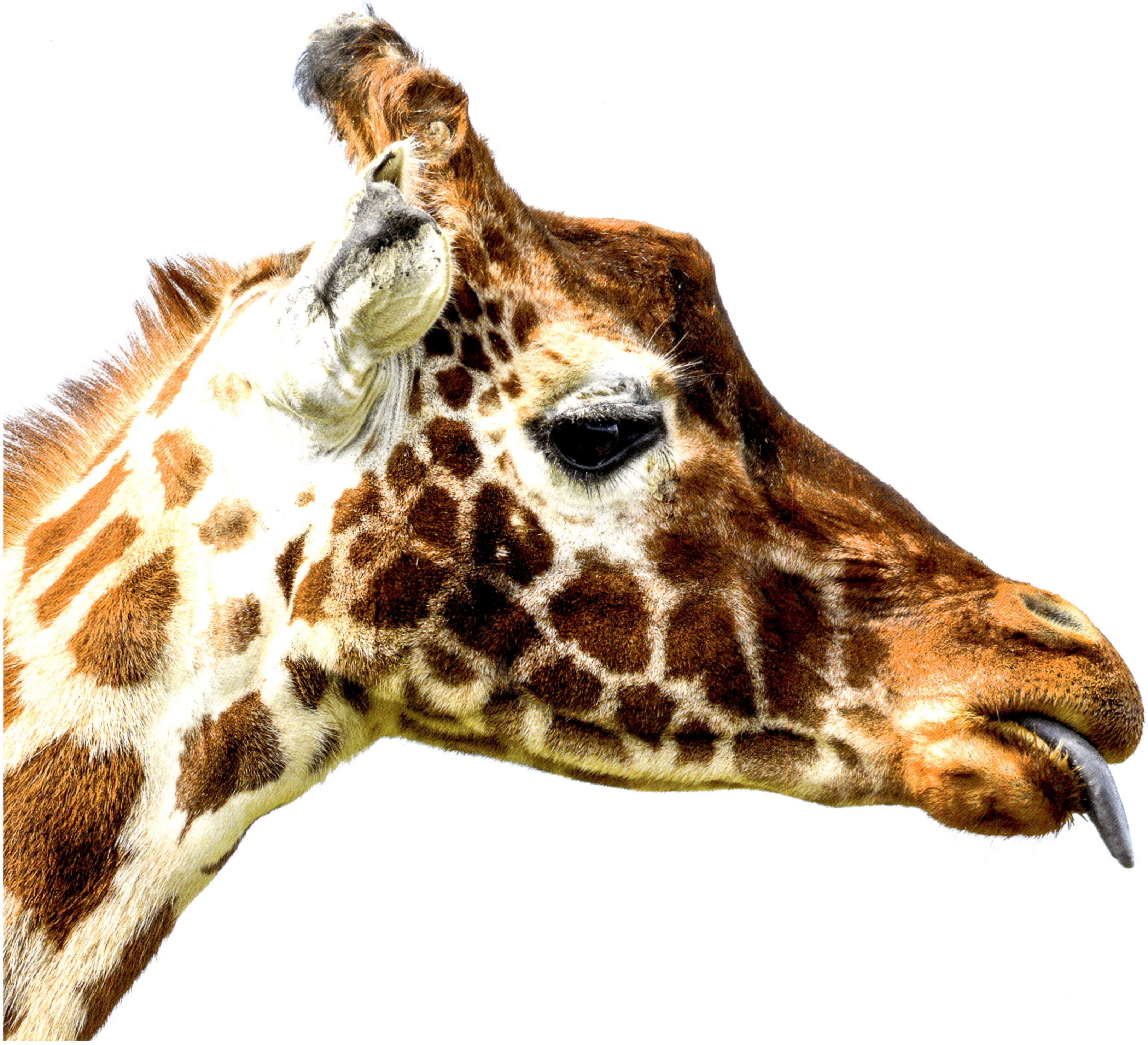

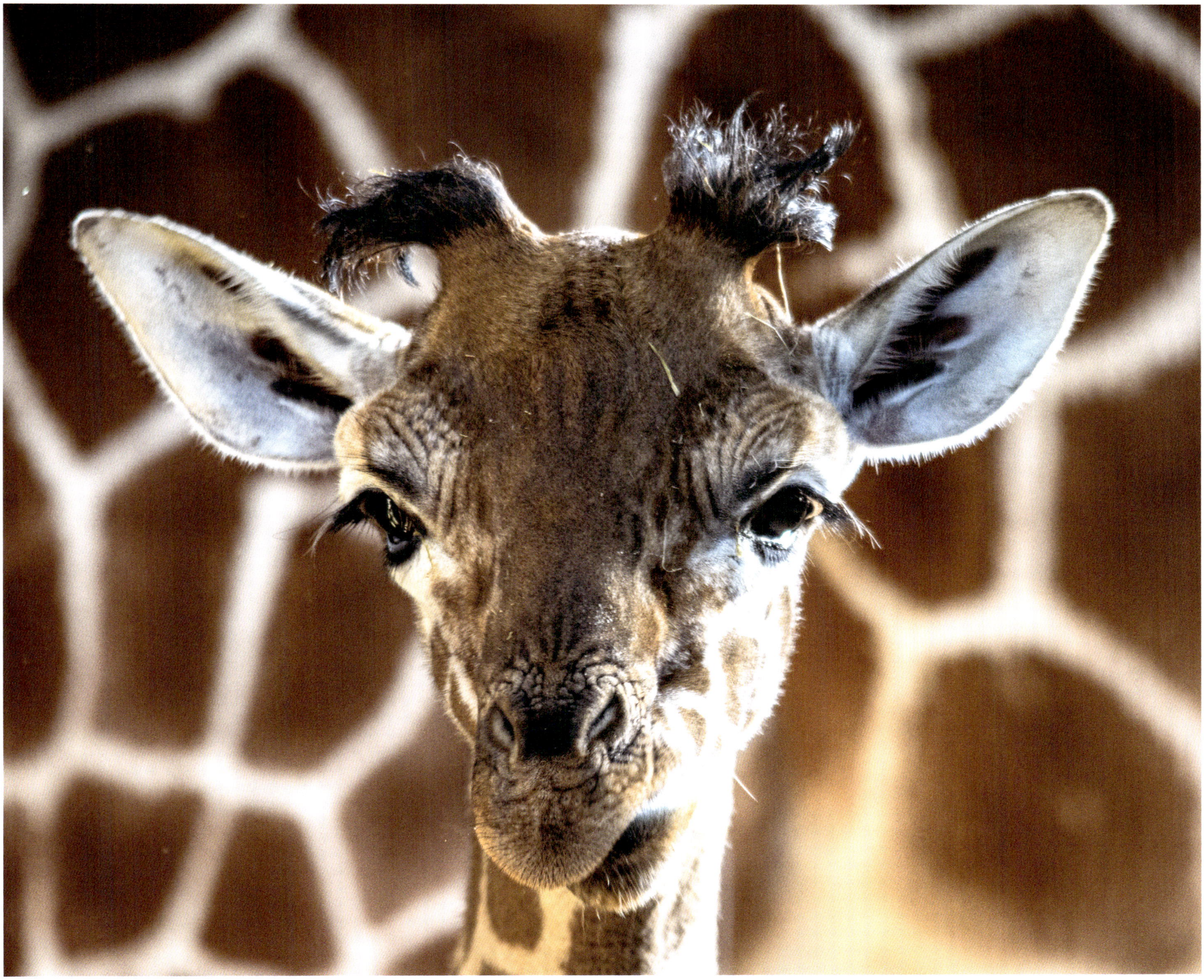

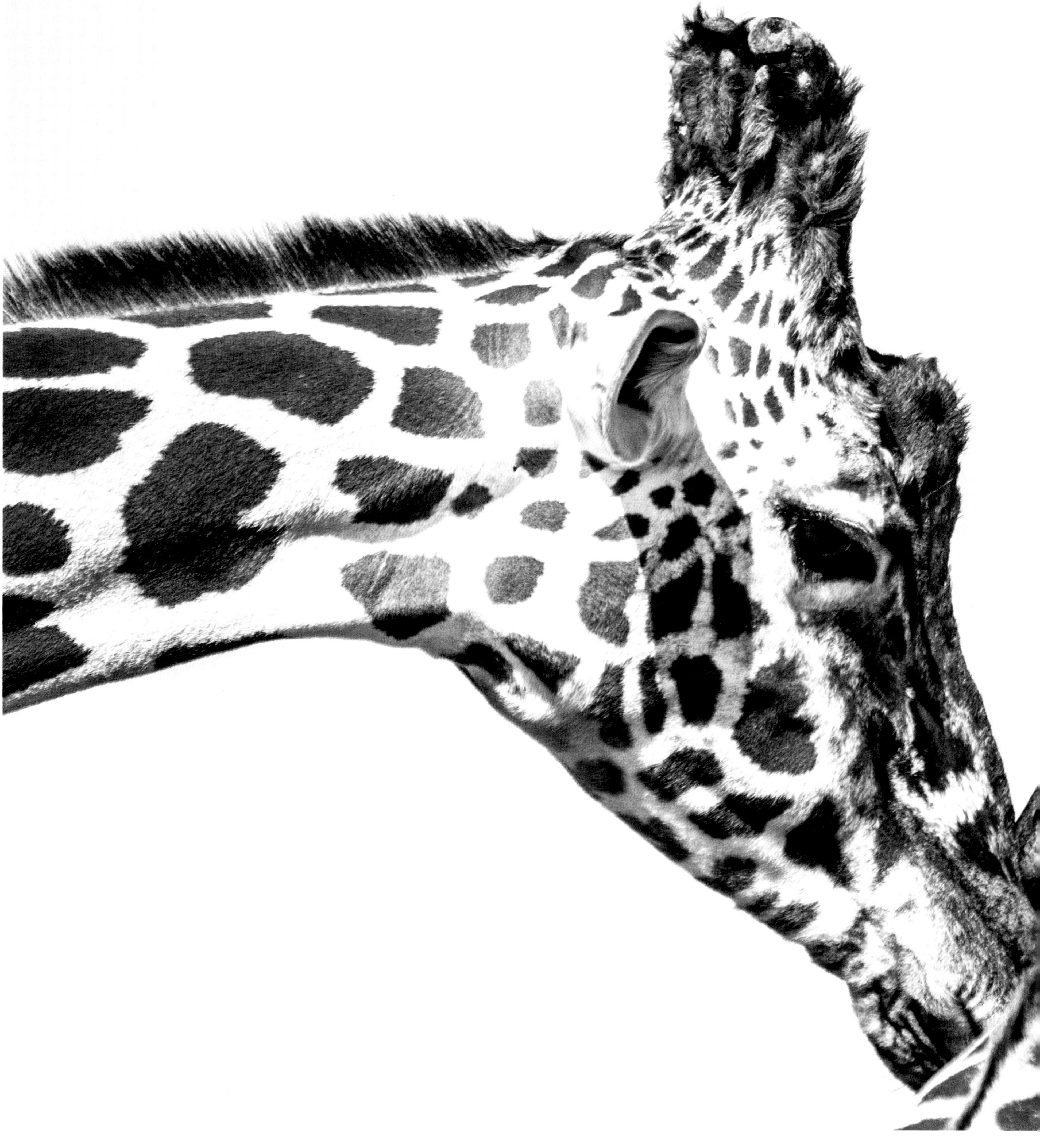

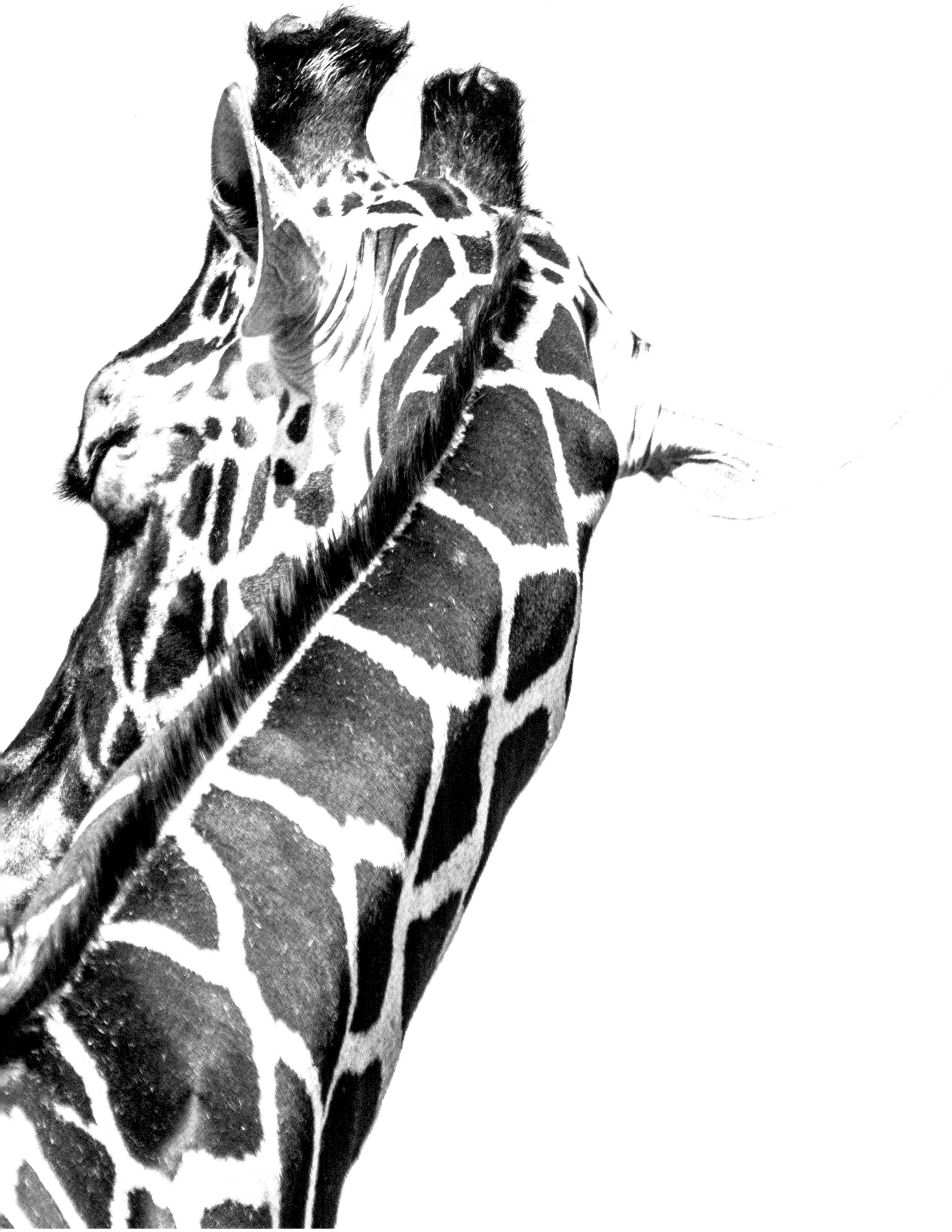

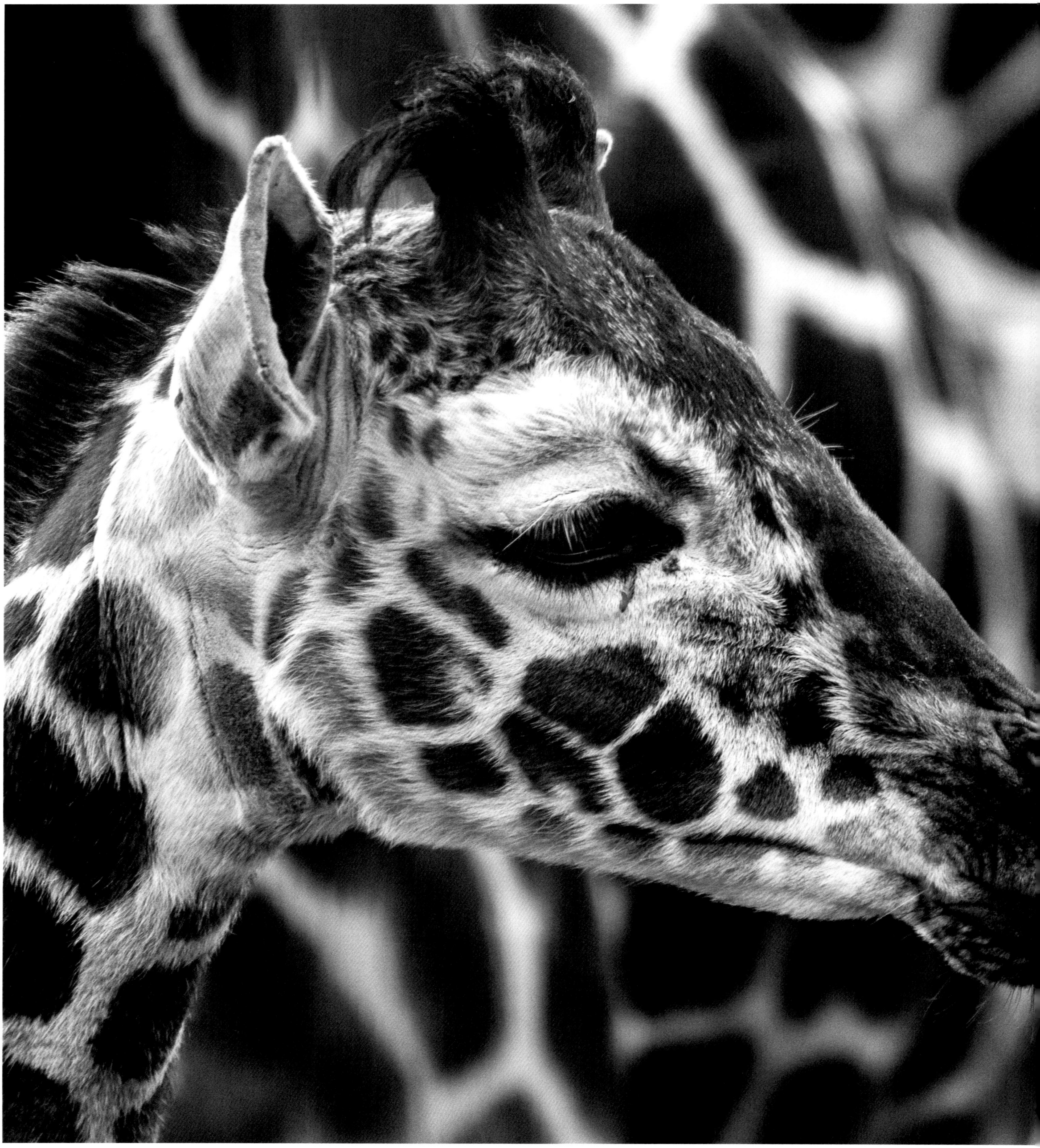

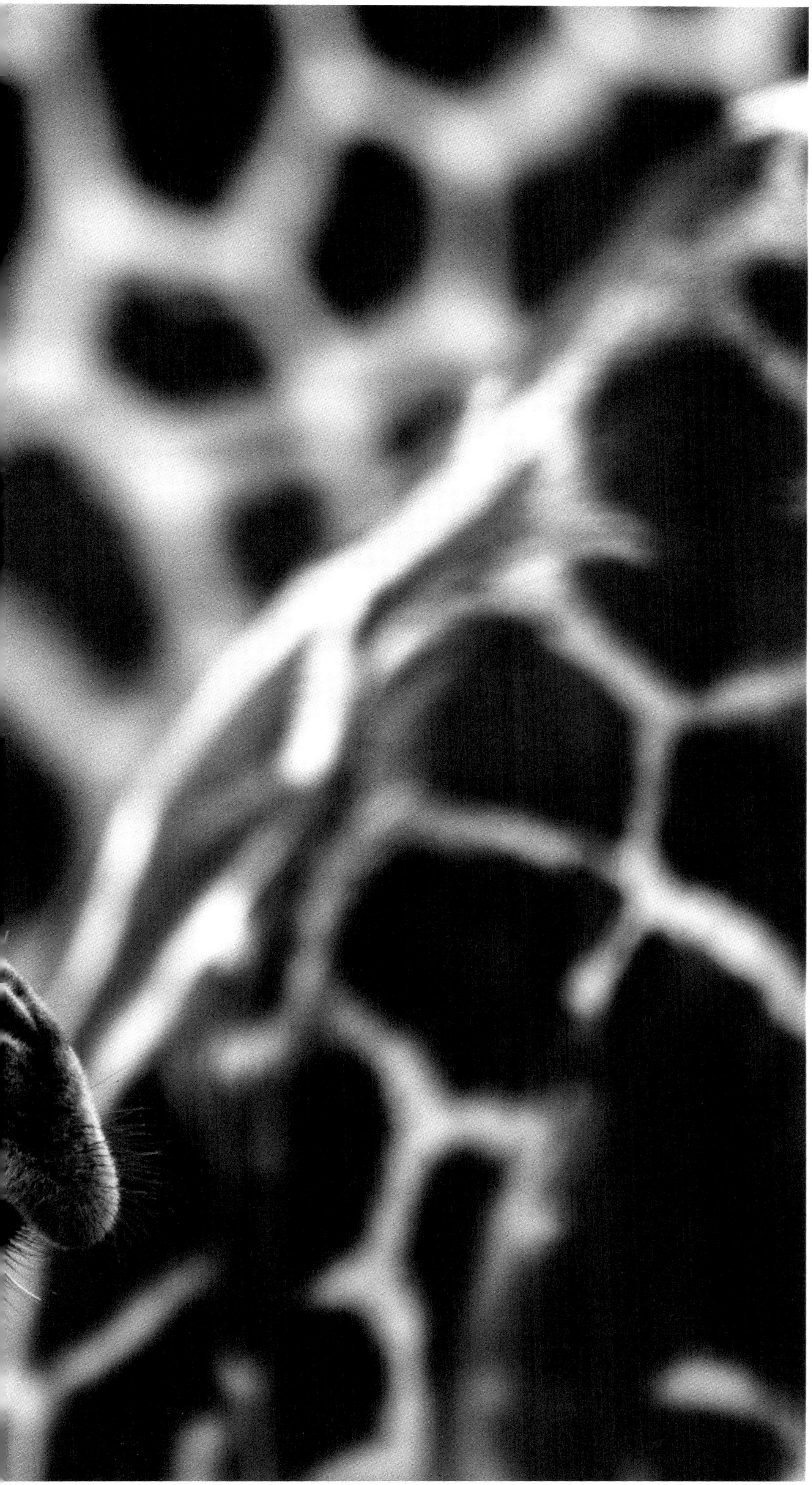

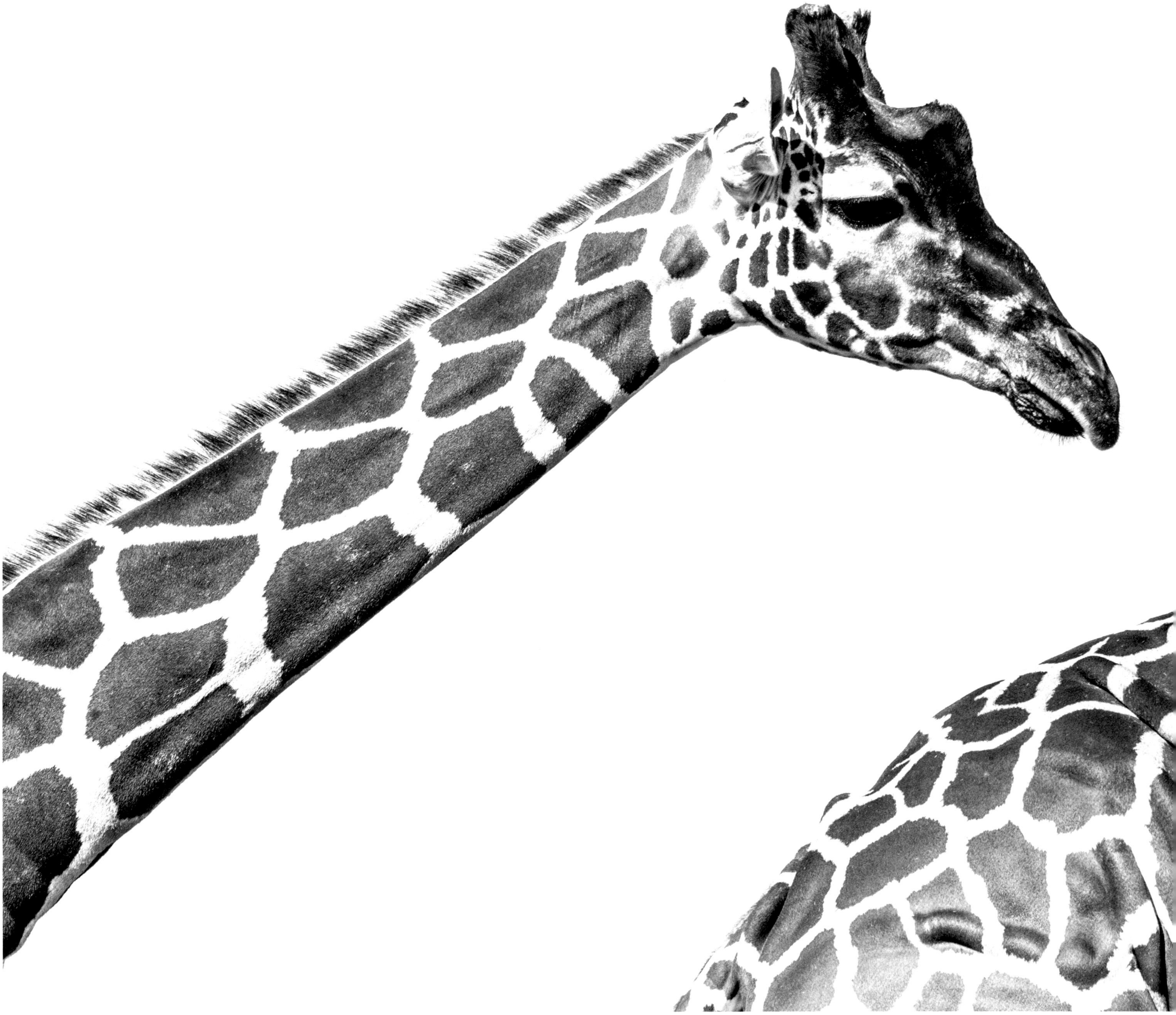

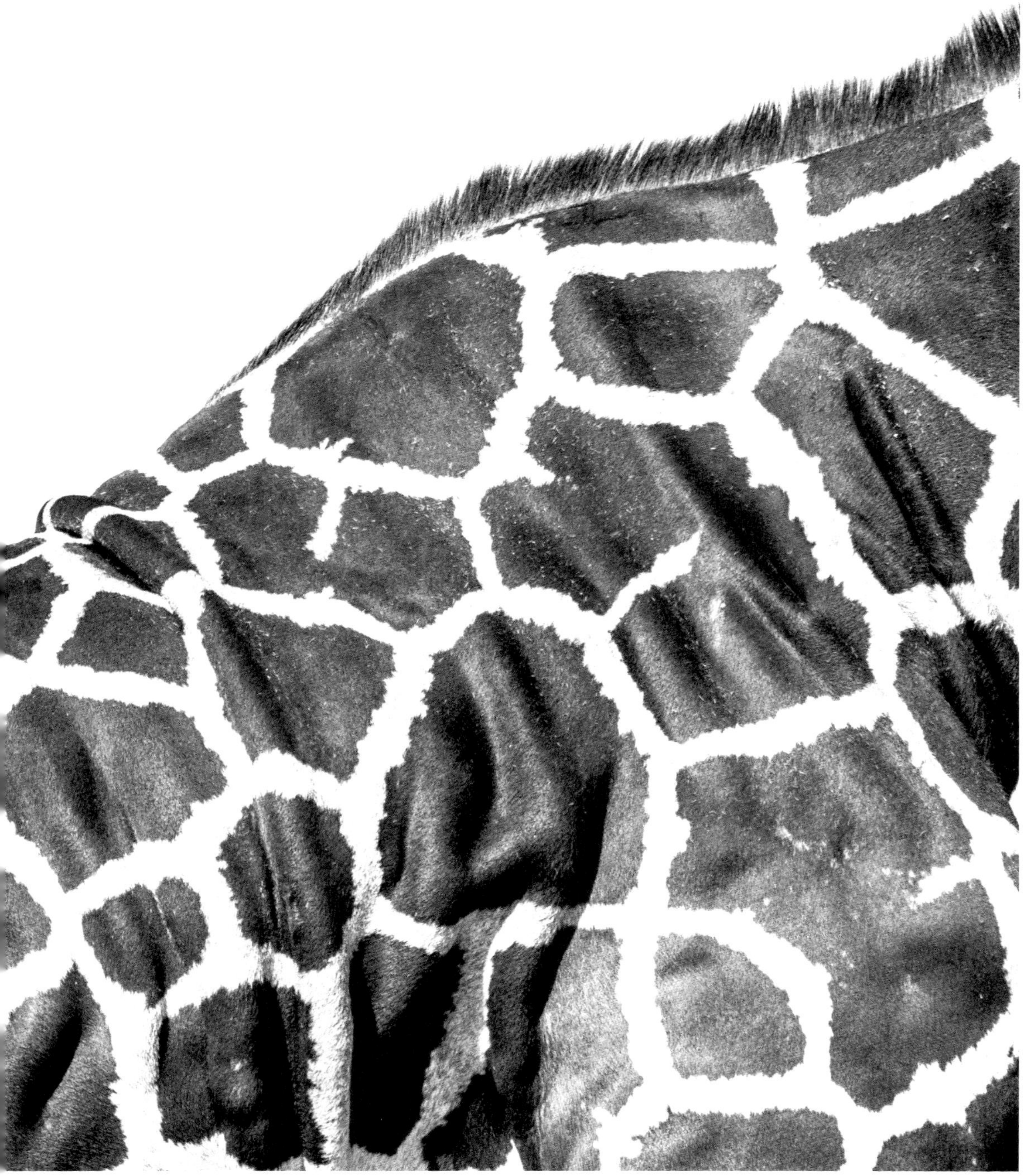

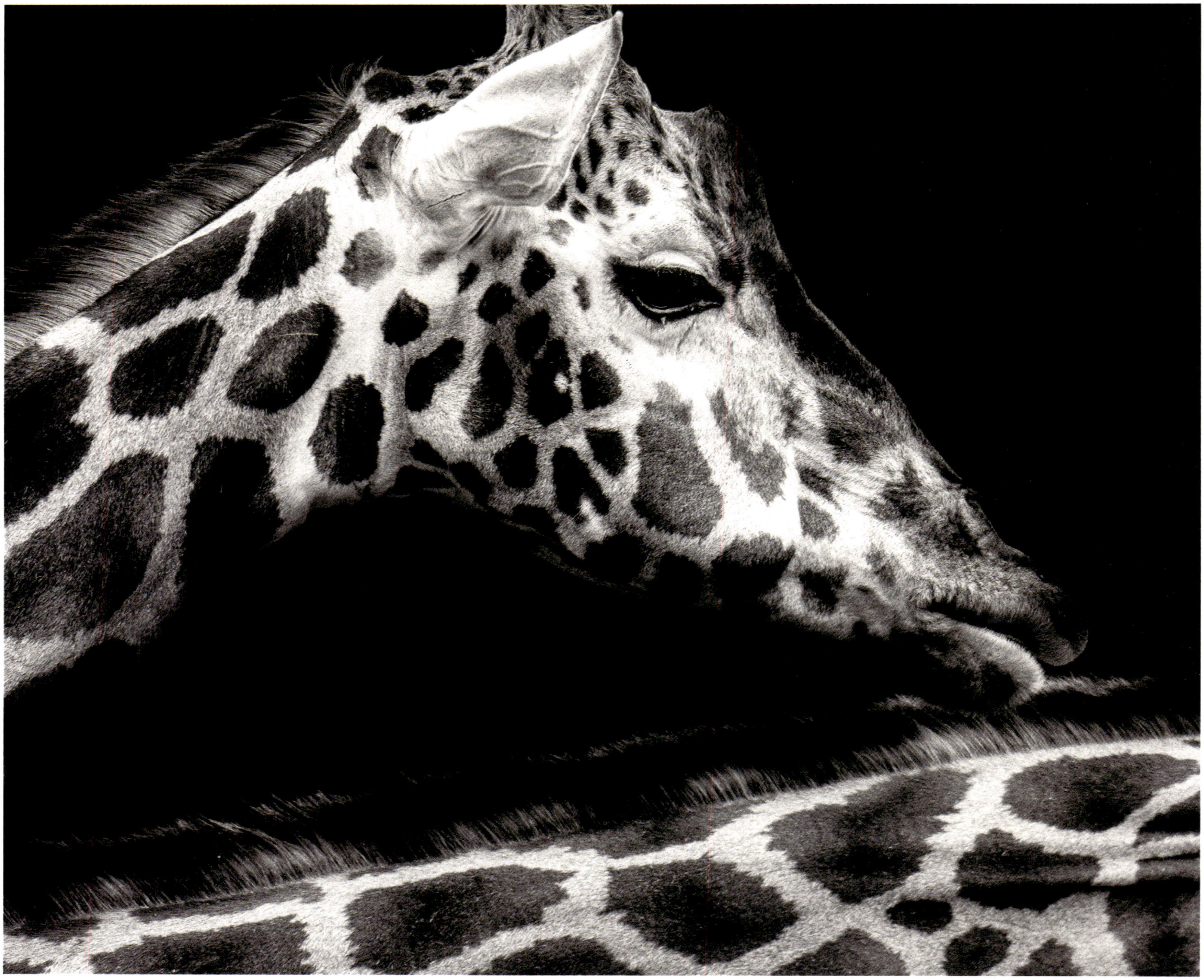

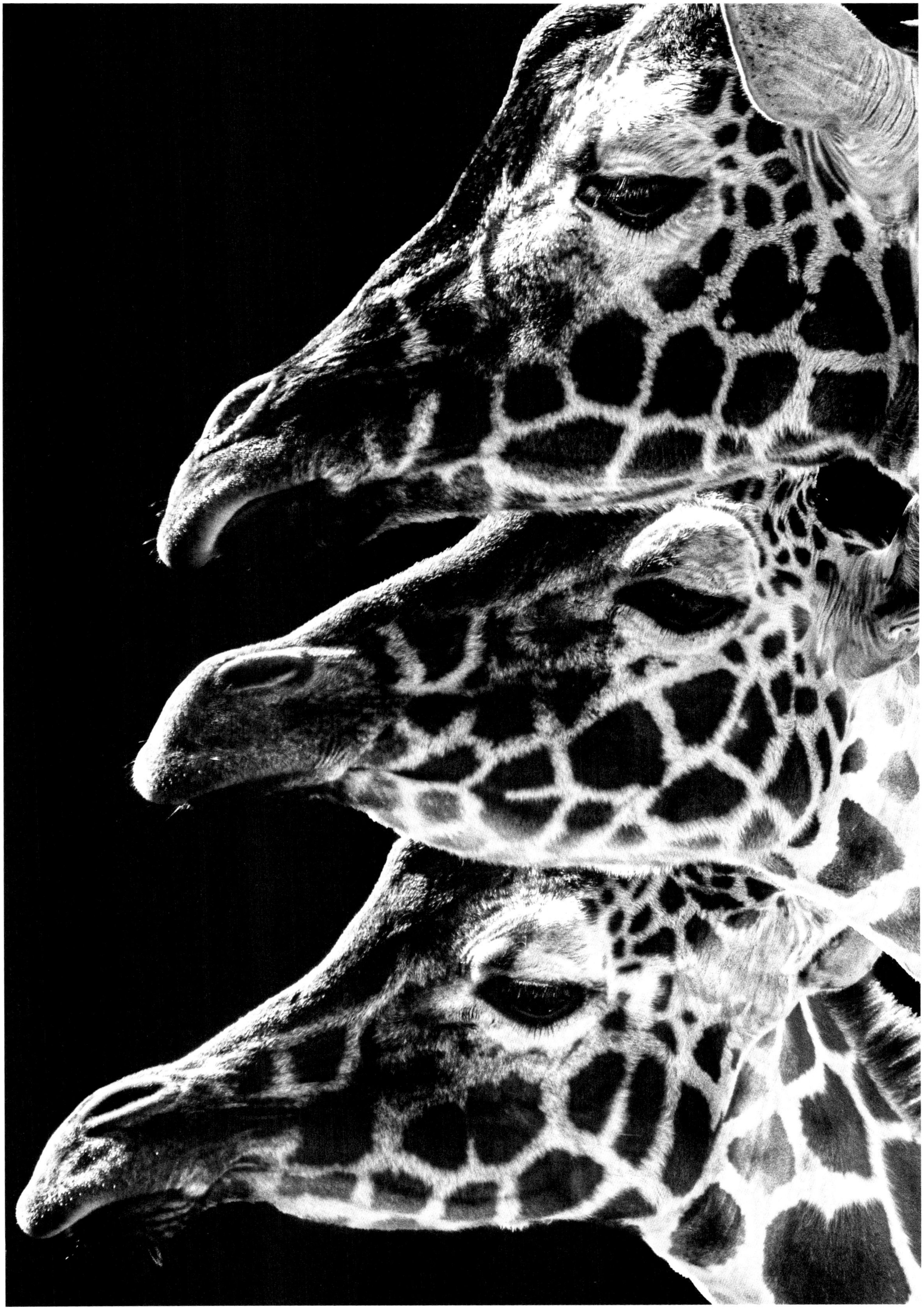

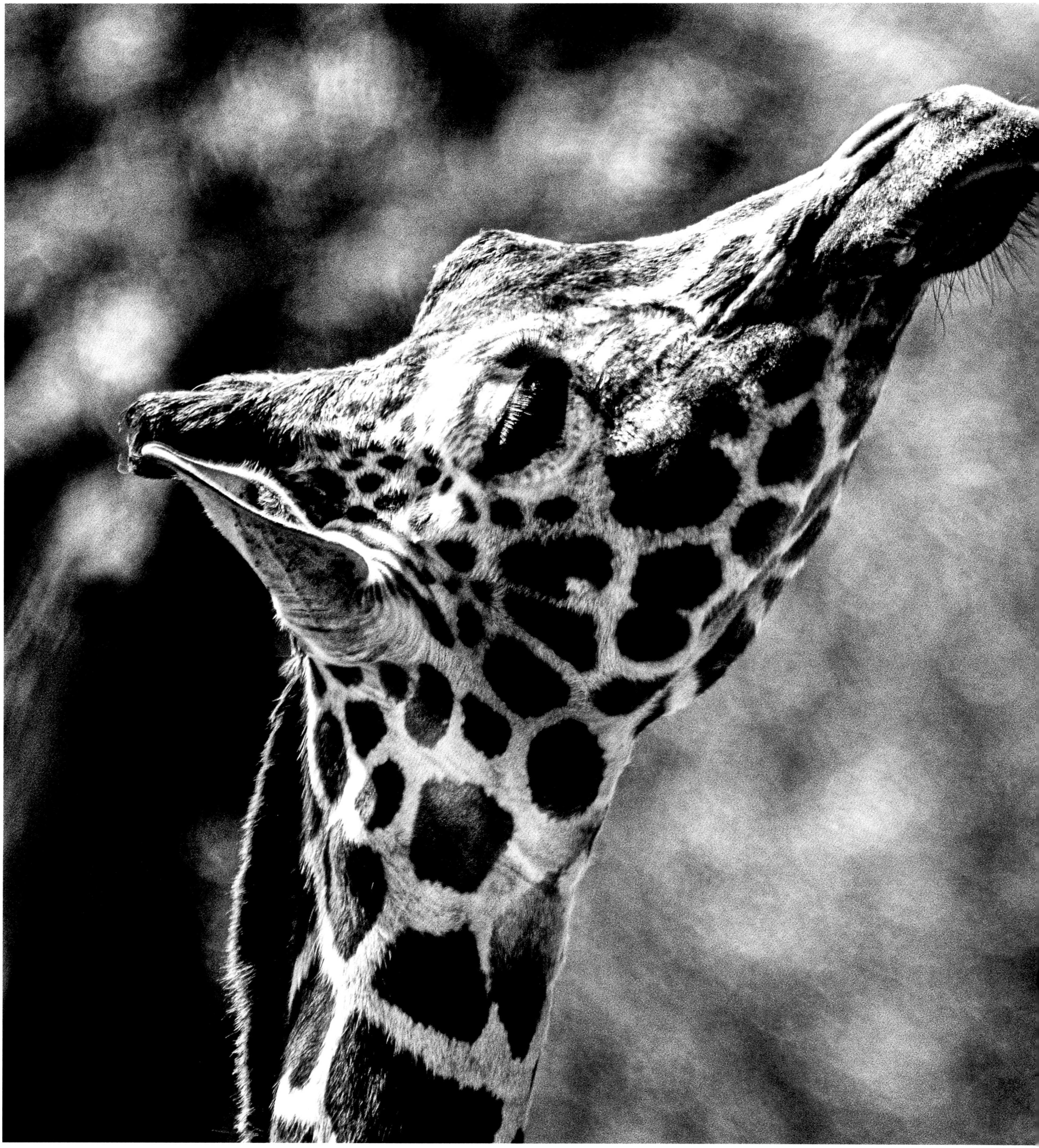

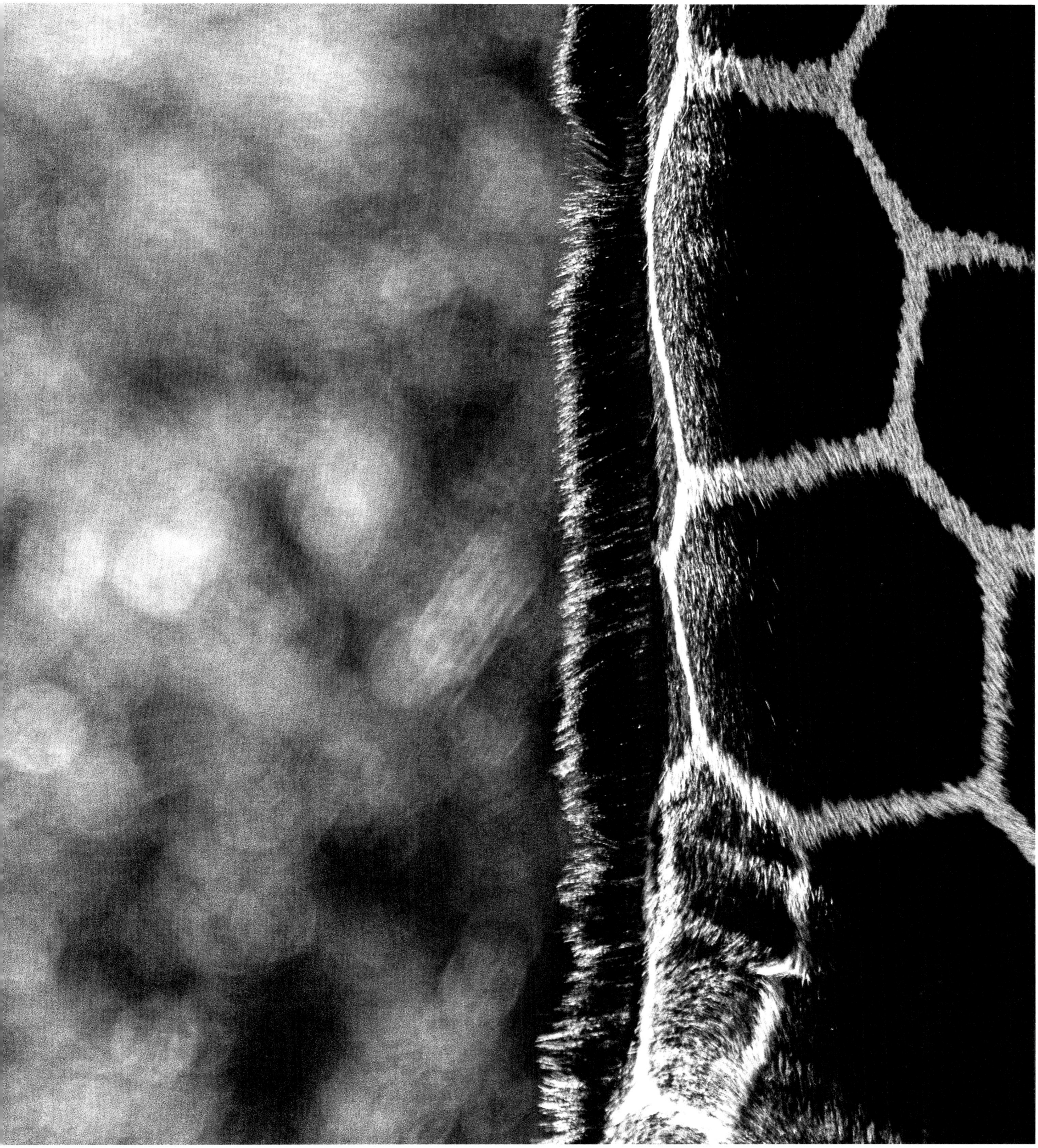

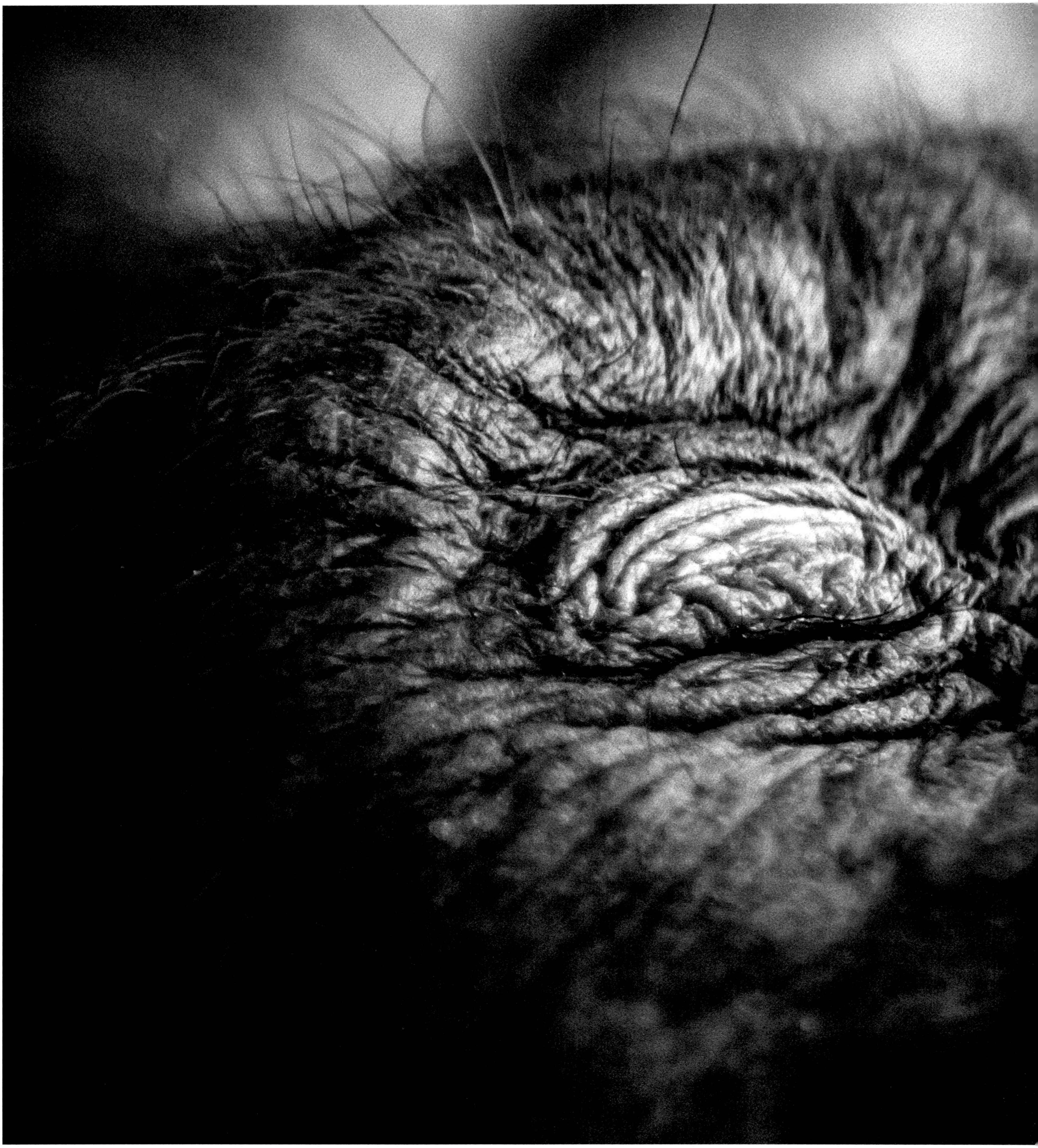

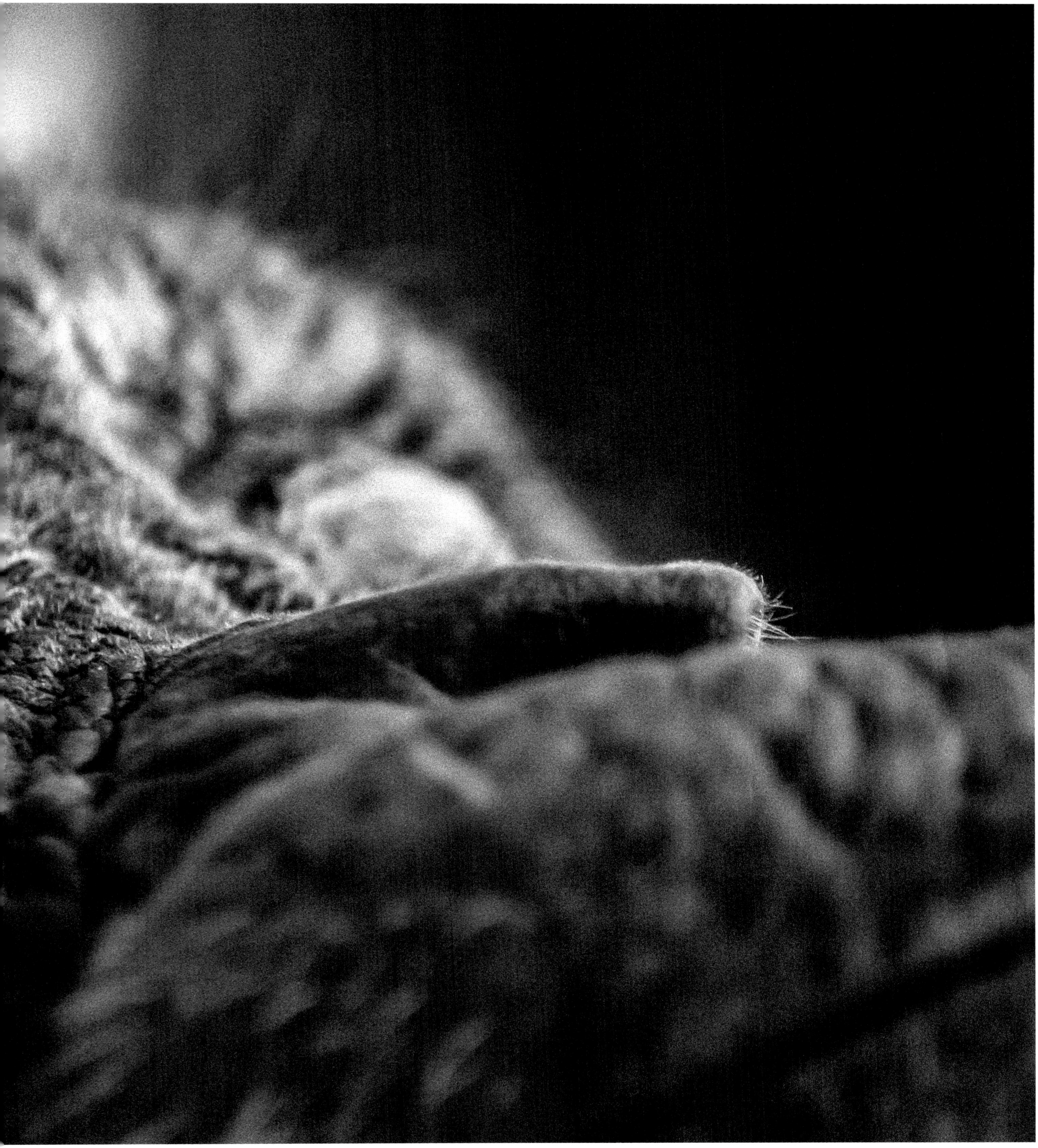

I have been patient over the last few years, and have spent countless hours with chimpanzees, resulting in a handful of images. The idea that you can return with 200 photographs and publish them all is viable if you are only looking to show the animal's physical beauty. I want to show their soul, and glimpses of that are rare, which is why it took five years to capture this moving collection.

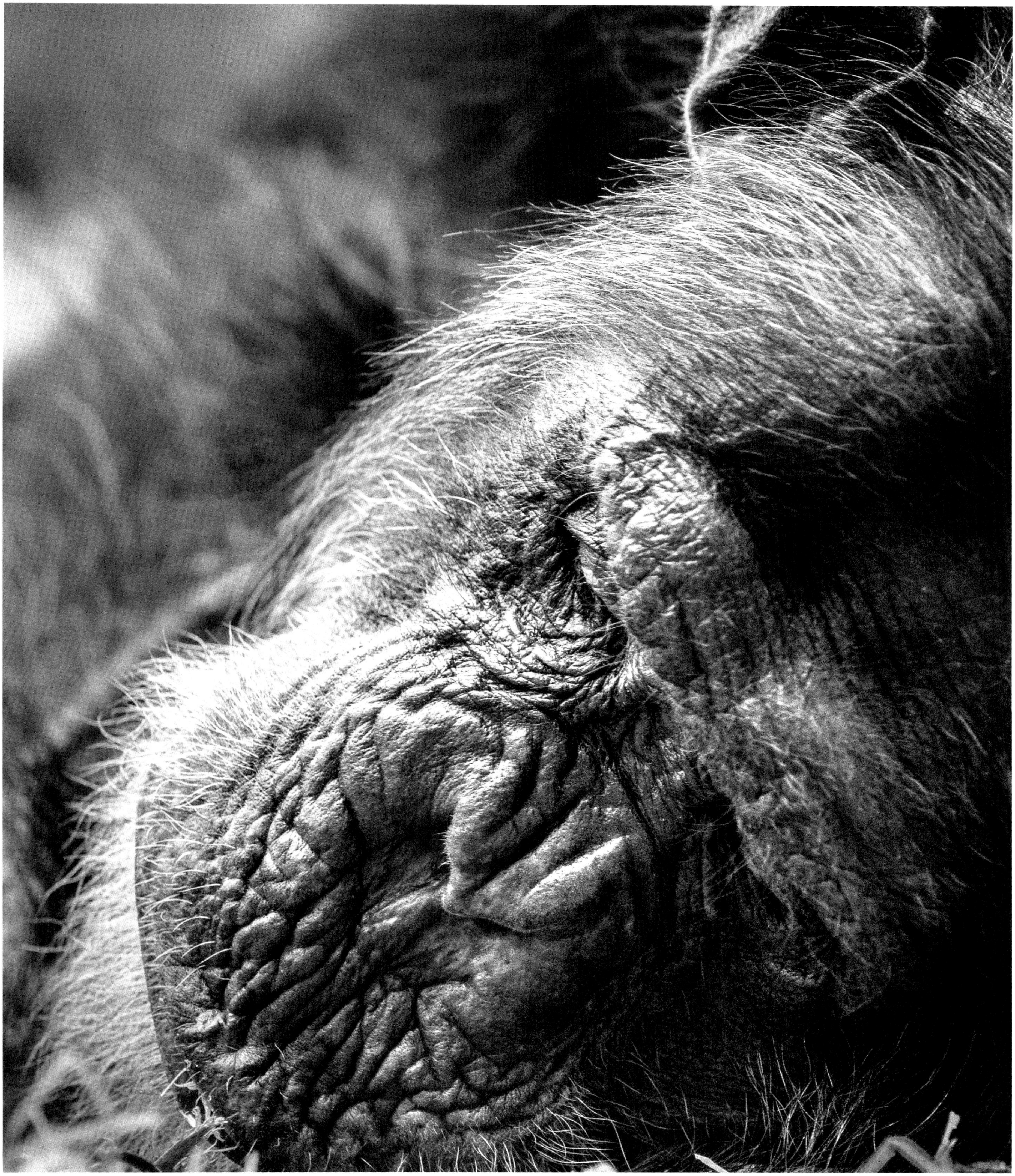

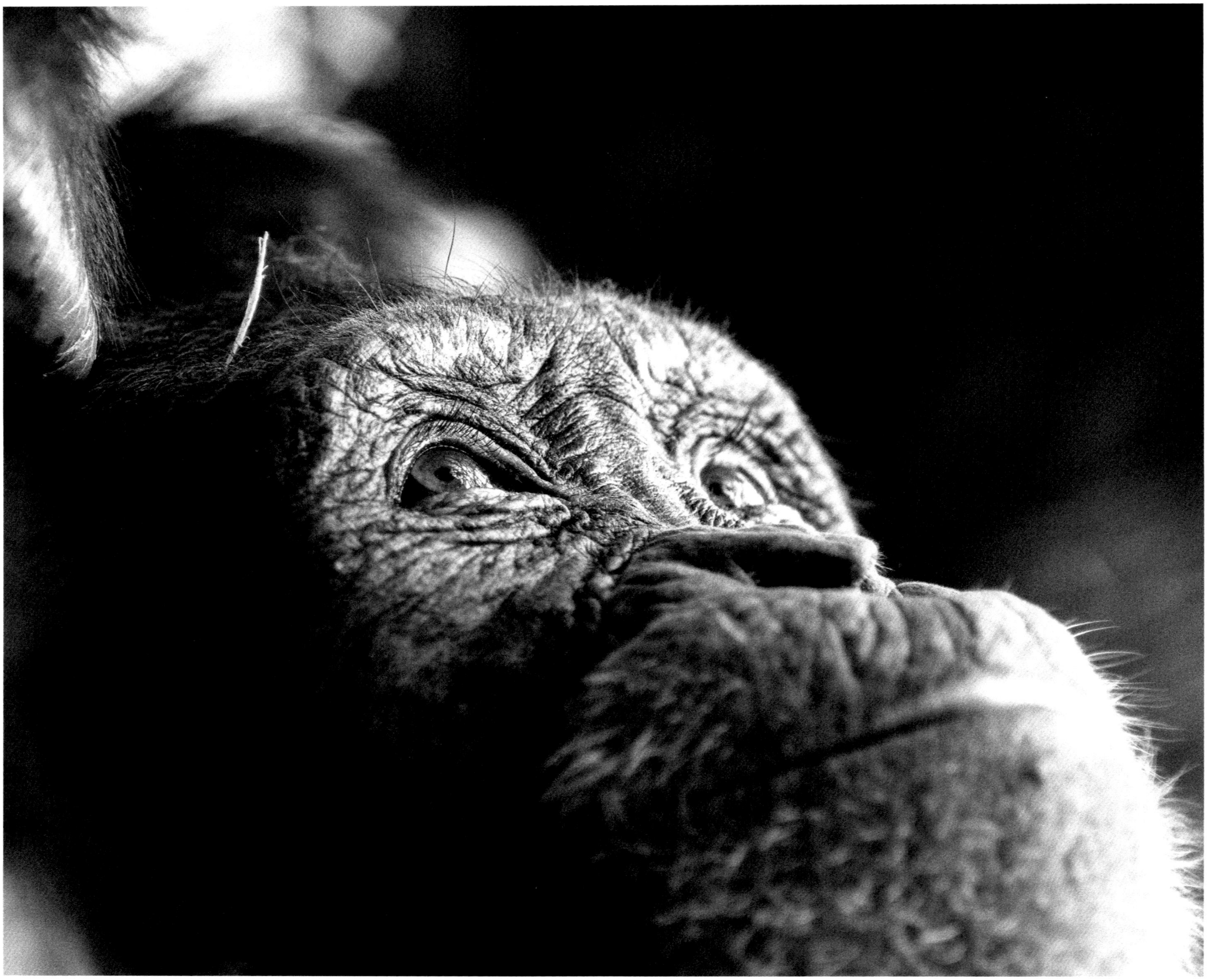

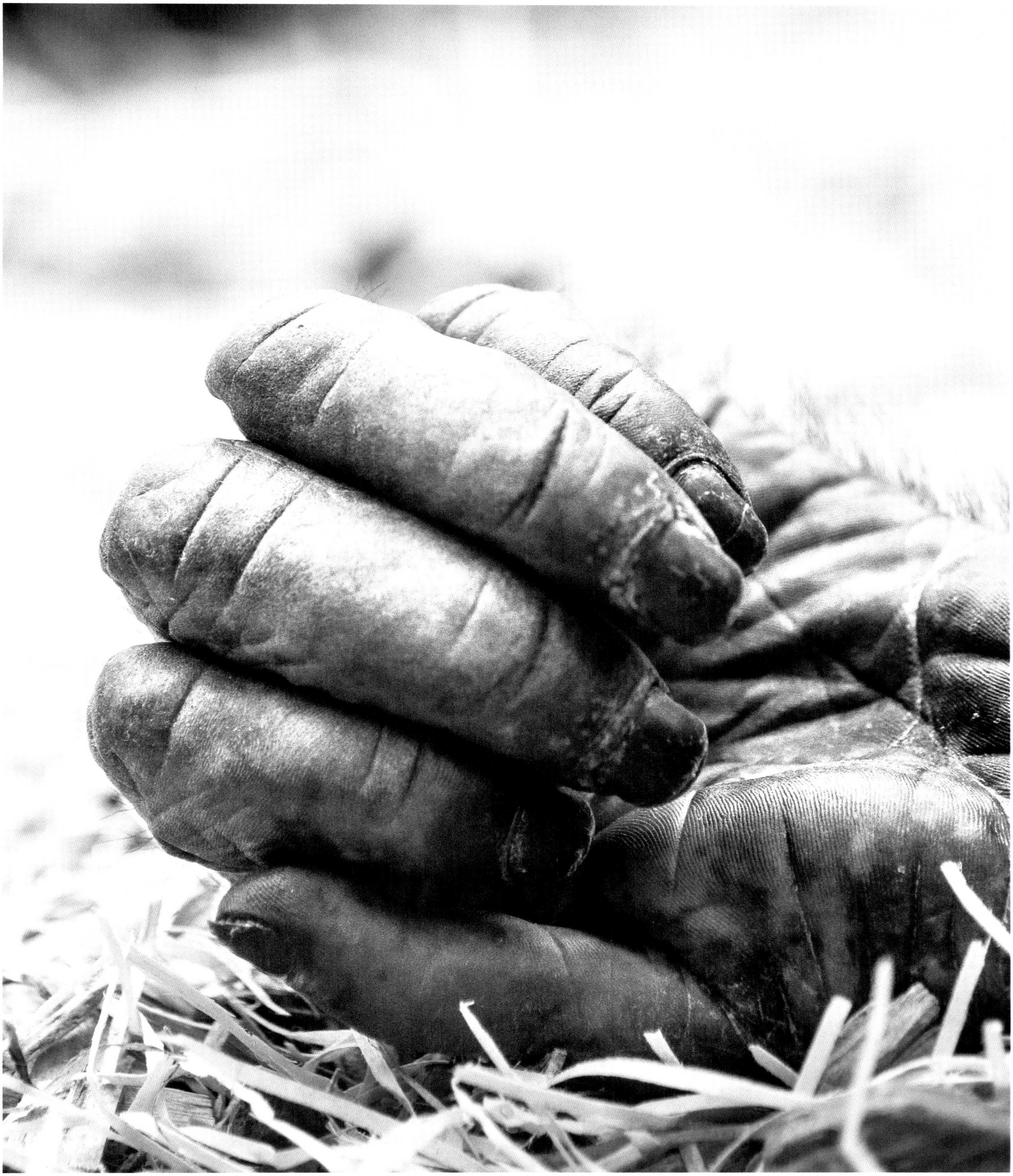

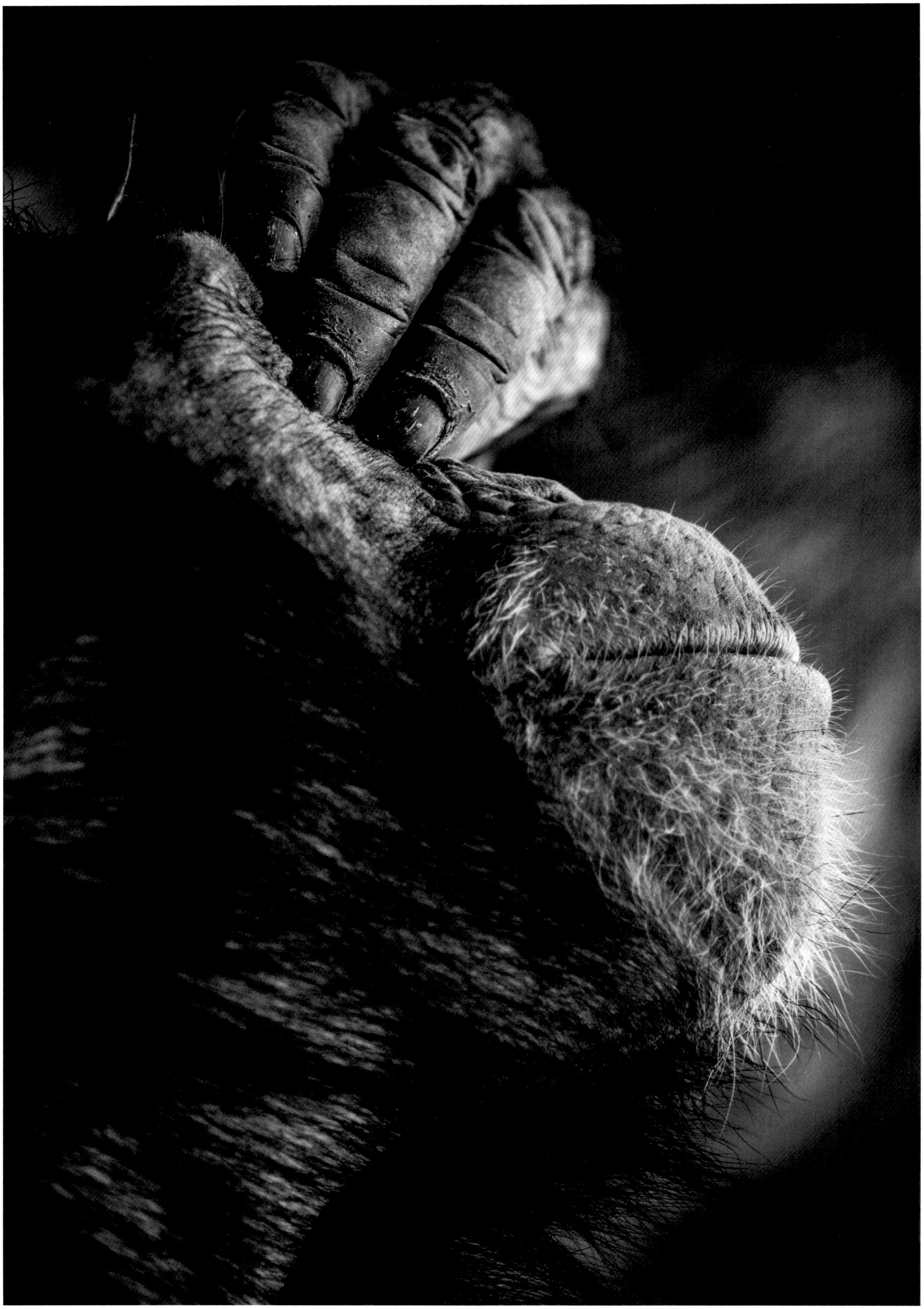

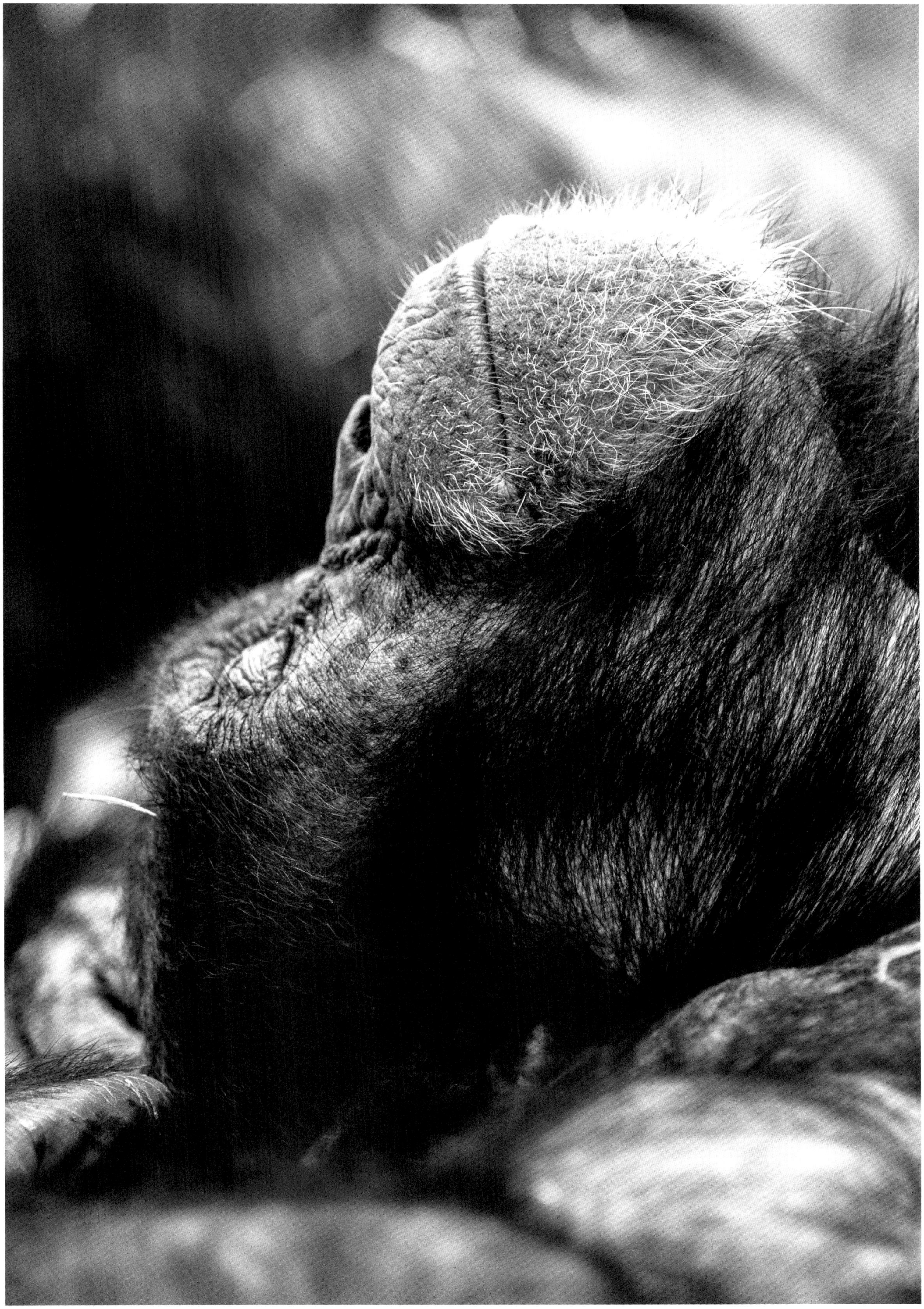

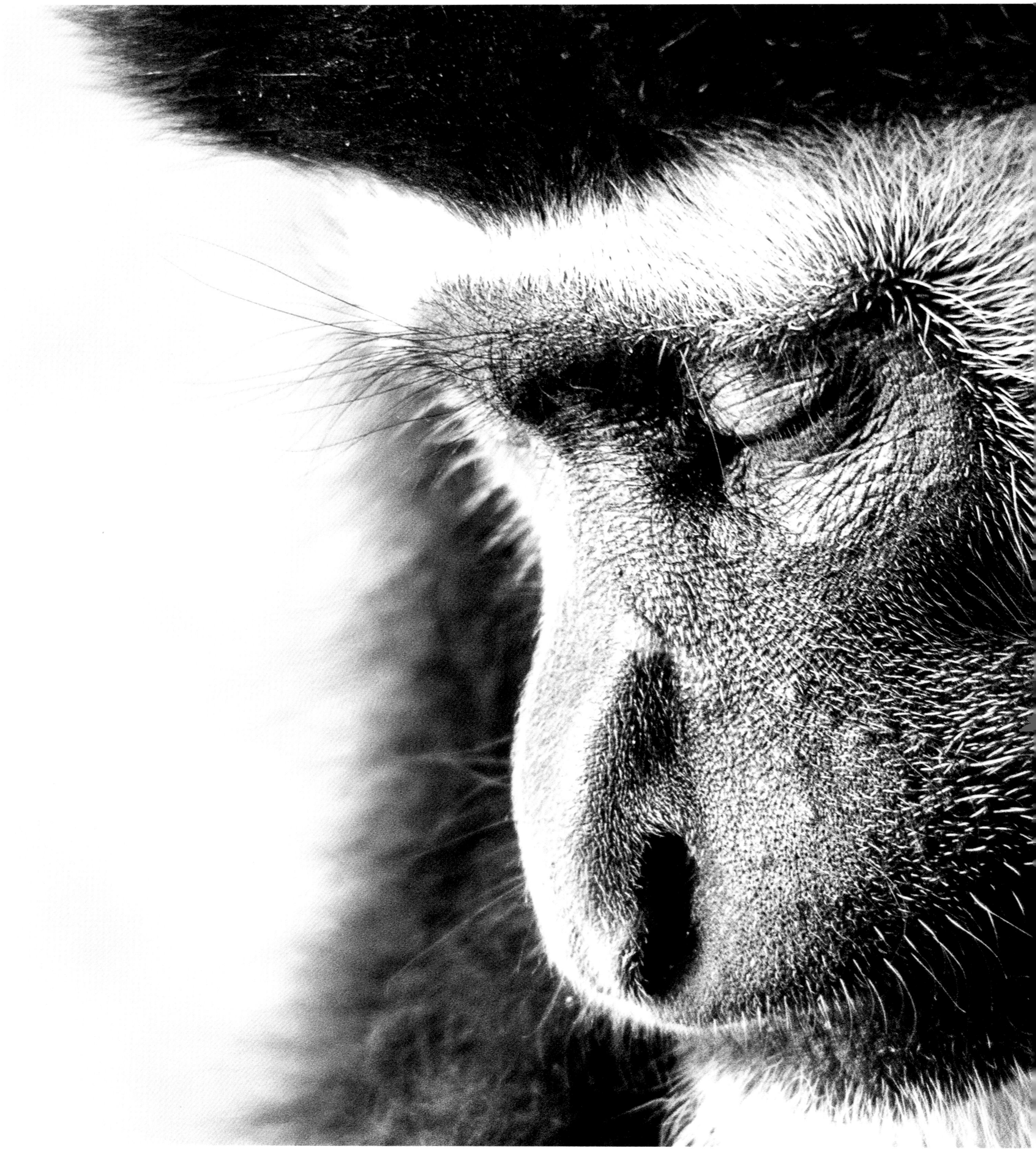

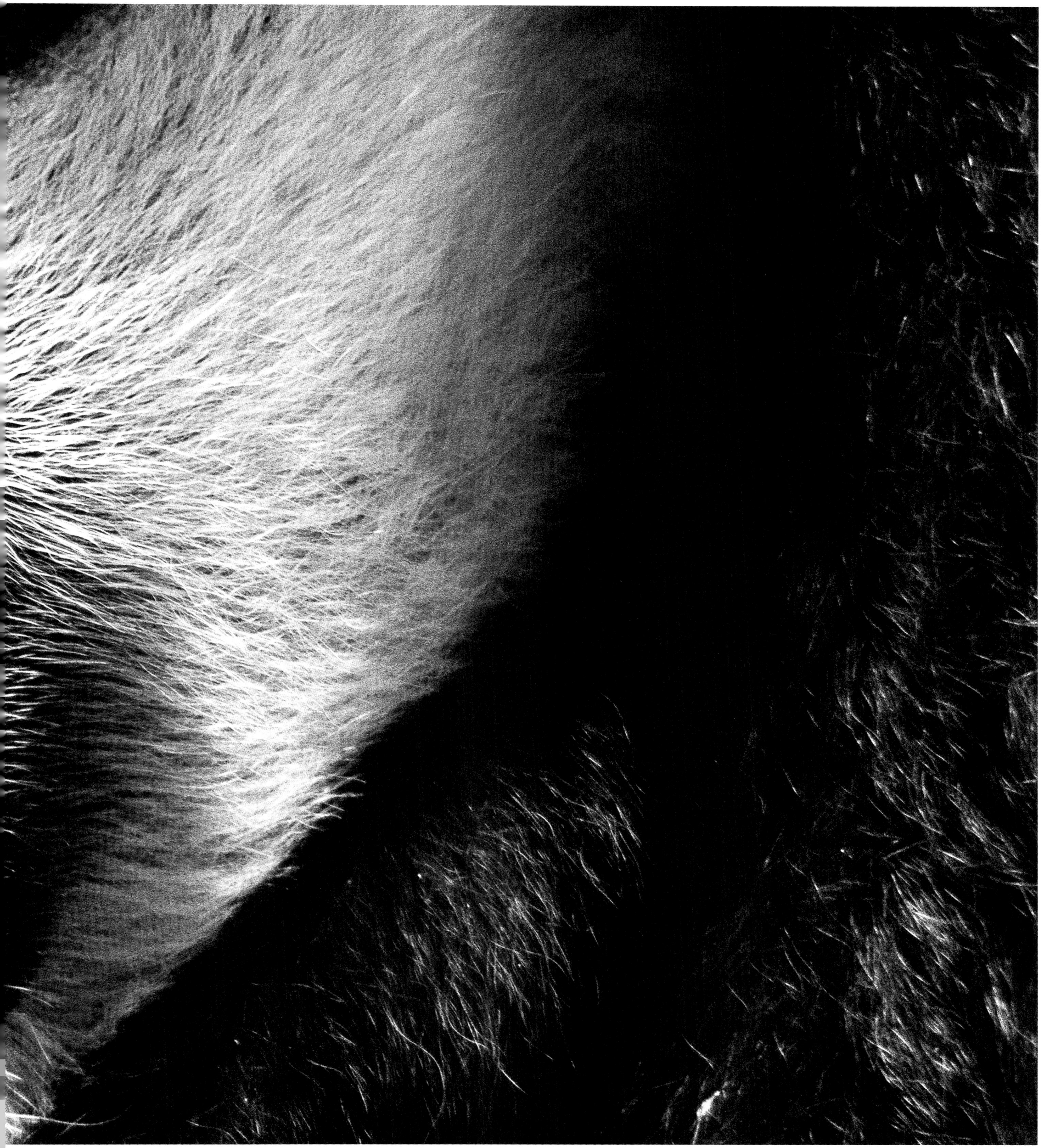

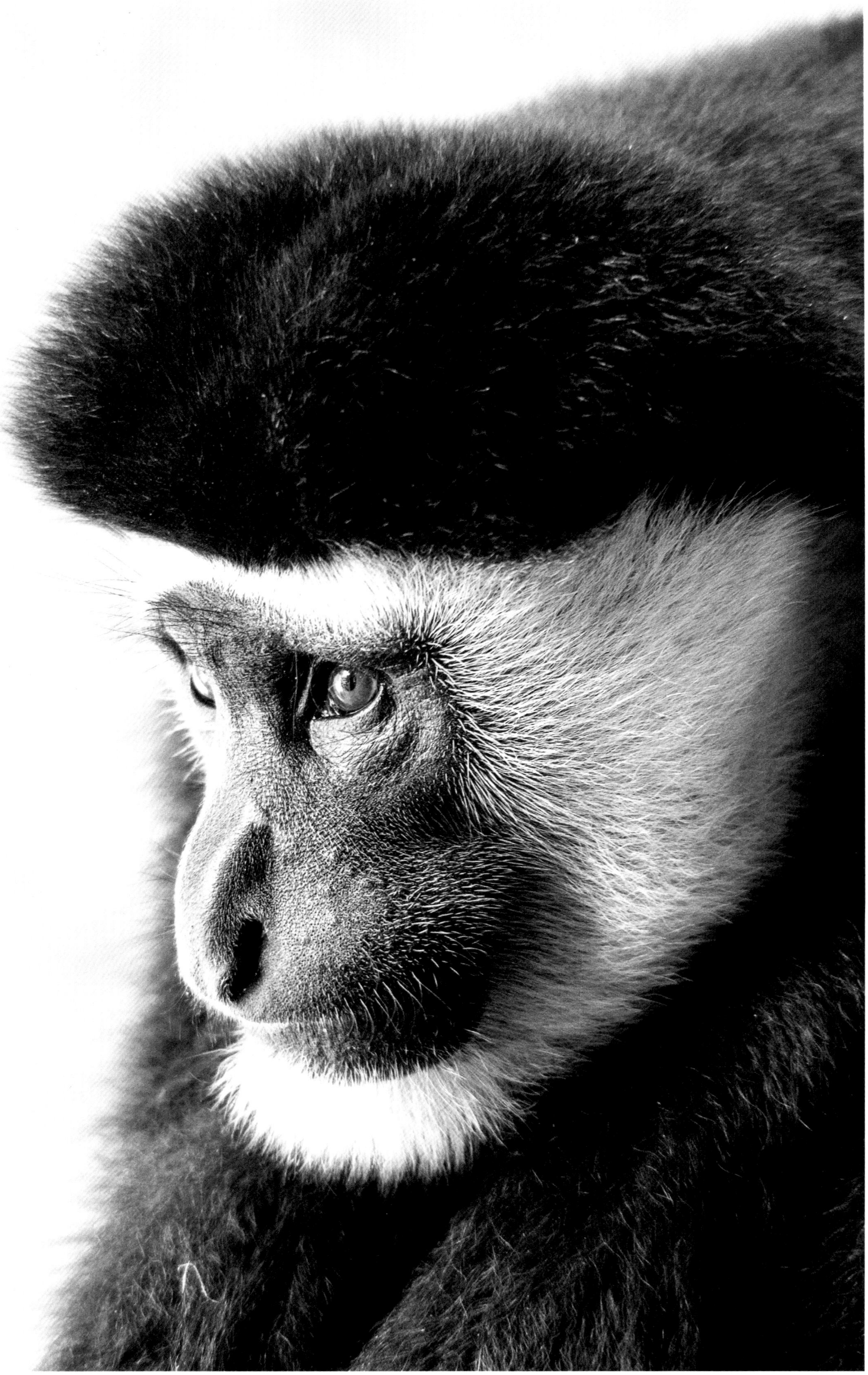

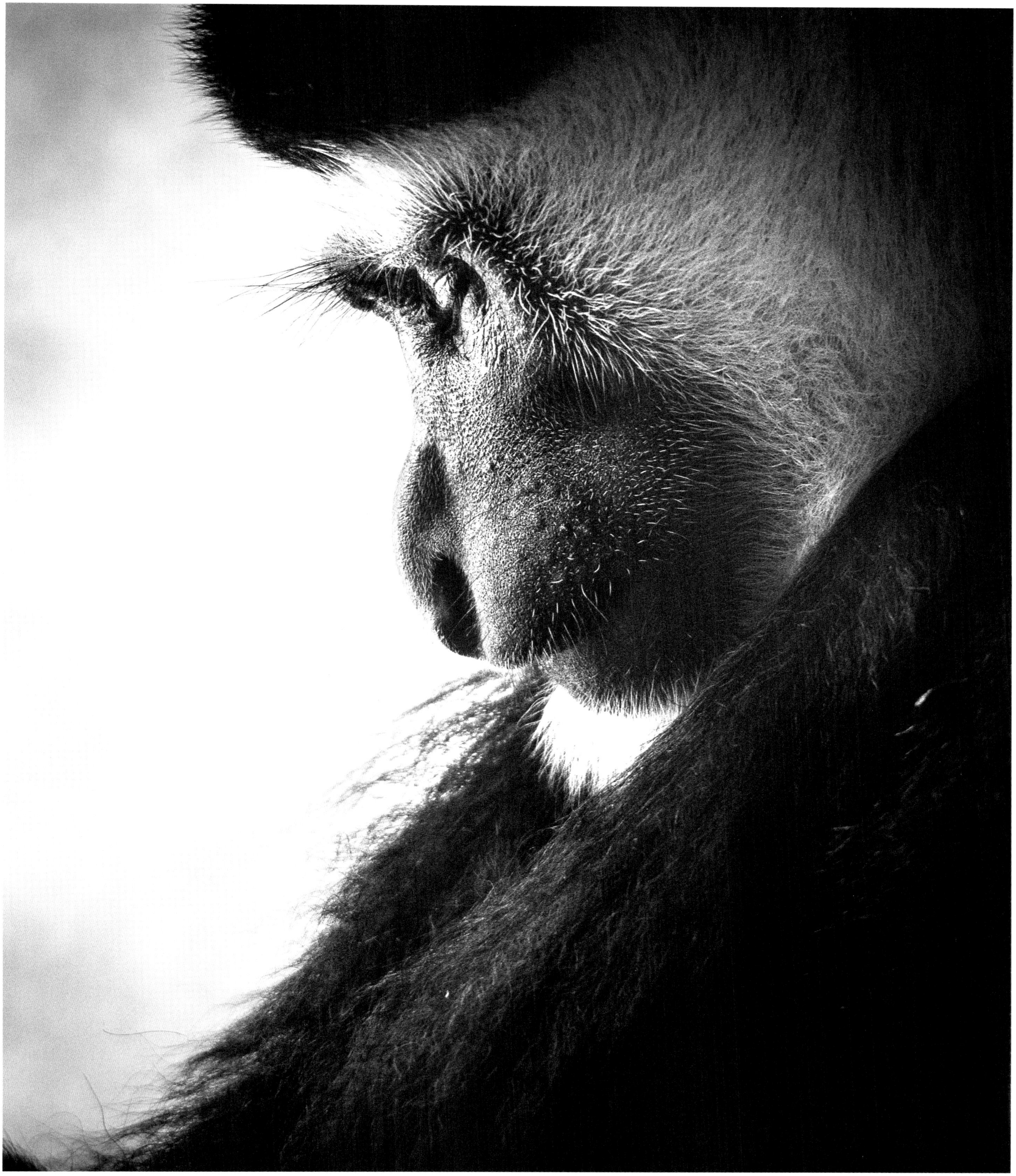

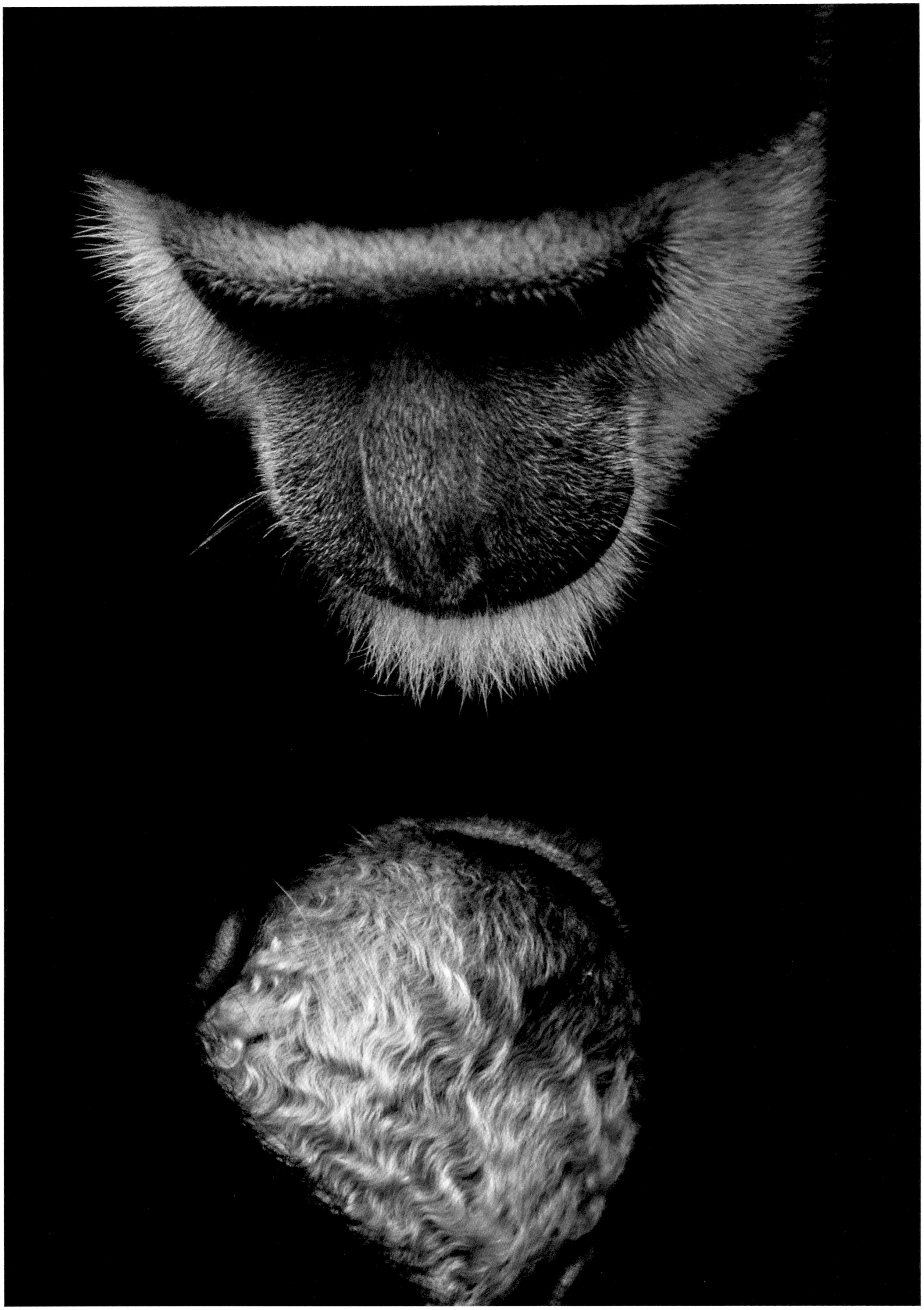

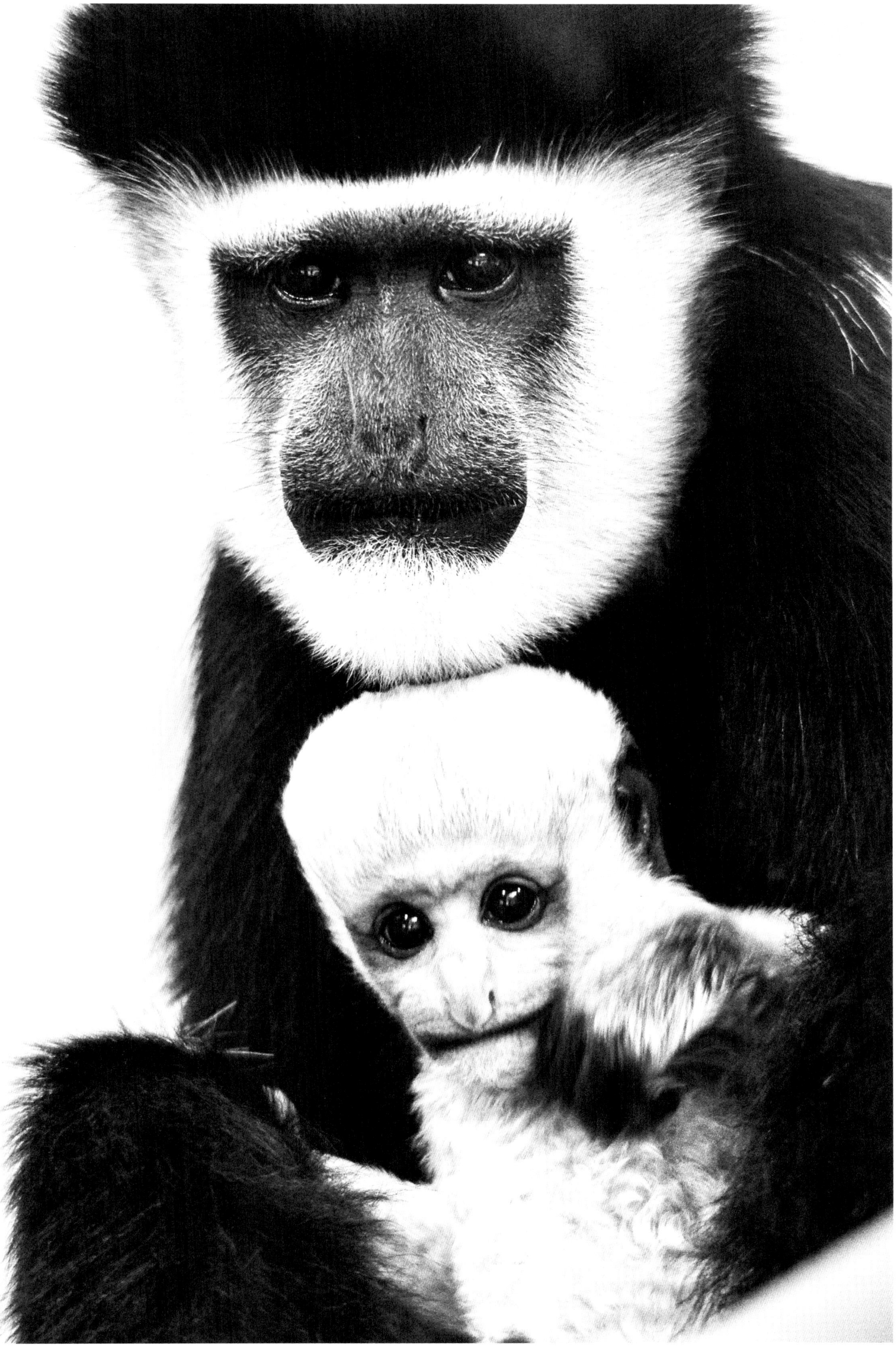

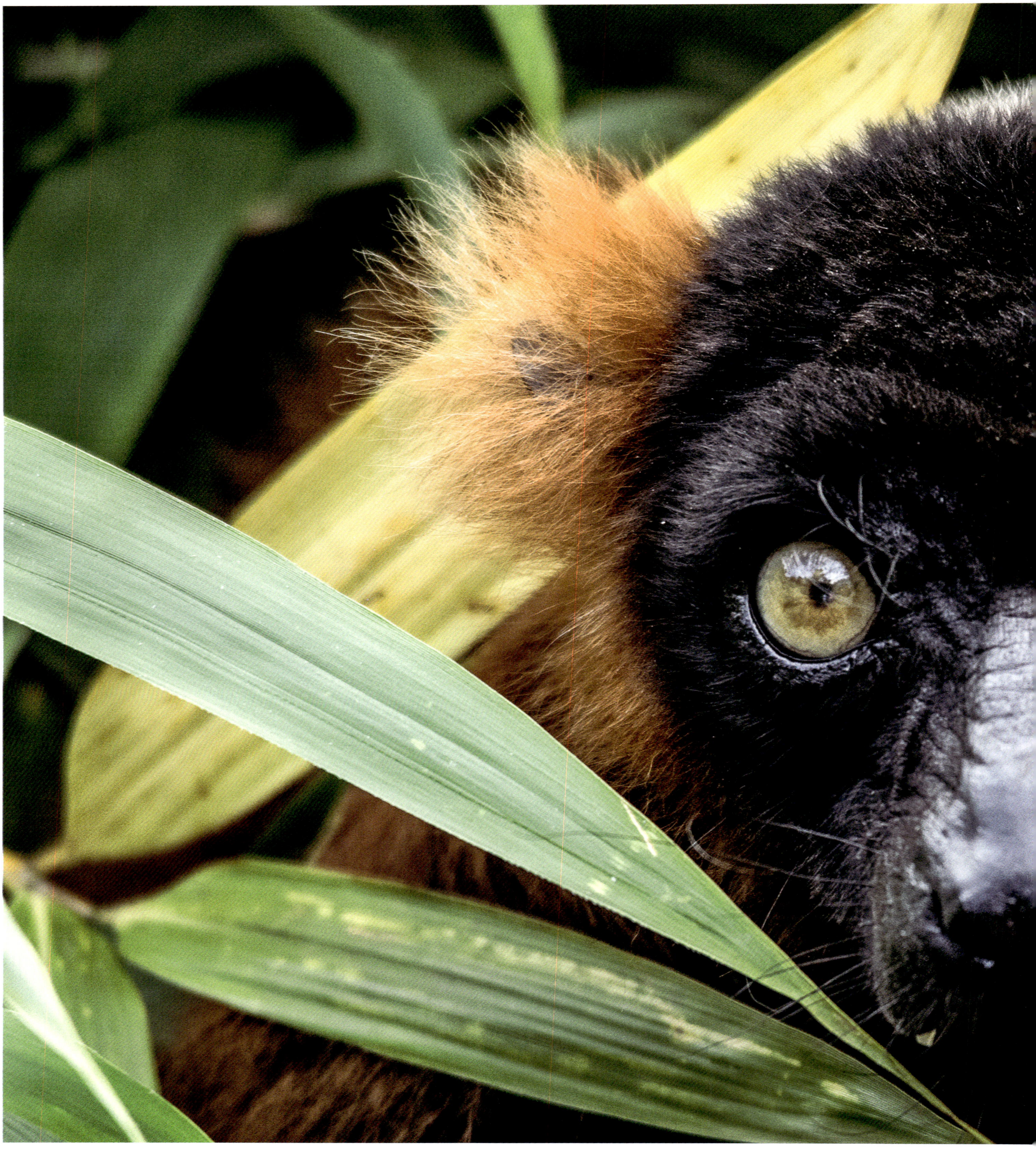

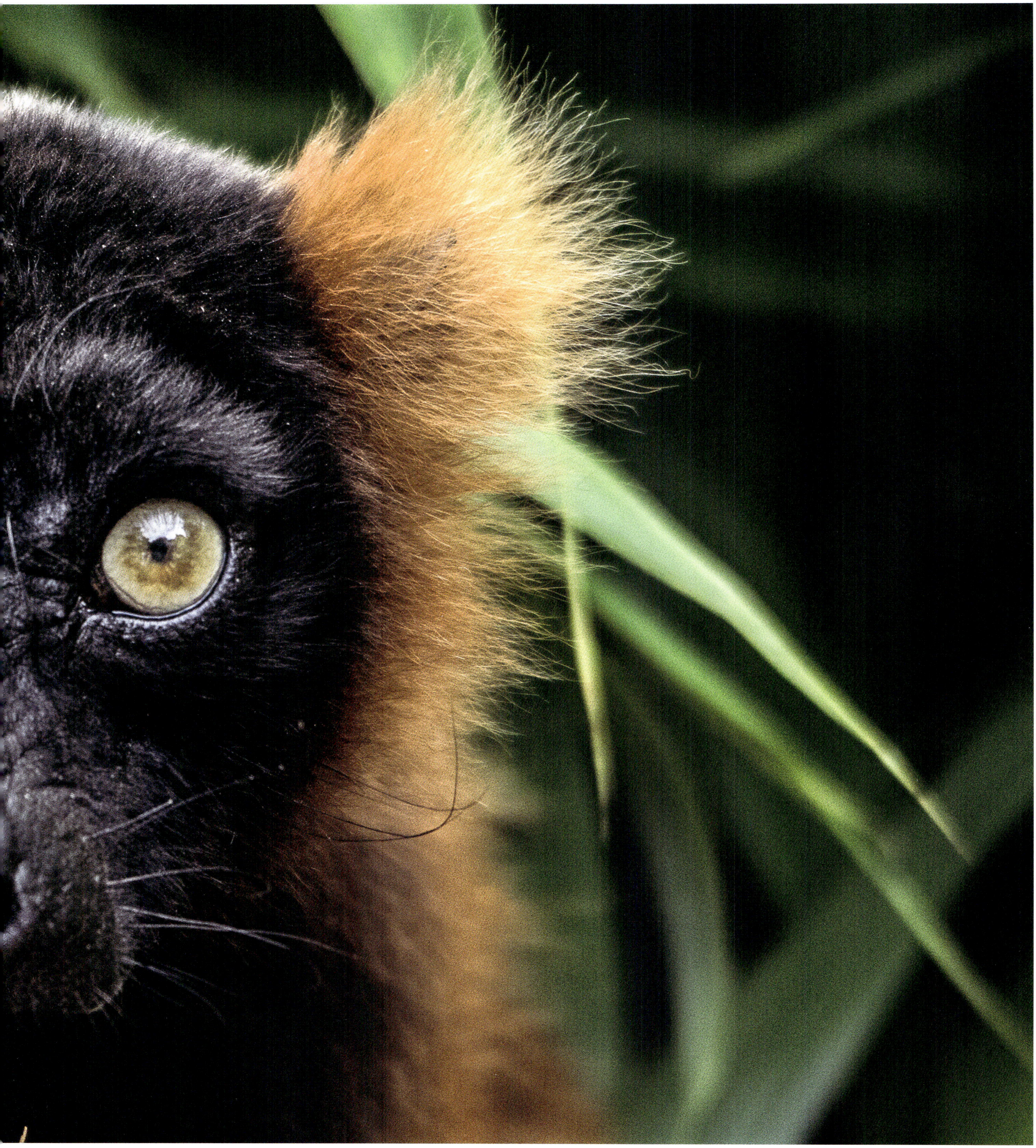

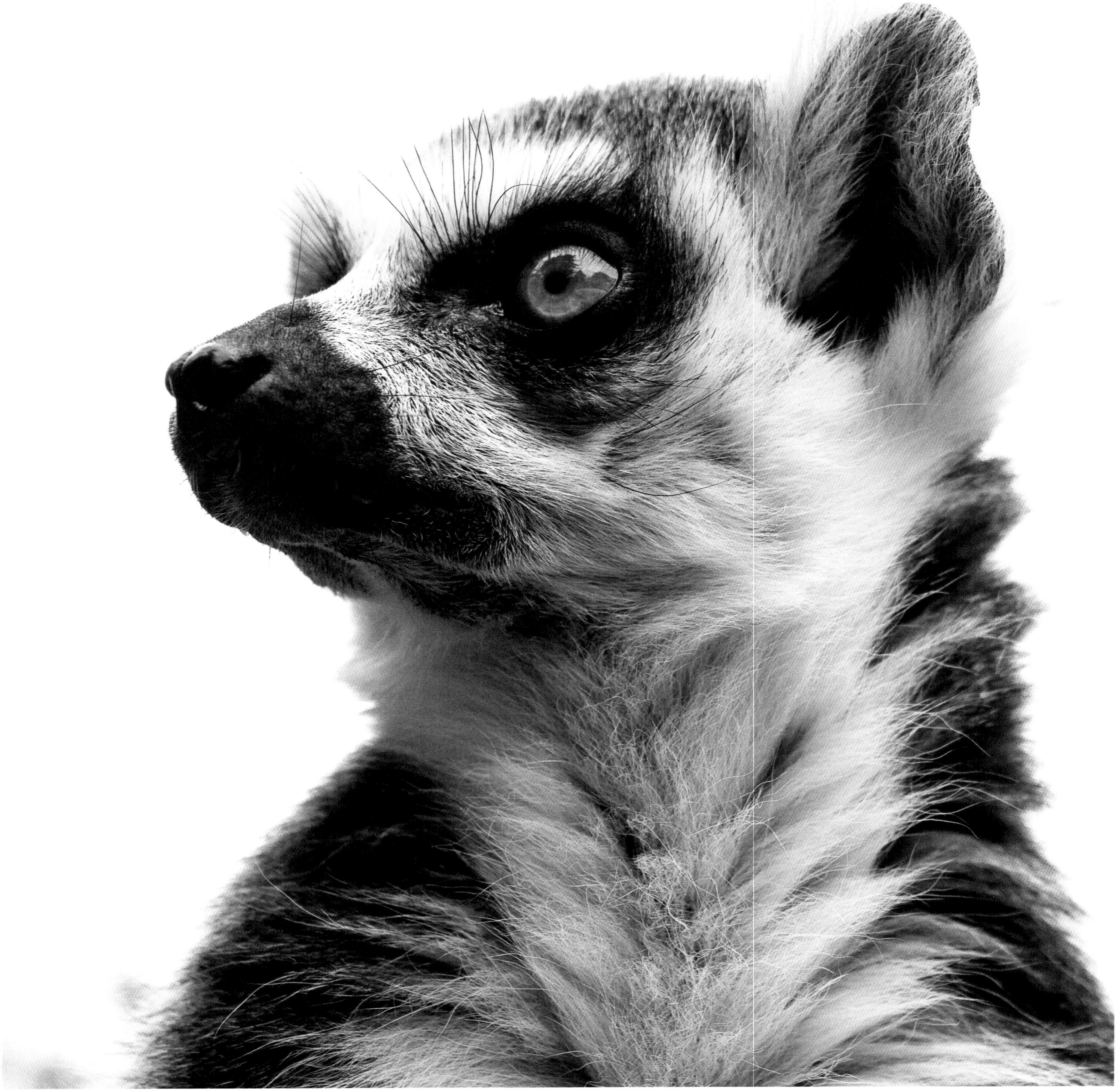

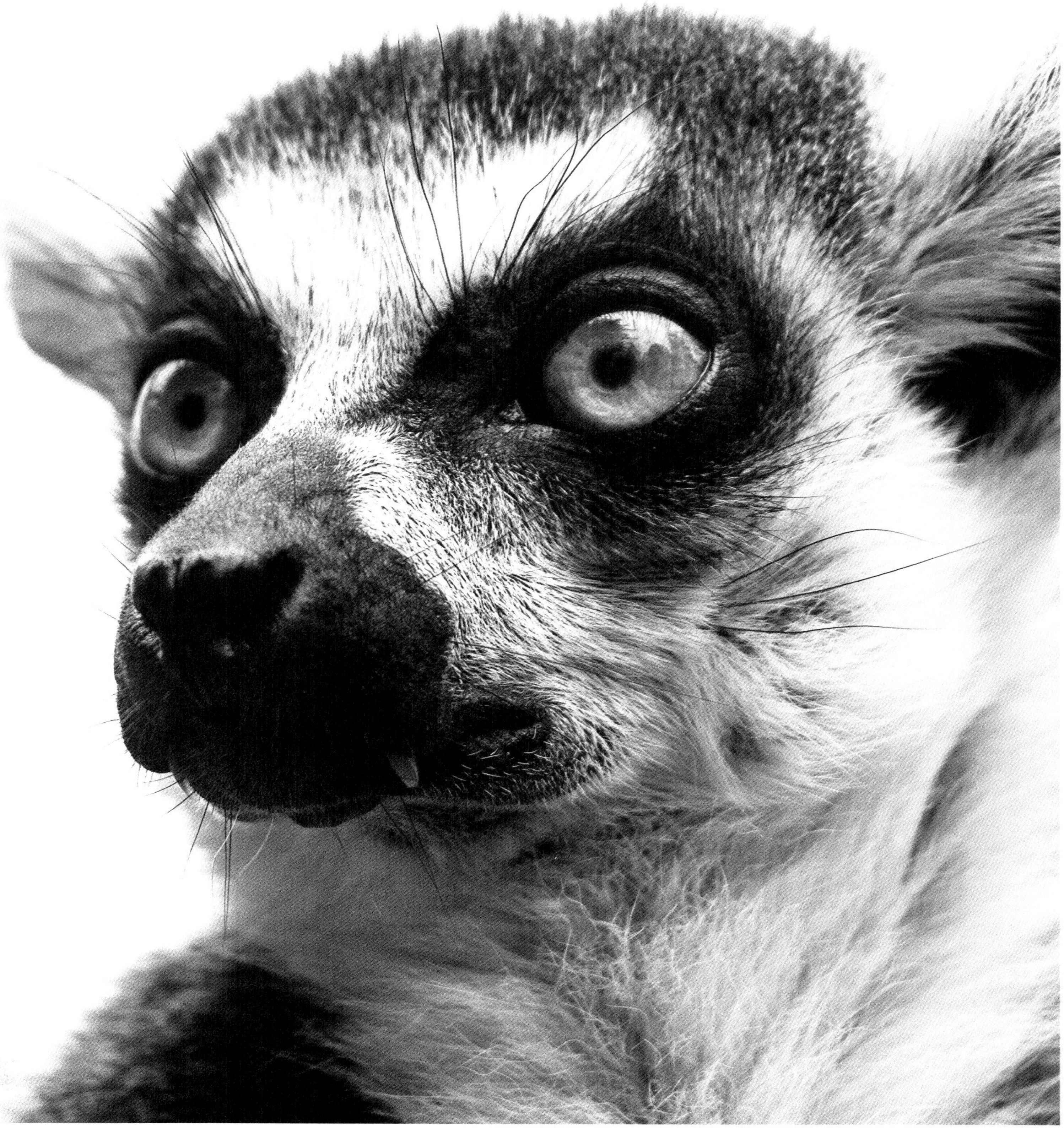

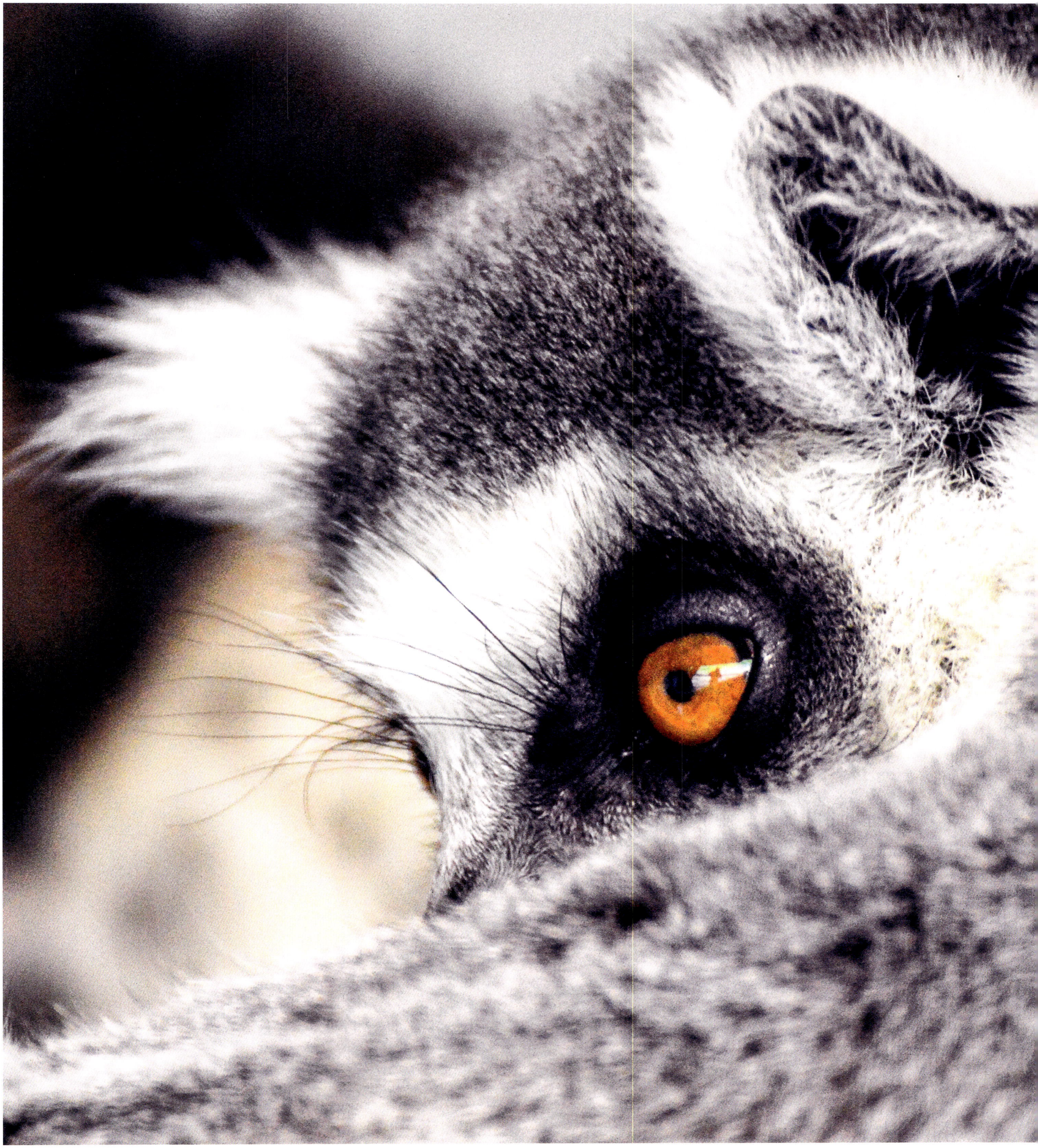

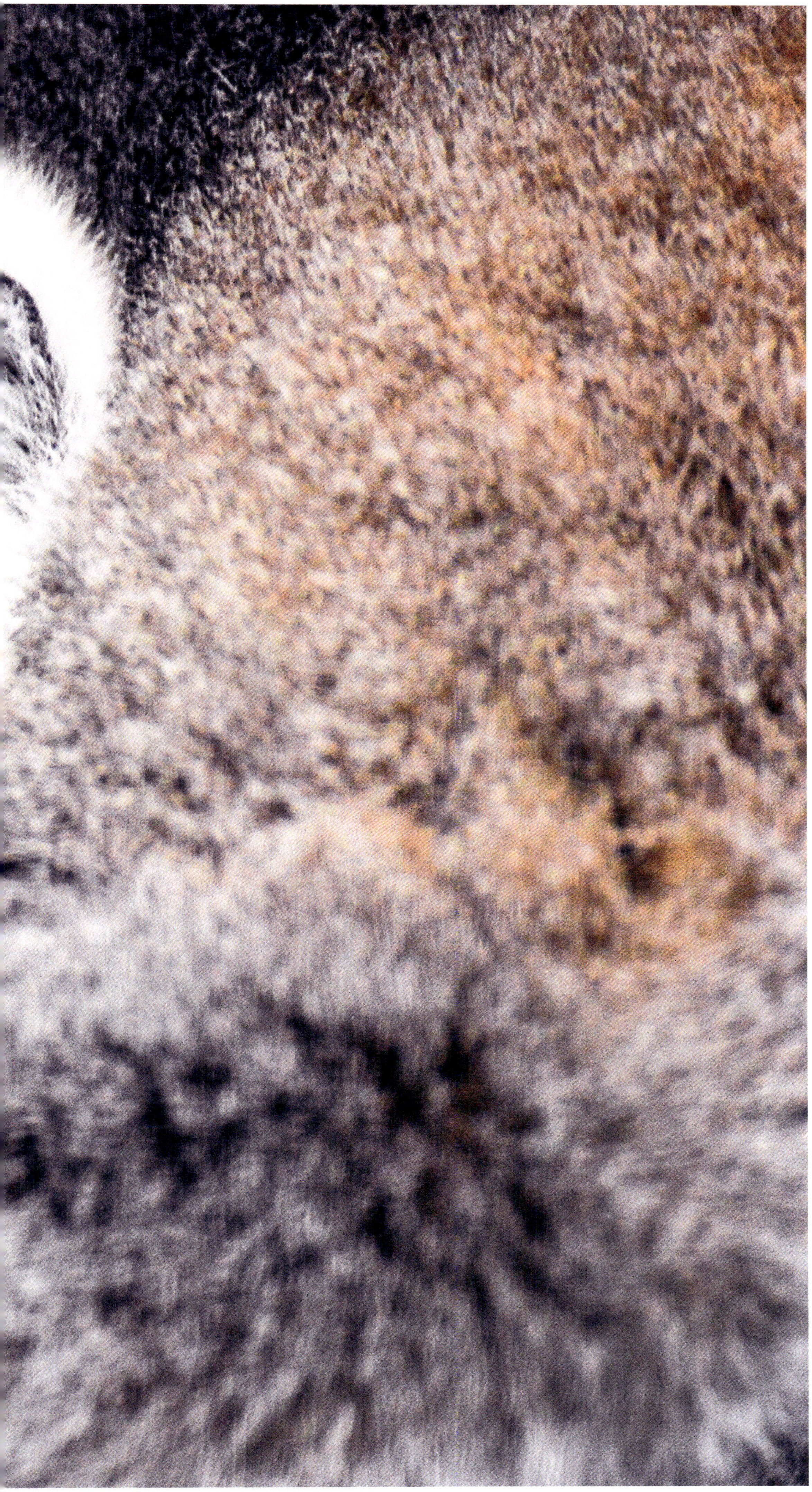

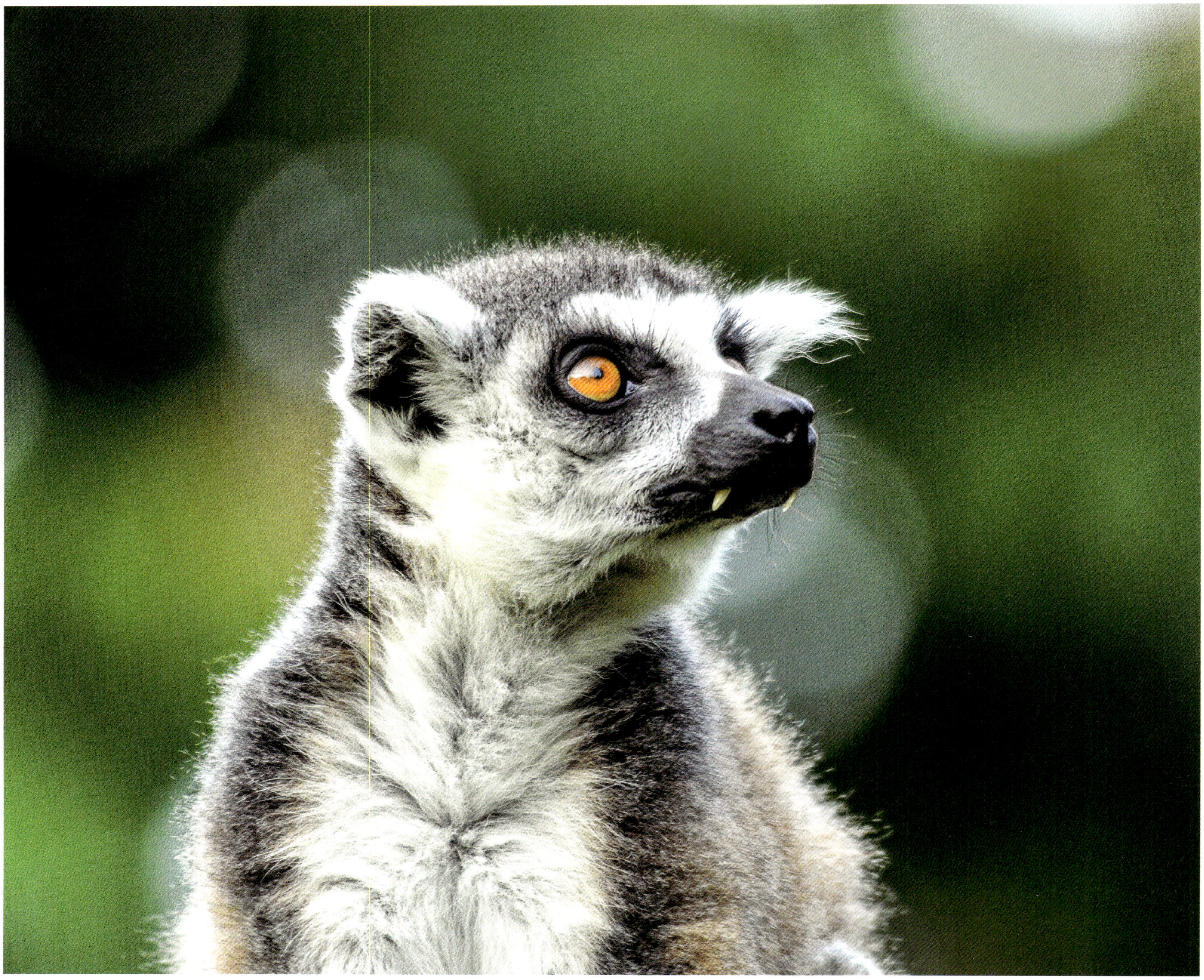

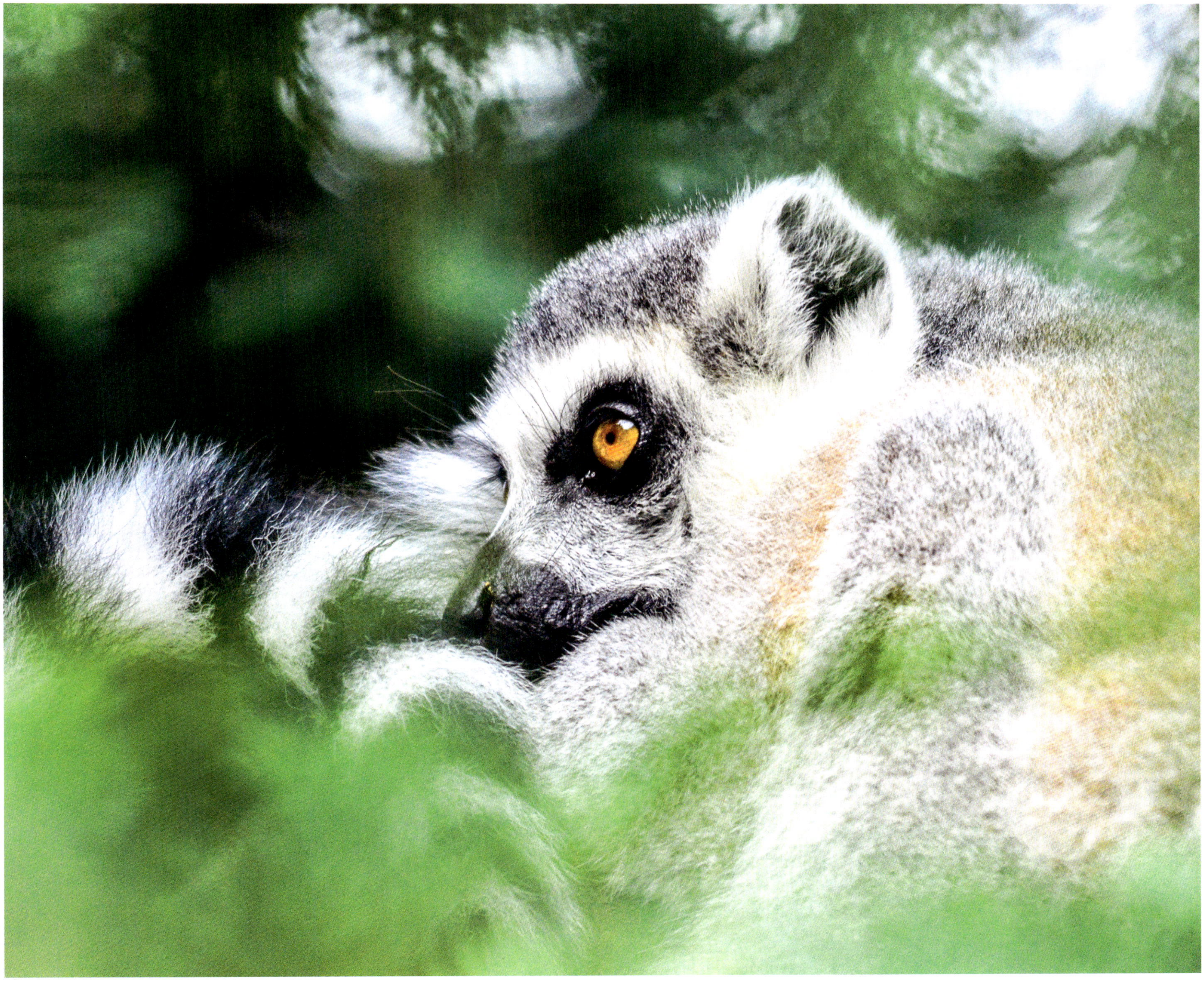

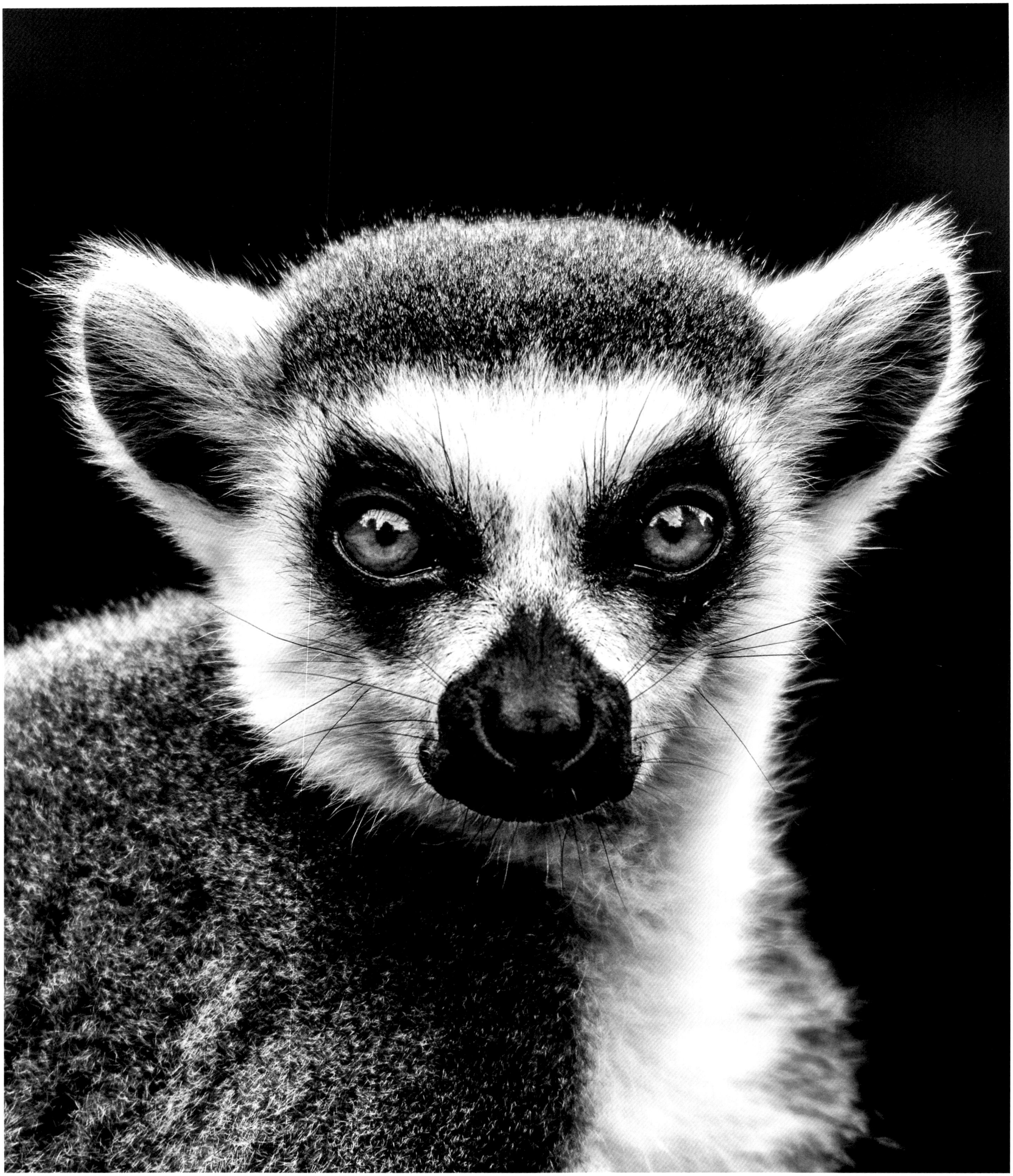

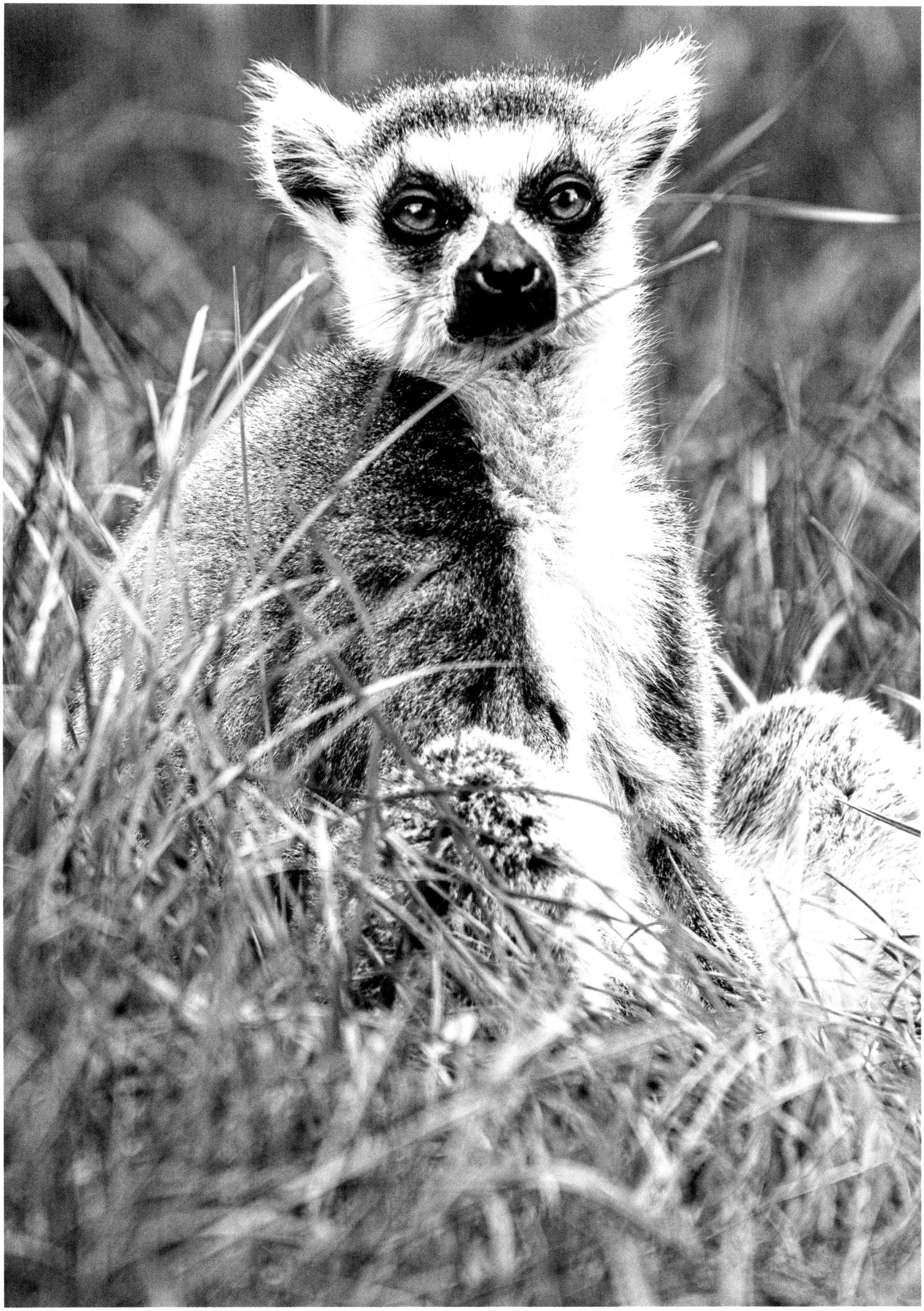

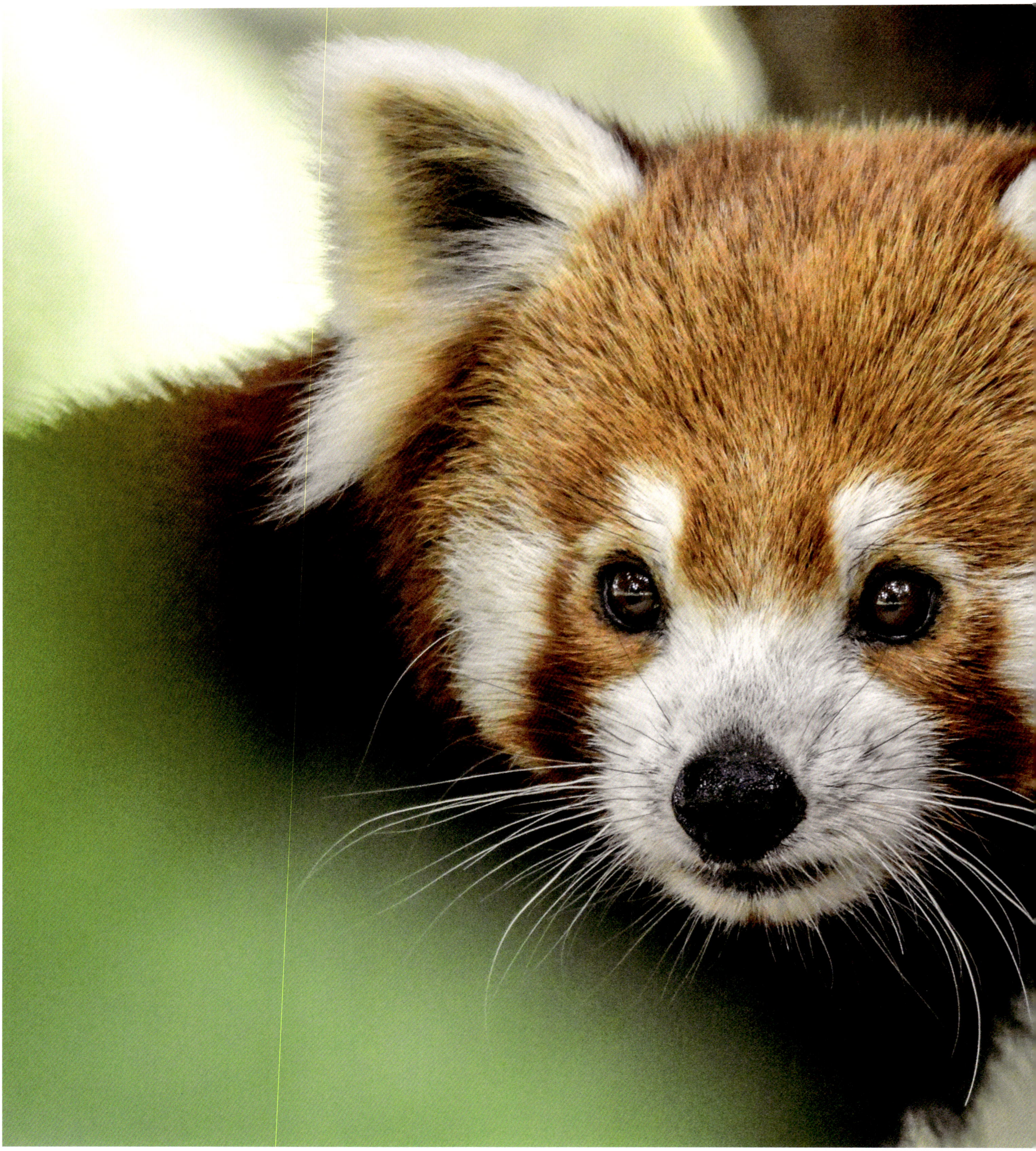

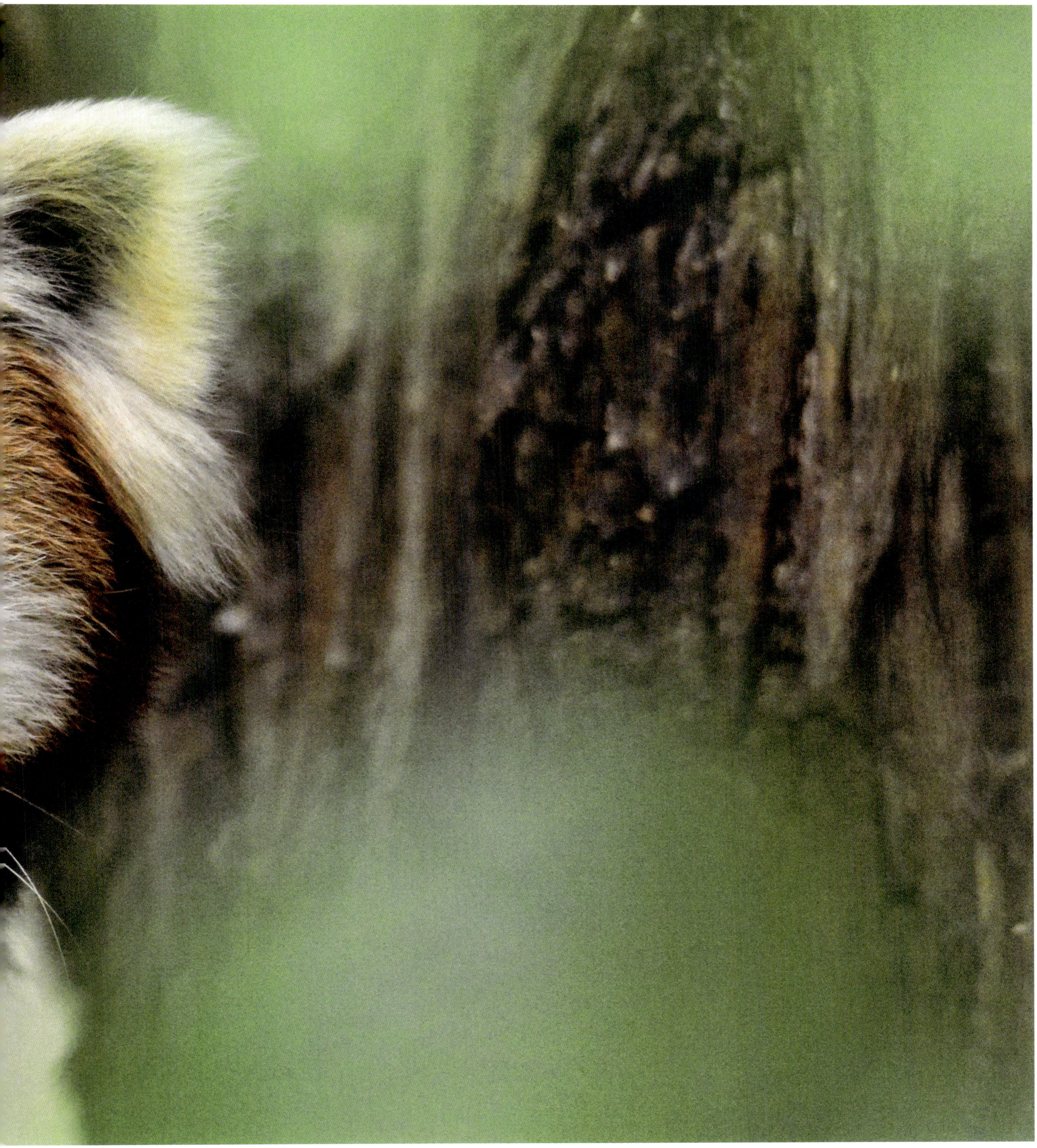

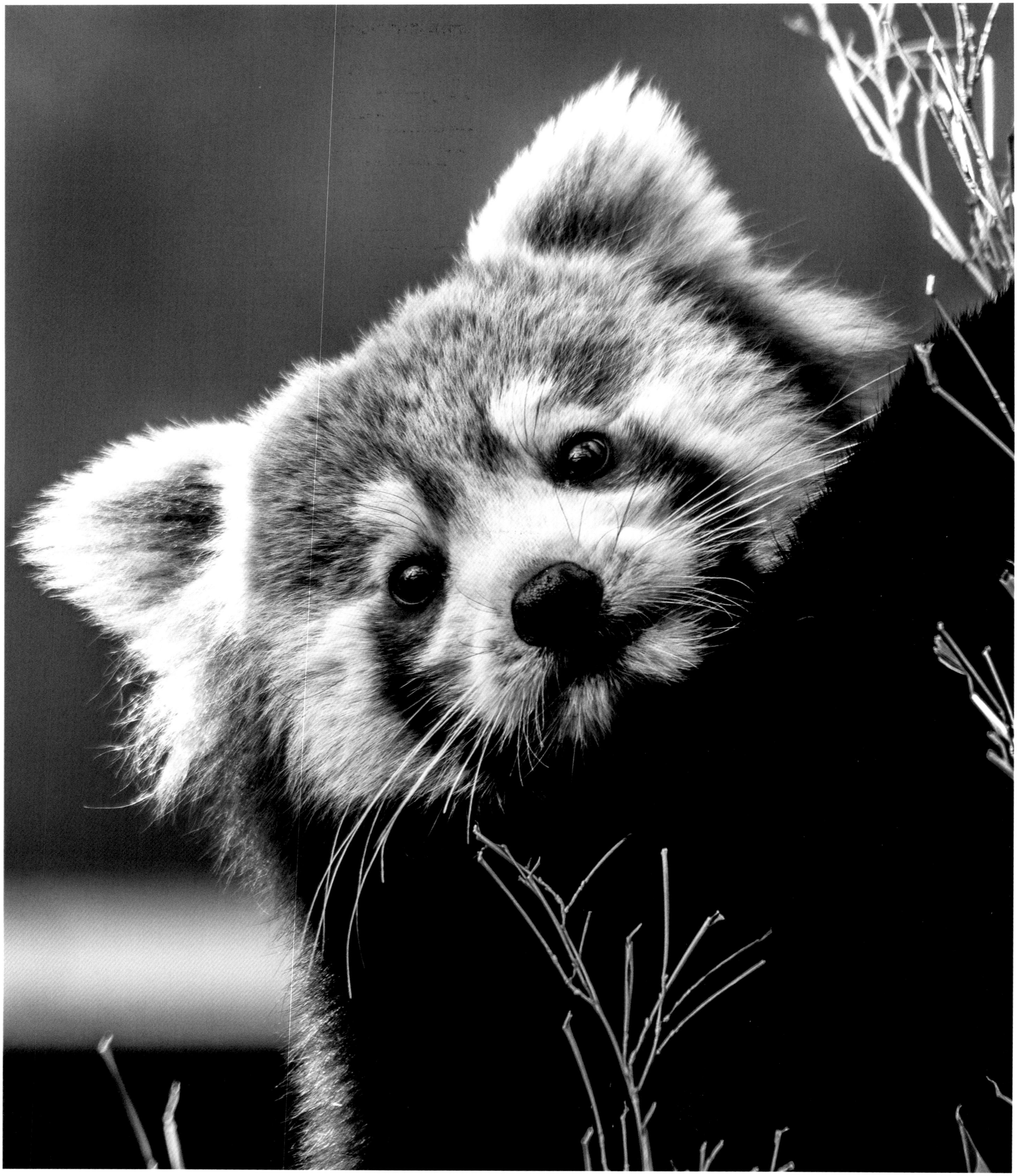

I find it very disheartening that there are now just 10,000 mature individuals in the world, a number that continues to decline due to habitat loss and fragmentation, poaching and inbreeding depression.

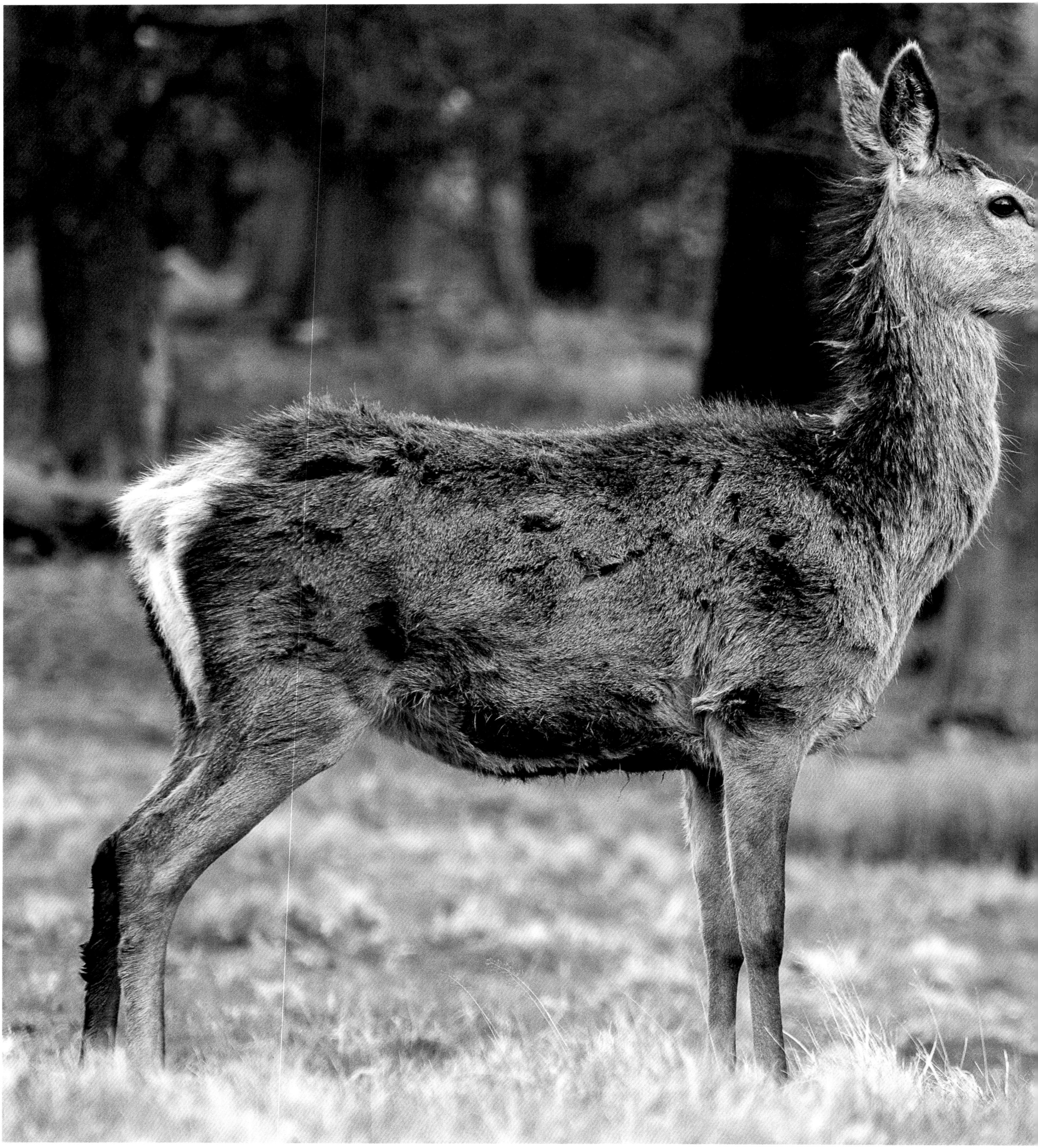

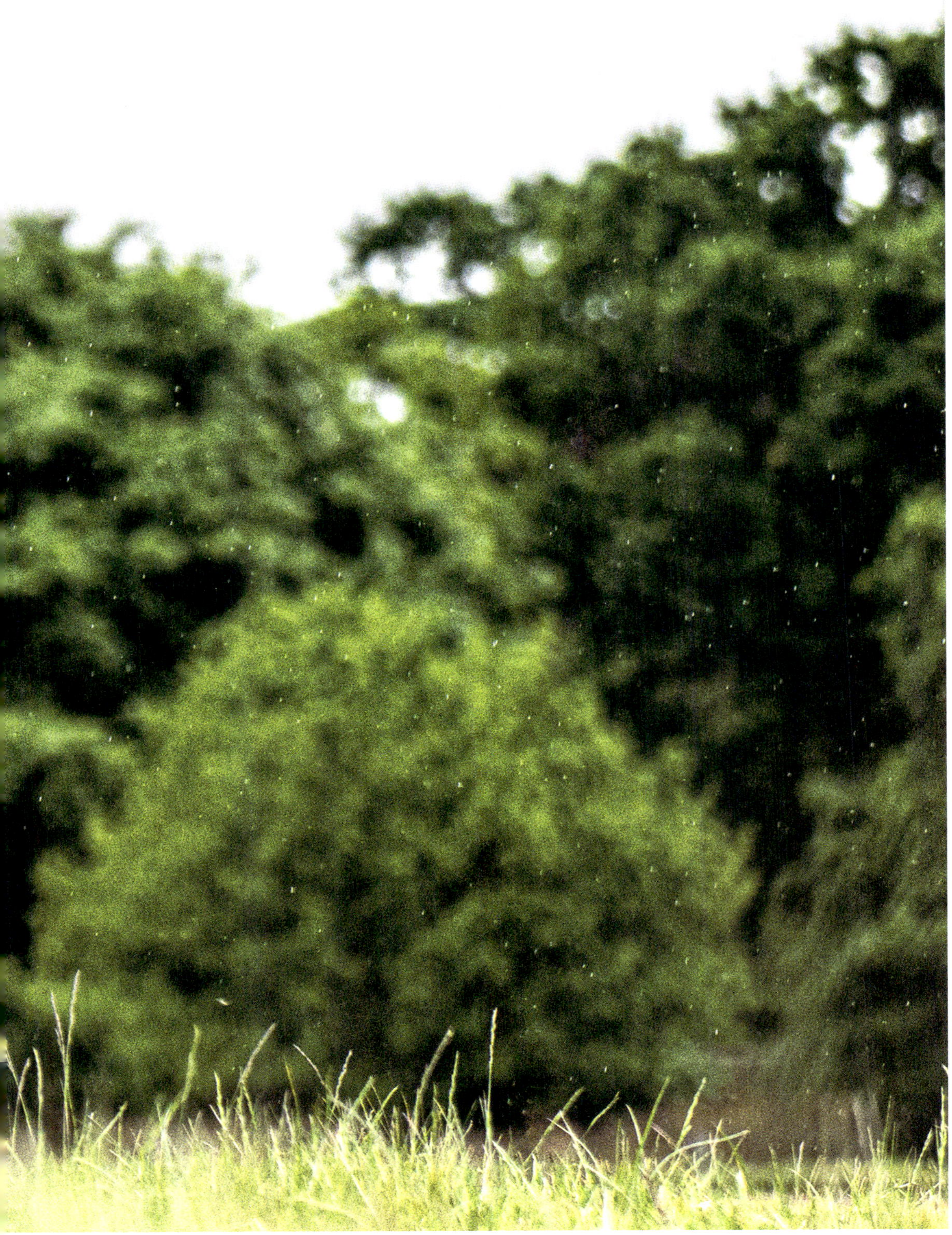

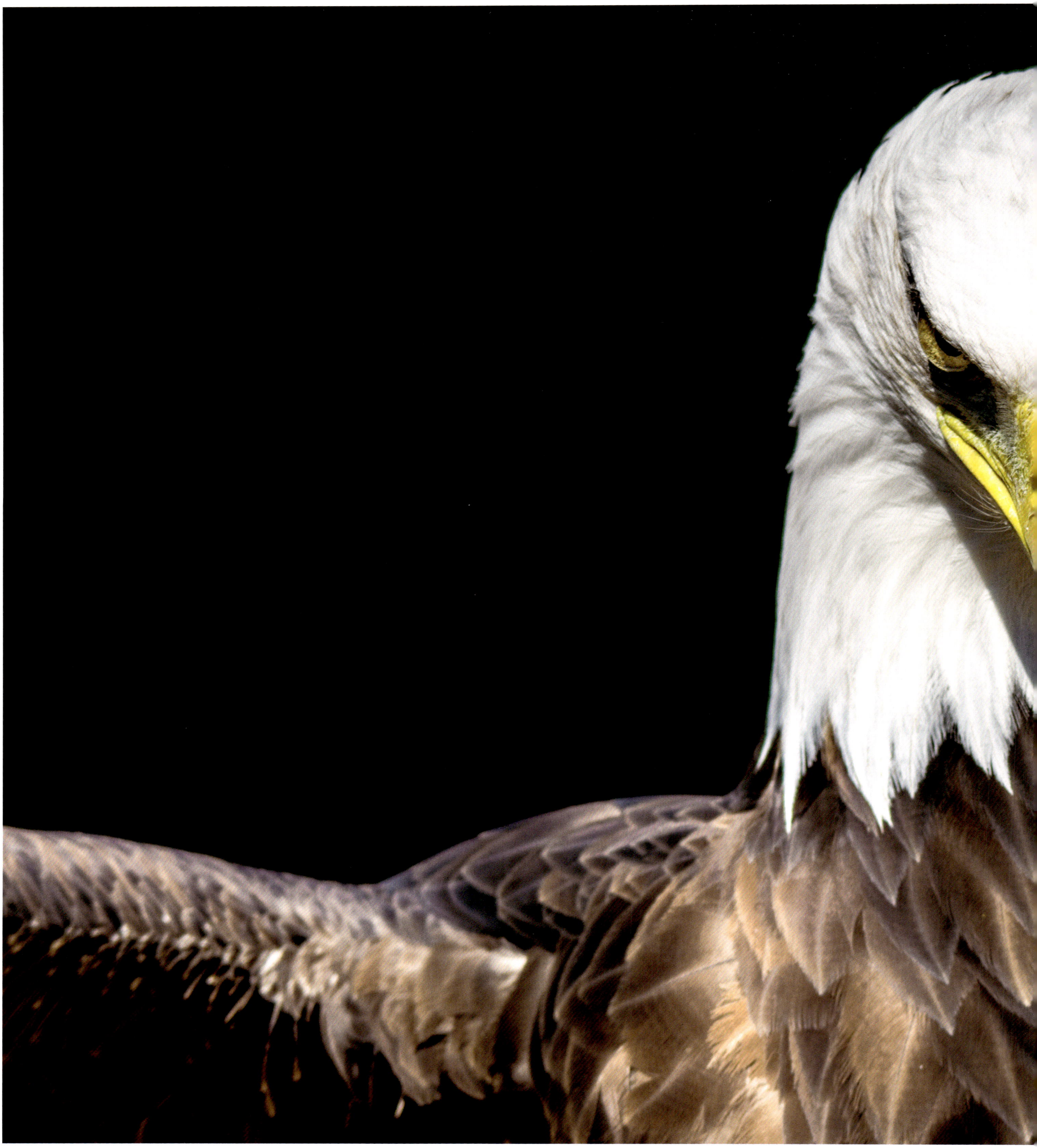

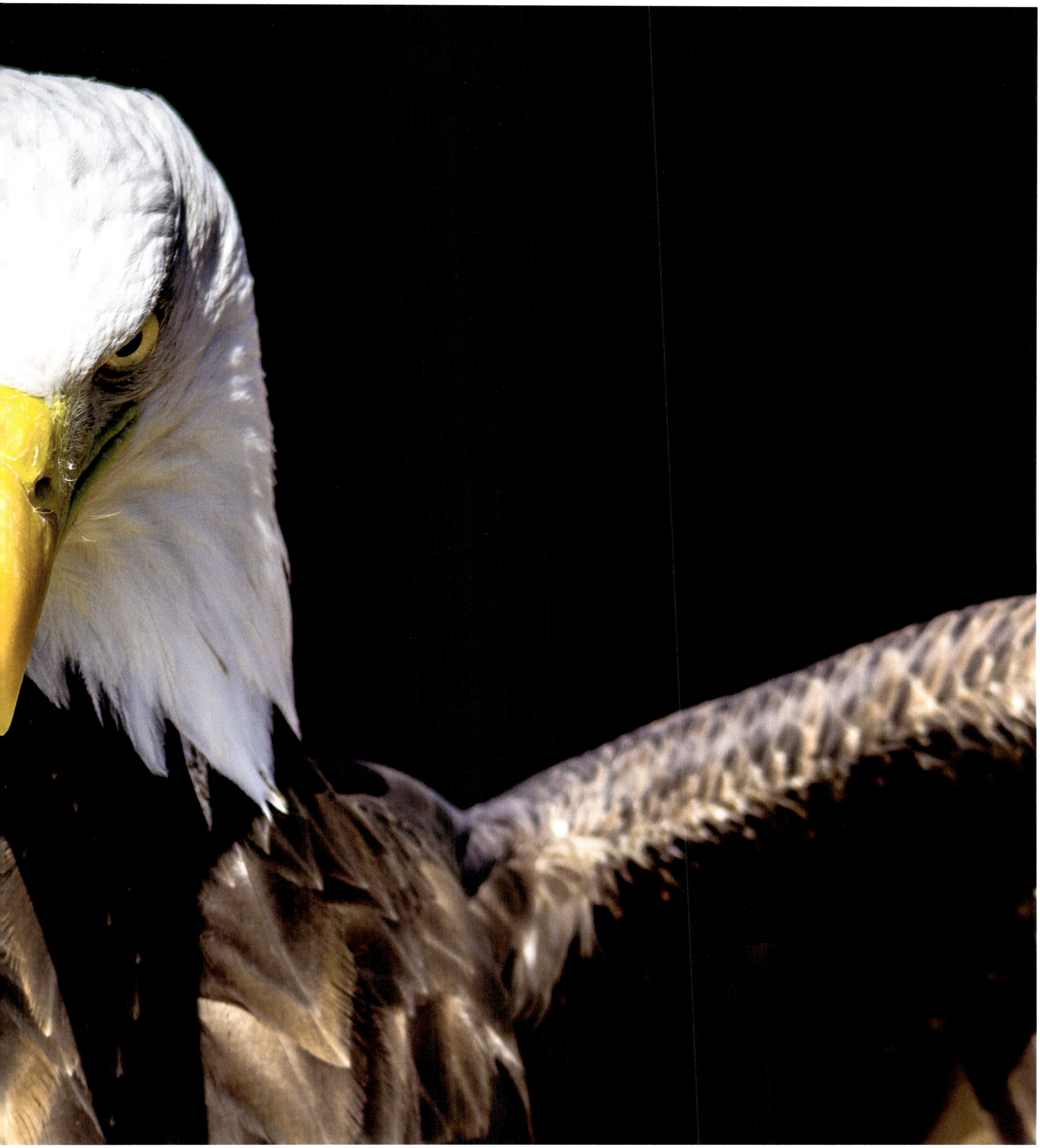

I invested many hours into desk research, learning about the American Bald Eagle, and also about the work of others to ensure that my resulting images would capture the personality and grandeur of the eagle, whilst also ensuring that the compositions were unique and powerful.

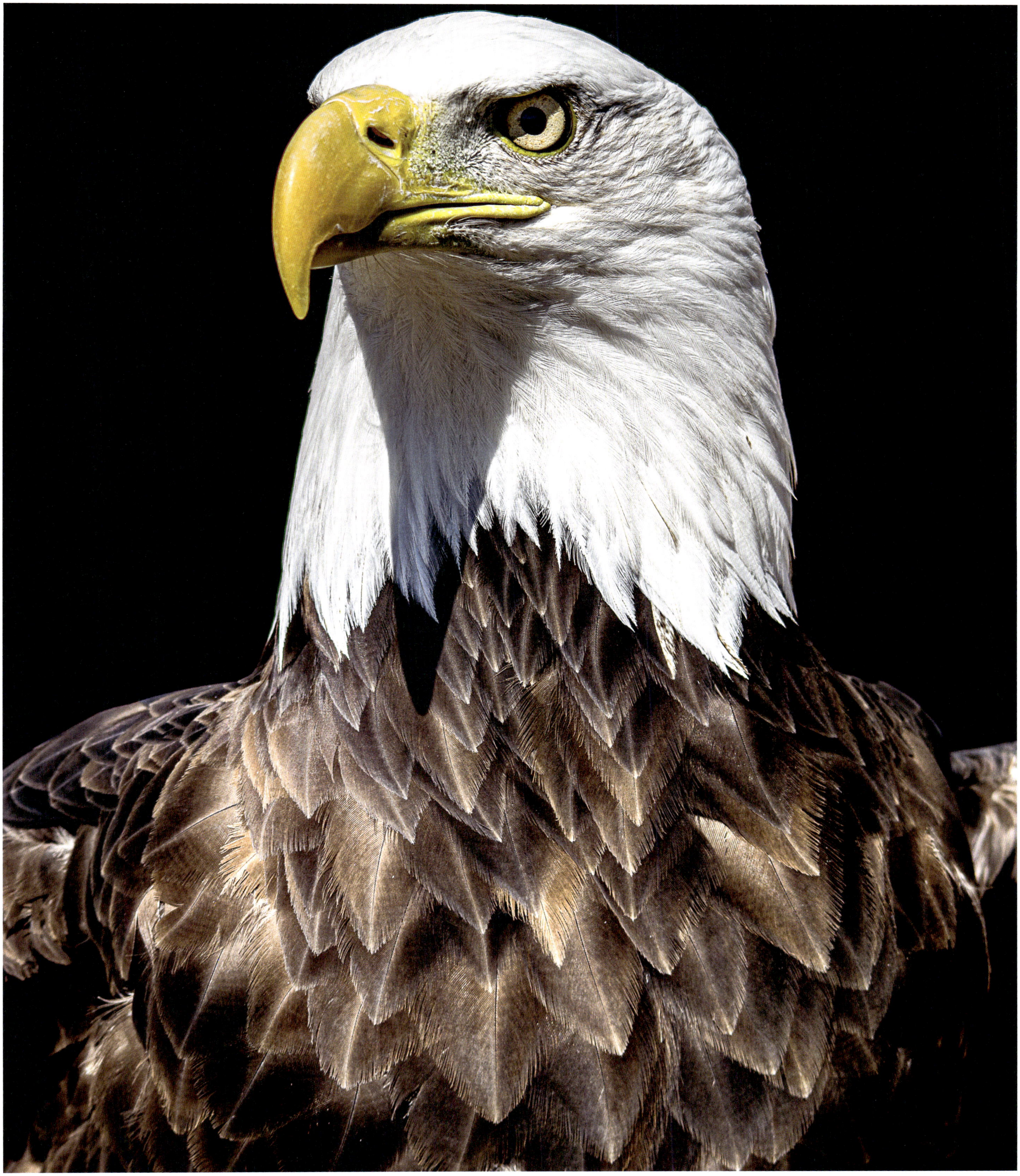

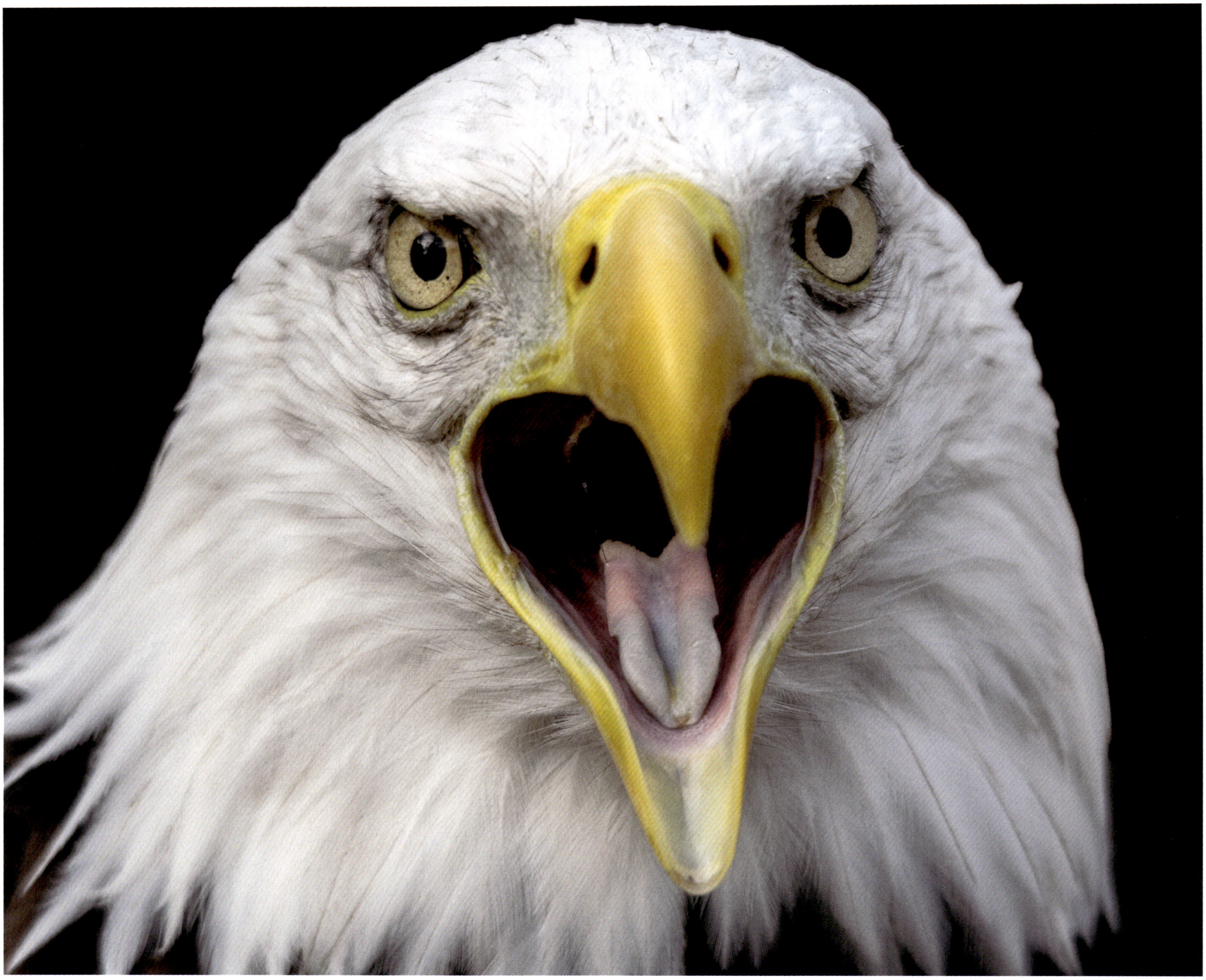

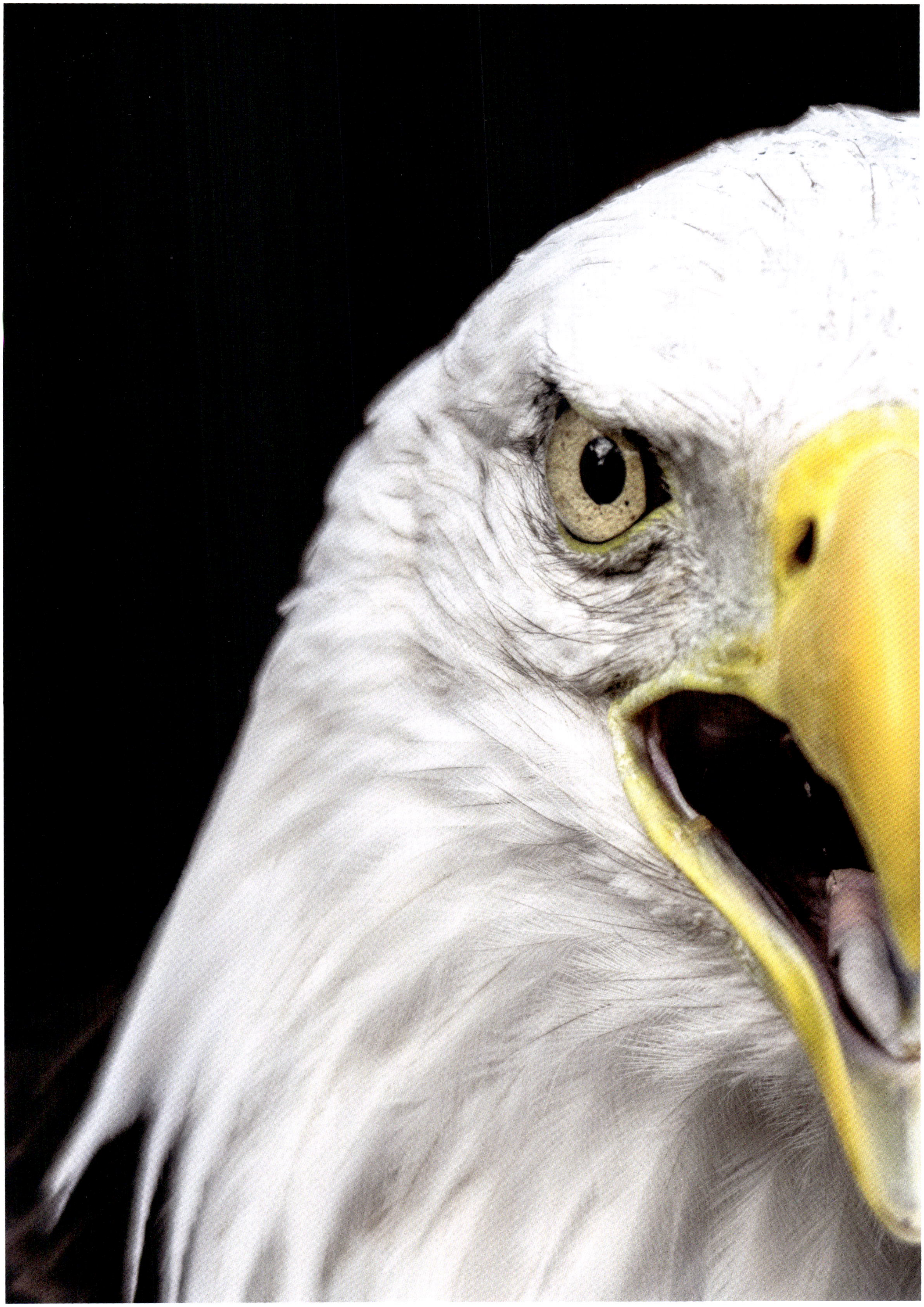

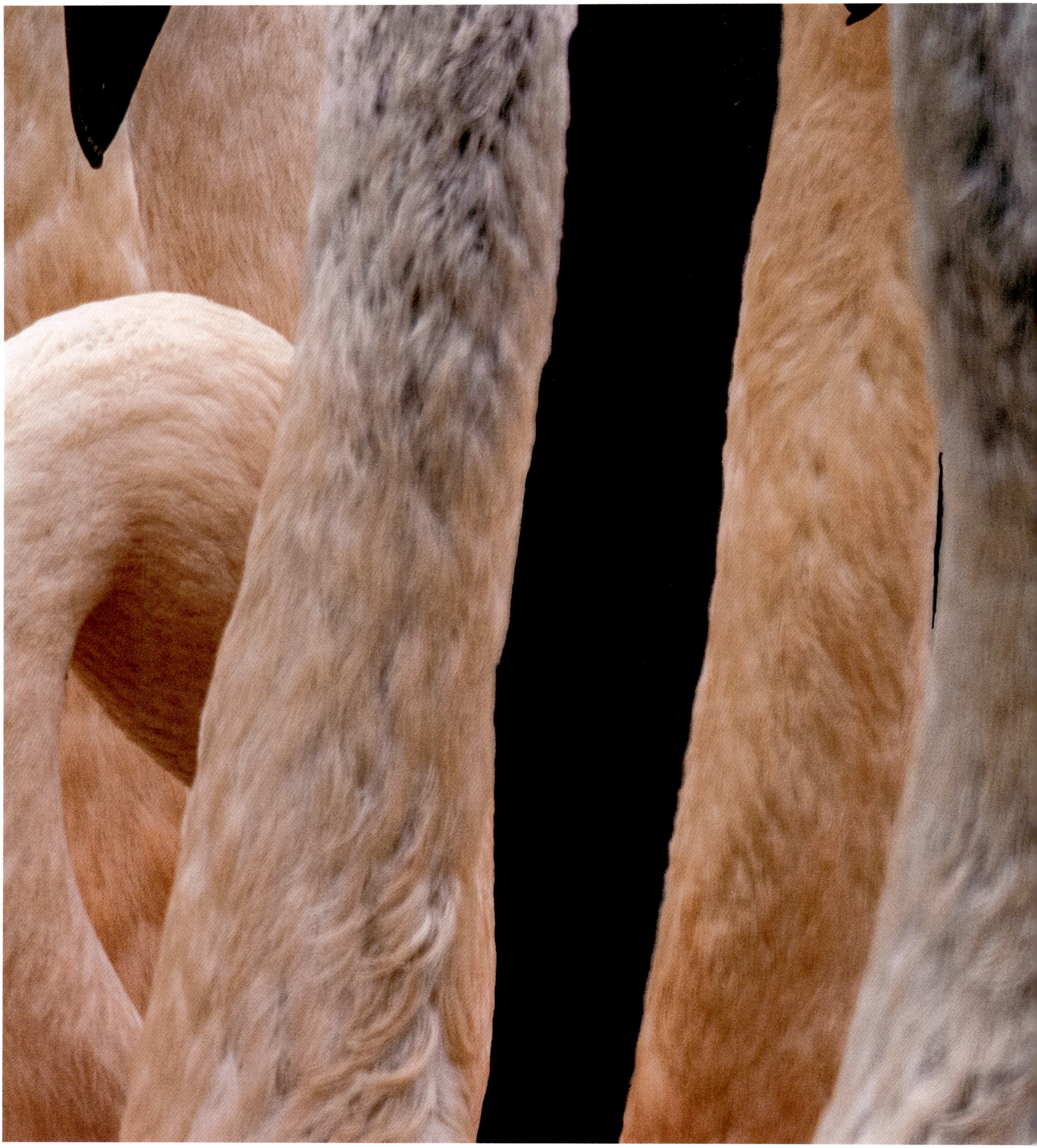

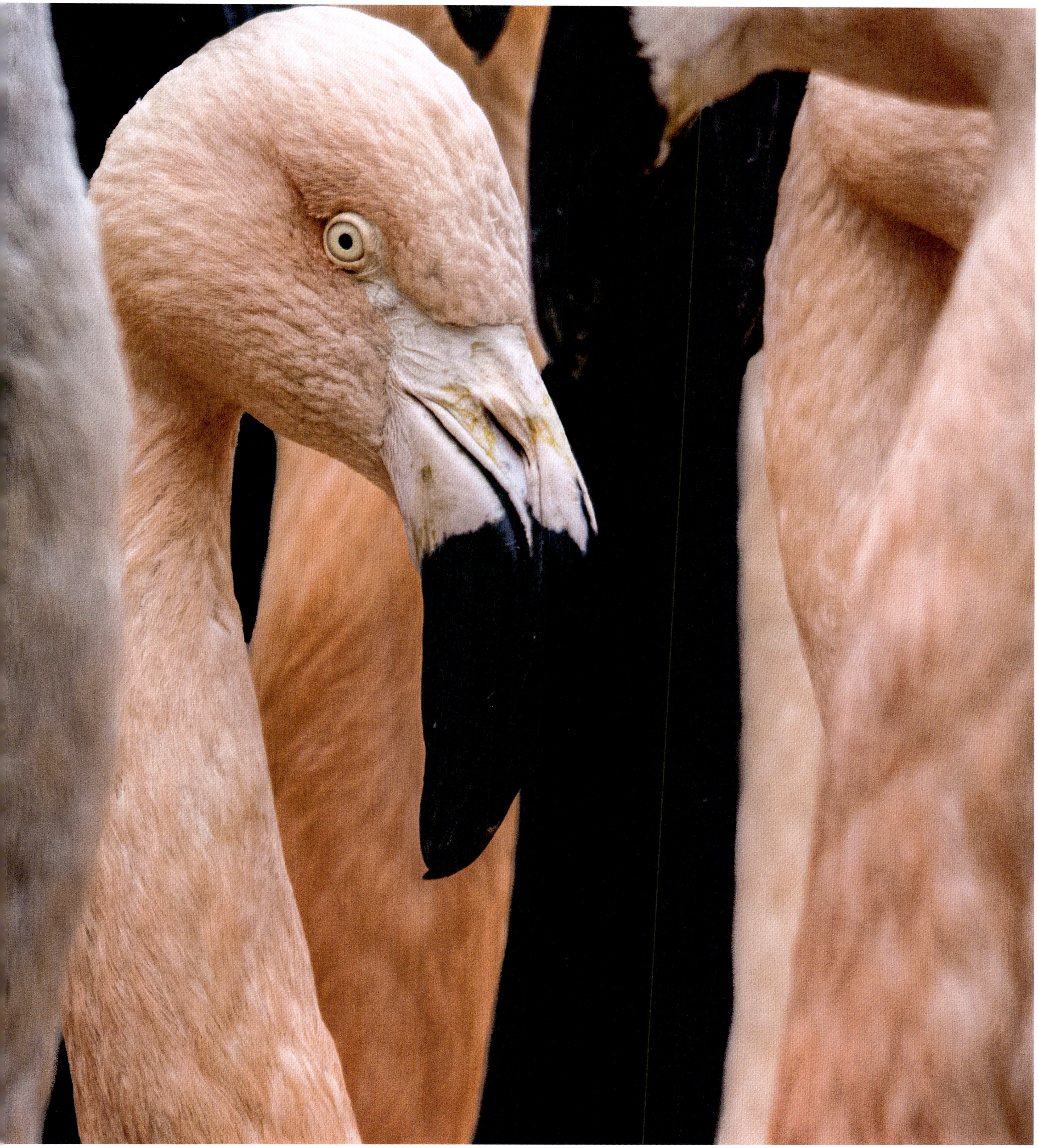

Flamingos: there can be no doubting their beauty, their grace or their photographic appeal. The question is how to make images that capture their personality and soul?

They are incredibly intelligent beings and can sense rain falling hundreds of kilometres away! So, before I could even consider which camera body or lens to employ, I had to gain their trust.

I spent many hours sitting beside the lake that this flock called home and, eventually, they began to relax around me. I soon got to know the birds on an individual basis; much like humans there were grumpy ones, happy ones and the occasional trouble-maker.

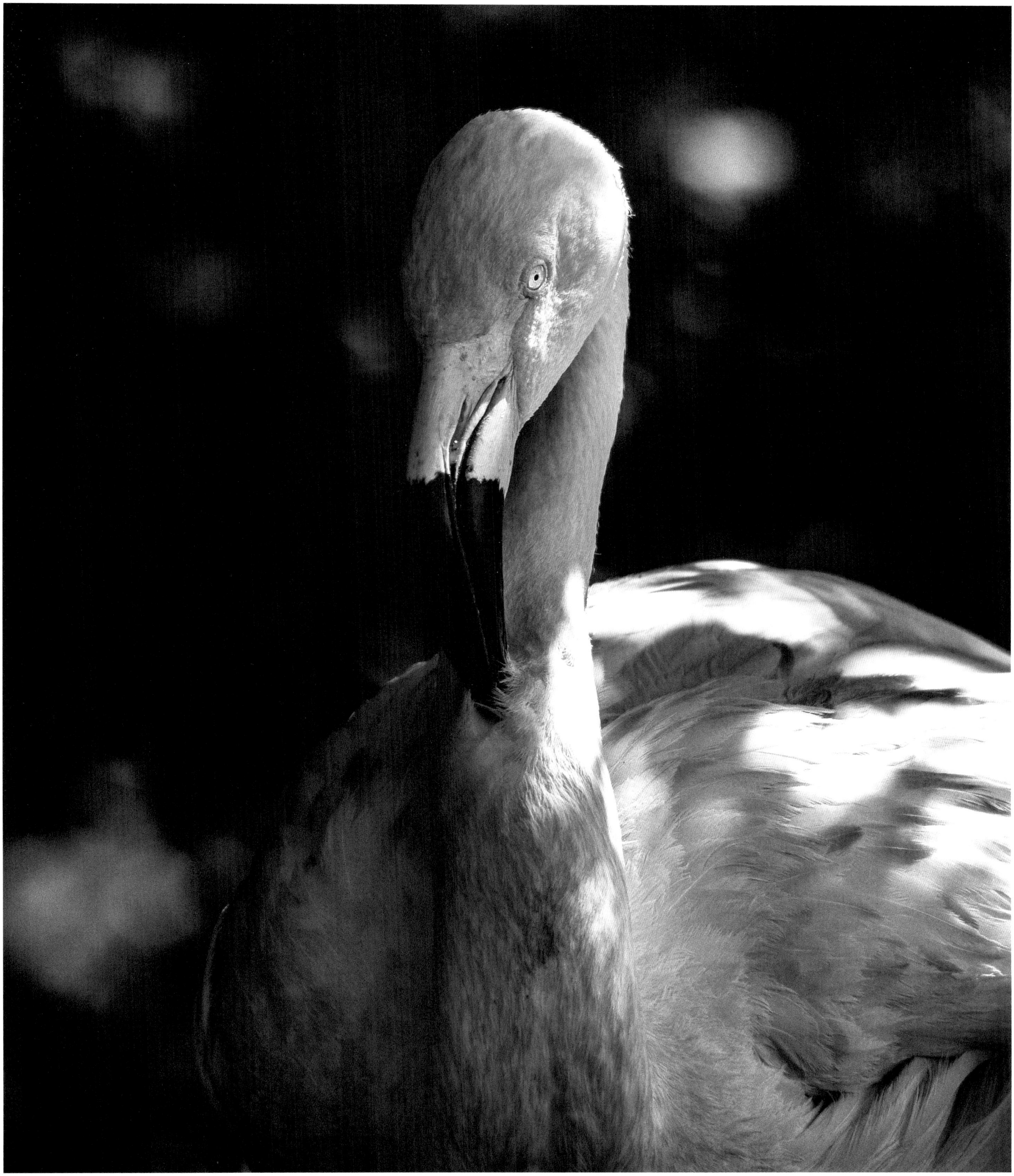

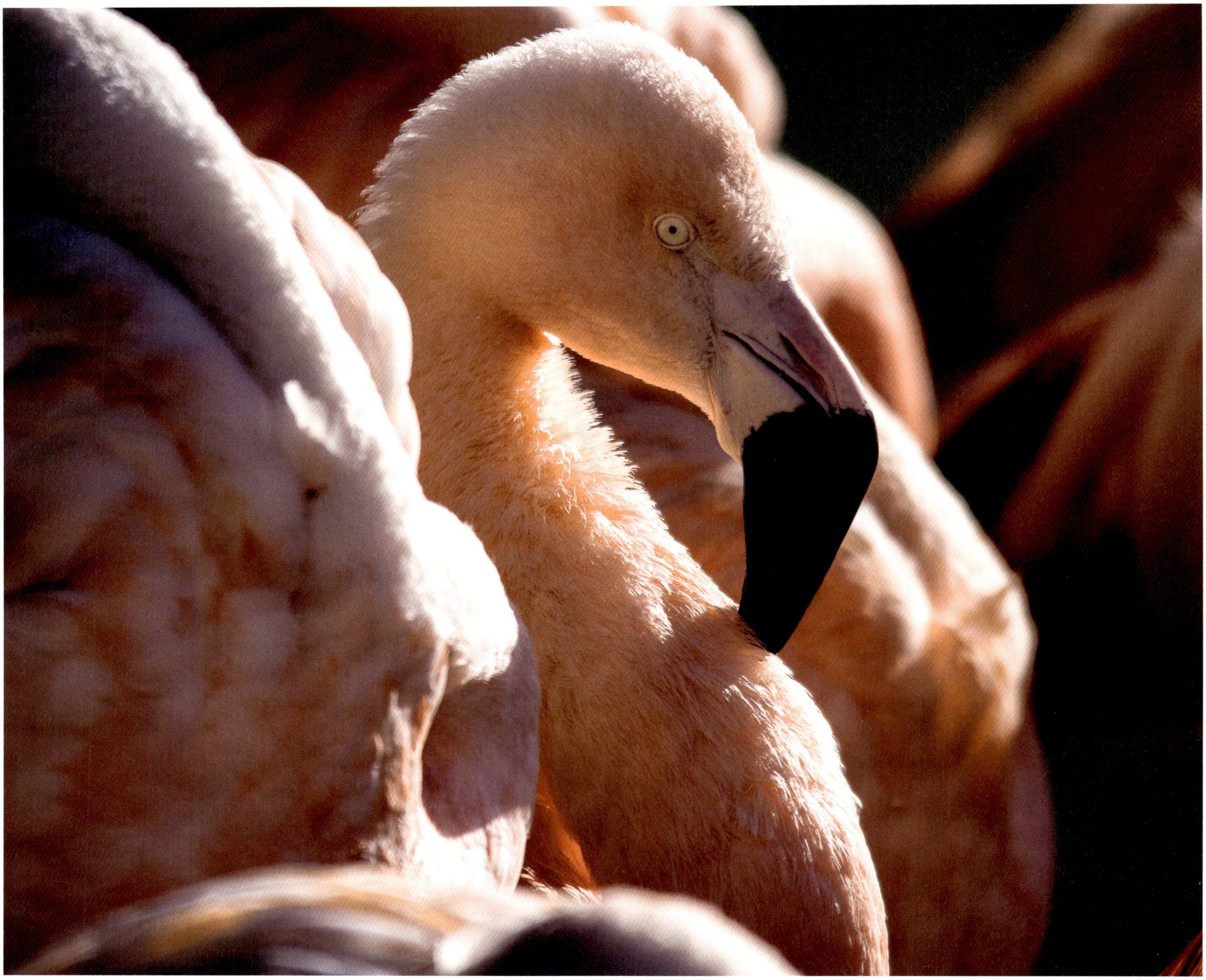

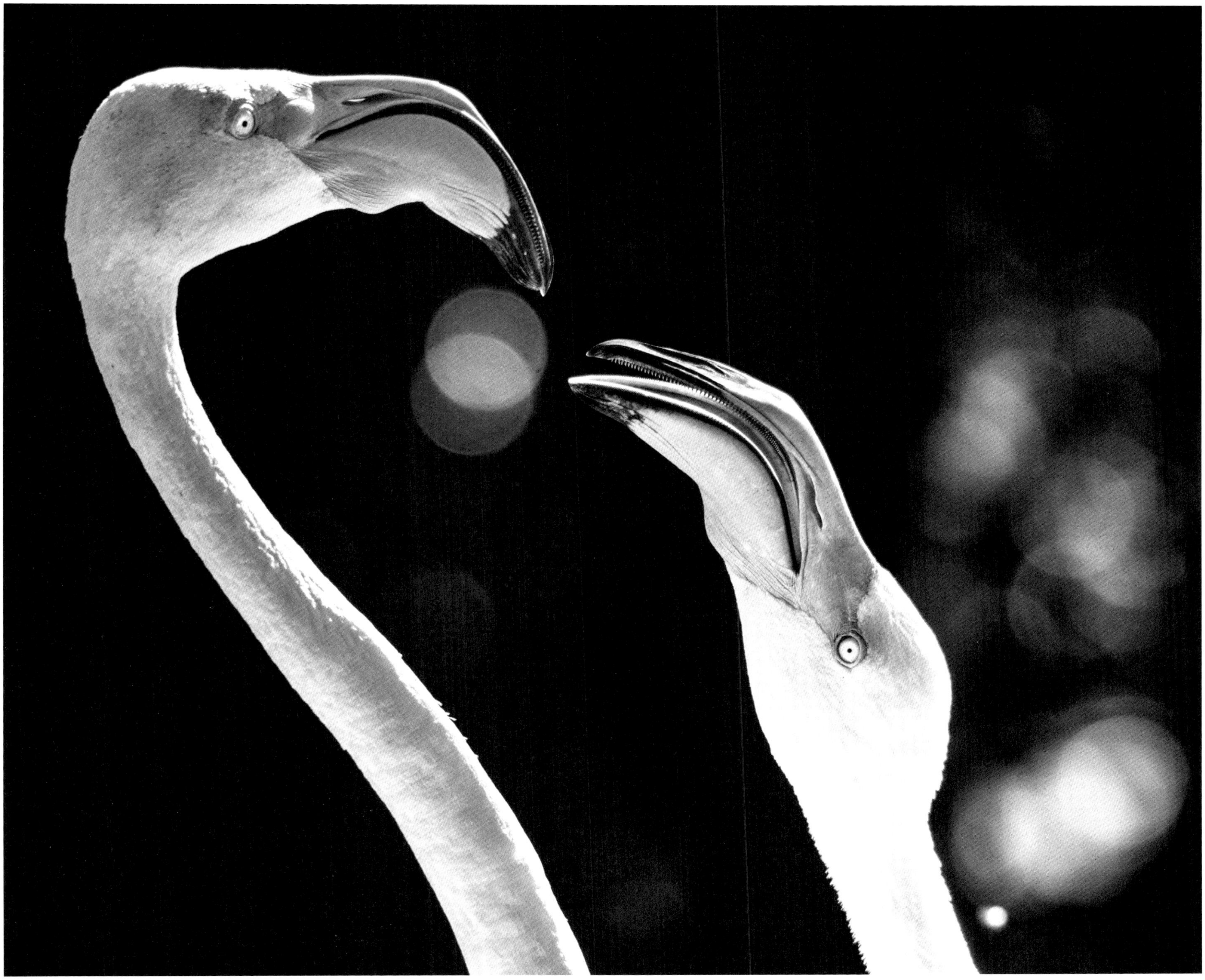

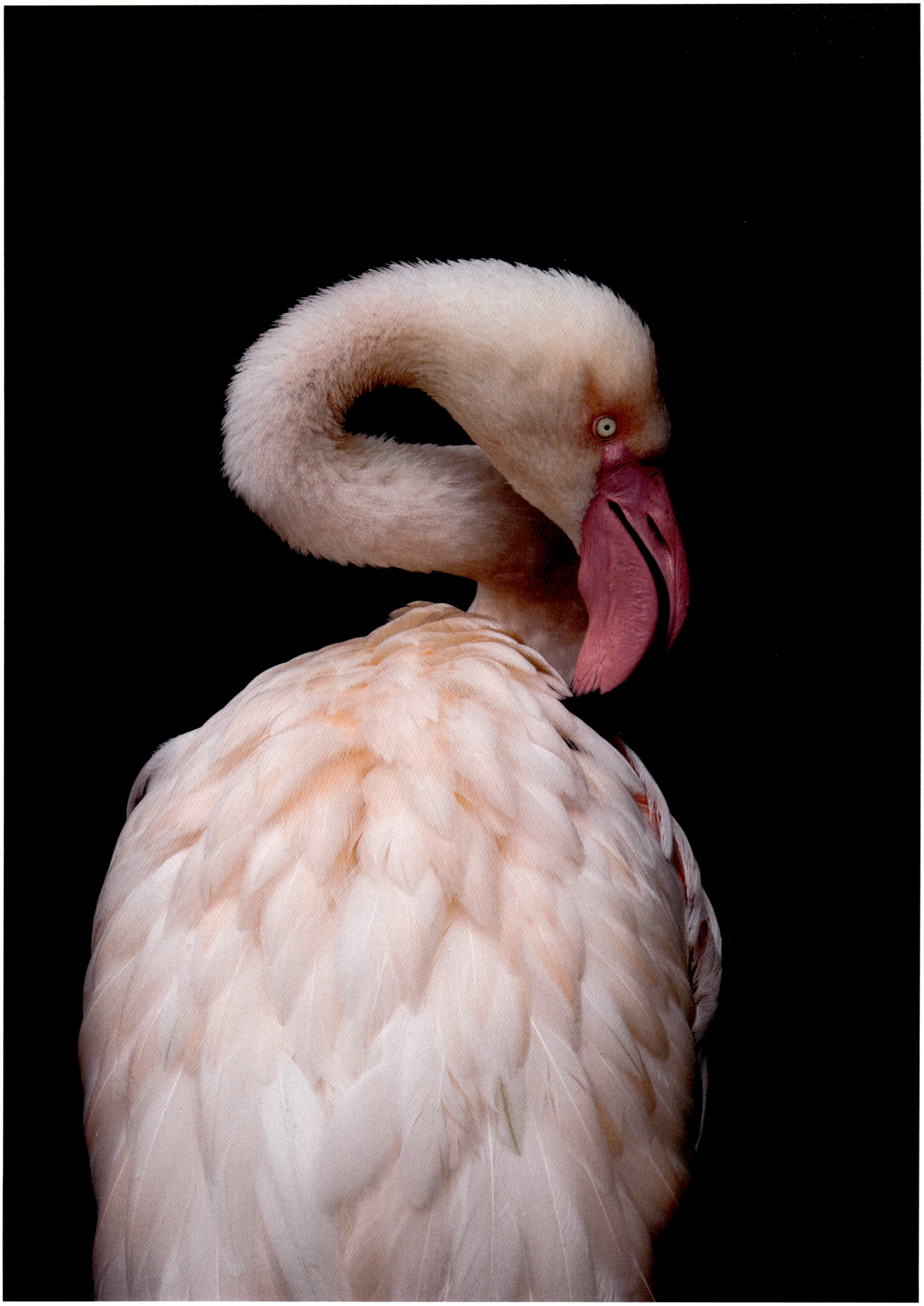

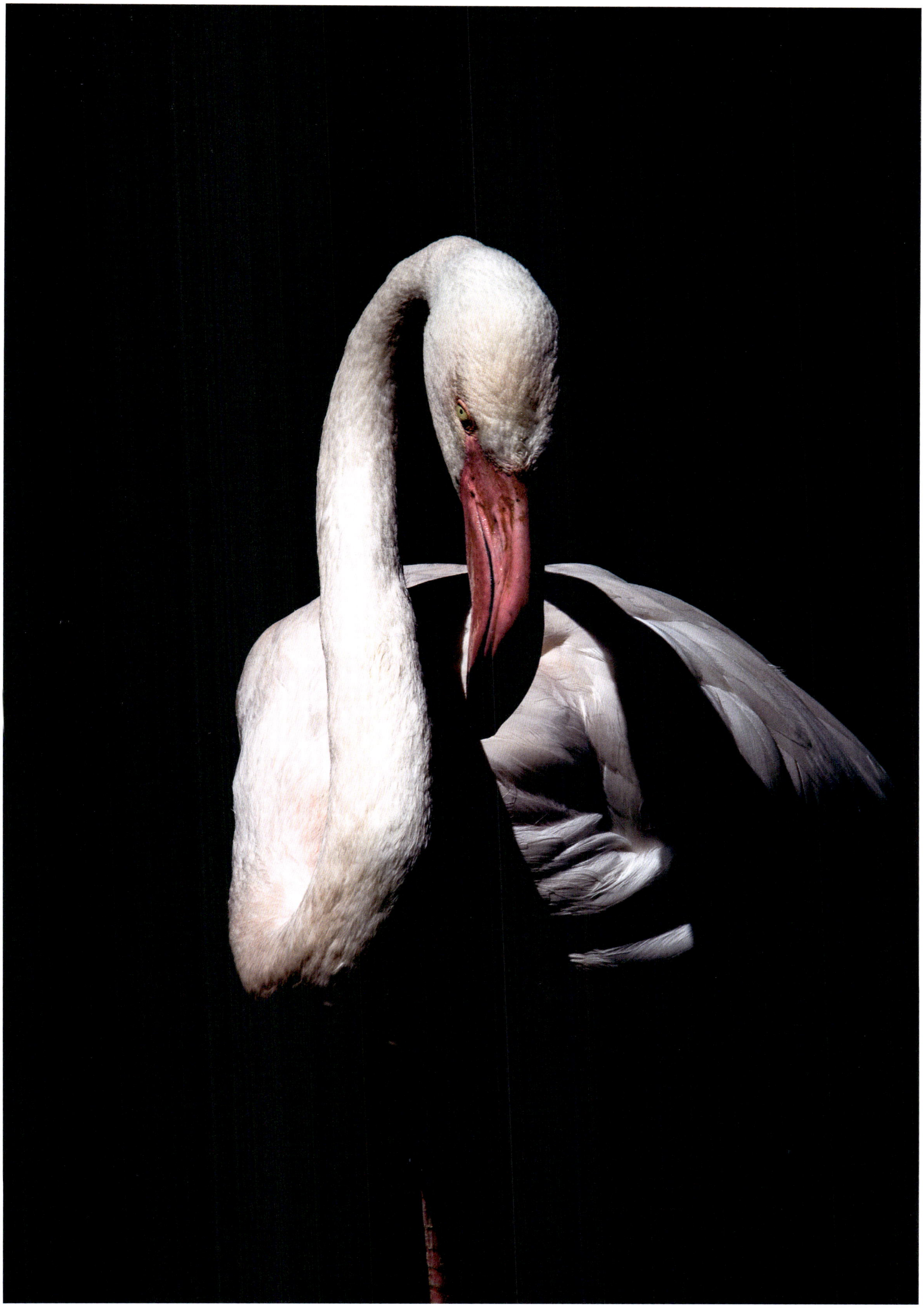

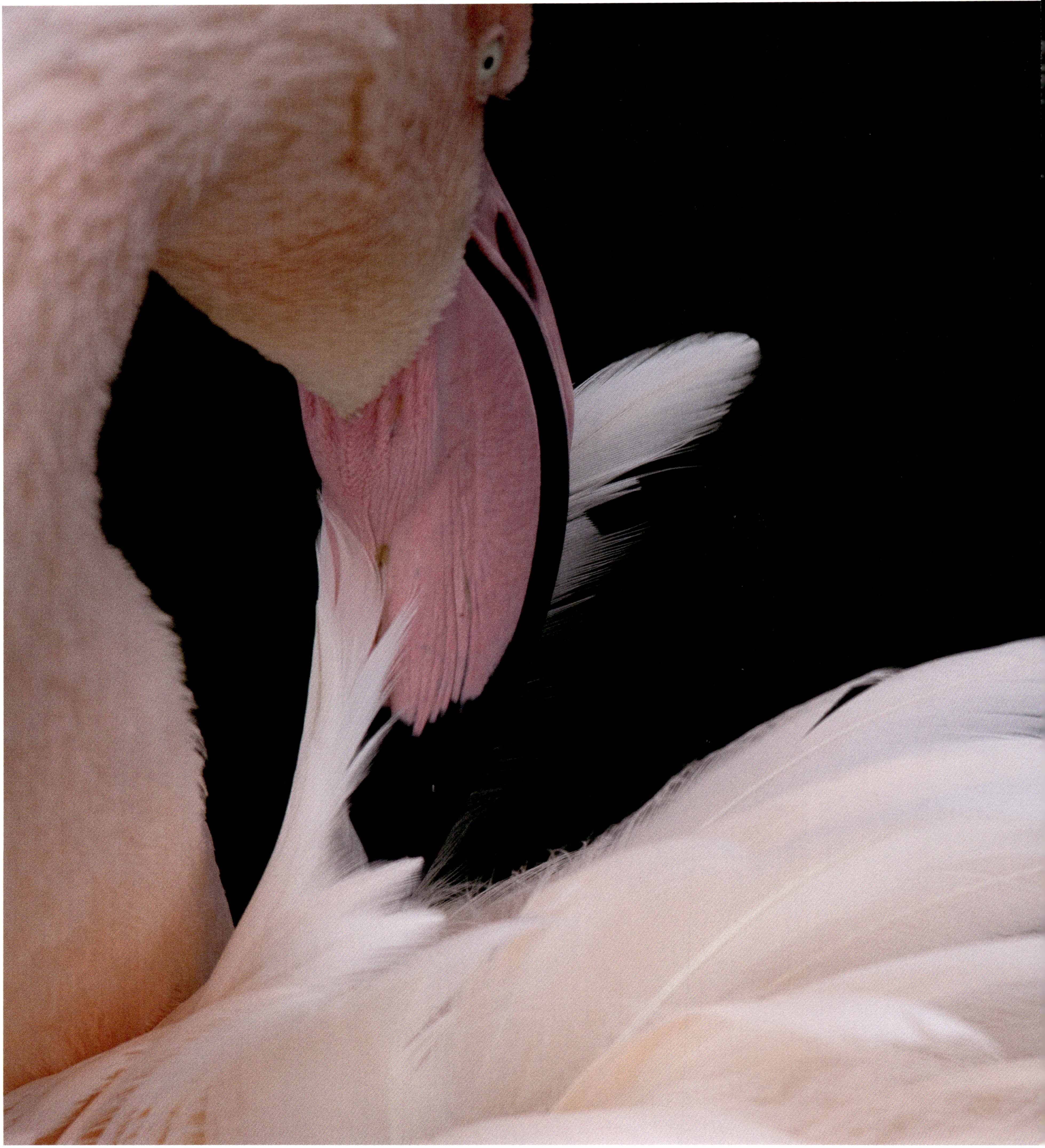

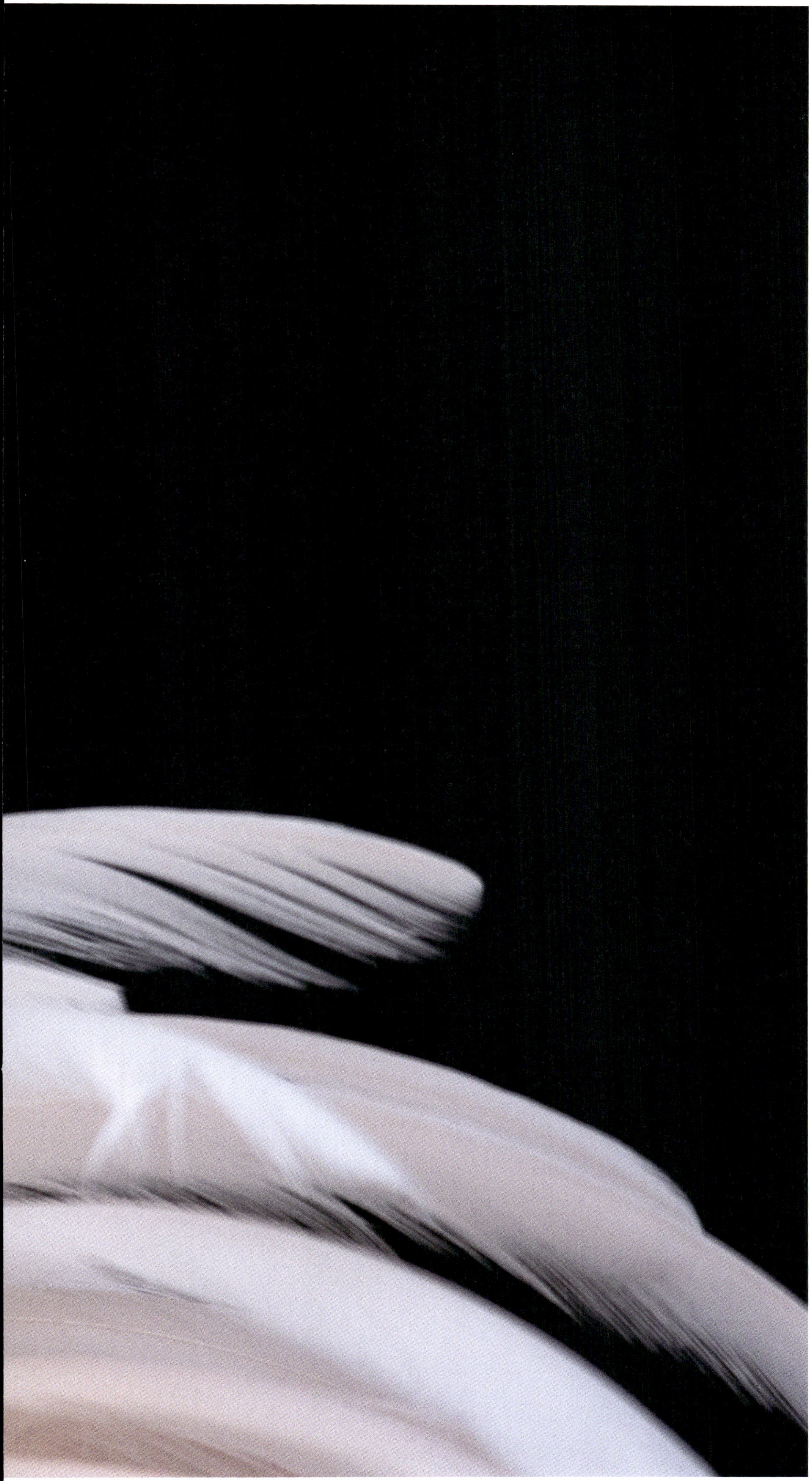

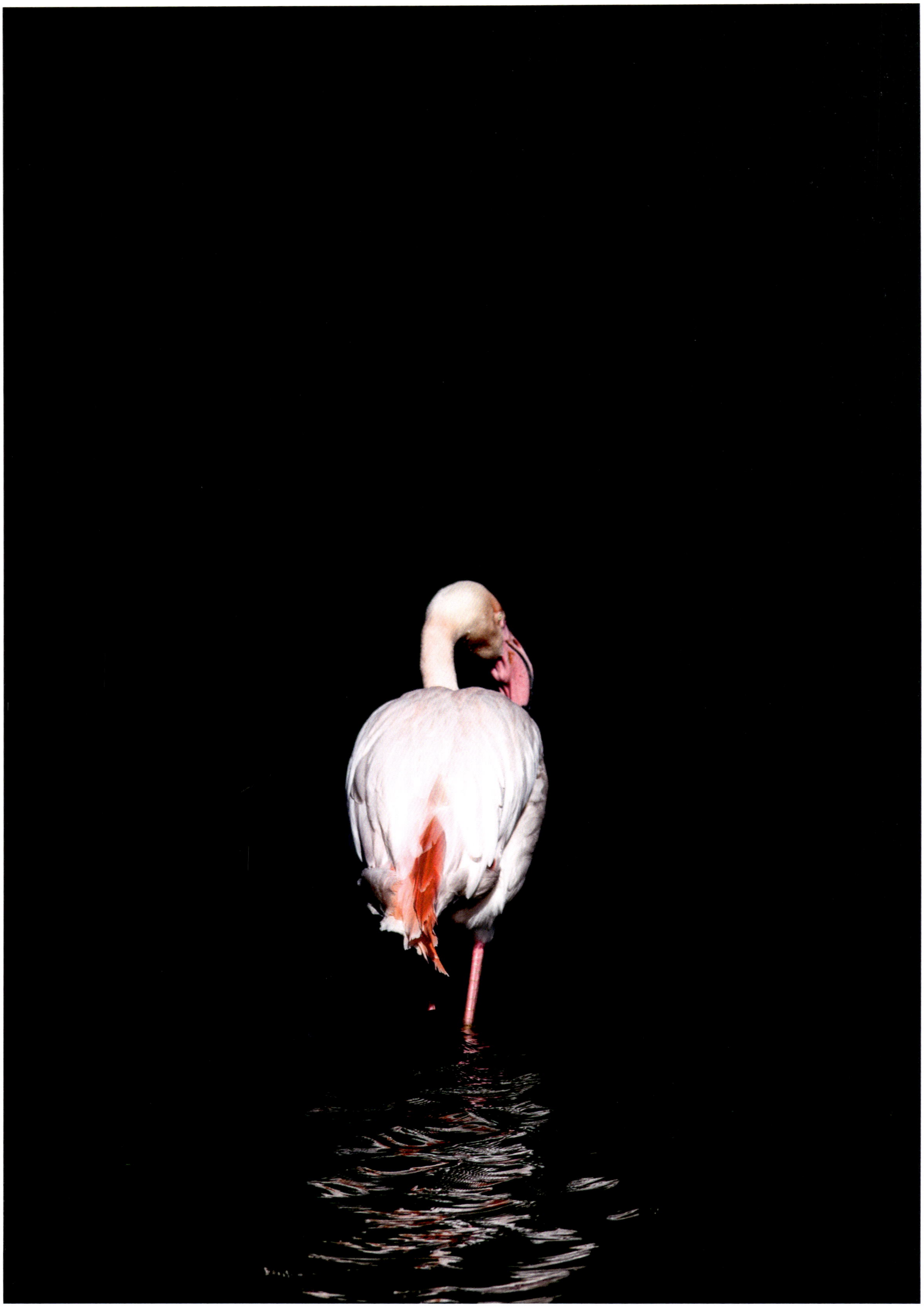

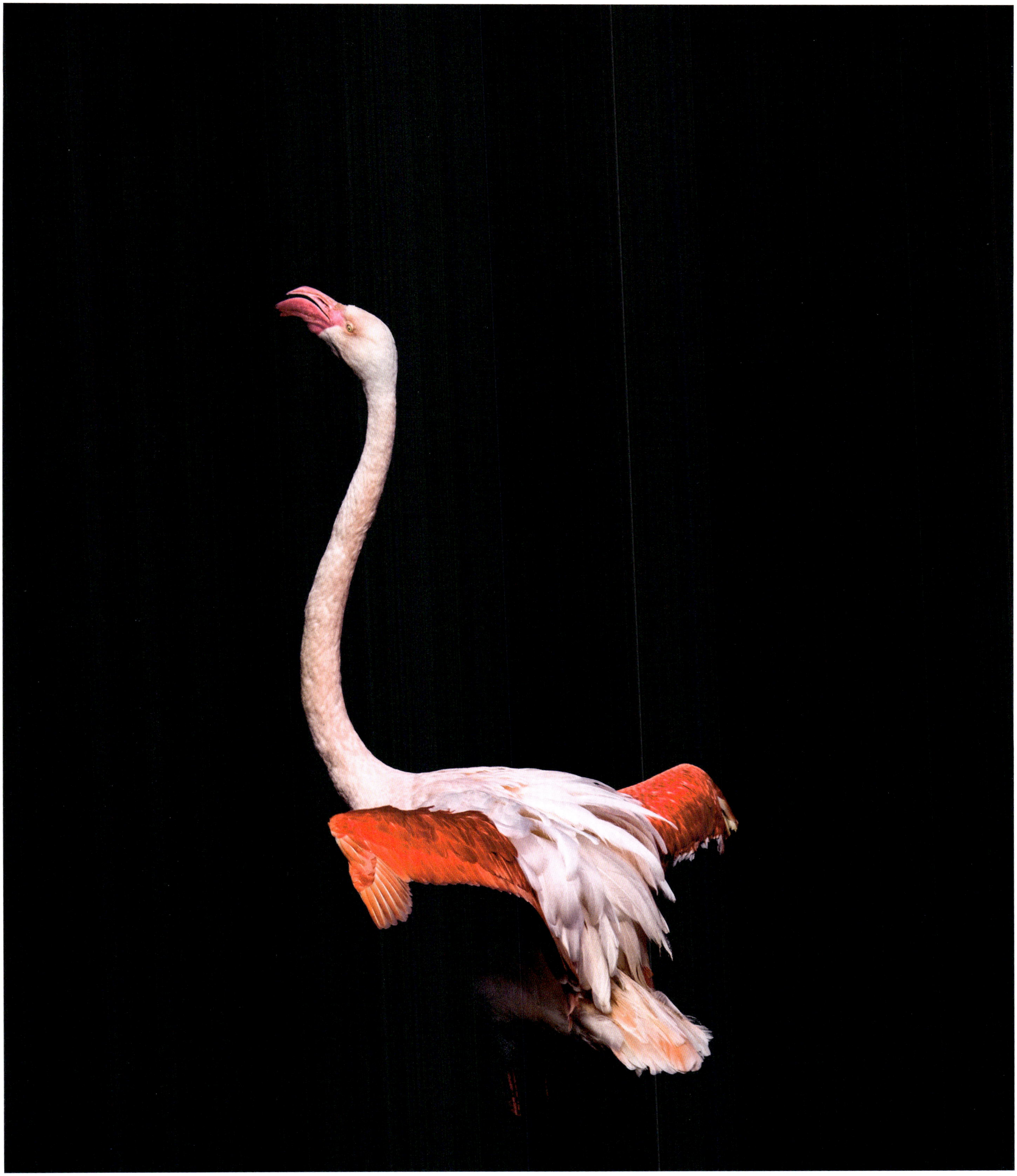

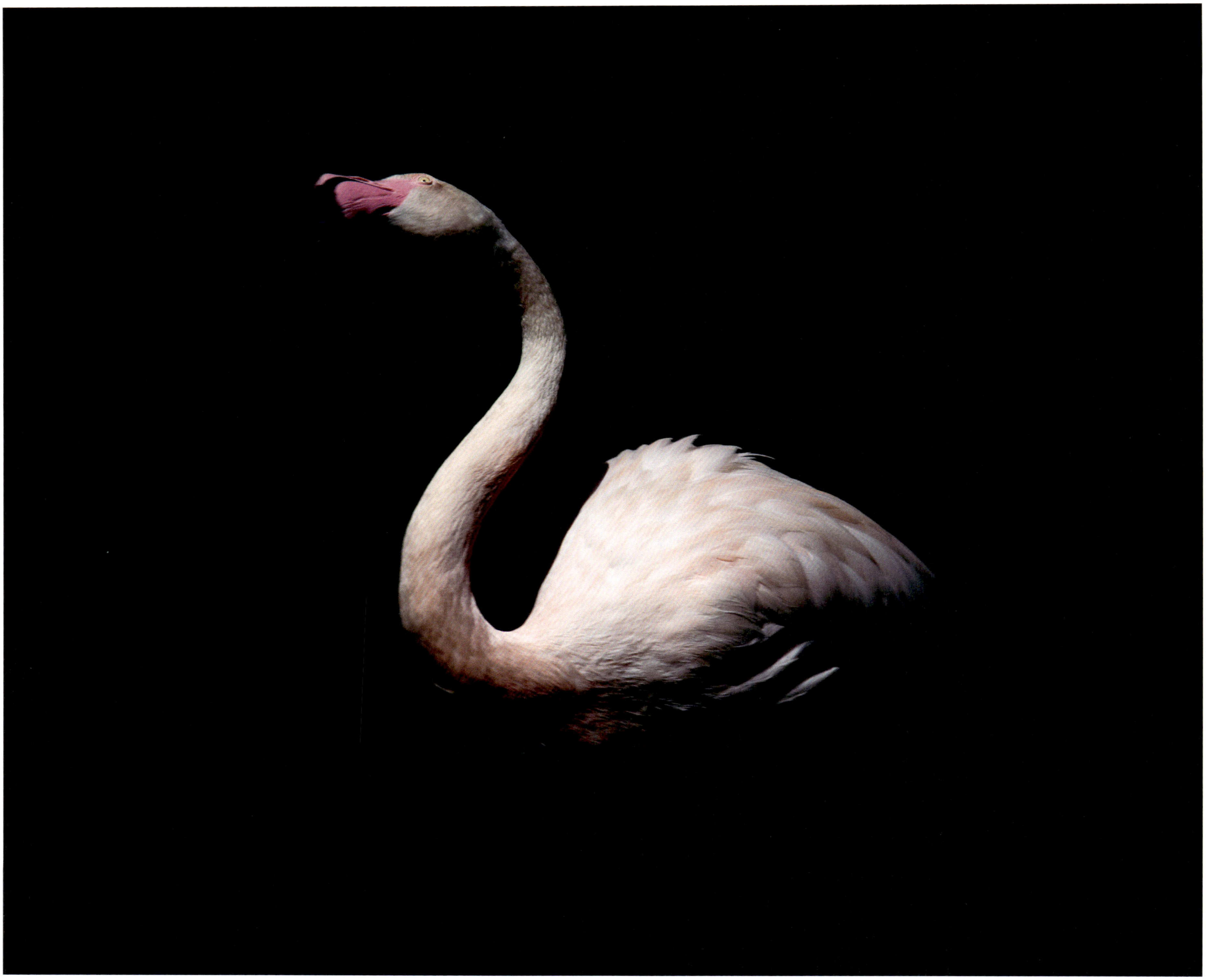

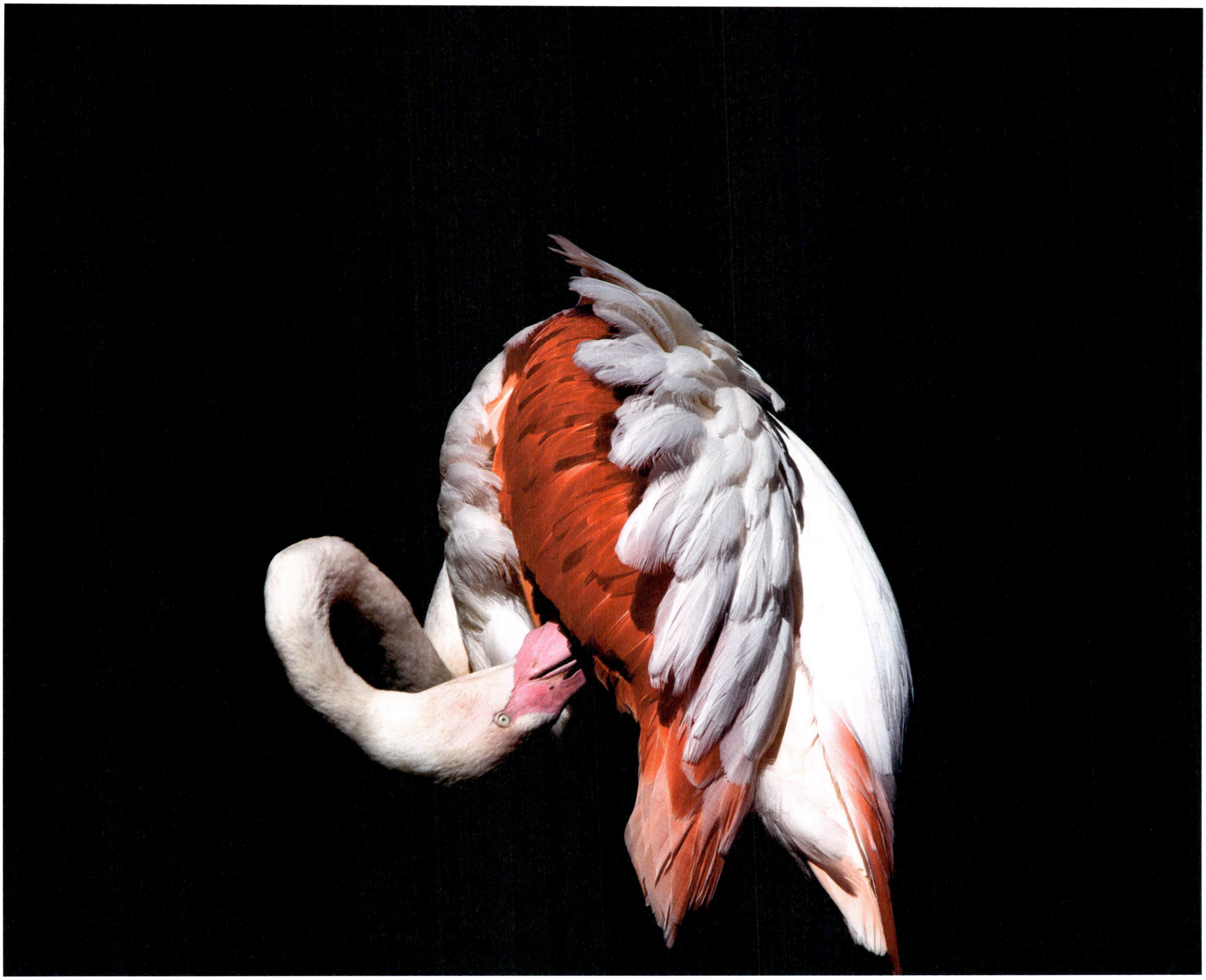

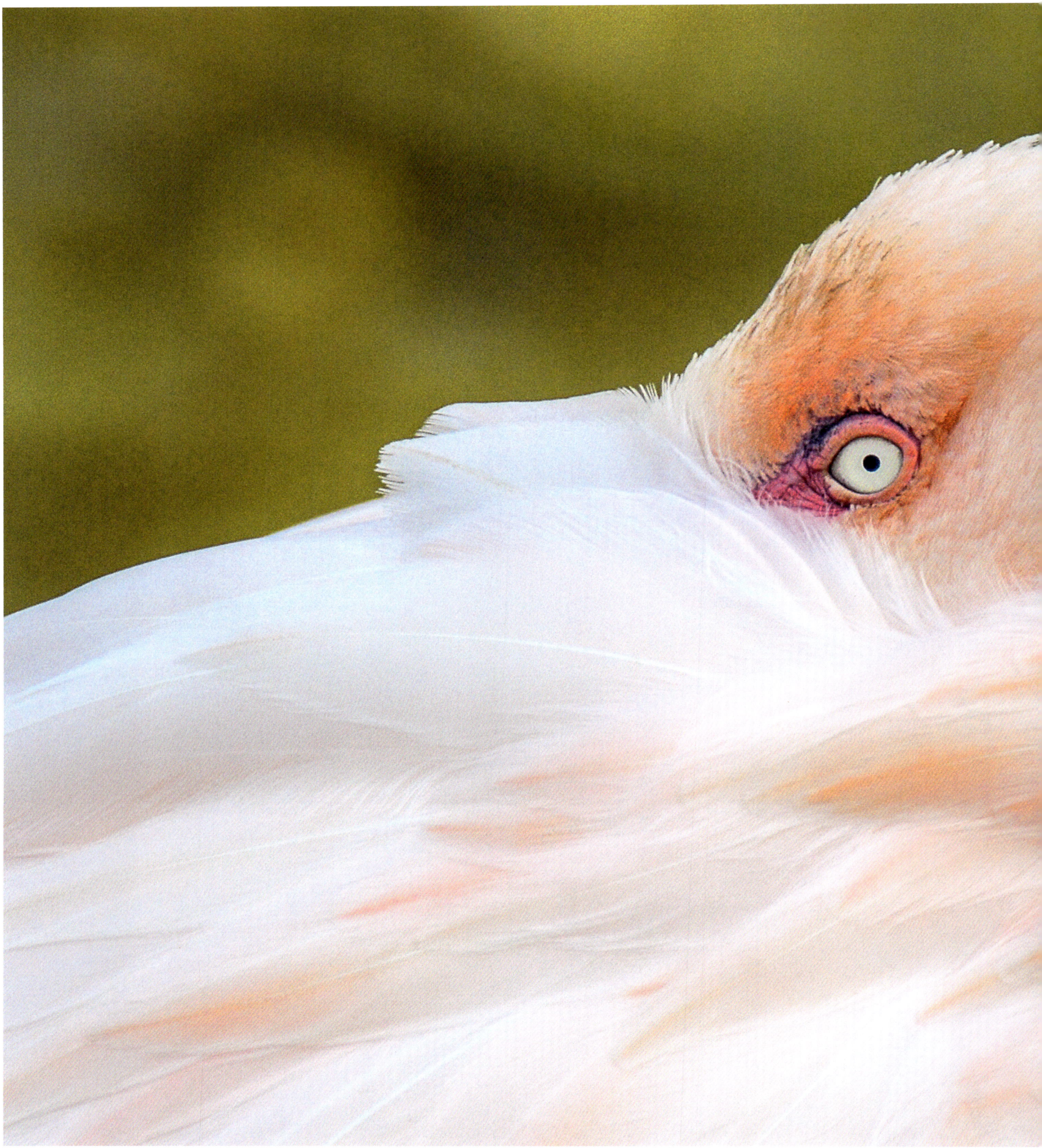

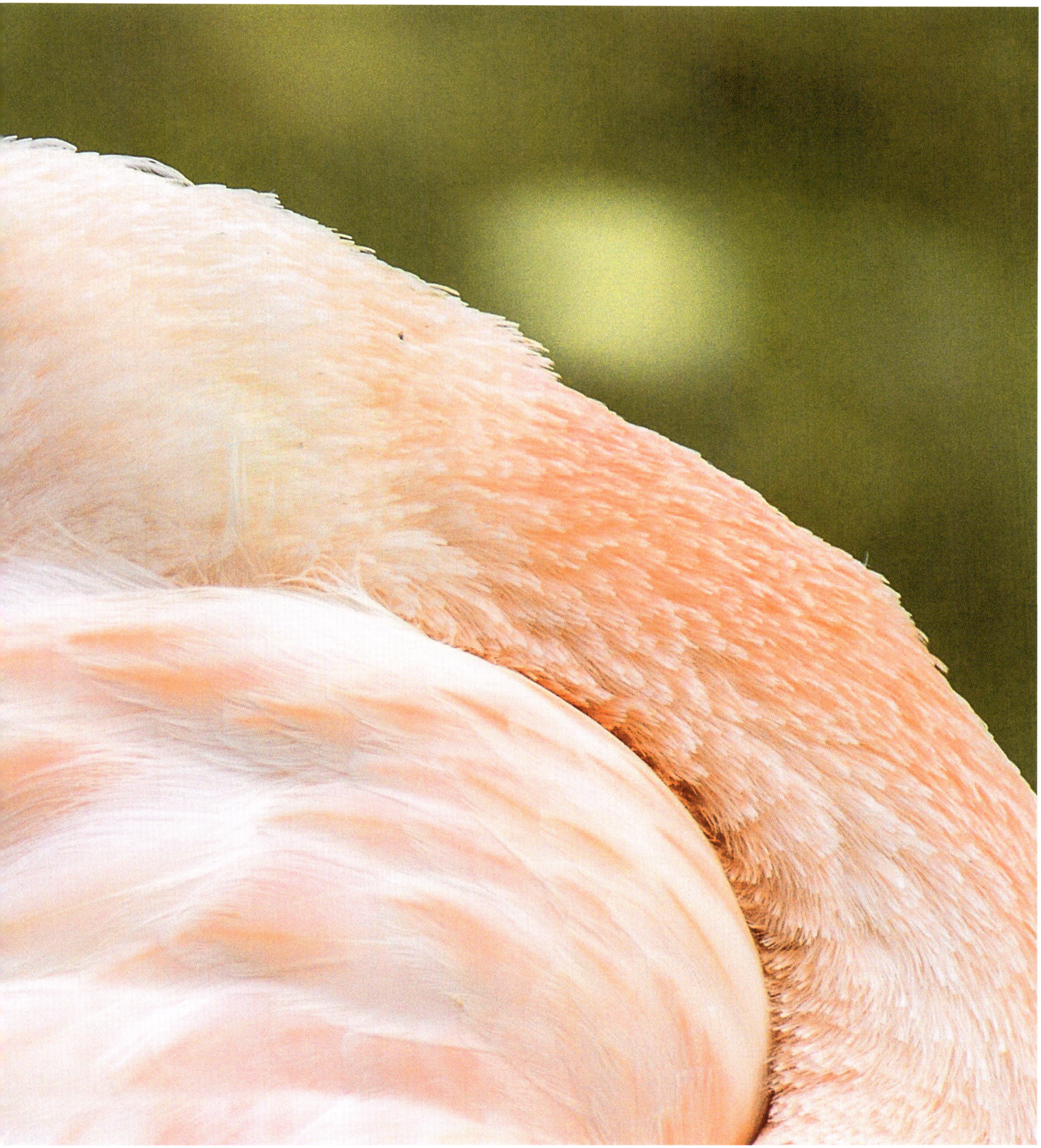

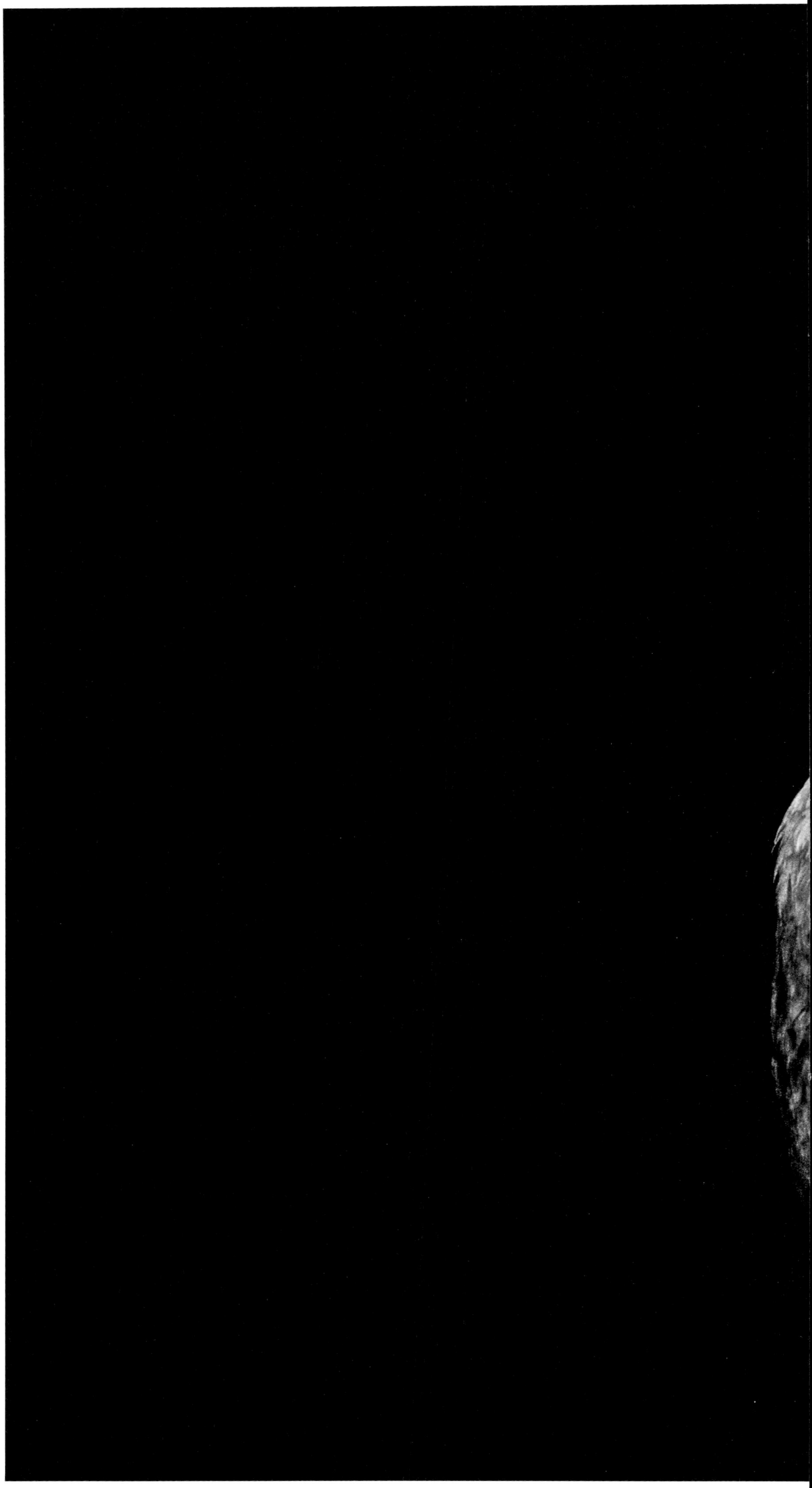

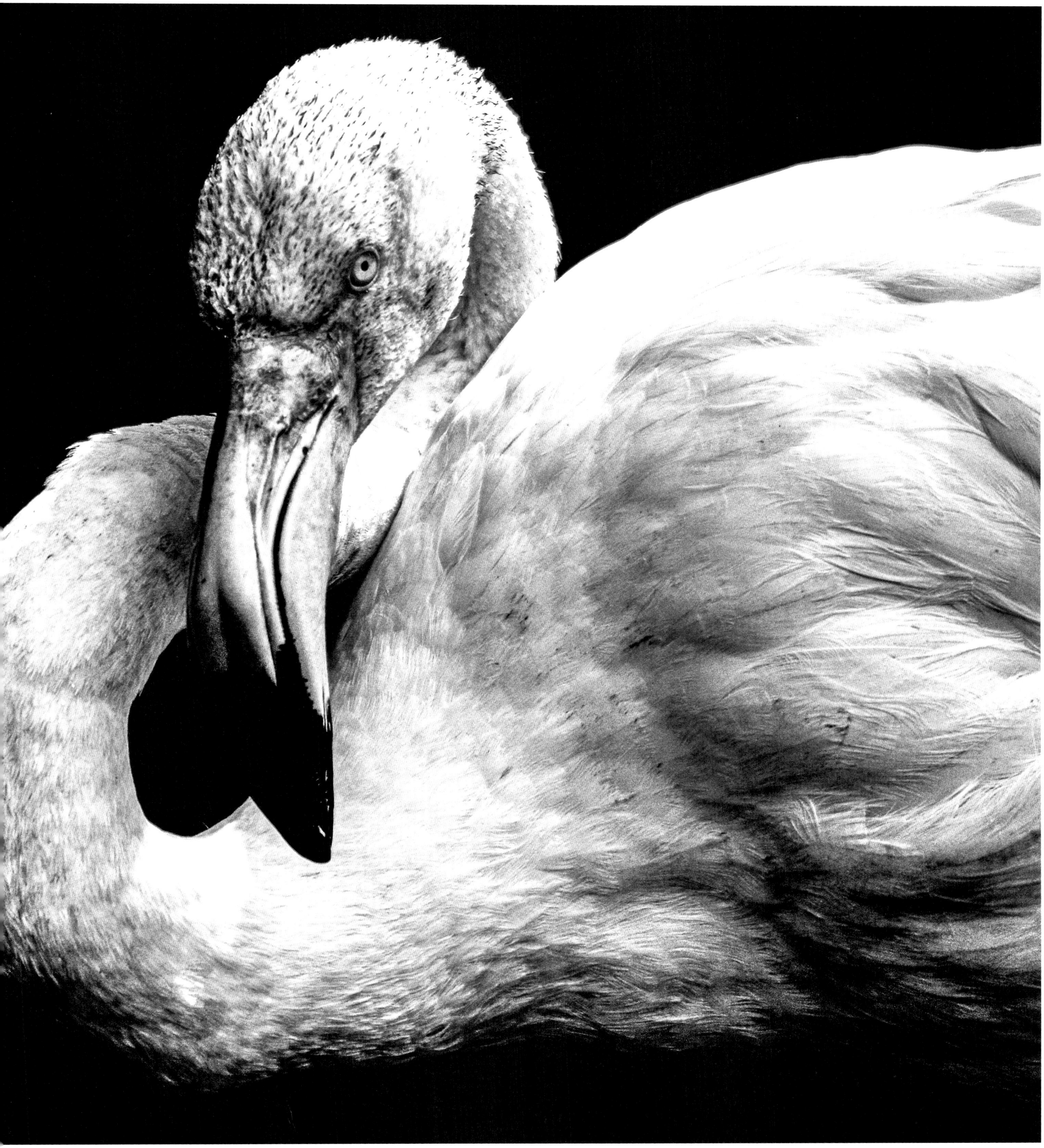

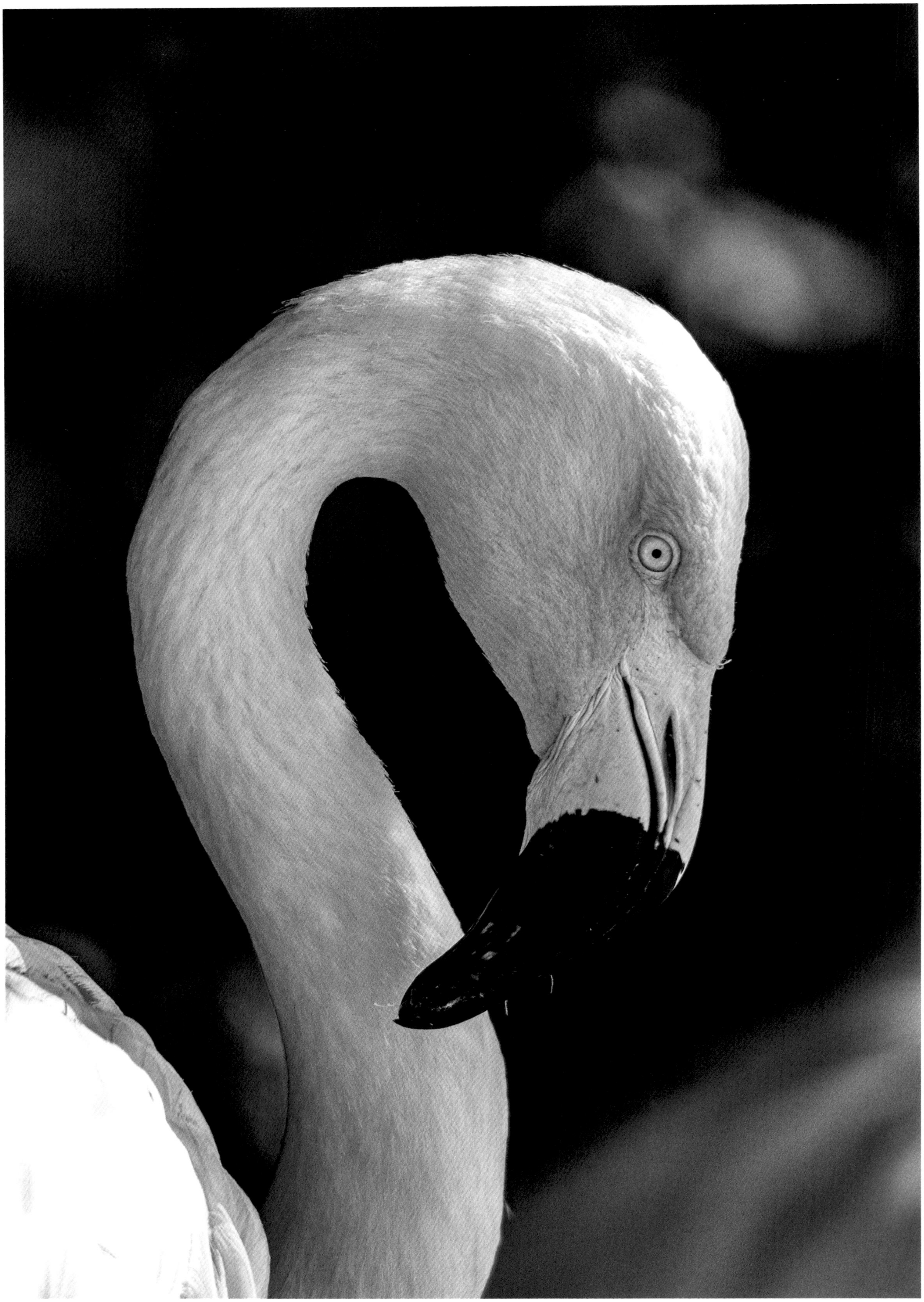

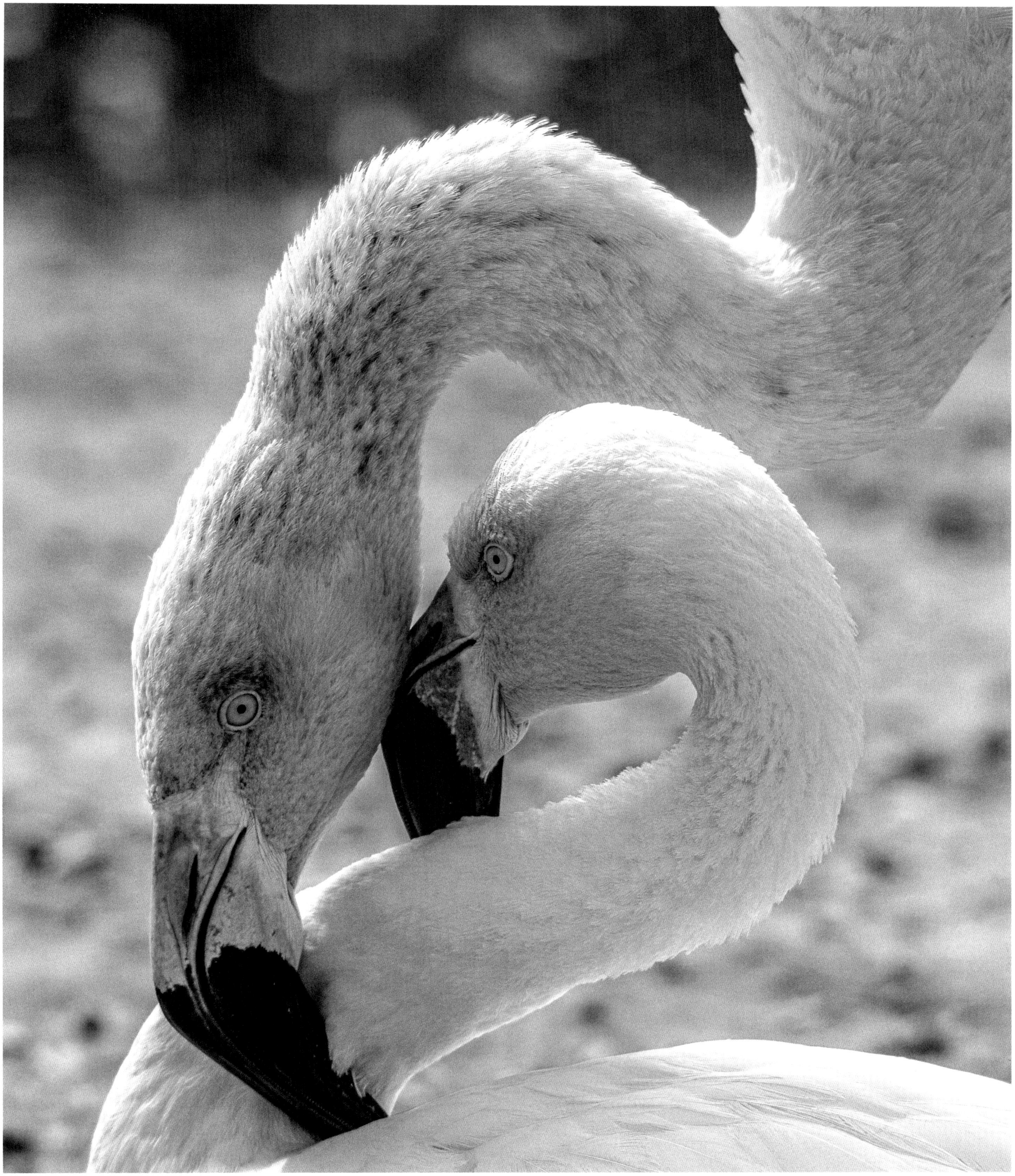

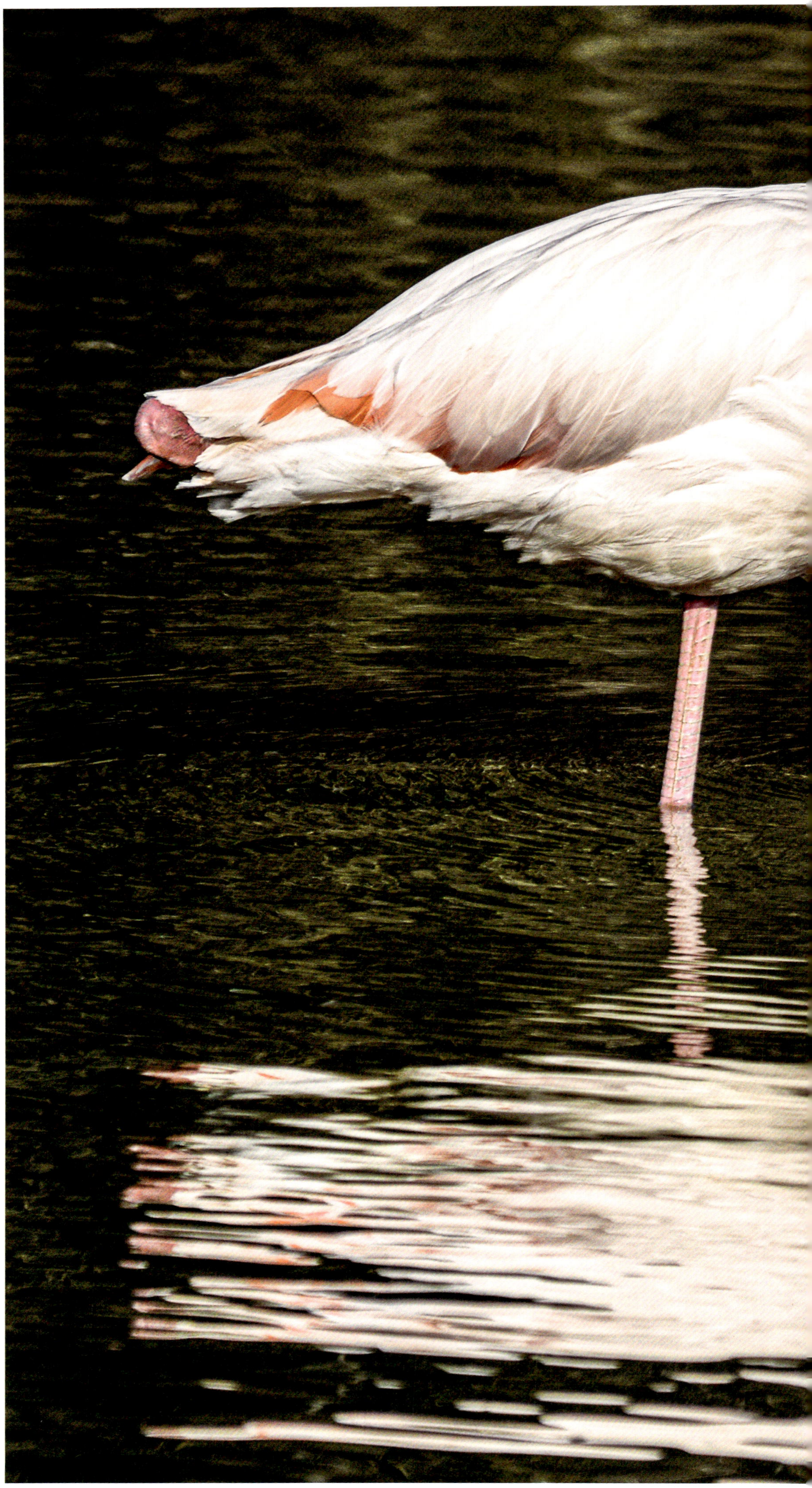

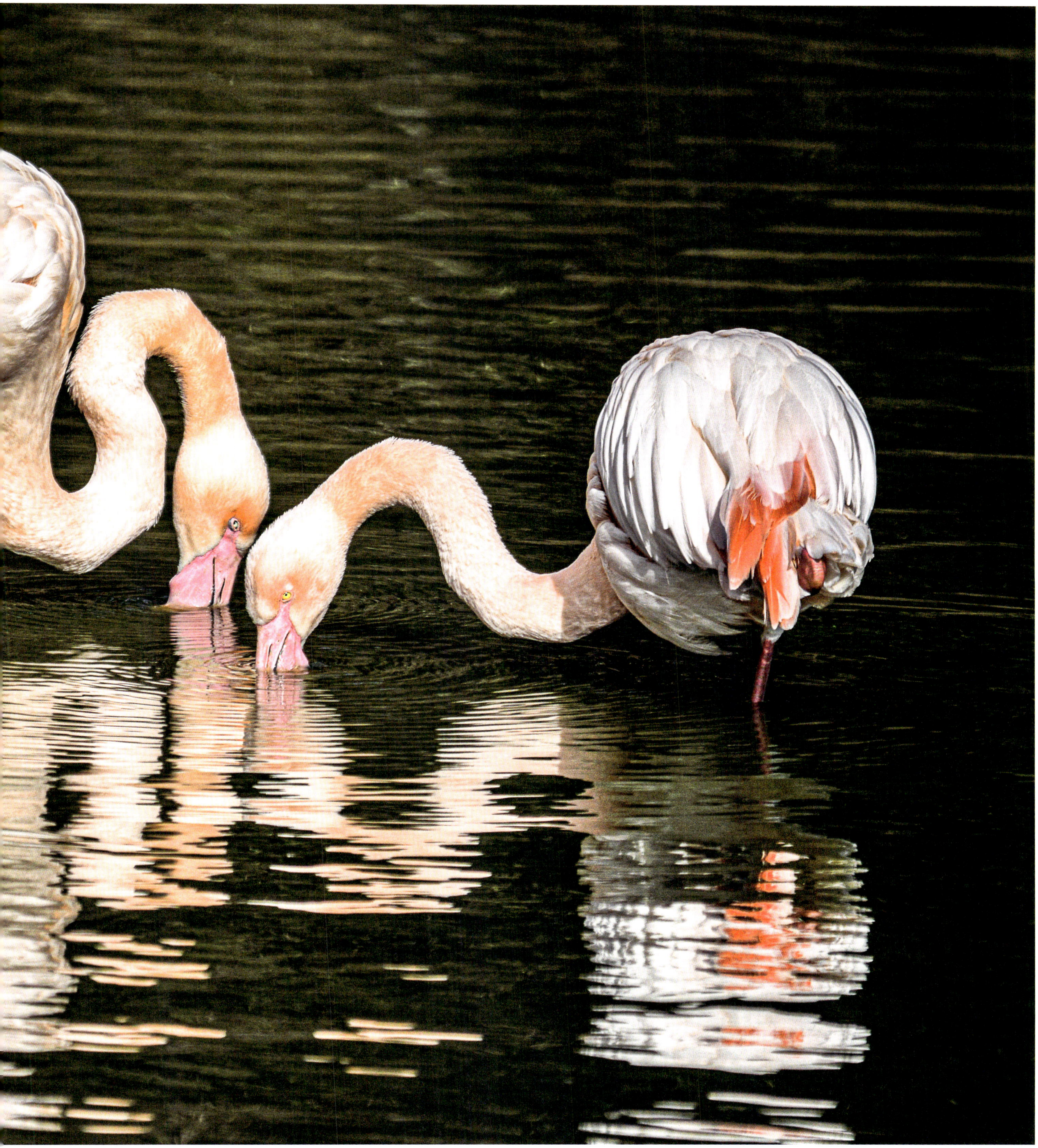

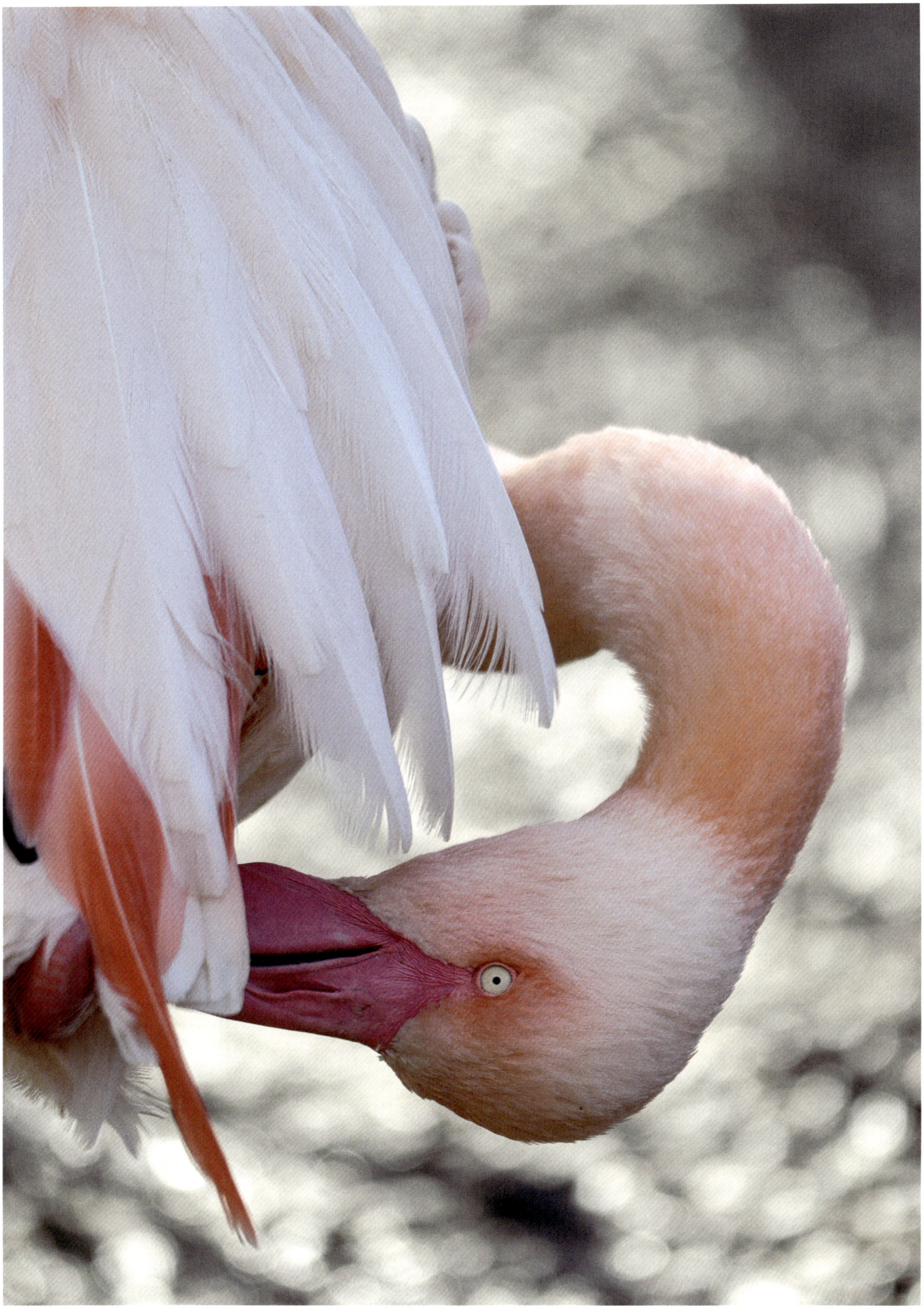

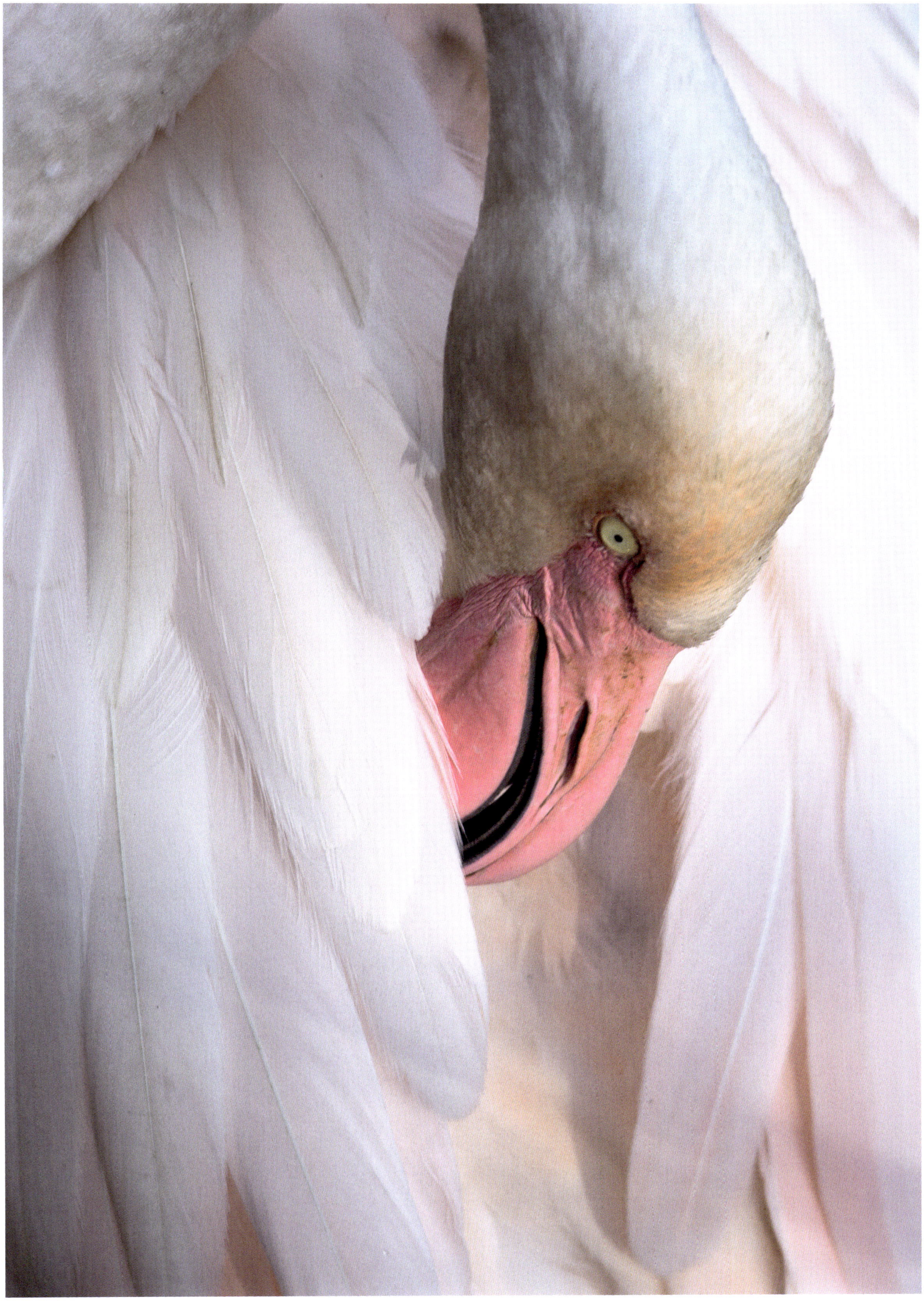

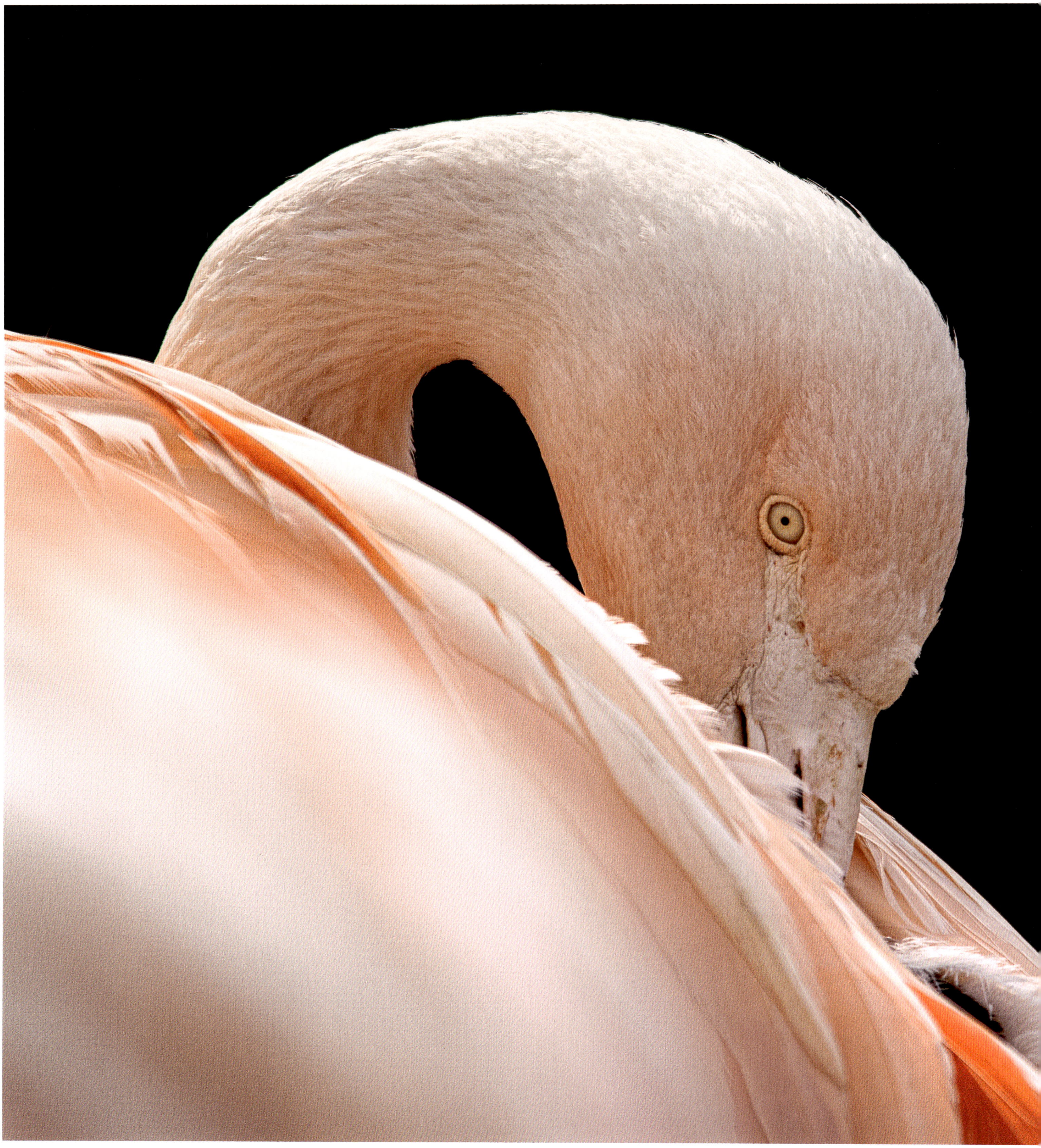

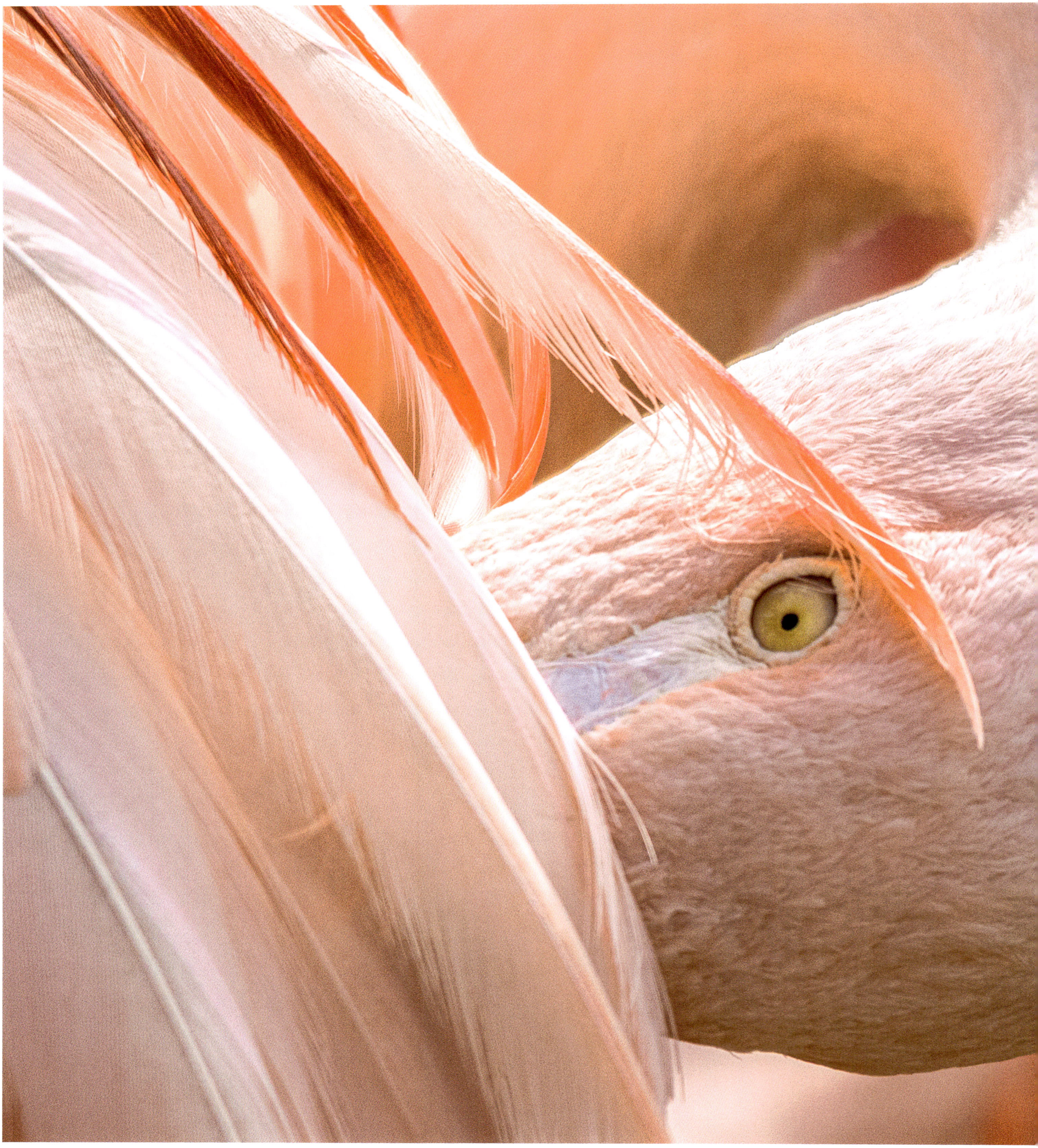

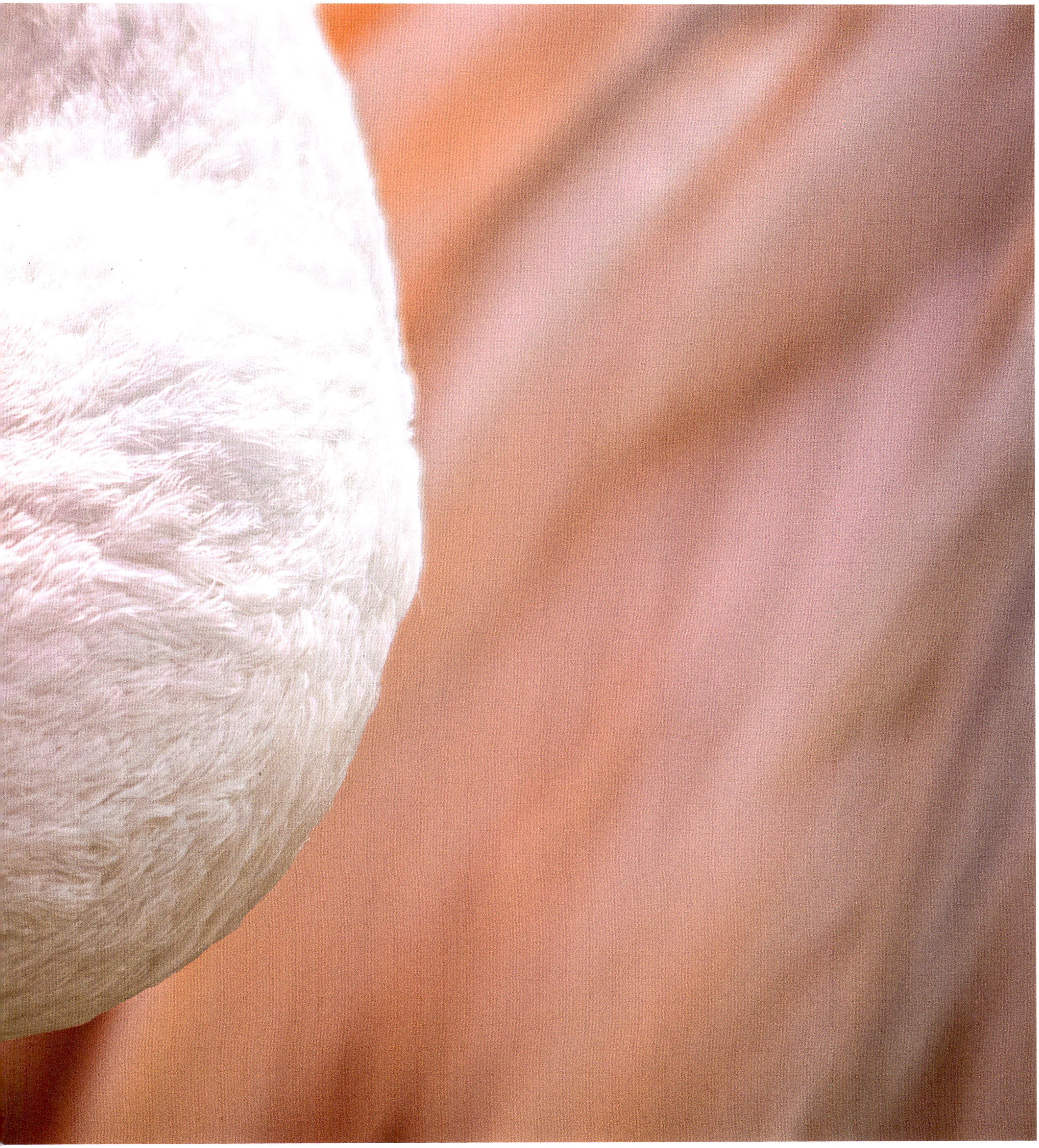

Alfie's Story

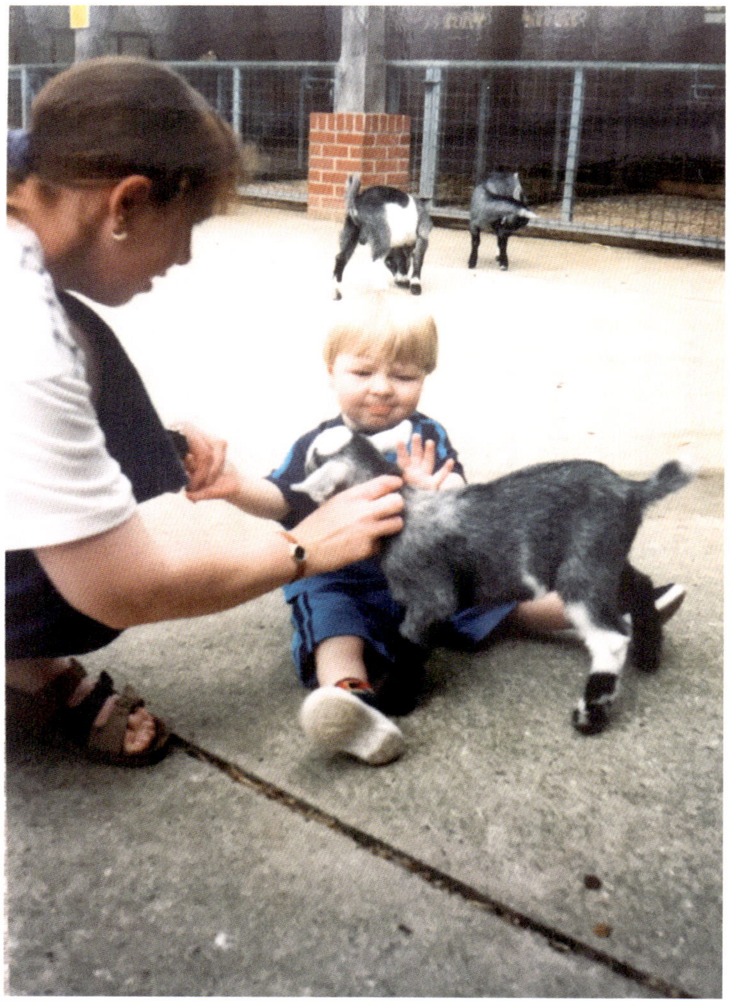

I was diagnosed with autism at an early age, after my mum had fought for years to get an accurate diagnosis so that I would get the best support throughout my life.

Education was always a tough experience for me, with many people judging me because of my lack of social skills or inability to 'fit in'. Primary school was possibly the easiest period in education because I hadn't yet realised that I was different from the majority of my peers. I went about my daily business and didn't really care about not talking to people; I was used to being in my own bubble with a wildlife magazine.

High school was like a kick in the teeth for me as it became abundantly clear that I didn't entirely fit in with the people that I was surrounded by. Getting laughed at for constantly reading about animals was a painful wake-up call and knowing that I was no longer accepted for exploring my passion was stressful. The high school I attended had a population of over 1,000 students, and I was placed in a form group of over 30 students – a scary prospect for a child who struggled to speak to one person, let alone 30.

I dreaded class time each and every day. I would spend the entire duration sitting at my desk, watching the clock hung on the wall in front of me, praying that it would soon strike three o'clock so that I could escape and return home to my wildlife magazines. I will always remember that class; it felt as though everyone around me was speaking a foreign language that I could not understand. I did not fit in at all. Every lesson was with those same 30 students, every minute of every day was with them . . . and not even one ever bothered to say hello.

It was during this time that I watched and tried to listen to what the majority of those around me were discussing – cars, motorbikes, celebrities, dating – and then there was little me, only interested in wildlife. But I'd had enough of feeling alone and clock-watching, so I tried to develop an artificial interest in the more 'normal' topics of discussion amongst teenagers. I forced myself to research these topics, that were really of no interest to me, just so that I could attempt to chat with the others . . . although this ultimately failed, and I was still shunned from their discussions.

This alienation led to severe mental health issues, resulting in several suicide attempts and a refusal to leave my bedroom for a period of time.

I left that school a broken person. I had given up on everything and had become very short-tempered and foul-mouthed – characteristics I hated, but struggled to control because deep down I knew for the first time that I didn't – and wouldn't ever – fit in. My social skills were non-existent and I couldn't be in a busy room without feeling dizzy.

Following months of hard work and numerous legal battles from my mother, I finally joined a private special educational needs school in the heart of the English countryside. I joined Centre

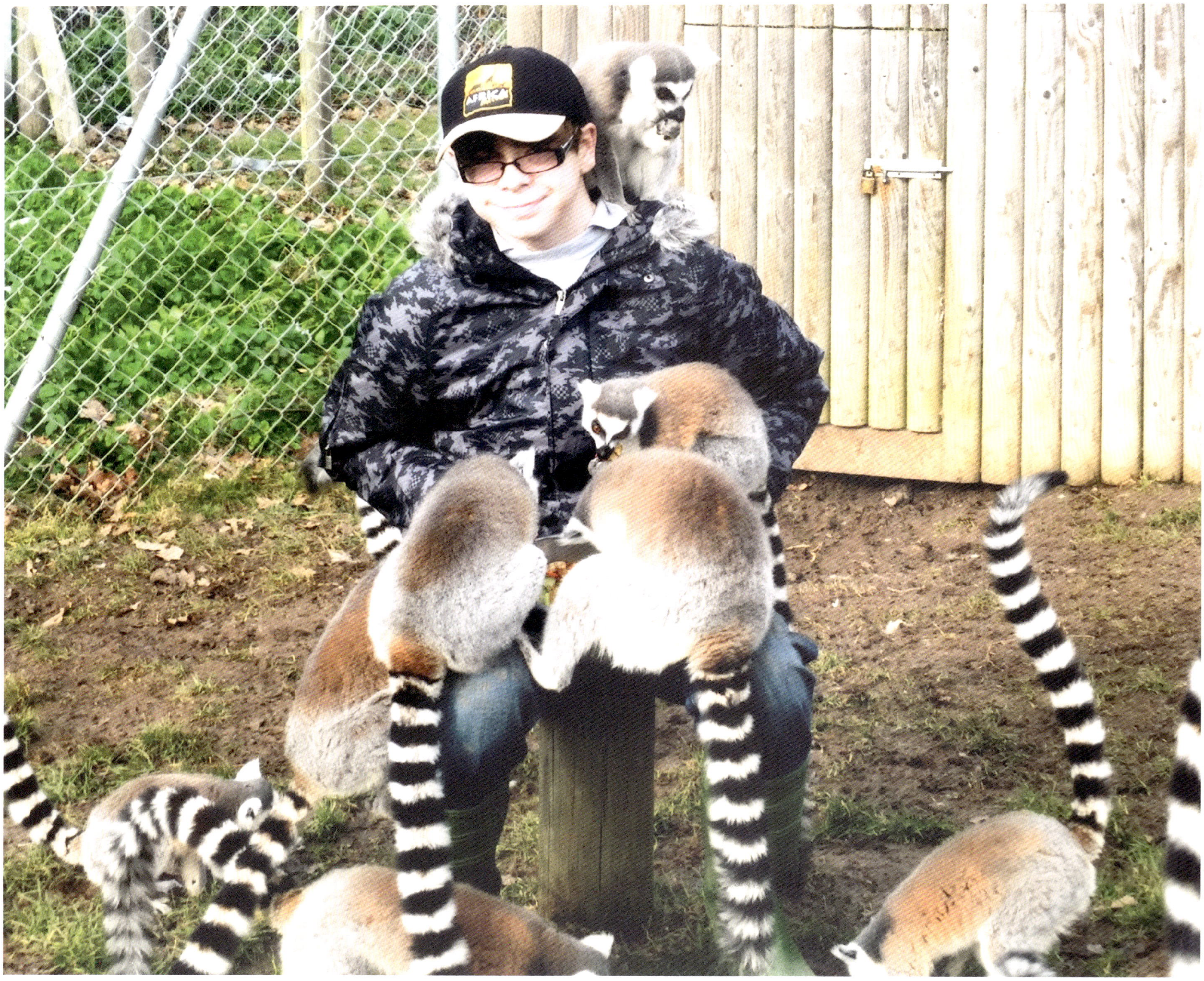

Academy East Anglia (CAEA) as a shy and broken person. I spent the first year getting by, getting used to the massive change, and spending a lot of time in my own silent company, for that was what I was used to doing. At my previous school, I had been told that I would never be able to take GCSEs, but in my first year at CAEA, I successfully sat six GCSEs. CAEA slowly breathed a renewed degree of confidence into me, and I began boarding away from home for the first time in my life – an experience that moulded me into the man I am today.

In my second year at the school, I took a scary step: I began the American High School Diploma. I remember sitting in the principal's office shaking at the prospect, before saying, "I can't do that." He responded confidently, stating, "Yes you can, Alfie." I reluctantly began the course.

Three years later I graduated from the school with A and B grades in American Literature, American History, Environmental Science, Current Affairs, Quantitative Mathematics, Media Studies and Advanced Writing; I was also Head Student, Head of the Student Council and President of the Eco Council. I owe so much to Centre Academy East Anglia and the passion invested by every single staff member. Without them, I am not sure where my life would have taken me.

They further fuelled my love of photography, and I haven't looked back since. The school also gave me the confidence to apply for university to study a degree in Photography and, following numerous nerve-wracking interviews, I received five unconditional offers. I decided to attend a university in London. I managed just three weeks before suffering from psychosis. This was probably the scariest period of my life; it felt as though one side of my brain was constantly fighting with the other and I was unable to establish if my surroundings were real.

Leaving university was heart-breaking, but turned out to be a blessing in disguise as it allowed me to invest my time in carving a career as a fine art photographer. I am now a globally-renowned fine art photographer, signed with Castle Fine Art – something I still struggle to believe!

Many people have suggested that it is extremely brave and slightly bonkers to release such a revealing essay in what is a very judgemental and often cruel world; but change does not happen by sitting back, it happens when we stand up and educate.

Afterword

by Dr. Duncan Rollo

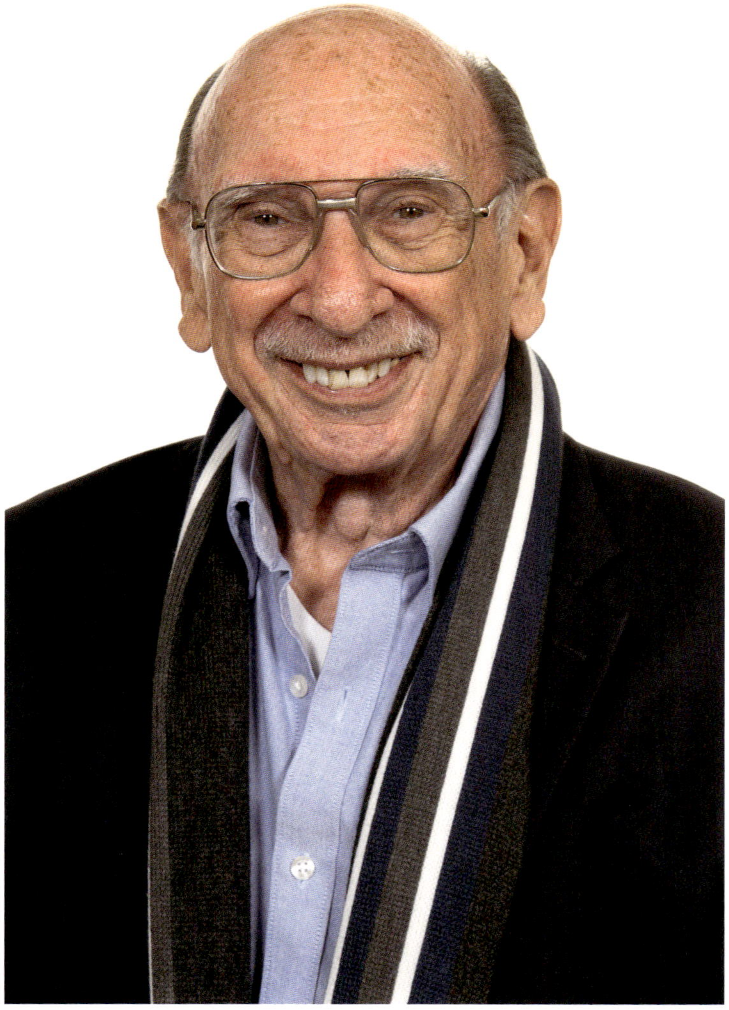

I suspect that every educator seeks that special student, the one who, through his own genius, validates all that education stands for, all that education can be. For most, it's an exercise in futility. But not for all.

Alfie Bowen came into my life large. Only 15, he was already well over six feet tall – probably more, but it was hard to tell because he would only look down. That posture was emblematic of Alfie's world, one in which the educational establishment had let him down. He was told that he couldn't take the regular exams, that his crippling anxiety was such that education for him had to be kept simple. Thus, he spent years attending school part-time, with other students who "didn't fit in". What, the Head of my school asked, had he learned. "I learned to tell time. I learned to tell time again and again. That was all I learned: to tell time."

Had any educator taken just a few minutes to talk with Alfie, they would have discerned his intelligence. But there were no takers. So he arrived at my school, a special school for bright kids with learning challenges. Eyes down, he said he wanted to try the exams. Within a year, he succeeded. Then he tried our most advanced Diploma. He excelled. He could write, he could analyse, his insights bordered on the profound, his kindness to other students belied what had previously happened to him.

Alfie became our School Captain, the first in our history. He was elected as Head of the Student Council. He gained admission, unconditionally, to five universities. He could have read English. He could have read History. But Alfie envisioned something else: Photography. During his too few years with us, he spent virtually all his weekends and holidays photographing wildlife at various zoos. My colleagues and I were staggered at the results. We were not alone, as word of his genius was getting around. When you open this book, you'll see.

In a sense, Alfie Bowen's life has been all about vision. A youngster who, despite all odds, saw himself as others failed to see him. A young photographer whose thousands of images are now emblematic of his genius. A young man whose craft is a *paeon* to the indomitable human spirit. Perhaps Henry David Thoreau, the 19th-century American philosopher, best captures what Alfie Bowen is all about: "The question is not what you look at," Thoreau noted, "but what you see."

Alfie is now the young professional. He looks through lenses. He sees elements of life that most of us miss. He no longer looks down. And rightly, he is very busy. He is in demand.

Good thing he has learned to tell the time.

Dr. Duncan Rollo
Principal and CEO, The Centre Academy Schools

Acknowledgements

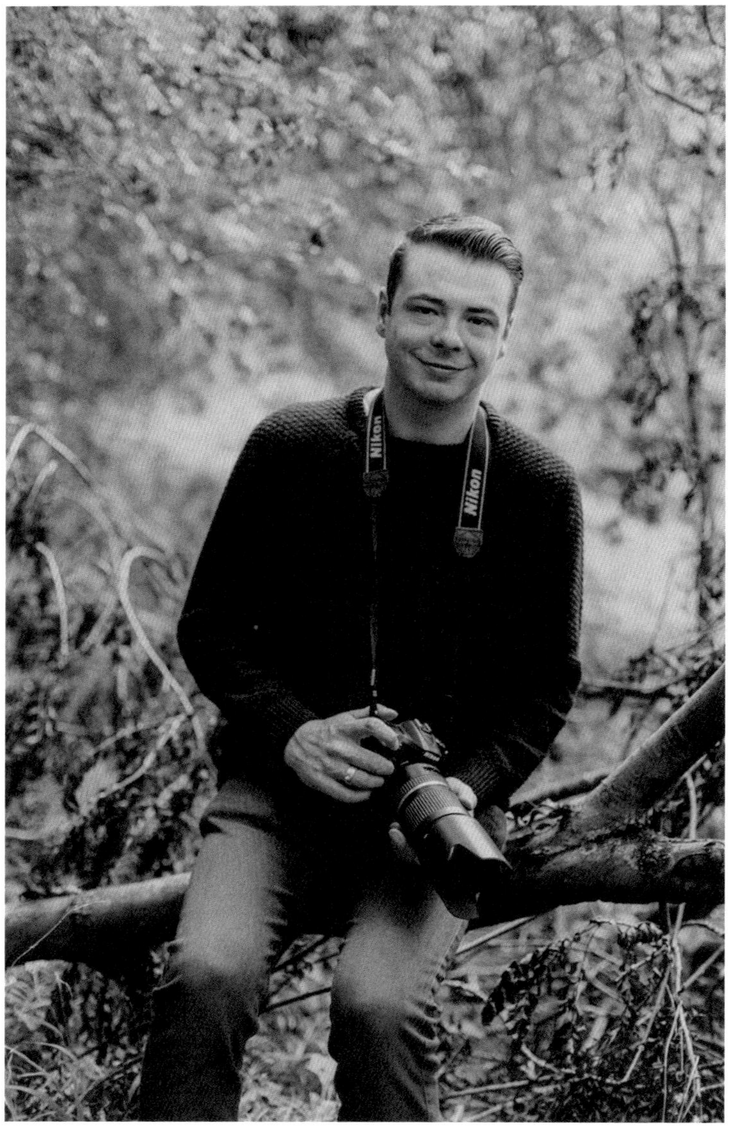

There is no climactic ending to this book, just a simple message. My message is one of immense gratitude, not just to those who helped in the making of this book but also to those who, most importantly, shaped and continue to shape the person behind this book.

I will use the last few pages of this book to personally thank as many of those who have played a significant role in my twenty-two years of life as space permits, but first, a short message that I hope will trigger some serious thought and reflection.

Life can be tough for all of us, but it is even tougher for those of us who live with a disability daily. I have spent many hours being bullied and, consequently, considering and attempting to end my life. No one should have to suffer for being themselves; all anyone wants is to feel accepted and valued, not bullied and worthless. I will continue to fight for those without a voice until everyone is treated with the same level of respect and I hope that this shows what can be achieved when we make someone feel valued.

Contributors

I should begin my acknowledgements by thanking those that have kindly penned contributions to this book.

Firstly, Dr Duncan Rollo of Centre Academy East Anglia. When considering whose shoulders to place the responsibility of penning some words for this book, I quickly came to a decision. Dr Duncan Rollo is a highly-respected university professor, teacher, author and special educational needs expert whom I have known closely for several years. Thank you for your very flattering words.

I have long admired the genius of Chris Packham, the autistic naturalist, TV presenter, author and photographer. Society lacks role models for those with disabilities, there are very few, but Chris Packham is a fine example and made growing up with autism a little less lonely for me. I never imagined that Chris would one day contribute to my book — that was the stuff of dreams until my recent appointment as a judge for Young Bird Photographer Of The Year opened some doors. I am extremely proud to share the pages of my debut book with this legendary autistic broadcaster and honoured to call Chris a friend.

Family

I want to pay tribute to my mother. I was by no means an easy child, but you always stuck by me, fought for me and showed me that not every human is a bully. I often think of you as a soldier, not because I would want you to risk your life for country or crown, but because you fought with resilience and determination until you got the very best for your children. A hero, a beautiful human being and my mother, this is for you. Thank you.

Amie, my solider-like sister. I still remember the first time I held you some eighteen years ago and I have been full of pride ever since. You have fought your battles with anxiety, bullying, depression and autism head-on and I am so proud to call you my sister.

Two key and consistent figures in my life have been my grandparents, Ann and Phil. Thank you Grandma and Grandad for being my rocks, always inspiring me to be a better version of myself, to fight my anxiety and most importantly, to follow my dreams.

School

School was a difficult experience until, thanks to my mum, I moved to Centre Academy East Anglia. I credit this small, friendly private special school in the heart of the East Anglian countryside with my transformation into the young man I am today. I joined as a broken person but this school and its amazing staff spent many hours putting those broken pieces back together, filling me with self-belief and supporting my dreams of becoming a photographer from day one.

Thank you to Dr Duncan Rollo and Mrs Kim Salthouse for their unwavering support throughout my time at the school and, indeed, since my departure. Centre Academy East Anglia is a credit to your hard work, dedication and determination to transform those neglected by the mainstream education system into strong and successful people. As my dreams turn into reality, I am aware that none of this would be possible without your wonderful school.

I also want to pay tribute to Mr Daniel Stott, and, indeed, all of the wonderful staff at Centre Academy East Anglia for their dedication and determination to have a positive impact on everyone who passes through the school gates. Keep up the great work.

Work

I was very lucky to begin my artistic career under the management of Da Vinci Fine Art / The Da Vinci Group and owe so much to both Natasha Lands and Hayley Courtney-Smith, the brains behind the operation. Thank you to Hayley for instigating our initial meeting; it has changed my life. Natasha, thank you for championing not only my work, but also me as a person.

I am honoured to now be managed by Castle Fine Art, the leading art publisher and gallery network in the UK. It is a wonderfully well-oiled machine of creativity, and I extend my sincere gratitude to the entire team at Castle for their hard work. Exciting times ahead.

Friends

Thank you to my friend Freddie Miles for his unconditional love and support and for, along with the gorgeous Madeleine Venn, gracing the world with your incredible music. I am, and always will be your biggest fan.

A sincere thank you to Karis Smith for the love, support and laughs during six years of friendship. There have been many great highs, but also many deep lows, and you have been beside me throughout.

I must also pay a heartfelt tribute to fellow artist and dear friend Georgie Hadingham. My confidence was demolished during my short stint at university, and Georgie has played a considerable role in my attempts to rebuild that confidence. I also want to thank Natalie, Jan and the entire Hadingham family for their incredible support – it means so much.

Thank you to Beth Delaney for shooting the portrait photography for this book, our social media channels and press coverage. You made me feel totally at ease and you possess great photographic talent.

Thank you to Daisy Godbolt, a very special friend. This young lady has been through more in her 18 years of life than some face through their entire lives, yet she still has the kindest heart, the bravest soul and the warmest smile. That, in my eyes, constitutes a hero.

Thank you to Rachel and Millie O'Driscoll and her wonderful family for being such important and unconditional friends.

There are simply too many people to thank individually for all they have done, but my sincere and ever-lasting gratitude to Mike Jackson and family, Doeke Dobma and all at Clinks Care Farm, African Revival, Global Animal Welfare, ZSEA, Nikon, WaterBear, OffTheFence, Talia Melesi, Helen Roden, Phoebe Smith, Ashley Turton, Toby Alexander and family, Diana Miles, Rosie Venn, Lesley Neesham, Charles Neesham, Jade Neil, Mel Seager, Sue Willgoss, Benjamin Davy, Rosie Lee, the Owen Family, Liz, Jordan & Libby Page and Joanne, Chloe, Ben & Henry Bazneh. I love you all.

You all played your part to remind me that not all humans are bad, and that some accept you for who you are, make you feel good about yourself and remind you to never give up. So, thank you for flicking that switch in me, which had been turned off for many years. I will do my best to ensure that it stays switched on.

Pictorial Index

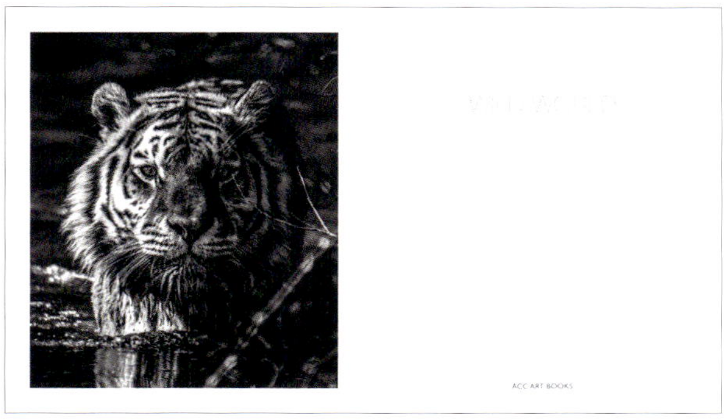

p2: *Yenisei*, Amur tiger, Banham Zoo, 2018

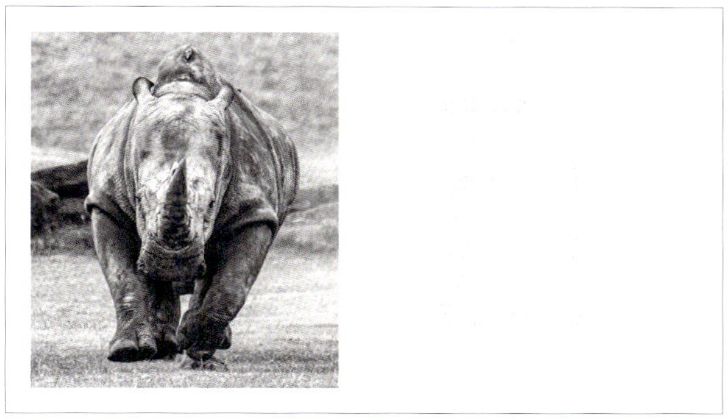

p4: *Full Speed Ahead*, white rhinoceros, Africa Alive!, 2019

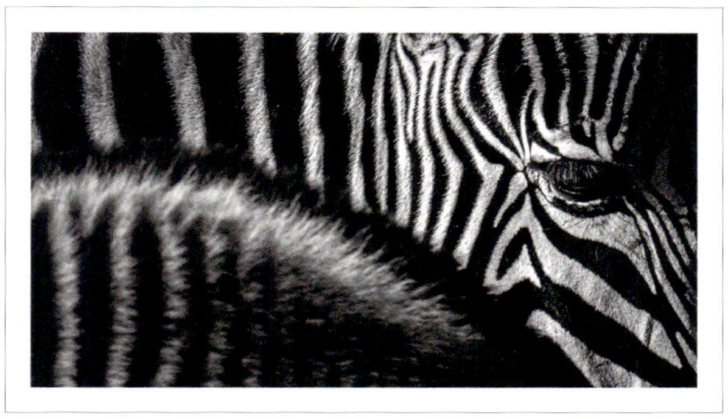

pp6-7: *Stripes*, Grevy's zebras, Banham Zoo, 2019

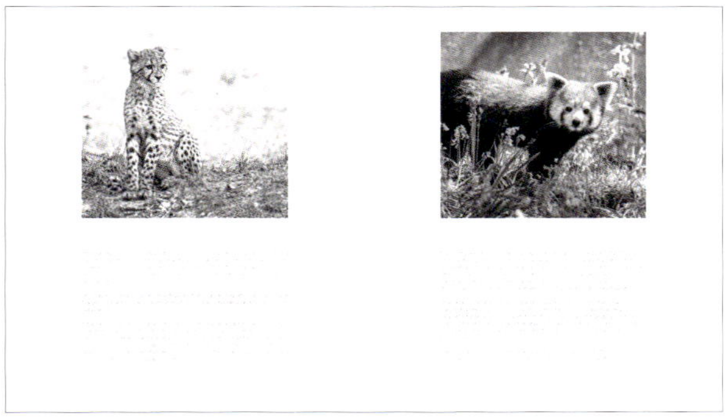

p12: *Duma*, cheetah, Colchester Zoo, 2020
p13: *Enchanted Forest*, red panda, Thrigby Hall Wildlife Gardens, 2020

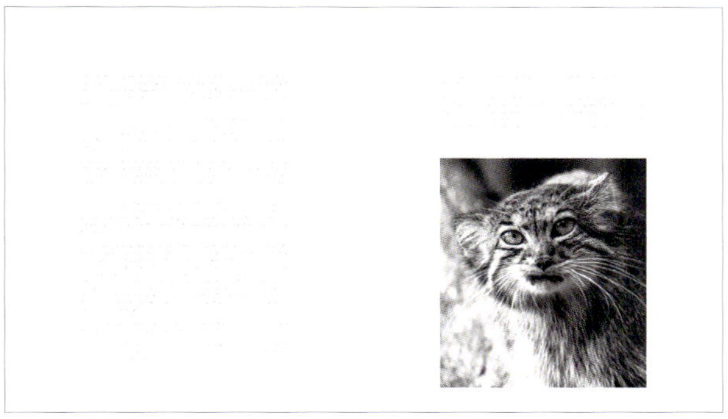

p15: *Manul*, Pallas's cat, Banham Zoo, 2020

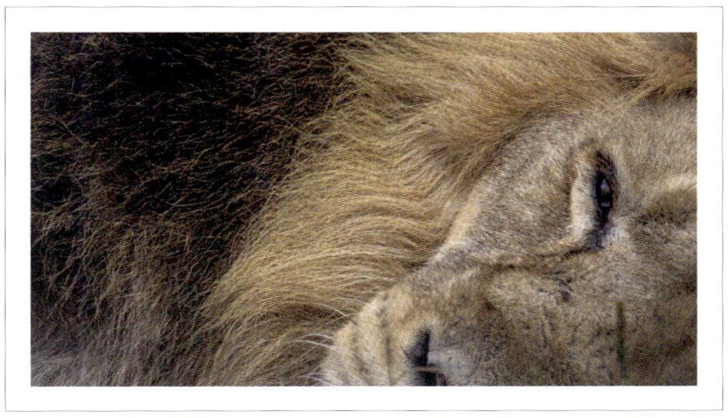

pp16-17: Asiatic lion, ZSL London Zoo, 2018

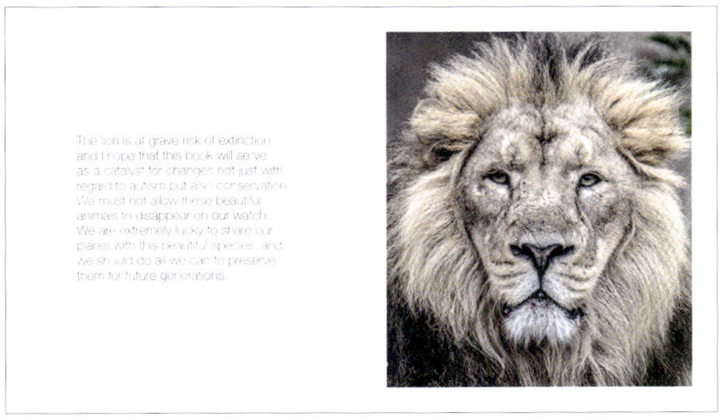

p19: Asiatic lion, ZSL London Zoo, 2018

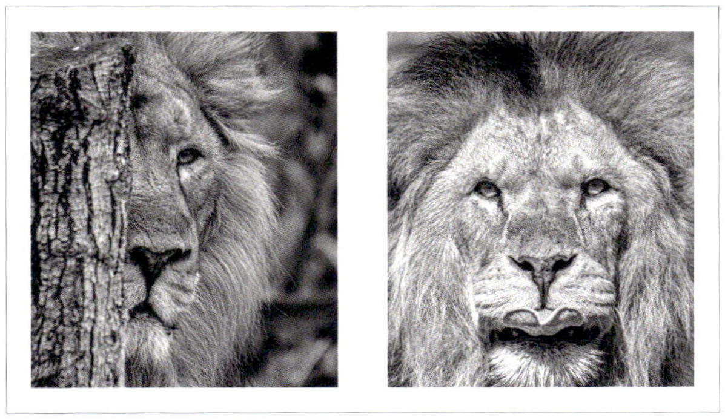

p20: *Silent Witness*, Asiatic lion, ZSL London Zoo, 2018
p21: *Hunger Games*, African lion, Colchester Zoo, 2021

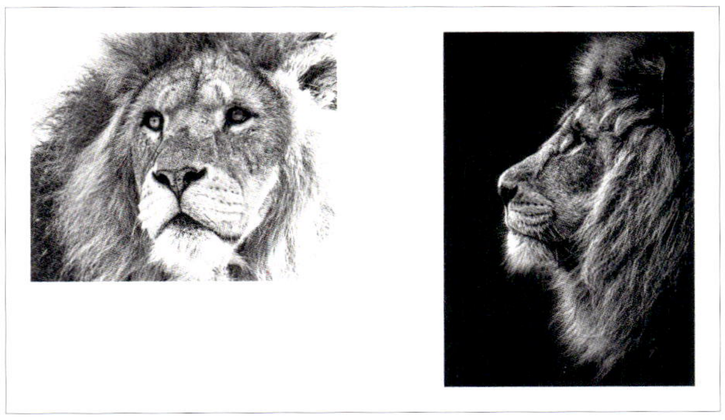

p22: Asiatic lion, ZSL London Zoo, 2018
p23: *Prince of Darkness*, African lion, Colchester Zoo, 2019

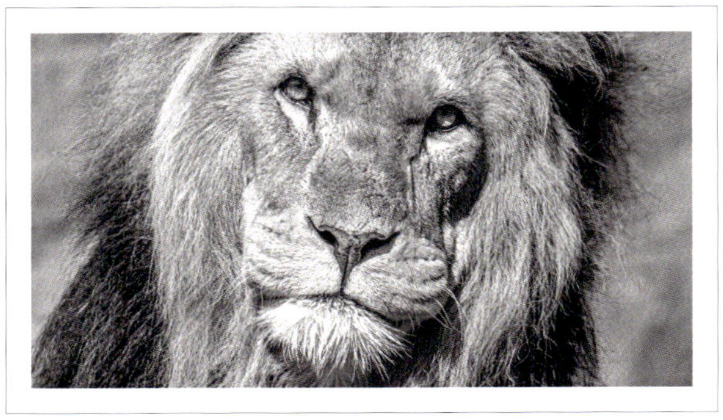

pp24-25: *Aslan*, African lion, Colchester Zoo, 2021

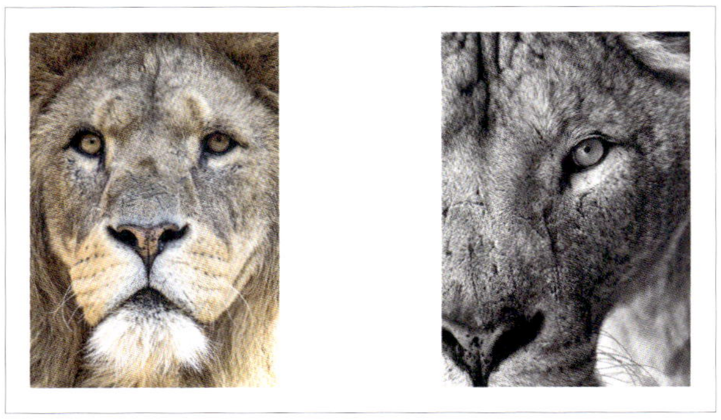

p26: *King*, African lion, Colchester Zoo, 2020
p27: *The Queen's Gaze*, African lion, Colchester Zoo, 2020

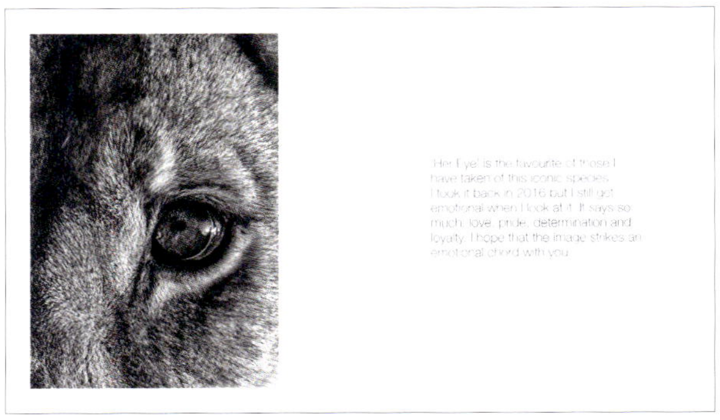

p28: *Her Eye*, African lion, Africa Alive!, 2016

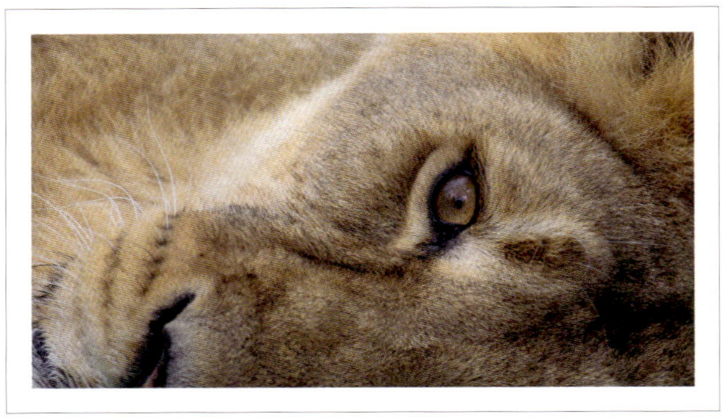

pp30-31: *Eye*, African lion, Colchester Zoo, 2018

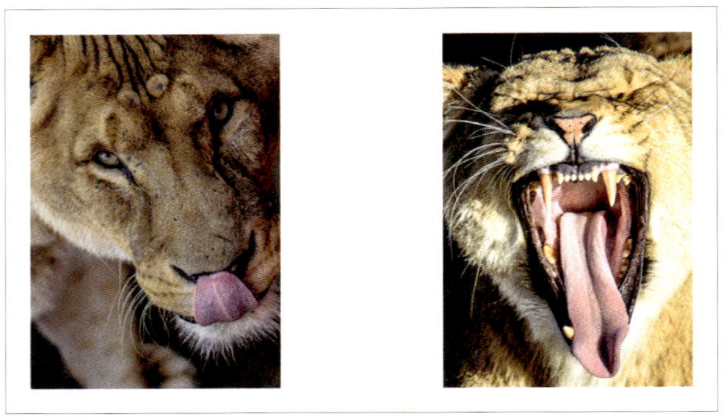

p32: *That Look You Gave Me*, African lion, Africa Alive!, 2019
p33: *Jaws*, African lion, Africa Alive!, 2016

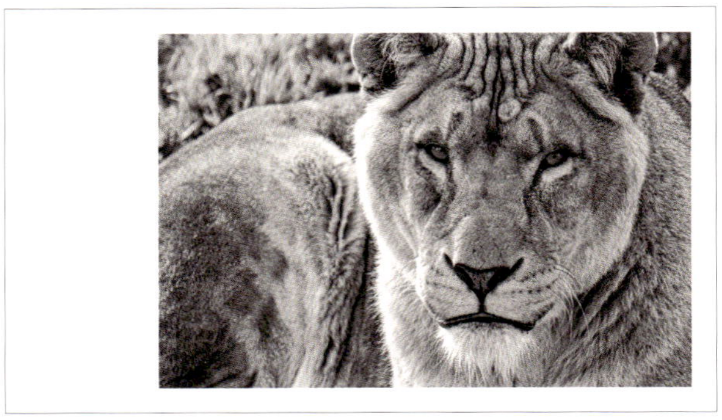

pp34-35: *Queen of Africa*, African lion, Africa Alive!, 2015

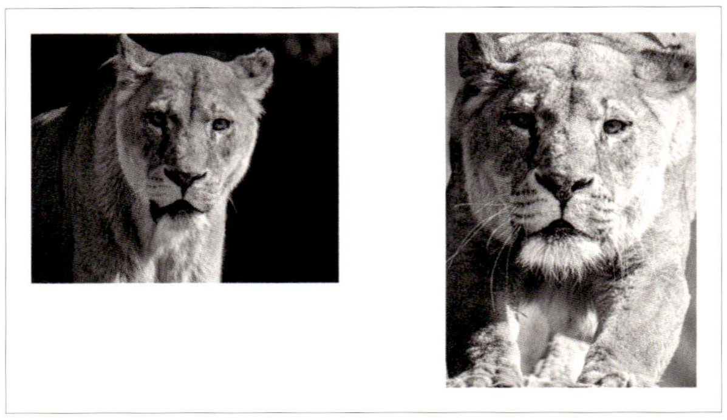

p36: *I Am Me*, African lion, Colchester Zoo, 2019
p37: African lion, Colchester Zoo, 2019

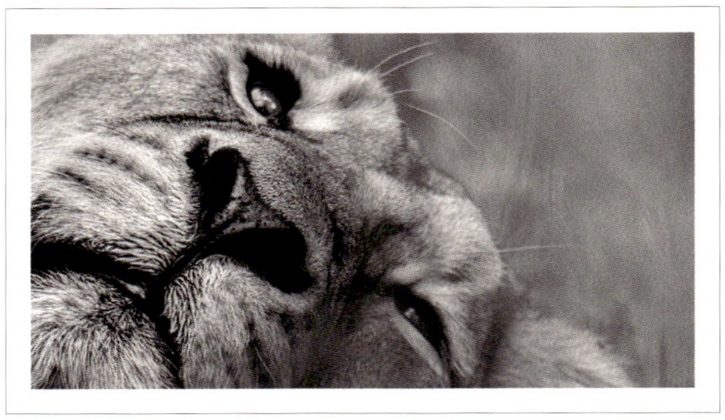

pp38-39: *Whiskers*, Asiatic lion, ZSL London Zoo, 2018

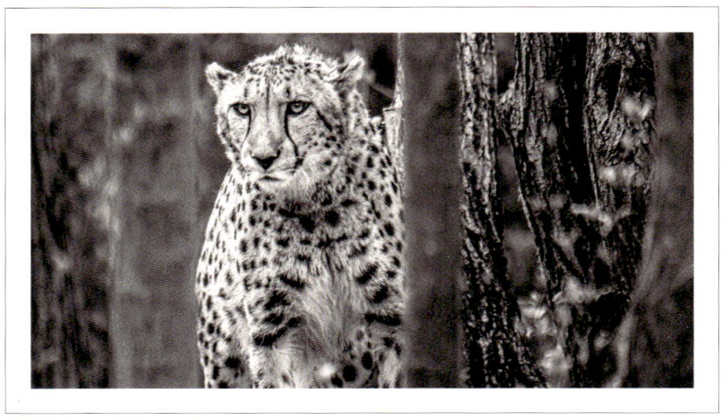

pp40-41: *Through the Trees*, cheetah, Colchester Zoo, 2019

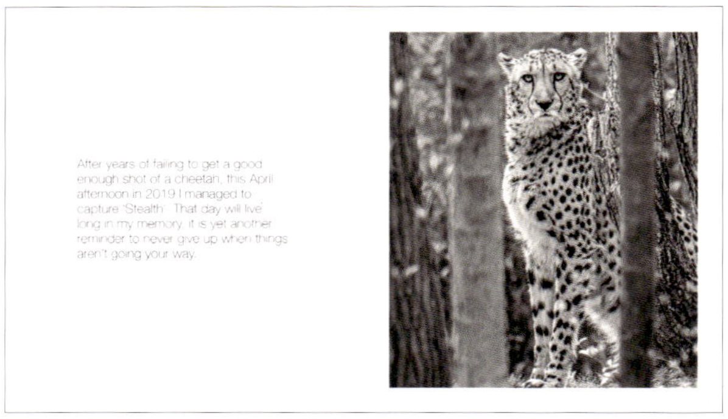

p43: *Stealth*, cheetah, Colchester Zoo, 2019

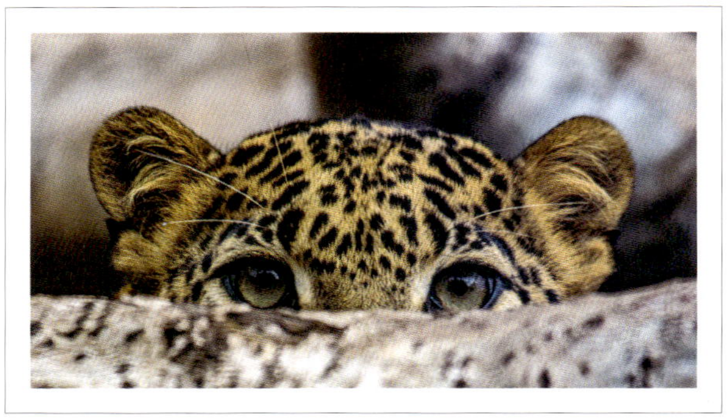

pp44-45: *Always Watching*, Sri Lankan leopard, Banham Zoo, 2018

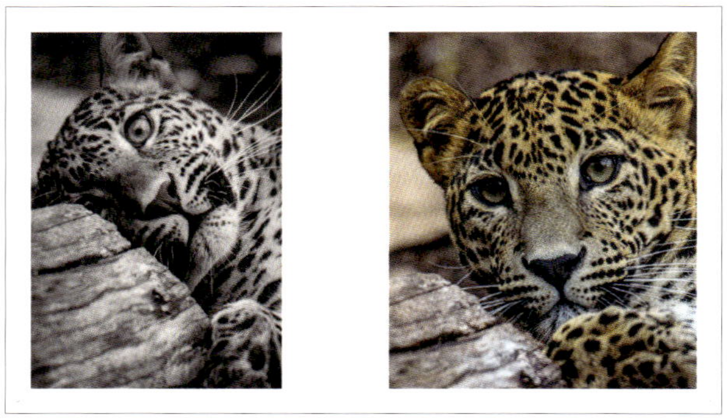

p46: Sri Lankan leopard, Banham Zoo, 2018
p47: Sri Lankan leopard, Banham Zoo, 2018

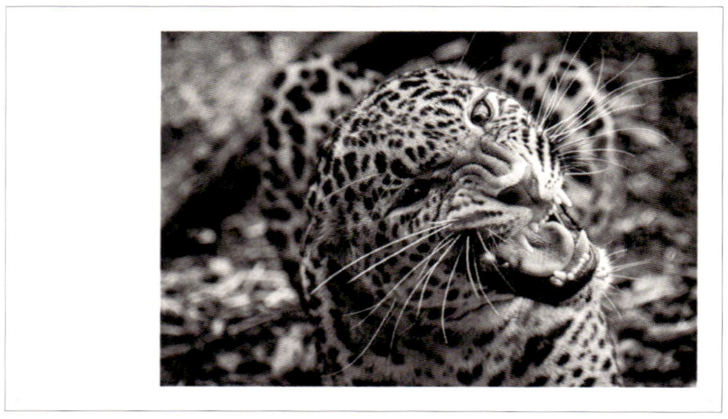

pp48-49: *Be Warned*, Sri Lankan leopard, Banham Zoo, 2018

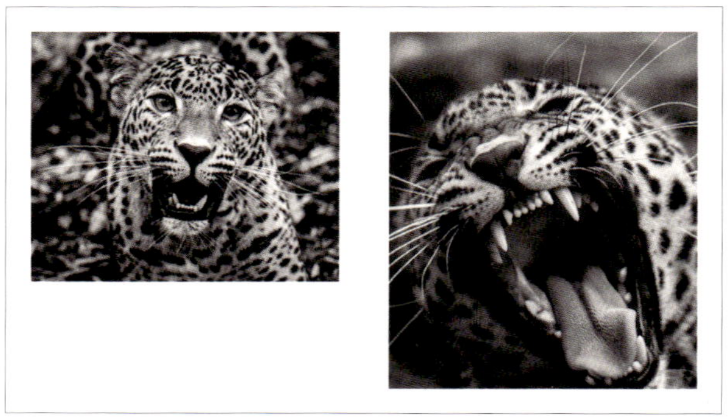

p50: *Sabor*, Sri Lankan leopard, Banham Zoo, 2018
p51: *Pearly Whites*, Sri Lankan leopard, Banham Zoo, 2018

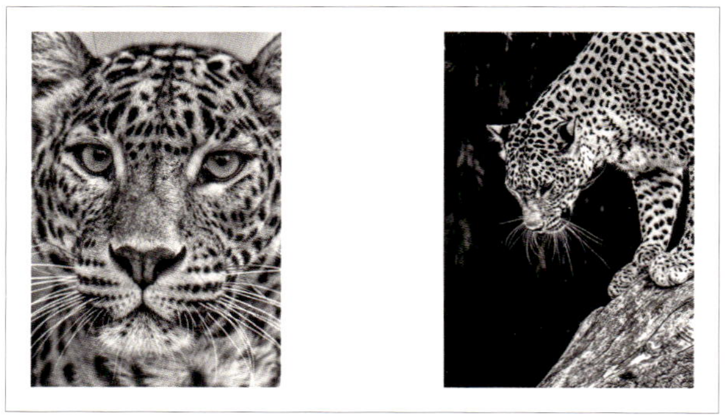

p52: *Her Royal Highness*, Sri Lankan leopard, Banham Zoo, 2020
p53: *The Descent*, Sri Lankan leopard, Banham Zoo, 2018

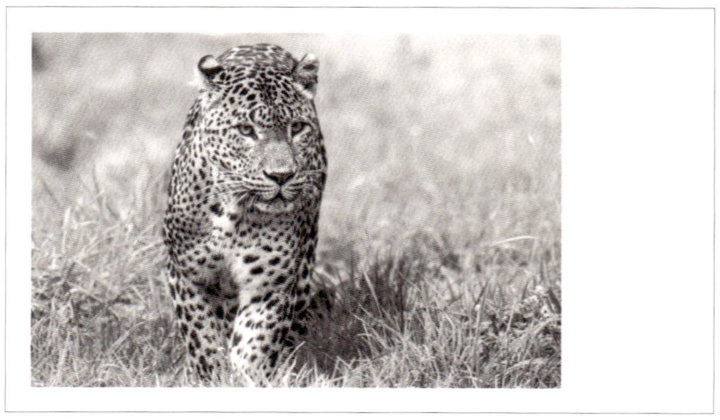

pp54-55: *Here She Comes*, Sri Lankan leopard, Banham Zoo, 2020

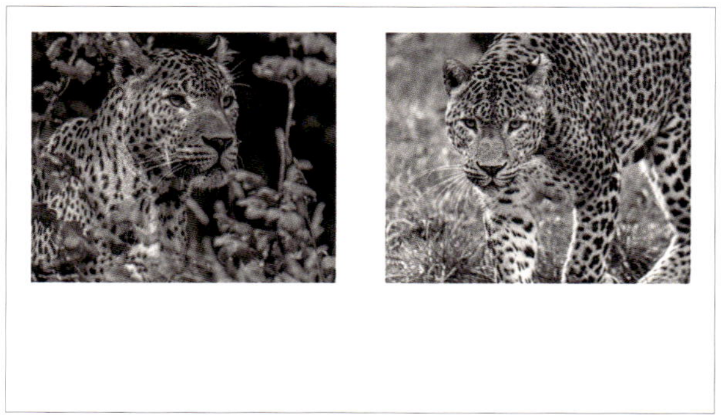

p56: *Through the Foliage*, Sri Lankan leopard, Banham Zoo, 2020
p57: *Here I Am*, Sri Lankan leopard, Banham Zoo, 2019

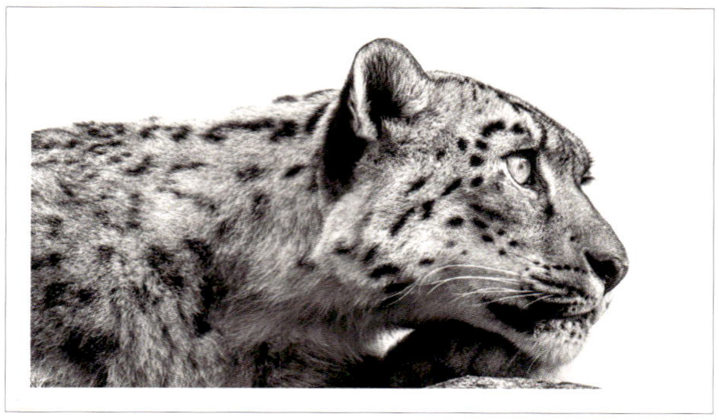

pp58-59: *Frozen*, snow leopard, Banham Zoo, 2018

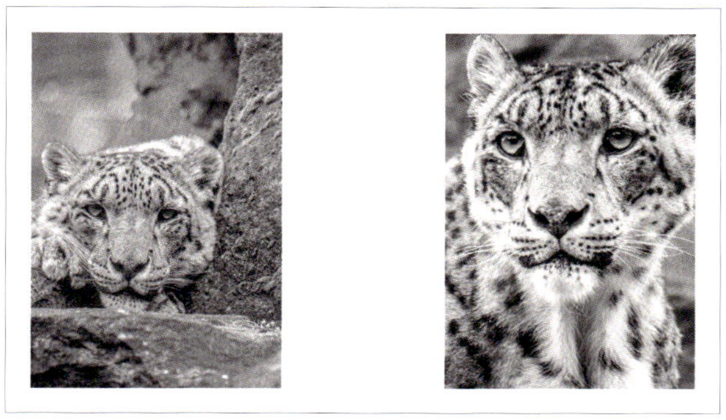

p60: *On the Rocks*, snow leopard, Banham Zoo, 2020
p61: Snow leopard, Banham Zoo, 2018

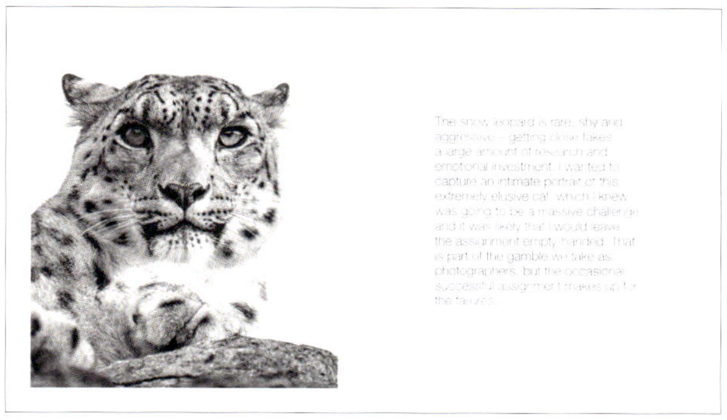

p62: *Frozen Beauty*, snow leopard, Banham Zoo, 2019

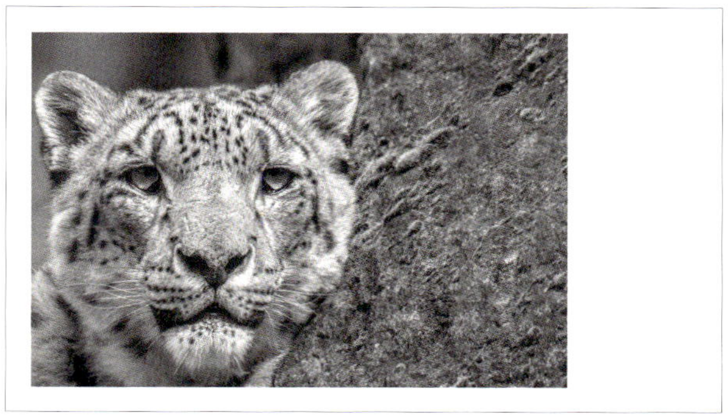

pp64-65: Snow leopard, Banham Zoo, 2020

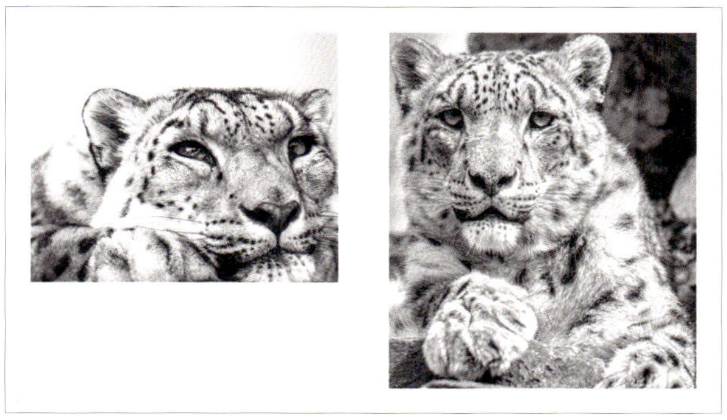

p66: *Cat Nap*, snow leopard, Banham Zoo, 2020
p67: Snow leopard, Banham Zoo, 2020

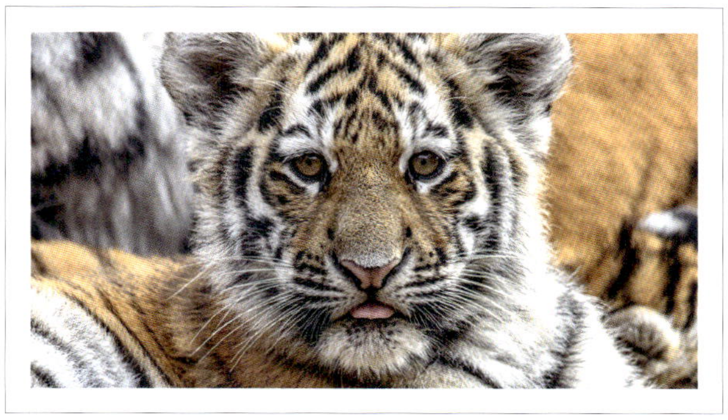

pp68-69: *Tiny Tiger*, Amur tiger, Colchester Zoo, 2019

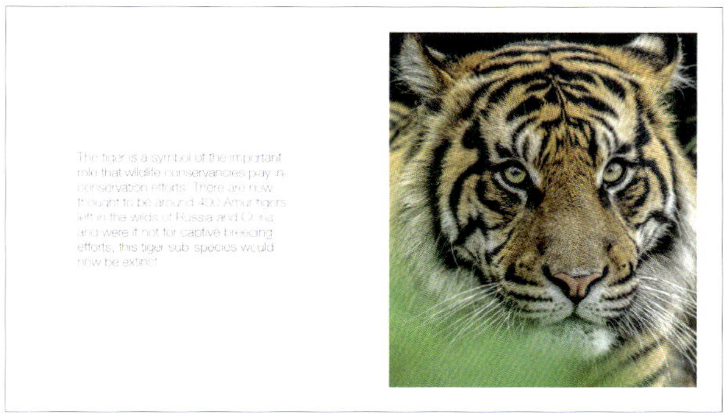

p71: Amur tiger, Banham Zoo, 2018

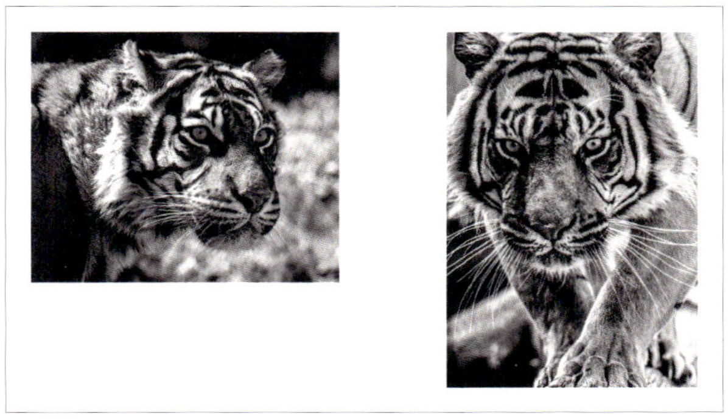

p72: Sumatran tiger, Thrigby Hall Wildlife Gardens, 2020
p73: Sumatran tiger, Thrigby Hall Wildlife Gardens, 2018

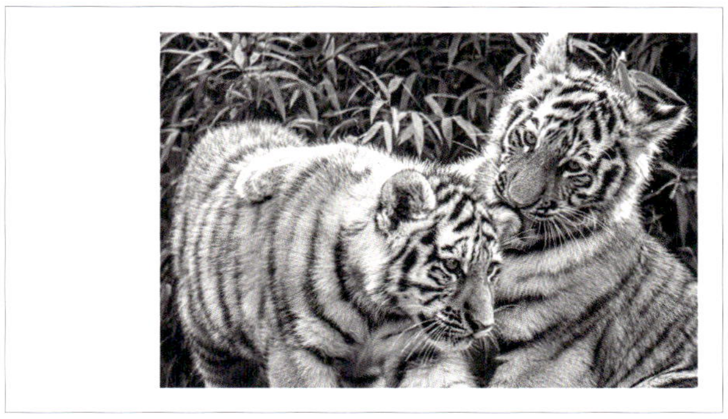

pp74-75: *I Got You*, Amur tigers, Colchester Zoo, 2019

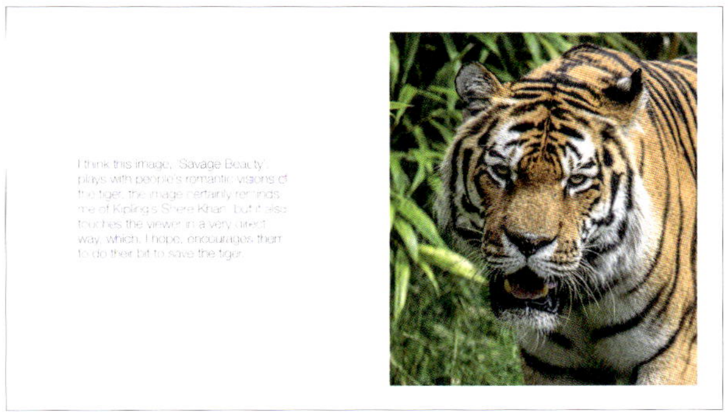

p77: *Savage Beauty*, Amur tiger, Colchester Zoo, 2019

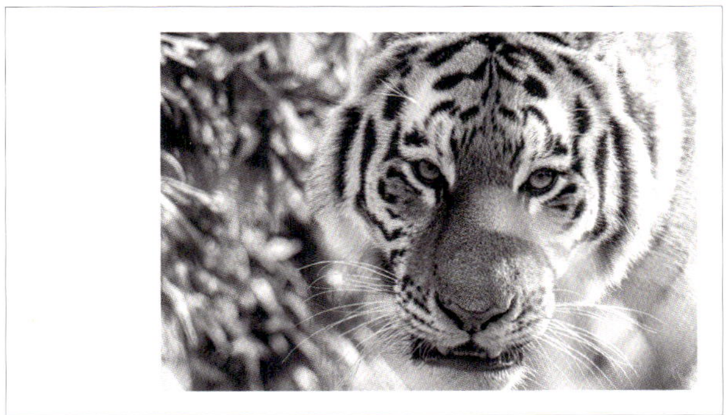

pp78-79: *Eyes On You*, Amur tiger, Colchester Zoo, 2020

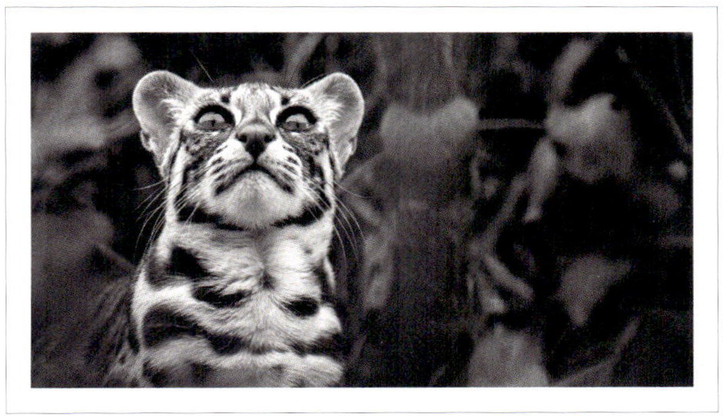

pp80-81: *Ghost*, Geoffroy's cat, Thrigby Hall Wildlife Gardens, 2018

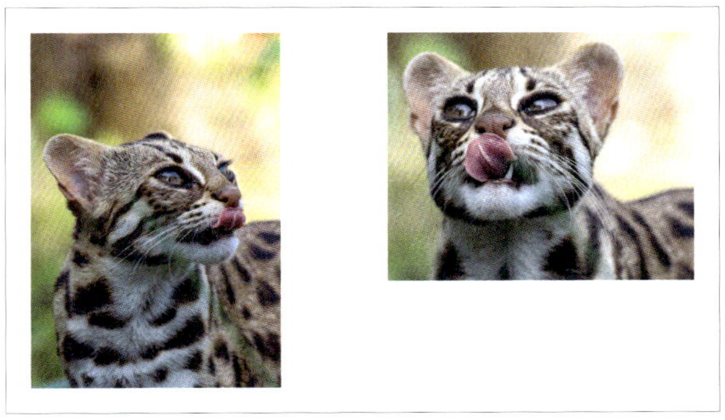

p82: Geoffroy's cat, Thrigby Hall Wildlife Gardens, 2018
p83: Geoffroy's cat, Thrigby Hall Wildlife Gardens, 2018

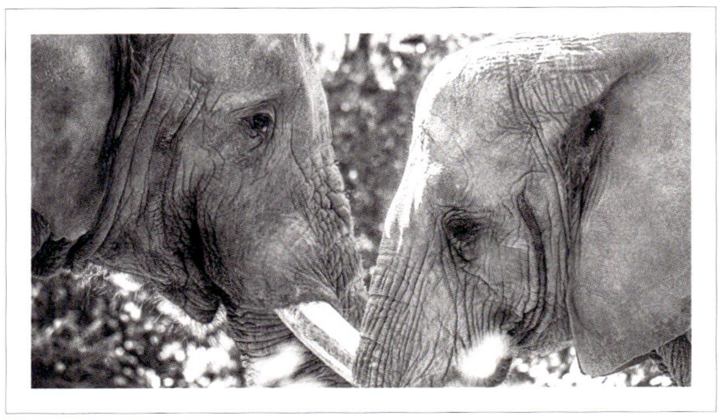

pp84-85: *You're My Favourite*, African elephants, Colchester Zoo, 2020

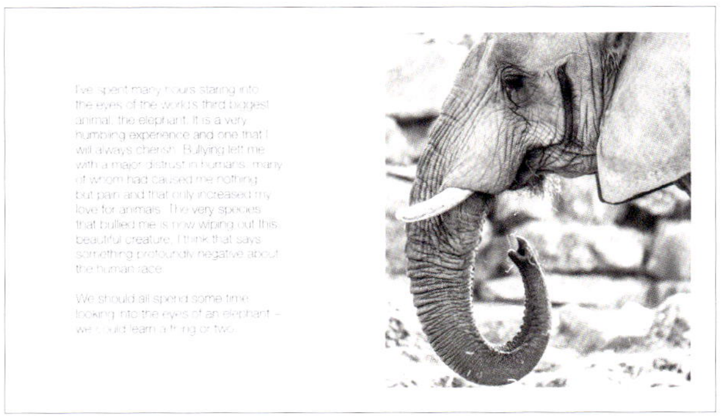

p87: African elephant, Colchester Zoo, 2020

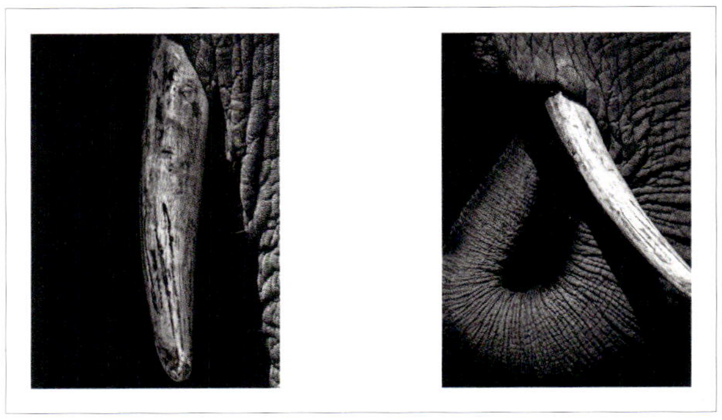

p88: *Tusk*, African elephant, Colchester Zoo, 2019
p89: *Trunk & Tusk*, African elephant, Colchester Zoo, 2019

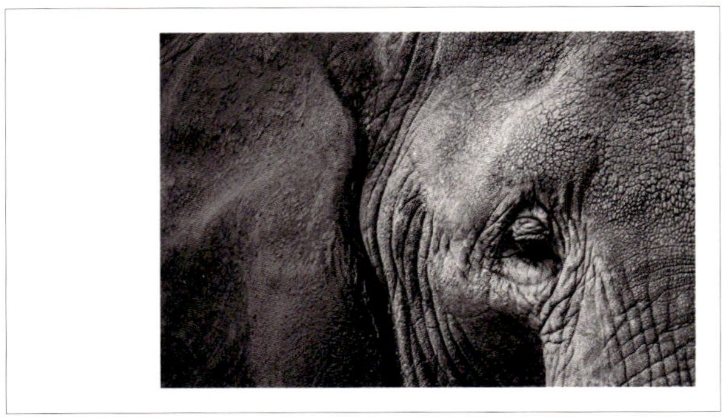

pp90-91: *Ethereal Giant*, African elephant, Colchester Zoo, 2018

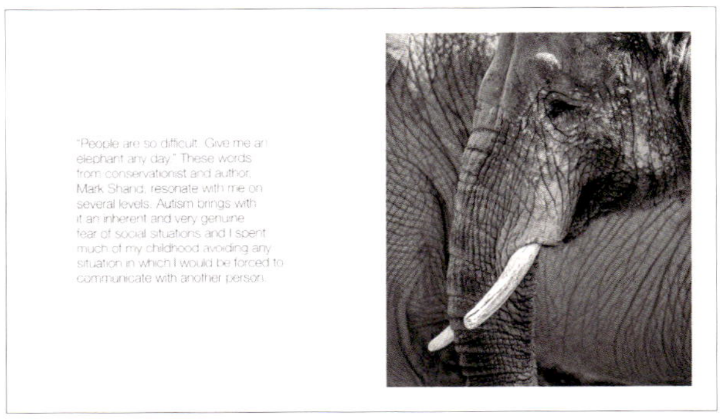

p93: *Tusker*, African elephant, Colchester Zoo, 2020

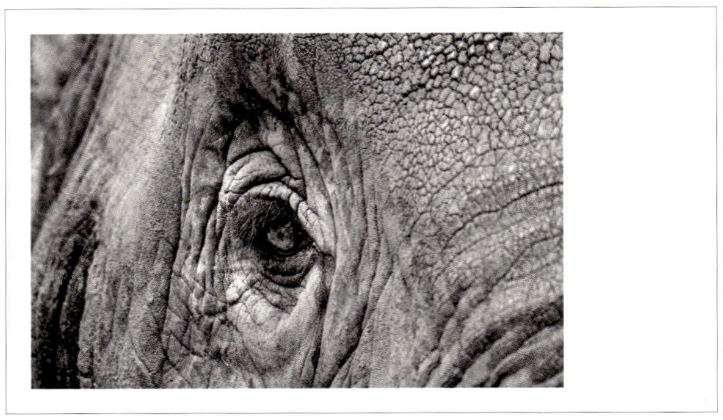

pp94-95: *Eye*, African elephant, Colchester Zoo, 2018

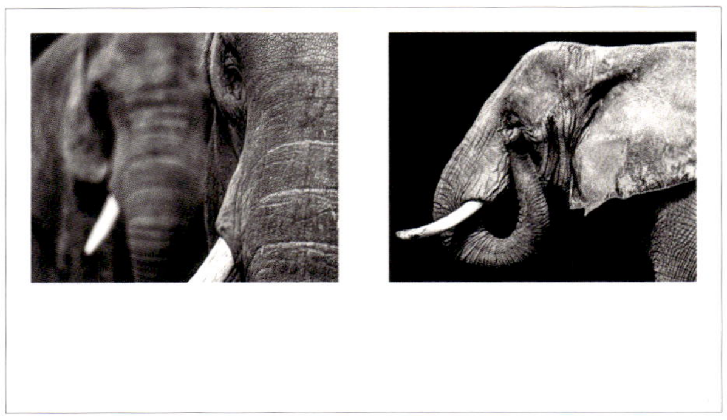

p96: *Two Tuskers*, African elephants, Colchester Zoo, 2020
p97: *Tears of the Vanishing*, African elephant, Colchester Zoo, 2019

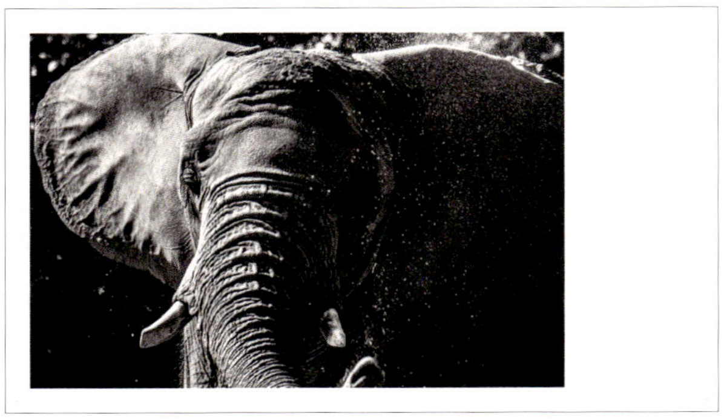

pp98-99: *Dust*, African elephant, Colchester Zoo, 2021

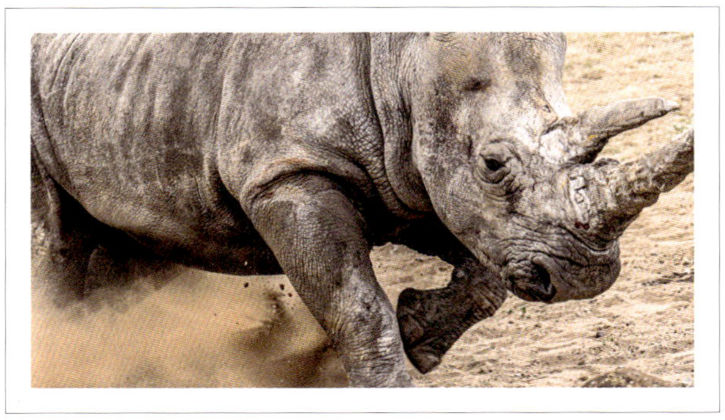

pp100-101: *The Charge*, white rhinoceros, Africa Alive!, 2019

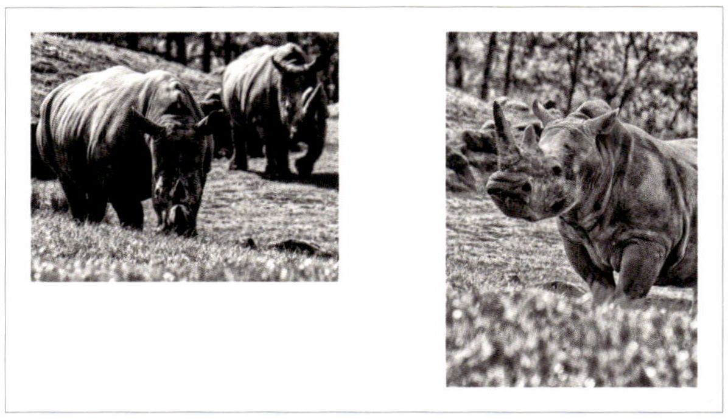

p102: White rhinoceroses, Africa Alive!, 2018
p103: *Fields of Silver*, white rhinoceros, Africa Alive!, 2018

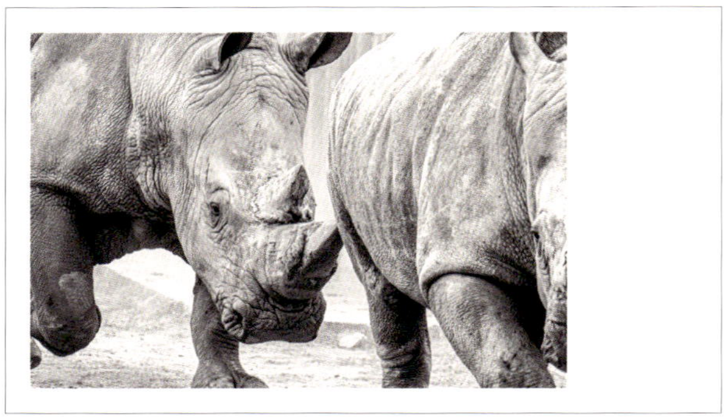

pp104-105: *Pursuit*, white rhinoceroses, Africa Alive!, 2019

pp106-107: *Stripes on Stripes*, Grevy's zebras, Banham Zoo, 2018

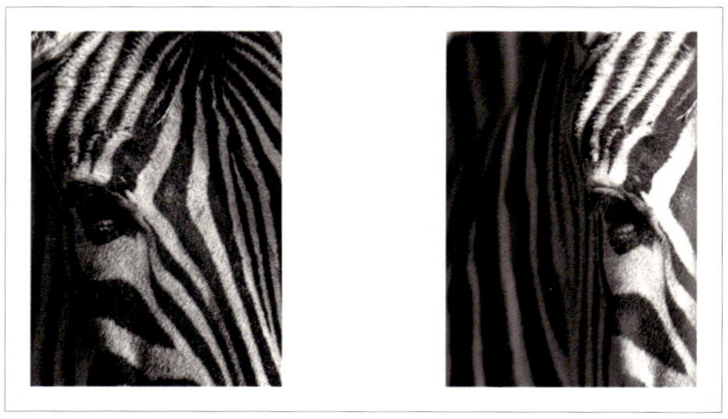

p108: *Light & Stripes*, Chapman's zebra, Africa Alive!, 2018
p109: Chapman's zebra, Africa Alive!, 2018

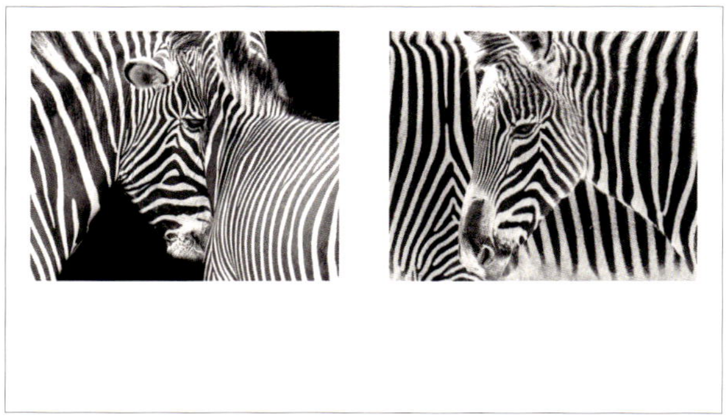

p110: *Against Stripes*, Grevy's zebras, Banham Zoo, 2019
p111: *Incognito*, Grevy's zebras, Banham Zoo, 2020

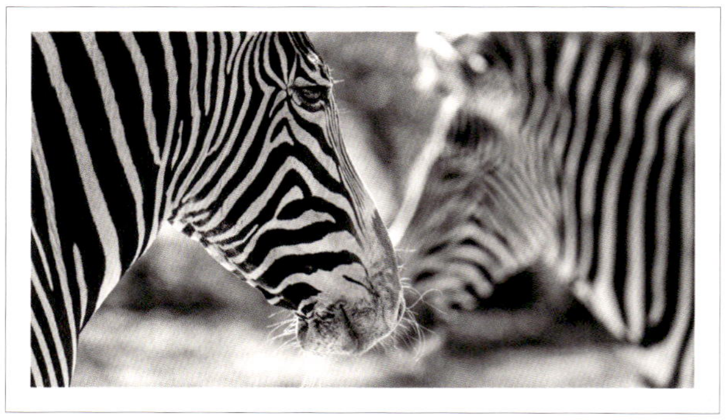

pp112-113: *Mirror Mirror*, Grevy's zebras, Banham Zoo, 2021

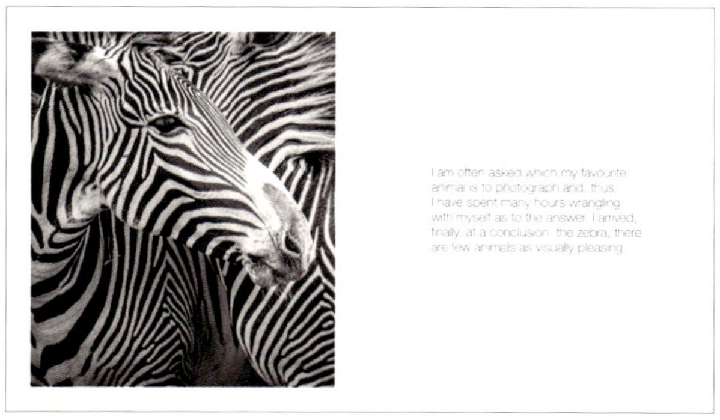

p114: *Intertwined*, Grevy's zebras, Banham Zoo, 2018

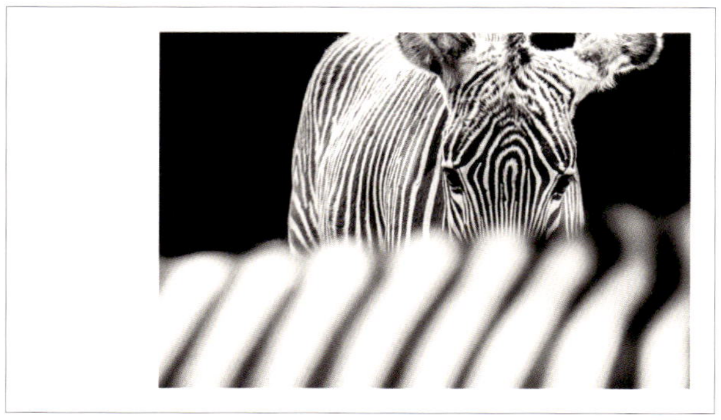

pp116-117: *Behind Stripes*, Grevy's zebras, Banham Zoo, 2018

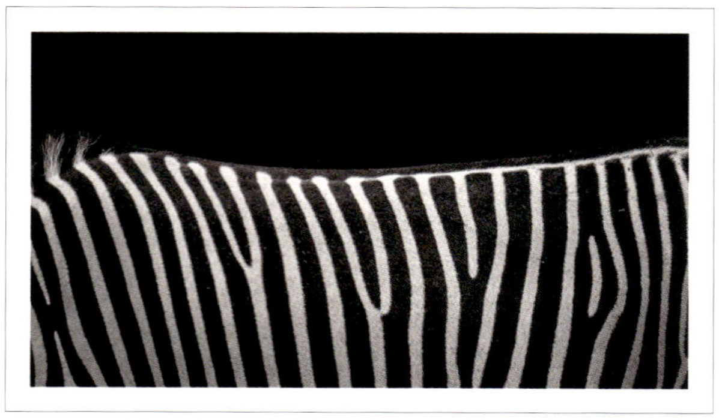

pp118-119: *Nature's Piano*, Grevy's zebra, Banham Zoo, 2018

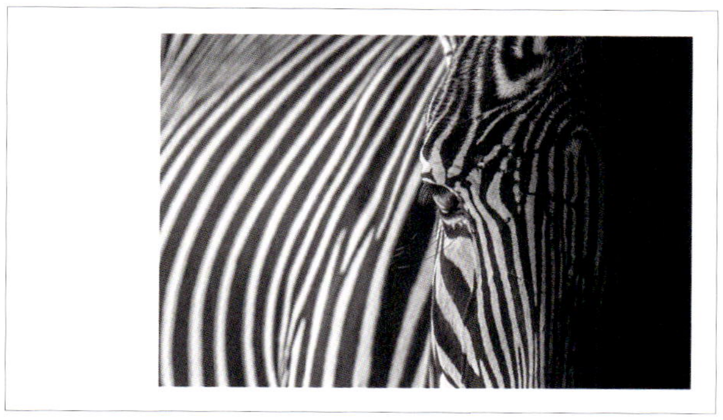

pp120-121: *Out of the Dark*, Grevy's zebra, Banham Zoo, 2018

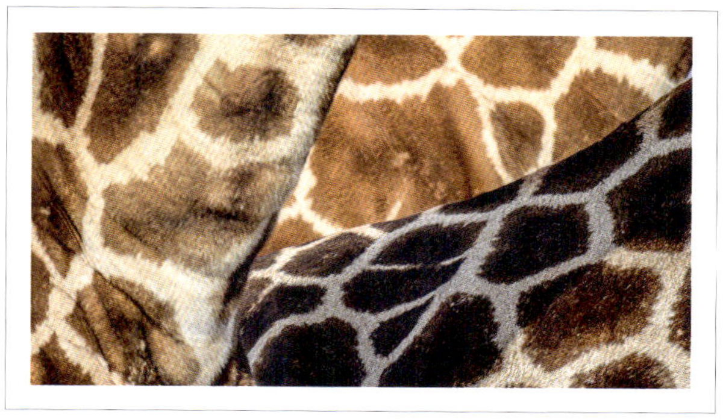

pp122-123: *Three of a Kind*, giraffes, Banham Zoo, 2017

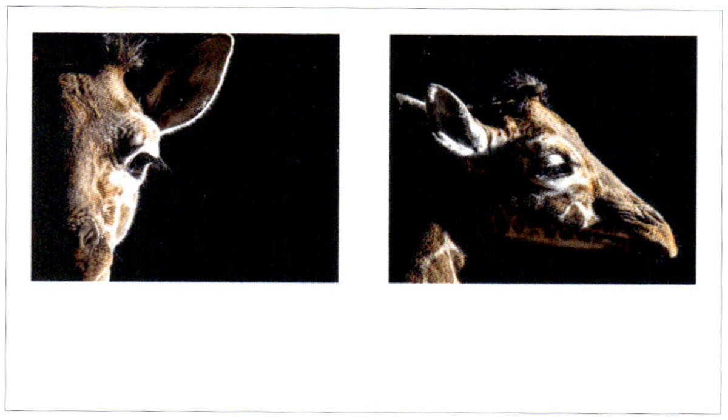

p124: Reticulated giraffe, Africa Alive!, 2021
p125: Reticulated giraffe, Africa Alive!, 2021

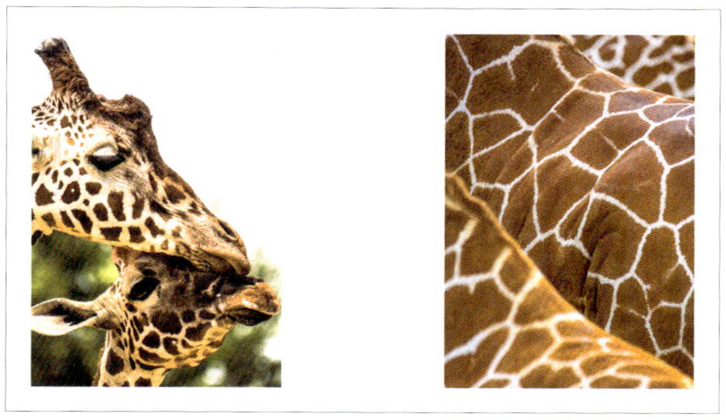

p126: *The Soft Touch*, giraffes, Africa Alive!, 2018
p127: Giraffes, Colchester Zoo, 2019

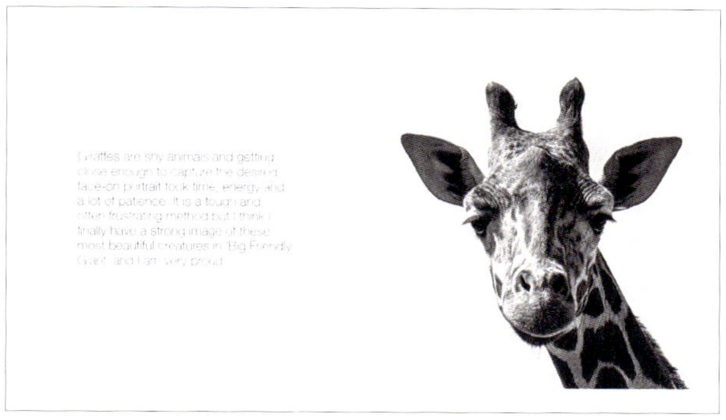

p129: *The Big Friendly Giant*, reticulated giraffe, Africa Alive!, 2020

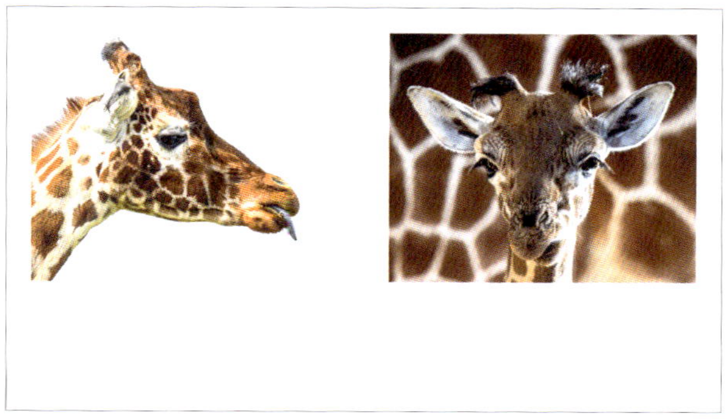

p130: *Cheeky*, giraffe, Africa Alive!, 2017
p131: *Tiny Twiga*, reticulated giraffes, Africa Alive!, 2021

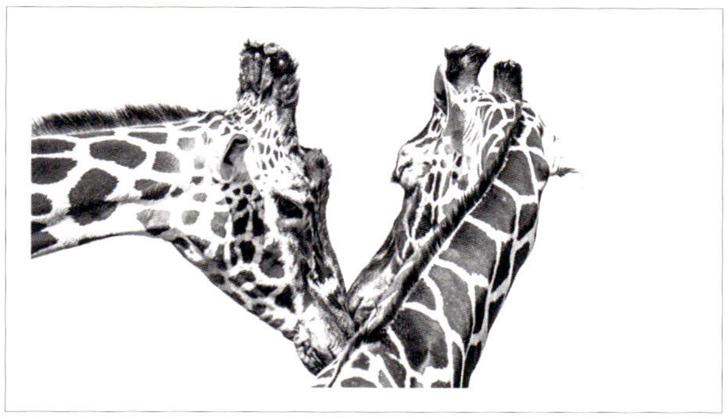

pp132-133: *Kiss*, reticulated giraffes, Colchester Zoo, 2021

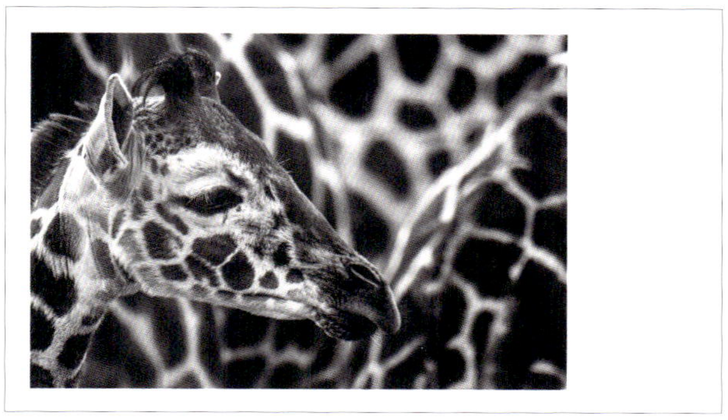

pp134-135: Giraffes, Africa Alive!, 2021

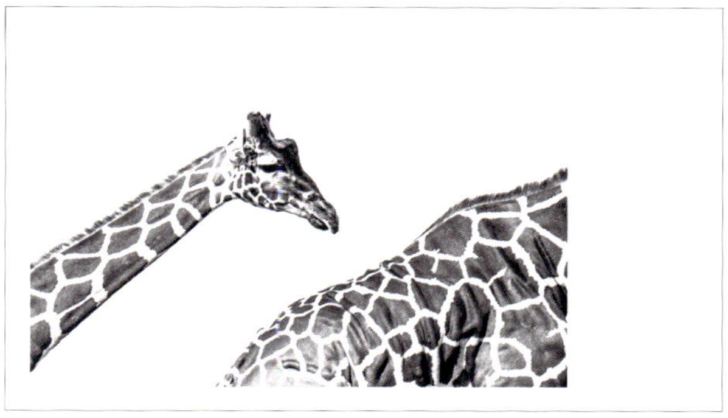

pp136-137: *Two Halves*, reticulated giraffes, Colchester Zoo, 2021

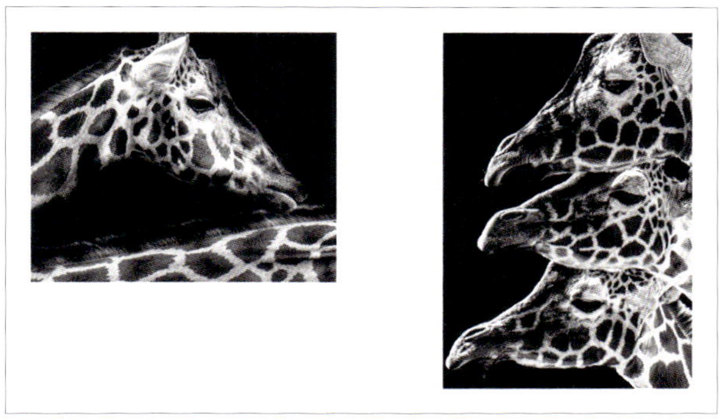

p138: Giraffes, Africa Alive!, 2016
p139: *Generation Game*, giraffes, Africa Alive!, 2019

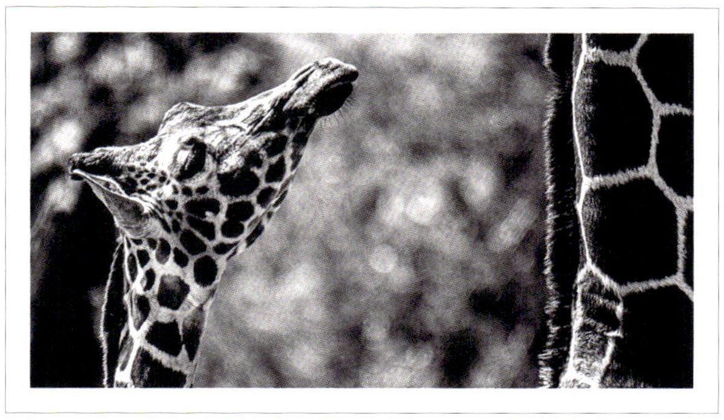

pp140-141: *When I Grow Up*, giraffes, Africa Alive!, 2019

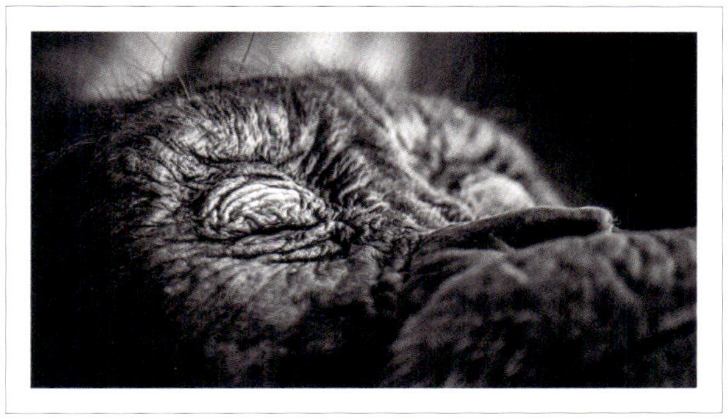

pp142-143: *Sweet Dreams*, chimpanzee, Colchester Zoo, 2018

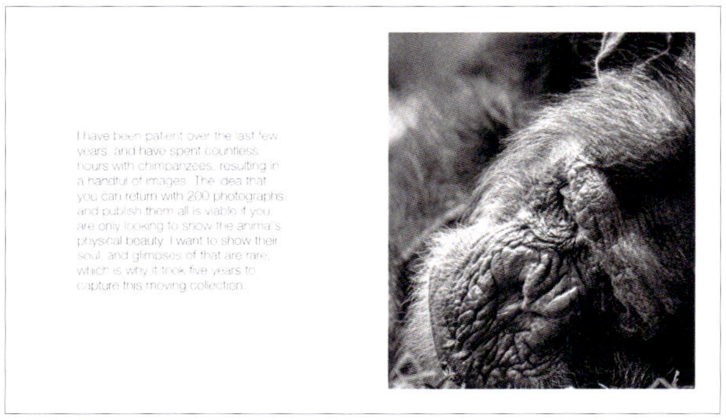

p145: *Wrinkles*, chimpanzee, Colchester Zoo, 2018

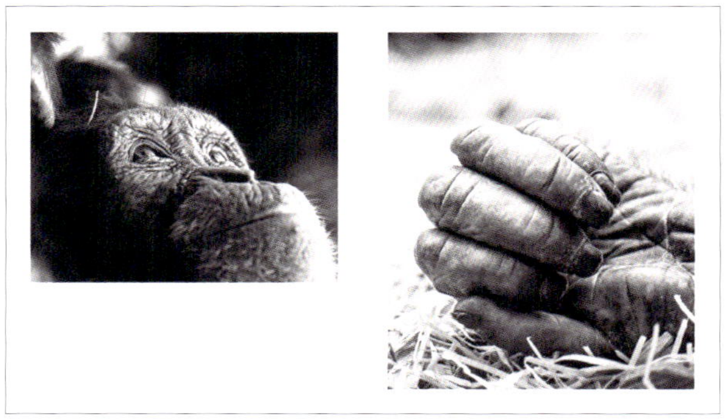

p146: *Daydreams*, chimpanzee, Colchester Zoo, 2018
p147: *Hand*, chimpanzee, Colchester Zoo, 2018

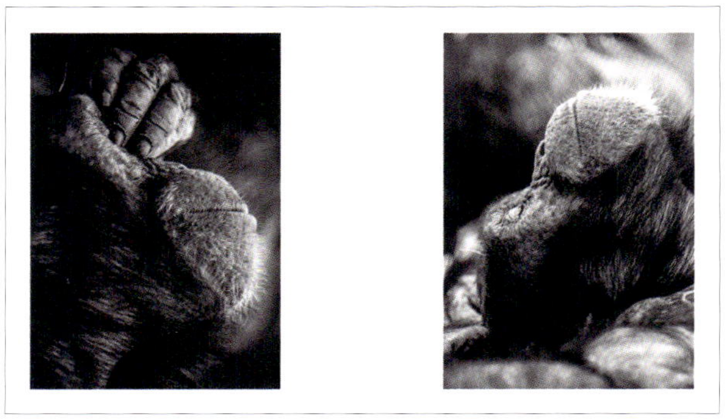

p148: *It's Been a Long Day*, chimpanzee, Colchester Zoo, 2018
p149: *Something about Sundays*, chimpanzee, Colchester Zoo, 2019

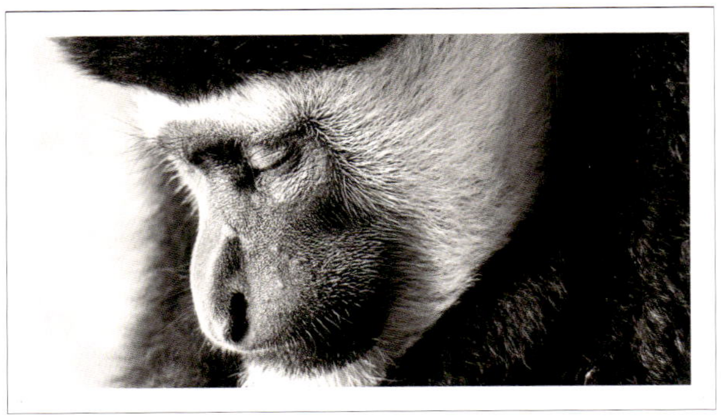

pp150-151: Black-and-white colobus monkey, Colchester Zoo, 2019

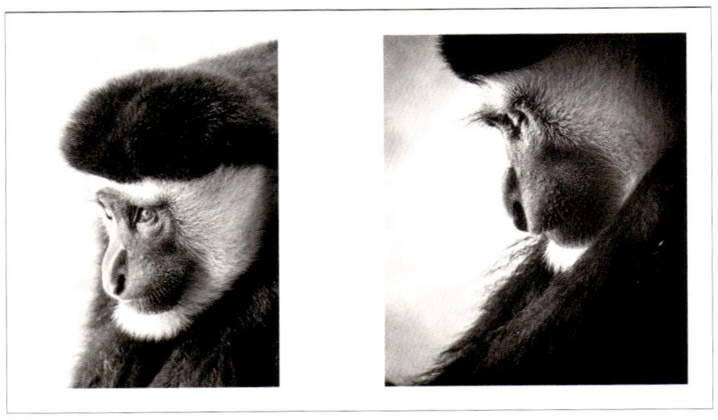

p152: *Contemplation*, black-and-white colobus monkey, Colchester Zoo, 2019
p153: *Sunday Prayers*, black-and-white colobus monkey, Colchester Zoo, 2019

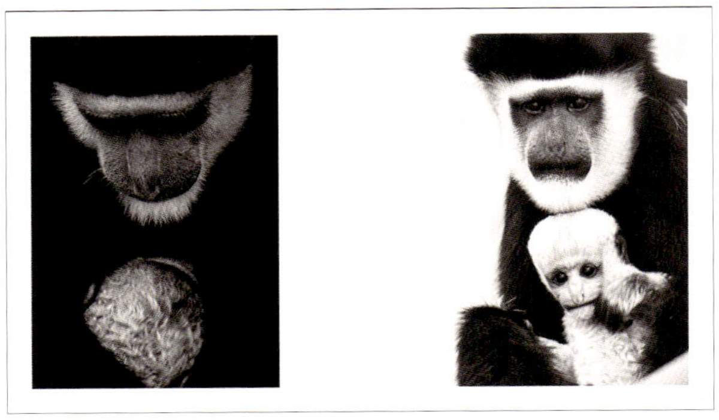

p154: *The Most Important Job in the World*, black-and-white colobus monkeys, Colchester Zoo, 2017
p155: *Motherhood*, black-and-white colobus monkeys, Colchester Zoo, 2016

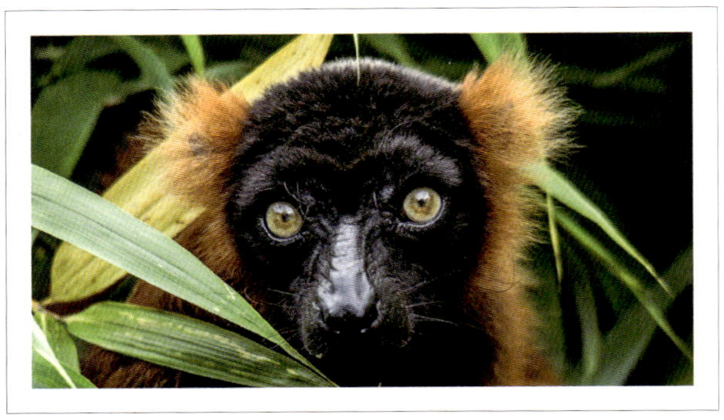

pp156-157: *Jewels*, red ruffed lemur, Banham Zoo, 2020

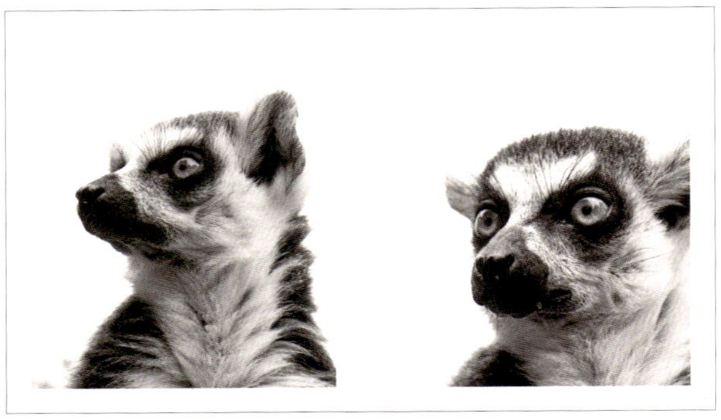

p158: *Portrait I*, ring-tailed lemur, Banham Zoo, 2019
p159: *Portrait II*, ring-tailed lemur, Banham Zoo, 2019

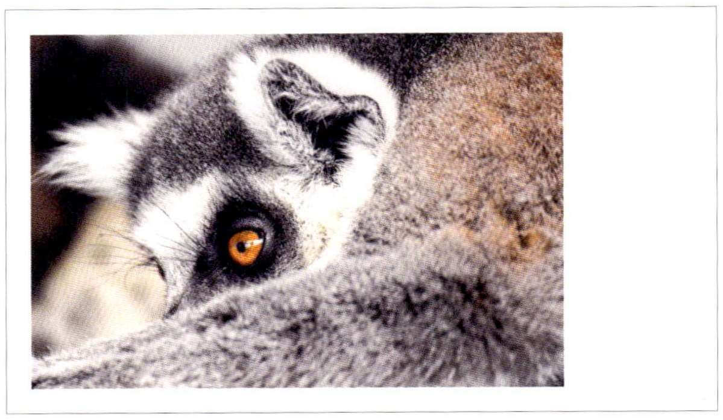

pp160-161: *Focus*, ring-tailed lemur, Africa Alive!, 2017

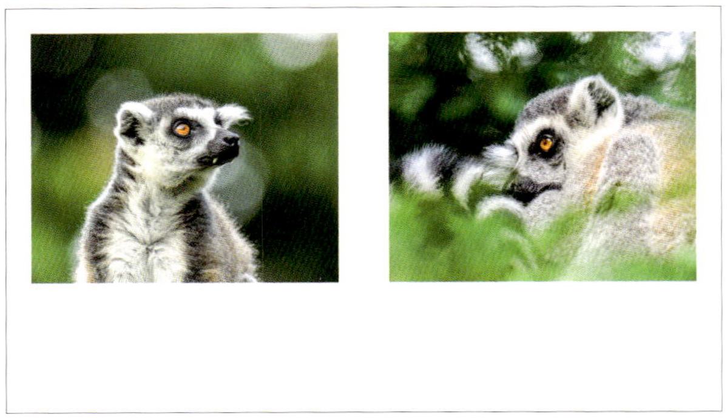

p162: *Lemur Dreams*, ring-tailed lemur, Africa Alive!, 2017
p163: Ring-tailed lemur, Africa Alive!, 2018

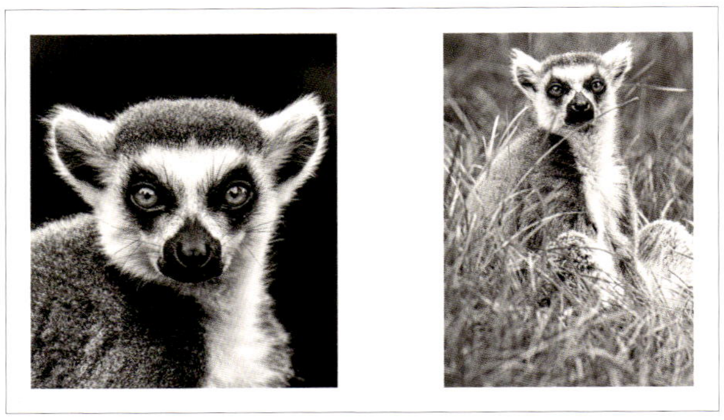

p164: *The Emperor*, ring-tailed lemur, Africa Alive!, 2020
p165: Ring-tailed lemur, Africa Alive!, 2020

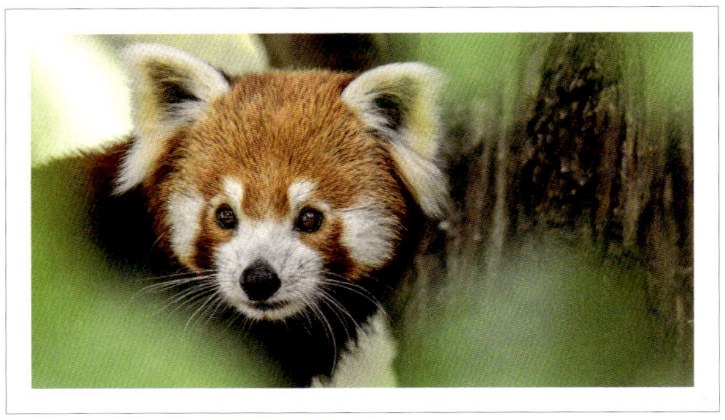

pp166-167: *Fire Fox*, red panda, Thrigby Hall Wildlife Gardens, 2018

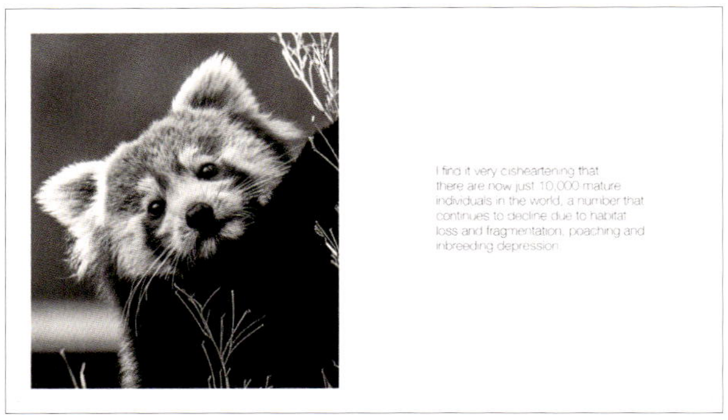

p168: Red panda, Thrigby Hall Wildlife Gardens, 2020

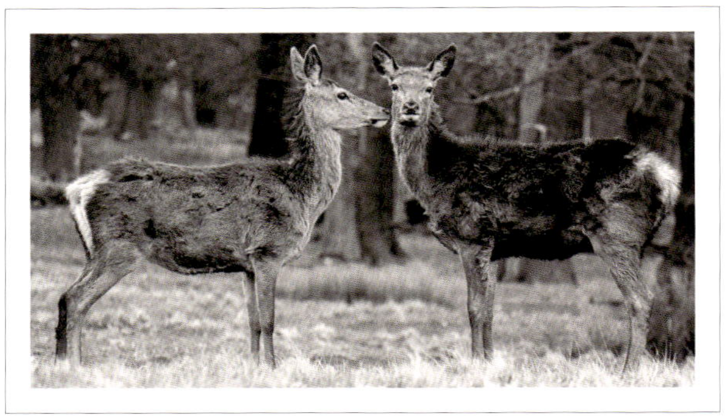

pp170-171: Red deer, Richmond Park, 2019

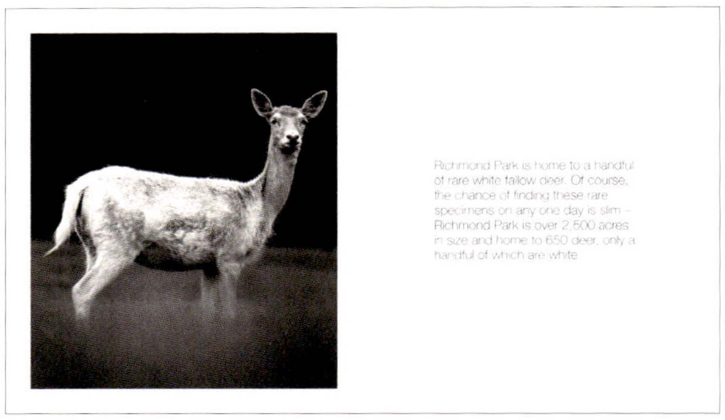

p172: *Snow White*, fallow deer, Richmond Park, 2017

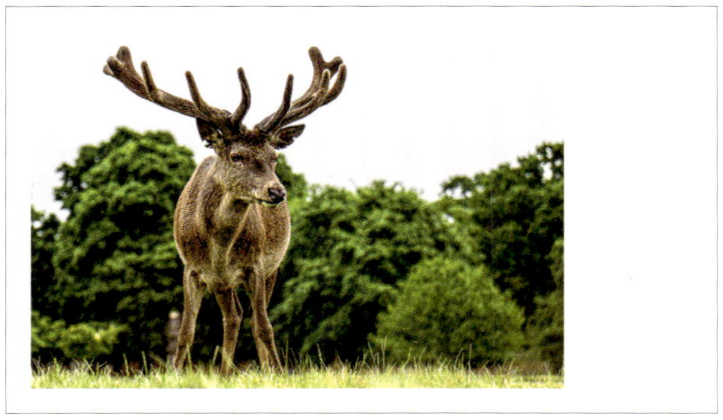

pp174-175: *Gladiator*, red deer, Richmond Park, 2017

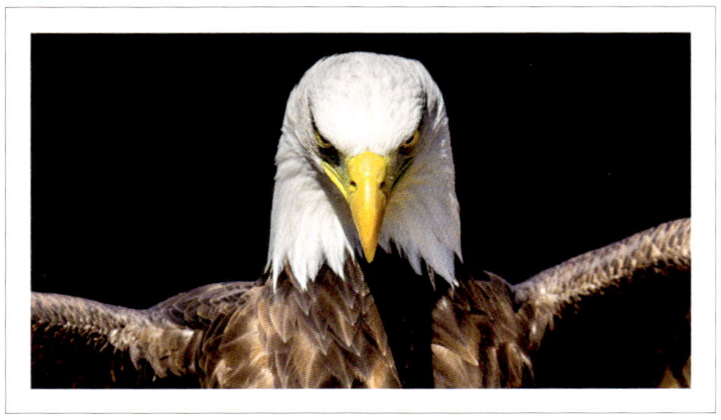

pp176-177: *Nemesis*, bald eagle, Banham Zoo, 2020

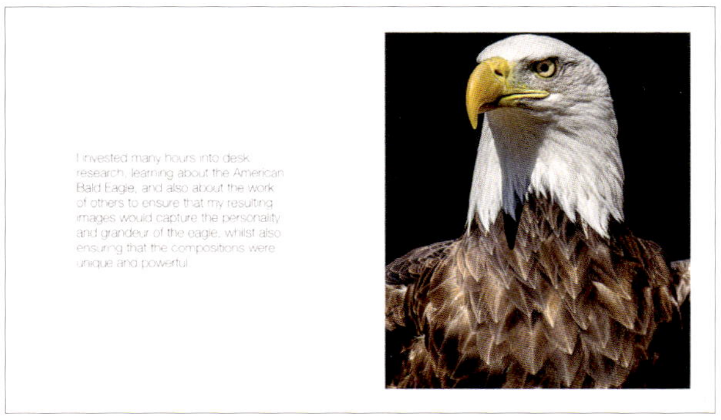

p179: *American Eagle*, bald eagle, Banham Zoo, 2020

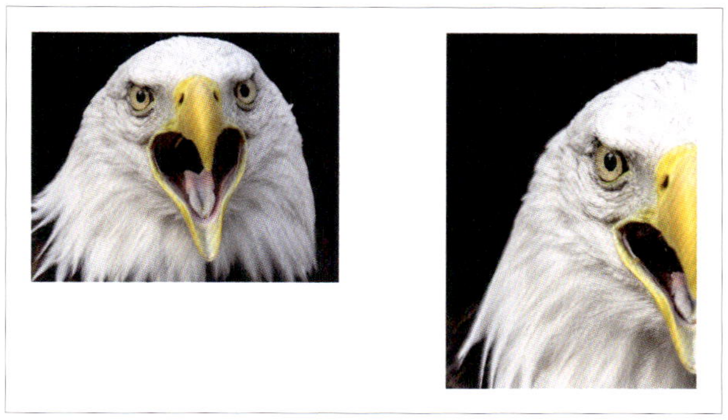

p180: Bald eagle, Banham Zoo, 2020
p181: *Eagle Eyed*, bald eagle, Banham Zoo, 2020

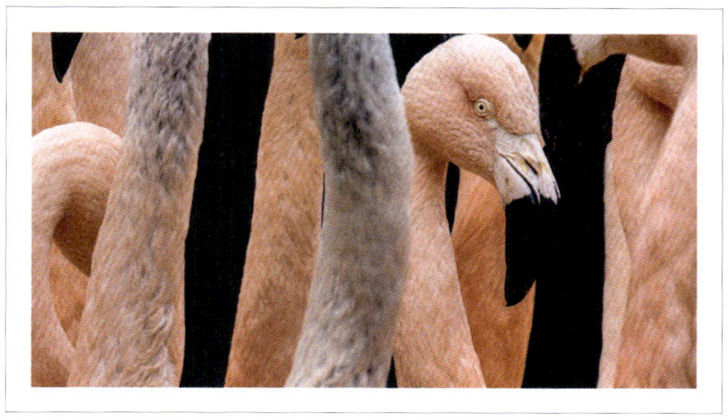

pp182-183: Chilean flamingos, Banham Zoo, 2019

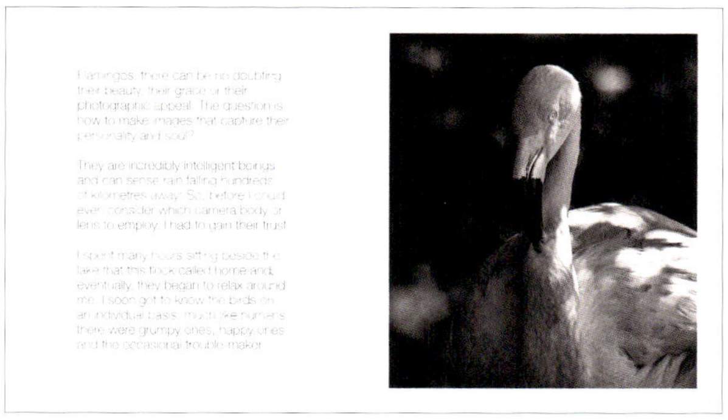

p185: *Serenity*, Chilean flamingo, Banham Zoo, 2020

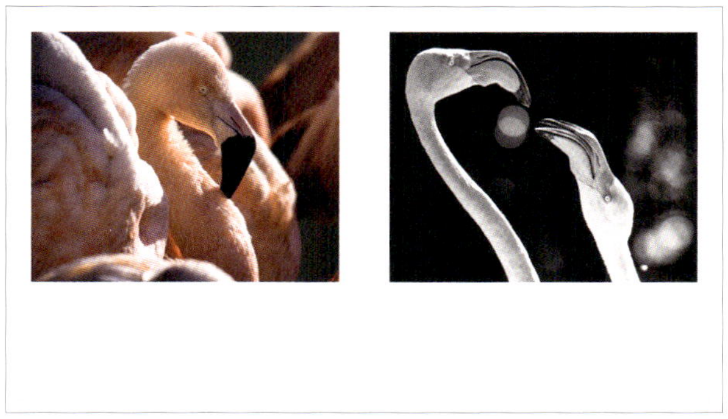

p186: *Star of the Show*, Chilean flamingos, Banham Zoo, 2019
p187: *Feud*, Chilean flamingos, Banham Zoo, 2020

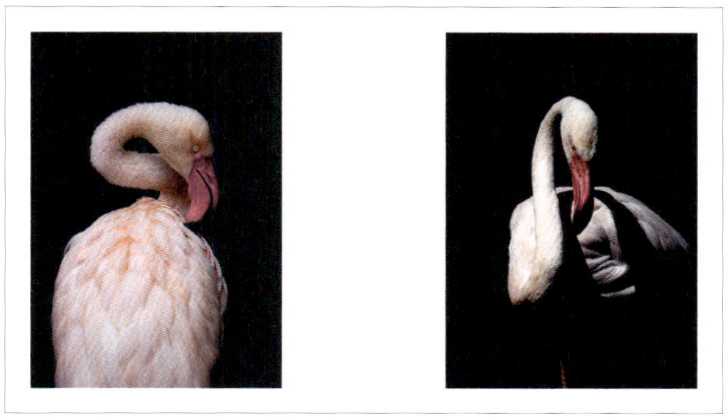

p188: *Candy*, greater flamingo, Africa Alive!, 2018
p189: *Shadows*, greater flamingo, Africa Alive!, 2018

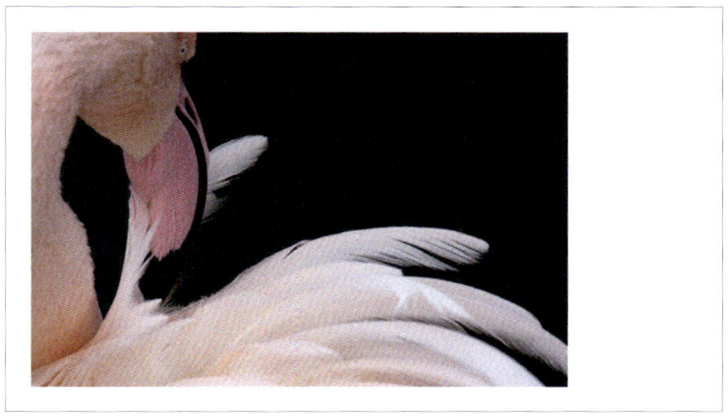

pp190-191: *Feathers*, greater flamingo, Africa Alive!, 2018

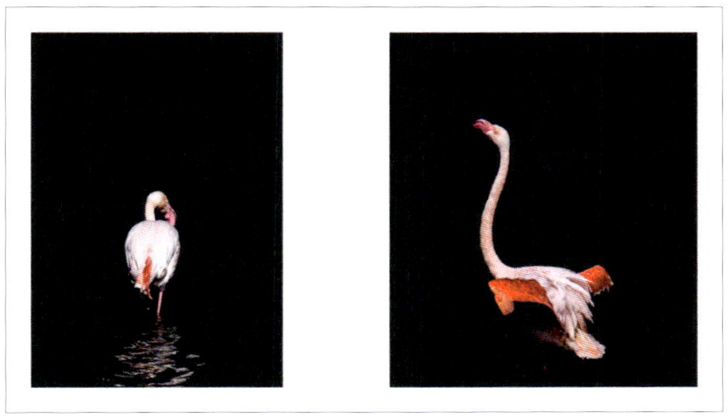

p192: *Stronger Alone*, greater flamingo, Africa Alive!, 2019
p193: *Ballerina*, greater flamingo, Africa Alive!, 2020

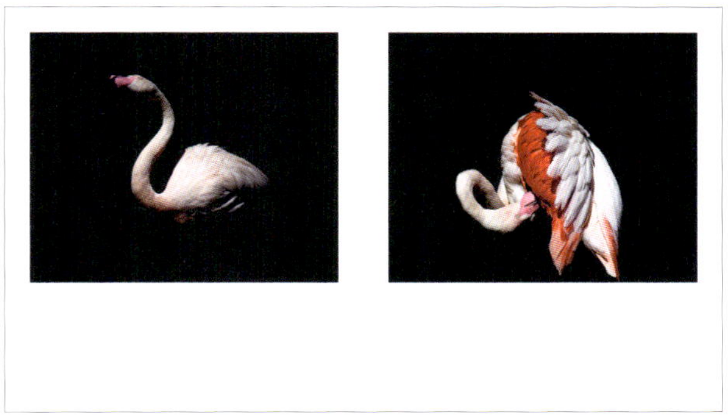

p194: Greater flamingo, Africa Alive!, 2018
p195: *Fiesta*, greater flamingo, Africa Alive!, 2018

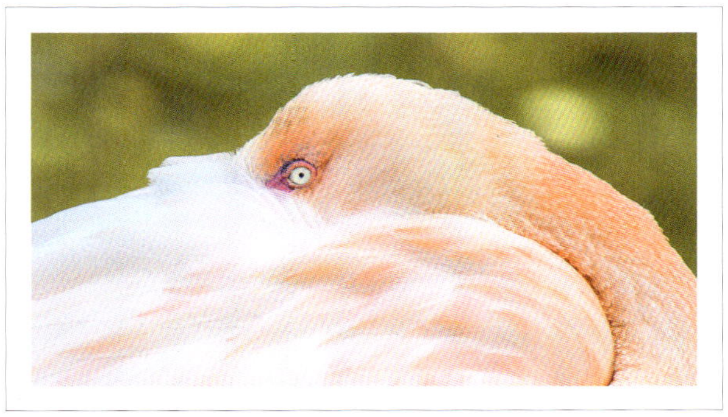

pp196-197: *The Original Flamingo*, greater flamingo, Africa Alive!, 2015

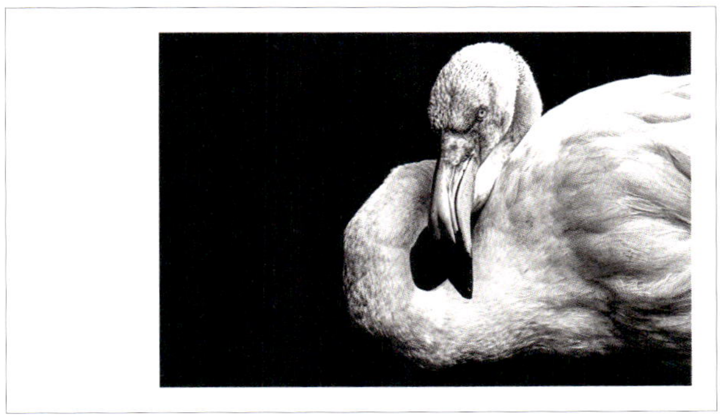

pp198-199: Greater flamingo, Africa Alive!, 2015

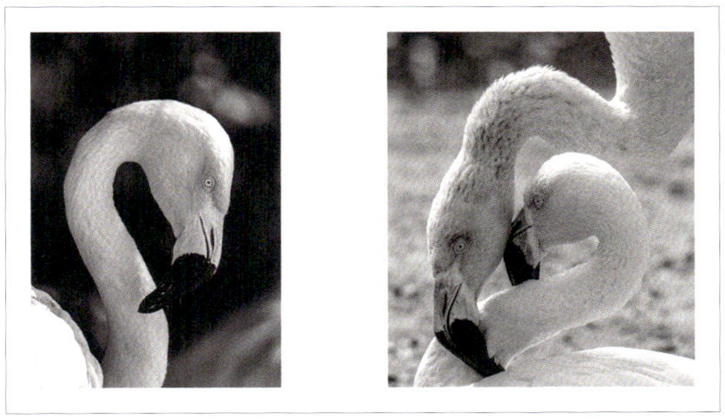

p200: *Innocence*, Chilean flamingo, Banham Zoo, 2020
p201: *Entwined*, Chilean flamingos, Banham Zoo, 2020

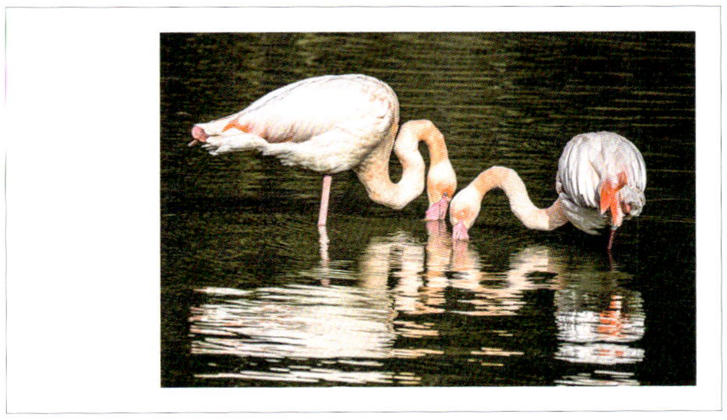

pp202-203: *Crimson Reflections*, greater flamingo, Africa Alive!, 2015

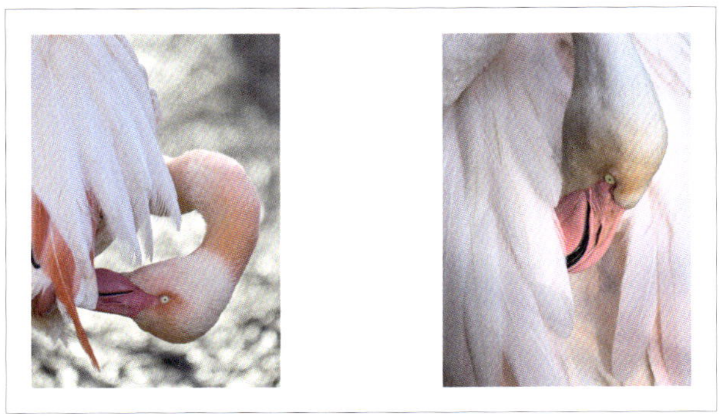

p204: *Pink on Silver*, greater flamingo, Africa Alive!, 2015
p205: Chilean flamingo, Banham Zoo, 2020

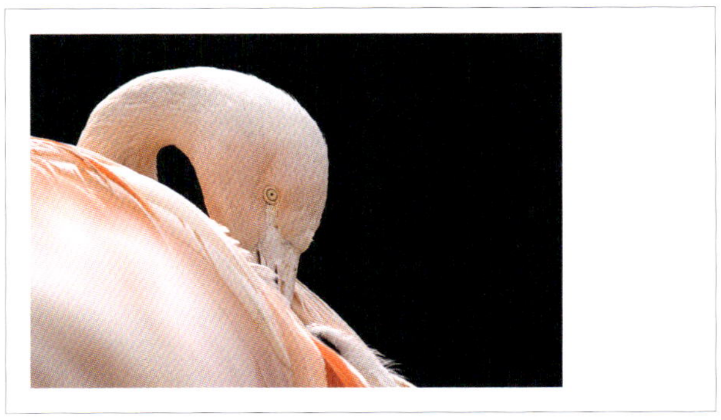

pp206-207: *Grace*, Chilean flamingo, Banham Zoo, 2020

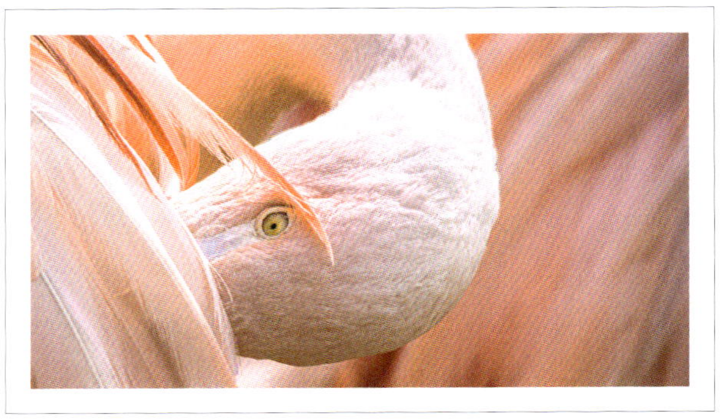

pp208-209: *Honour*, Chilean flamingo, Banham Zoo, 2020

ISBN: 978-178884-123-8

British Library Cataloguing-in-Publication Data
A catalogue record for this book is available from the British Library

The author and publisher gratefully acknowledge the permission granted to reproduce the copyright material in this book. Every effort has been made to trace copyright holders and to obtain their permission for the use of copyright material. The publisher apologises for any errors or omissions in the text and would be grateful if notified of any corrections that should be incorporated in future reprints or editions of this book.

Front cover: *Fiesta,* greater flamingo, Africa Alive!, 2018 (see p.195)
Back cover: *Prince of Darkness*, African lion, Colchester Zoo, 2019 (see p.23)

MIX
From responsible sources
FSC® C014767

Printed in Belgium
for ACC Art Books Ltd., Woodbridge, Suffolk, UK

www.accartbooks.com

ACC ART BOOKS